French Romanesque
and Islam

Andalusian elements in French architectural decoration c. 1030–1180

Katherine Watson

Part i

Text

BAR International Series 488(i)
1989

726.5
W339f
v. 1

B.A.R.

5, Centremead, Osney Mead, Oxford OX2 0DQ, England.

GENERAL EDITORS

A.R. Hands, B.Sc., M.A., D.Phil.
D.R. Walker, M.A.

BAR -S488, 1989: 'French Romanesque and Islam'

Price £30.00 post free throughout the world. Payments made in dollars must be calculated at the current rate of exchange and $8.00 added to cover exchange charges. Cheques should be made payable to B.A.R. and sent to the above address.

© Katherine Watson, 1989

ISBN 0 86054 625 X

For details of all new B.A.R. publications in print please write to the above address. Information on new titles is sent regularly on request, with no obligation to purchase.

Volumes are distributed from the publisher. All B.A.R. prices are inclusive of postage by surface mail anywhere in the world.

Printed in Great Britain

CONTENTS

SUMMARY, FOREWORD and ACKNOWLEDGMENTS (p. v)
Glossary (p.viii)

CHAPTER I INTRODUCTION. THE TOPIC OF ISLAMIC INFLUENCE.
NOTES. (p. 1)

CHAPTER II. THE GREAT MOSQUE OF CORDOBA. ITS PLACE IN
     ANDALUSIAN ARCHITECTURE (p. 9)
Building Campaigns in the Mezquita. The First Mosque. The
     First Extension.
The Puerta San Esteban (Bab al-Wuzara´), Pioneer of
     Mediaeval Doorways. Tripartite design: façade
     articulation, recessed opening, voussoired lintel,
     tympanum and discharging arch; extrados, alfiz, arcade
     above; projecting cornice on roll corbels. Stepped
     merlons. Flanking niches: stepped lintel on carved
     roll corbels, motifs in spandrels, blind arch above
     niches, marble grilles.
Further Features of 9th century Andalusian Architecture:
     double tiers of arches, superposed columns, saw-tooth
     moulding.
Torre San Juan: ajimez, arcading.
The Sources of these Andalusian Features. The Western
     Character of Andalusian Art.
The Tenth Century. The Minaret. The Second Extension, the
     Climax of Caliphal Decoration. The Villaviciosa
     Chapel. The Mihrab and Maqsura Tract. The Chocolate
     Door. The Third Extension. The Anomaly of the 11th
     Bay.
Cristo de la Luz in Toledo.
Caliphal Decorative Motifs. Linear and Geometric Motifs:
     intersecting arches, polychrome inlay. Plant and
     border motifs: down-turned leaf, asymmetrical plant
     scrolls, naturalistic acanthus stem, leaf cross,
     relief studs, rosette and hollowed coupolettes, little
     florets, spiral stems.
Motifs used in Woodwork: the Ceiling of the Mezquita. The
     Fez Mimbar.
Architectural Decoration in 11th Century Andalusia. Malaga.
     Granada. Toledo. Tudela. San Millán de Segovia.
     Aljafería, Zaragoza: interlacing and mixtilinear
     arches, spandrel coupolettes, secondary lobing,
     capitals, the dome and its supports.
Non-Architectural Secular Decoration, Caliphal and 11th
     Century. Marble, the basins. The stilt motif. The 11th
     Century Játiva basin. The Játiva Atlas Figures and
     Related Compositions (Silos, Poitou, Saintonge, Saint-
     Benoît-sur-Loire, Berry. Turban Hair Style. Carved
     Marble in Toledo: the well-heads. Ivory.
NOTES, CHAPTER II (P. 41)

i

UNIVERSITY LIBRARIES
CARNEGIE MELLON UNIVERSITY
PITTSBURGH, PA 15213-3890

CHAPTER III. ARABIC SCRIPT AND ITS IMITATIONS (p. 65)

The Romanesque Examples. The Wooden Doors of the Velay. Le Puy: The Inscription on the Nativity Doors, Plant Motifs, Colour, Interlace.

The Lavoûte-Chilhac Door: The Inscription, The Cross, The Latin Inscription, Cording, Fan-knot Interlace, Scrolls, Construction.

The Chamalières Door.

The Blesle Doors.

Discussion of the Workshop. Parallels in Catalunya. Script-Scroll Ambiguities. The Rôle of Roofing. Flat Relief and Chip Carving.

Saint-Pierre-de-Rhèdes.

Textiles and Woodwork.

The Mock-Kufic Inscription at Moissac. The Impost. The Inscription. The Style of Lettering. Andalusian Examples of Wedge-shaped Hollows.

The Capital 50 Scroll and variants. Further Comparisons, and Affiliations of the Scroll. Spanish Romanesque Scrolls: Frómista, Nogál.The Standing Frontal Figure. Loarre. Conques.

NOTES. CHAPTER III (p. 87)

CHAPTER IV. ANDALUSIAN FEATURES IN ROMANESQUE DECORATION II. THE LOBED ARCH

The Lobed Arch in Andalusia. Types of Lobing in the Mezquita. Applications of Lobing to Architecture in the Mezquita. Andalusian Lobed Arches other than those in the Mezquita.

Lobed Arches in Mozarab and Early Romanesque Architecture in Northern Spain.

The Lobed Arch in France. Previous Studies and Classifications. The Present Classification:

I. Cluny: The Transept Arcades. Associated Features in Cluny Transept. Altar Table Influence. Cluny Doorway. Summary of Cluny lobe characteristics. Examples of Influence of Cluny (a). Similar Lobe Types, Combination with Chevron: Overlapping Points, Scalloped Profile. (b). Similarity of Application, 1. Lobed Interior Arcades, 2. Lobed Doorways.

II. The Velay and Rhône Valley: Concentric Trilobes and Polylobes and Other Trilobes. Le Puy. Rhône Valley. Trilobes in the Limousin and Further West. Trilobes in the Rouergue: Saint-Pierre-Toirac, Bessuéjouls. Nivernais and Auvergne.

III. Quercy and Central France: Cahors South Door. IIIa. Arches with Lobes with Volute or Elaborated Points. Waisted Voussoirs. The Volute. The Jointing. Three Restorations reconsidered: Moissac, Saint-Antonin, Collonges. The Spanish Elements at Moissac. Meymac. Vigeois. The Volute Cusp. Junction with the Jambs. IIIb. Torus (Limousin) Moulding with Lobes.

IV.   Arches with Convex Lobes. Examples in the Saintonge.
V.   Lobed Arches with Edged Lobes. The Outlined Extrados.
VI. Lobes Portrayed in Sculpture.
Summary
NOTES. CHAPTER IV (P. 150)

CHAPTER V. ANDALUSIAN FEATURES IN ROMANESQUE DECORATION
      III. THE ROLL CORBEL

Three broad classes, all with antecedents in Andalusia.
Roll Corbels in Andalusia: Shape. Rod Corbels in the
      Mezquita: Decoration.
Fillet Roll Corbels: the Corbels of the San Esteban Door
      Cornice. The Corbels of the North façade of the
      Mezquita. Interior Arcades of the Second Extension.
      Almanzor´s Extension. Decorative Fillet Roll Corbels.
Plaster Corbels.
The Down-turned Leaf Motif.
Mozarabic Roll Corbels.
Wooden Corbels. Ceramic Corbels.
Corbels in North Spain. Double and Composite Rolls.
      Problems of the Transmission of the Roll Corbel Form
      from Andalusia to Romanesque: the Fillet Corbel and
      its Rarity in Spain. Early Corbels in León. San Miguel
      de Fluviá. Corbels at Frómista, Jaca and Santiago. The
      Platerías Doorway: rosettes and corbels. Corbels at
      Iguácel. Corbels at Loarre.
The Roll Corbel in France and Compostela. La Trinité,
      Vendôme. Corbels in the vicinity of Vendôme. Saint-
      Benoît-sur-Loire. Le Mans. Poitiers, Saint-Hilaire.
      The cornice slabs. Fillet Roll Corbels in Poitou.
      Political Affiliations. Relations of Poitou with
      Spain. Other types of roll corbel in Poitou.
Roll Corbels and other Andalusian Features in Normandy.
      Jumièges. La Trinité in Caen. Relations of Normandy
      with Spain.
Roll Corbels in the Rhône/Saône Valley: Tournus, Ile Barbe
      and Saint-Martin d´Ainay. Auvergne. Brionnais: Anzy-
      le-Duc, Saint-Laurent, Charlieu, Nivernais. Berry-
      Bourbonnais. Corbel Types. Volute Stems with Curls. In
      Spain.
Roll Corbels in Sainte-Foy-de-Conques: 3 Types. Type 1.
      North Door and Chapels. Type 2. South Transept Door.
      Type 3. Ambulatory, Apse and Transepts. The Spread of
      Influence from Conques. Further Andalusian Elements at
      Conques. The Relations of Conques with Spain, and
      Wider Affiliations.
Roll Corbels at Saint-Sernin in Toulouse. The Eaves
      Corbels. The Porte des Comtes and the Fragment in the
      North Nave Tribune. The Porte Miègeville. The Paris
      Cornice Fragment. Further Andalusian Elements at
      Saint-Sernin.

Roll Corbels in the Lower Garonne Valley and Gascony. Type 1: Small Curls: La Sauve, Saint-Sever, Saint-Pierre-du-Mont, Roquefort, Lagrange, Cadillac, Saint-Sardos, Moirax. Type 2: Plain and Plain Fillet: Saint-Macaire, Aubiac, Layrac, Engayrac, Peujard, L´Hôpital-Saint-Blaise, Oloron.
Other Areas. Limousin. Dordogne.
Summary
NOTES. CHAPTER V (p. 216).

CHAPTER VI. THE CONTRIBUTION OF ANDALUSIA TO ROMANESQUE DESIGN (p. 247)

Features and Motifs. Foliage. Rosettes.
Doorway Design and Lobed Arches. The West Door of Cluny III. Other Romanesque Doorways. The Lobed Arch.
Roll Corbels and General Problems of Distribution. Two Early Types of Roll Corbel. Agents of Transmission
NOTES. CHAPTER VI (p. 255).

APPENDIX I. (p. 260). A NUMBERED LIST OF SOME ANDALUSIAN FEATURES AND MOTIFS SHARED WITH ROMANESQUE.
APPENDIX II. (p. 271). "CAHORS TYPE" LOBED ARCHES. (a). Intrados with Volute, Split or Elaborated Points. Limousin. Quercy. Dordogne and West. (b). Archivolts with Lobed Limousin Moulding (Map III)
APPENDIX III. (p. 274). DOCUMENTED DATES FOR EARLY SPANISH ROMANESQUE BUILDINGS
APPENDIX IV. (p. 276). A CHRONOLOGICAL LIST OF MILITARY ENCOUNTERS IN SPAIN WITH PARTICIPANTS FROM FRANCE

BIBLIOGRAPHY (p. 279)
LIST OF ILLUSTRATIONS (p. 283-294)

MAPS . I, France, general. IIa, Spain in 1050. IIb, Spain c1095. III, Distribution of Lobed Limousin Moulding and Trilobes. IV, Distribution of Roll Corbels. V. The Cluny/Santiago Axis.

ILLUSTRATIONS Figures 1 - 332.

SUMMARY.

An examination of all types of Islamic monument (buildings, carved marble, wood, ivory and metalwork) in Spain dated before 1100 AD has provided a lengthy list of structural and decorative features and decorative motifs sufficiently distinctive to imply the likelihood of a degree of Andalusian (Spanish Islamic) influence in comparable features of French Romanesque decoration. A selection of some 40 of these has been listed (Appendix I) and numbered, and they are noted in the text in parenthesis as they are found associated with the three main features discussed - Kufic writing, lobed arch and roll corbels - in order to assess the recurrence and extent of an Andalusian influence as a whole. Many of these features appear on the San Esteban doorway of the Great Mosque of Cordoba (the "Mezquita"), and this doorway is shown furthermore to be of special importance as the earliest example, on a religious building west of the Euphrates, of a doorway with a declamatory function, and thus to be the pioneer among all western mediaeval doorways on religious monuments.

There are no more than four examples of Kufic script in French architectural contexts: two wooden doors in the Velay, a lintel in Languedoc and an impost block in Moissac cloister bear this decoration. All four are connected with a workshop tradition that includes both Andalusian wooden ceilings of the 9th to 14th centuries AD, and carvings of the 10th and 11th century in wood and marble found on the north-west coast of the Mediterranean. Toledo can be identified as the source of the Moissac example, and the antecedents of the scroll decoration associated with it are traced in early Spanish Romanesque as well as Andalusian decoration.

Lobed arches in France are compared with the Andalusian precedents. Previous classifications are discussed and revised in the light of recent chronologies, with groupings suggested to take account of typology and geographical distribution. Convergent incentives are considered for the adoption of this Andalusian practice, and Moissac is proposed as the originator of the "Limousin" type.

The diverse influence of Andalusian uses of the corbel for supporting eaves, decorative cornices and lintels in different regions of France is manifest in the early adoption of a form with rolls which was invented in the 8th century in Andalusia.

Andalusian influence can thus be seen to have operated in two areas of activity where the characteristics of Romanesque architecture are particularly marked: the method of roofing with overhanging eaves supported on sculpted corbels, and the adoption and design of monumental façades and doorways. There is justification in the historical record also for the conclusion that Andalusian influence was more integral and less exotic than has so far been allowed

FOREWORD.

References in brackets are to the list of Andalusian features (F) and decorative motifs (D) of Appendix I (p. 260). References to my illustrations are underlined (<u>fig.</u> 00). For published works to which frequent reference is made, the abbreviation (see Bibliography, p. 279) and figure or plate number are given in brackets (<u>AHIII</u> fig. 00). I have limited references to illustrations in foreign publications as far as possible to works easily accessible in England, and to as few works as possible. Since <u>AHIII</u> and <u>LTB 1957</u> are indispensable to a study of Andalusian architecture I have used them wherever possible.

The terms <u>France</u> and <u>Spain</u> are taken to describe the areas within the modern political boundaries and without historical connotations. <u>Andalusia</u> describes the parts of Spain under Islamic rule, until the end of the 11th century reaching nearly to the Pyrenees (Map II). <u>Maghreb</u> denotes the Islamic lands of North Africa west of Egypt.

After the second chapter diacritics are not used for Arabic words and names current in Spain.

ACKNOWLEDGMENTS

My warm thanks go first to Professor George Zarnecki, for a memorable visit to Moissac cloister, and for supervising the thesis that it inspired. Thanks also to Dr Geza Fehérvari for supervising the Islamic sections, and to Constance Hill and her staff at the Conway Library, Rupert Hodge at the Witt, John Hopkins at the Society of Antiquaries, the staff at the libraries of SOAS and the Warburg Institute, who all made it a pleasure to work under their care. I wish to express my special appreciation to the staff of the Percival David Foundation for their unfailing welcome, and among them Glen Ratcliffe for help with photography. My main debt over photography is to Paul Fox of SOAS at home, and Dr Oliver Watson especially on site, for their generosity with time and advice for my photography over many years. I thank, for their respective kindnesses, Monsieur H. Renou at the Photothèque of the Centre for Mediaeval Studies in Poitiers, Professors Marcel Durliat, Jacques Bousquet, Jean-Claude Fau and Eliane Vergnolle, Me Marie-Madeleine Gauthier, Me Aline Lapicque,

M. and Mme Francis Perrin, Me Geneviève Coste, Me Marguerite Guary, Dr and Mme Jean Sentex in France; in Spain, Dr Juan Zozaya at the National Museum and Dr C. Ewert at the DAI in Madrid, Don Antonio Duran in Huesca; in England, Dr G. Michell for the doorway drawings, Arun Weys and Benedick Watson for helping him, Mary-Lou Arscott for the use of her thesis on Cordoba, Mr Neil Stratford for help in many forms, Maxwell Watson for support on my travels and for photographs, particularly the bench at Durro, Dr Rowan Watson for discussions and advice on historical problems, Dr Oliver Watson on Islamic topics, my husband William Watson for every possible help and support; finally to all the members of my family and its extensions for their unending cooperation, stimulation and endurance.

GLOSSARY

Andalusia — The area of Spain under Muslim rule (Ar. al-Andalus)

Andalusian — The culture developed in Spain throughout the centuries of the Muslim regime

Mozarab — is strictly a term applied to Christians "arabized" by living under Muslim rule; it is extended to the people who emigrated to the Christian kingdoms of northern Spain at various periods, bringing their culture with them

Mudéjar — Muslims living under Christian rule in Spain, retaining many Andalusian cultural traits

Mezquita — The Spanish term for Mosque. The abbreviation of <u>Mezquita aljama</u> (Chief or Friday Mosque) is the name given by Spaniards to the Great Mosque of Cordoba to this day. It is used here for the building with all its extensions. <u>First</u> or <u>al-Hakam II´s Mosque</u> refer respectively to the original Mosque of 787 and to the second, 10th century extension which was virtually a "Mosque within a Mosque" (<u>LTB 1957</u>, p. 483). First and third extensions are referred to as such, or by their building patrons names, Abd ar-Rahman II and Almanzor.

alfiz (sometimes called arraba) — The rectangular frame outside an arch, sometimes a line of moulding, sometimes a band enclosed within two or several such lines.

ajimez — A small twin window, with colonnette and capital in the centre

extrados — "The upper or exterior curve of an arch; <u>esp.</u> the upper curve of the voussoirs or stones which immediately form the arch (O.E.D.)

intrados — "The lower or interior curve of an arch; <u>spec.</u> the lower curve of the voussoirs or stones which immediately form the arch (O.E.D.)

maqsura — The screened-off area round the mihrab and mimbar in a Mosque, reserved for the ruler

mihrab — arcade or niche denoting direction for prayer

mimbar — Pulpit

qibla — The direction of Mecca, and the direction in which Mosques were officially oriented, so that the end wall of the sanctuary holding the mihrab faced that way. In fact the Mezquita is oriented like Syrian Mosques and faces more to the south than towards Mecca.

CHAPTER   I

INTRODUCTION

The topic of Islamic influence on Romanesque architectural decoration embraces two fields of study that have
traditionally remained wide apart. On the one hand the observations of Islamic specialists on Romanesque features
have usually lacked the authority of first-hand acquaintance with French monuments (1), and on the other Andalusia, being included in the Islamic field, has been given
scant attention from all but a very few historians of West
European art. There has therefore been a lack of awareness
of the differences from the rest of Islamic art that make
Andalusian achievements part of the western tradition (2).

Mâle led the way in identifying a number of features of
Romanesque decoration with precursors in Andalusia (3), and
details of Andalusian decoration adopted into Romanesque,
but he presented them entirely as exotic references to an
alien world, and this is the current view: the lobed arches
and corbel forms whose Andalusian origin was noted by Mâle
are referred to with a similar vocabulary decades later by
Conant (4), though in Conant´s view Andalusian influence
was less superficial or solely decorative, and extended to
vaulting and occasionally to doorway design.

Focillon´s point of view (5) reflects the inter-
nationalist tendencies of the 1930s; he rejected the assumption of closed cultures held hitherto and sought for
indications of influence more in terms of stimulus (éveil)
and the propagation of methods and ways of seeing than of
direct imitations; his analysis of the "life of forms" introduced the idea of a complexity of levels at which sculptors could be expected to respond to different sources.
Most of the investigations into "oriental" or Andalusian
features in Romanesque sculpture that have since appeared
have been due to his inspiration; nevertheless in studies
of Romanesque the peculiar dimension of Andalusia still remains unexplored.

Among these investigations that of the monuments of
Le Puy by Fikry, the only specialist in Islamic architecture to study French monuments also, again tends to blur
differences between Cordoba and the rest of Islam in pur-
suit of his thesis that an architect trained in Islamic
methods worked at Le Puy. Fikry was dealing here in fact
with a unique case, for nowhere else could such a circum-
stance even be postulated; however the thesis is confounded
by recent work (6). Neither have the various studies of
French lobed arches shown them to relate significantly to
traditional or to contemporary Andalusian fashions in arch-
building (7); the current view now is that little beyond
the initial idea of a lobed arch, as conceived at Cordoba
in the tenth century, was owed to Andalusian models.   In
Chapter IV this view will be modified to include a second

1

wave of ideas from Andalusia, but this modification is of trivial import in comparison with the underpinning, given by the fact that lobed arches originated in Andalusia, to the contention propounded in the conclusion to this thesis that Andalusia is at the origin of the new function of the doorway in Romanesque church façade design: the monumental doorway of western architecture is first conceived at Cordoba.

Single monuments and single motifs have not yielded conclusive "proof" of the kind of Andalusian presence expected, and the enthusiasm of the 1930s in searching for Andalusian influence has given way, especially among French scholars, to a suspicion that the whole topic lacks precision and is tainted with a decidedly amateur overemphasis on pilgrimage routes or crusades. Ironically, just when Andalusian monuments became accessible with adequate illustration and analysis (8) in the decade after the second world war, French interest began to wane. Far from giving a place to Andalusia as a component of western civilization, the trend of thinking has been to discount the Andalusian participation in shared motifs or styles as irrelevant in comparison with their consistency with Carolingian or contemporary Mediterranean tradition (9).

This trend finds its most emphatic expression in a typical remark by Jalabert: "...it was not necessary [for Pyrenean marble workers] to go to Spain in the early 11th century to become acquainted with the horseshoe arch" [for example on the lintels at Suréda and Saint-Genis]. At this juncture the issue of influence needs raising once more, and from another side, in the following terms: considering the high level of Andalusian civilization from the early 10th century (11), the extent of French involvement in both Christian and Muslim Spain in the 11th (12), and the extensive and growing evidence for social and commercial traffic across the Pyrenees and through the ports of eastern and northern Spain throughout the 11th and 12th centuries (13), is it possible to regard similar motifs and equivalent methods as solely or even primarily the result of independent parallel developments from ultimate common sources? Since a few undeniable Andalusian motifs are persistent in Romanesque is it not likely that the adoption of a less obviously Islamic motif was encouraged when Andalusian and other models coincide? And is it not thus relevant to record the Romanesque motifs present in Andalusia in pre-Romanesque centuries, even if the same motifs may have been available as models elsewhere also?

This thesis sets out from the premiss that the presence and persistence of undeniably Andalusian elements in Romanesque decoration signify a cultural continuum on some artistic, technical or human level independent of the religious, political or other socially dominant institutions. This is in keeping with the three "Laws" governing the functioning of cultural influence observed by Hamilton Gibb (14), that predicate some common ground to allow borrowings to be vi-

2

able. Taken together these laws suggest that the most profound examples of influence will be the least immediately
recognisable as an alien element.

It will be argued here that Romanesque designers did
"go to Spain"; they went not only for fanciful details but,
among other things, for inspiration in two much more important, not necessarily related concerns. These are first,
the technique of roofing, in connexion with which both
"Kufic" motifs and, apparently separately, roll corbels
were adopted into the repertoire, and second the structure
and character of doorways. The evidence of the direct contact or common ground that could make possible such inspiration can be found in the number of features and decorative motifs shared between Andalusia and Romanesque France.
A preliminary survey of Andalusian monuments yielded a list
of some forty elements that can be matched in Romanesque
decoration; of these 22 are structural and miscellaneous
and 17 are decorative. They are numbered Fl-22 and D 1-17
(Appendix I) so that they can be noted in parentheses in
the text to show their presence at the sites considered in
Chapters III, IV and V. These chapters discuss the three
universally accepted "Islamic" features in Romanesque decoration: Kufic writing, lobed arches and roll corbels and
their associations. In the case of the two latter an Andalusian origin is generally agreed. In Chapter III it is
argued that the few Romanesque architectural examples of
Kufic all have the same derivation, and that the main agent
of transmission of Kufic and related motifs was the woodworking fraternity, who will be seen in Chapter V to have
been involved also in the introduction of corbels.   In
Chapters IV and V respectively lobed arches and corbels are
treated in broadly regional groups. for the former this
classification builds on earlier work by Fikry (1934),
Héliot (1946 and 1951), and Vergnolle (1966).

Romanesque corbels have enjoyed no such attention
(15).   The subject is vast and has hardly been broached.
Chapter V is therefore no more than an exploration of the
use of the Andalusian roll form. Detailed typological and
iconographic studies of all corbels forms, such as would
need a sizeable team to carry out, would reveal many cross
currents and movements of craftsmen and ideas, even from
the stone examples that alone survive, though the fact that
wooden examples have all perished means their history will
always be incomplete. As well as the processes of transmission from Andalusia, mapping the distribution of corbel motifs and forms would throw light on such questions as
whether corbels were normally produced on site or at quar-
ries (devices and themes recur at surprising distances),
whether they were the work of capital or doorway sculptors,
or apprentices, masons or specialists, or whether different
sites and regions were connected, as regards roofing practices, on the same pattern as for sculpture or other elements.

The uncertainties of chronology still impinge on all

questions affecting Romanesque sculpture. Awareness of the achievements of Andalusian builders and the opportunities for French patrons and designers to come in contact with them (16) encourages a preference for a "high" rather than a "low" chronology when there is doubt. Furthermore it is becoming increasingly difficult to accept that the decade 1095-1105 can possibly have concentrated as much activity as would have been the case were every attribution to it in recent years correct (17). Each correlation may be subject to doubt of some kind, but if in the aggregate some connexion is not allowed the paradoxical conclusion threatens that the buildings recorded were almost totally ephemeral or left unfinished, while what now stands is all the result of an activity for which no record survives (cf. Appendix III).

CHAPTER I   NOTES

1.   e.g. L. Torres Balbas, `Los Modillones de Lobulos´, AEAA 1936;  ). Grabar, `Islamic Architecture and the West: influences and parallels´, Islam and the Mediaeval West, Loan Exhibition, University Art Gallery, State University, New York, Binghampton 1975; M. Gomez Moreno knew both Andalusian and Spanish Romanesque art intimately, but not enough of France to compel attention to his views of architecture across the Pyrenees. H. Terrasse, L´Art hispano-mauresque, Paris 1932, devoted a few pages to speculating why, as he saw it, Andalusian art had a very minor effect in France. He concluded that the barrier was social: Romanesque art was popular, local and rural as against the urban aristocratic art of Islamic Spain. The exception to this divided specialization is A. Fikry, who in the same year published both La Grande Mosquée de Kairouan, Paris 1934 and L´Art roman du Puy et les influences islamiques, Paris 1934. This latter includes a full bibliography of the topic to date. A. Grabar is always specific: `Les mosaïques de Germigny des Prés´ Cah.Arch. 1954 gives evidence of considerable Mozarab and Andalusian influence in Carolingian France; H. Stern´s discussion in the same volume of the mosaics of Saint-Genès in Thiers, which he dates with those of Lescar in the early 12th century, likewise invokes a lasting tradition from Andalusia, with a link existing at Ripoll. It is now universally agreed that after c1040 artistic connexion between `France´ and Christian `Spain´ was so rapid as to make them part of a single sphere as far as architecture and decoration were concerned. The old debates of Kingsley Porter et al. as to priorities no longer arise.

2.   E. Lambert also bridges the gap: `Les voûtes nervées hispano-musulmanes du XIe siècle et leur influence possible sur l´art chrétien´, Hespéris 1928; and `Les premières voûtes nervées françaises et les origines de la croisée d´ogives´, Rev. Arch. 1933, but not concerned with decoration. It is symptomatic that not one of the twelve

annual meetings at Saint-Michel-de-Cuxa (CSCM 1970-1981 has given any attention to specific examples of Andalusian art, though passing references to "Cordoban influence" may be found in every volume. F. Garcia Romo, `Influencias Hispano-musulmanes y Mozarabes en general y en el Romanico Frances del siglo XI (Capiteles Corintios)´ AE 1953, was already writing of this neglect of Andalusia and its special situation "ignored even by Focillon" (p. 174). Romo's arguments for distinguishing a Mozarabic workshop in the Middle Loire region (`Un Taller Escultórico de Influjo Musulmán en el Loire Medio (antes de 1030-1050)´, al-Andalus 1960 - a search prompted by Focillon who was highly sympathetic to such ideas, cf. H. Focillon, L´Art des Sculpteurs romans, Paris 1964, p. 222) were based on such fine distinctions between the work of Unbertus in the tower porch of Saint-Benoît and that of his "Muslim-influenced workshop" that they did not carry conviction, and because the conclusions have been rejected his many pertinent observations have been ignored. La Escultura del Siglo XI (Francia-España) y sus Precedentes Hispánicos, Barcelona 1973 contains all his articles to date.

3.   E. Mâle, `La Mosquée de Cordoue et les églises de l´Auvergne et du Velay´, Revue de l´art ancien et moderne 1911 and `L´Espagne arabe et l´art roman´, Revue des Deux Mondes Nov.1923. The following list emerges from these two articles: lobed arches, alfiz, roll corbels, hollowed soffit rosettes, polychrome masonry wall patterns and arches, imitation of Kufic, low relief carving, horseshoe arch. At various times this had been added to by other writers to include twin windows, pointed arches, rectangular-rib vaults, double columns, angle columns, pierced oculi, blind arcading, slender columns. L.Courajod had already introduced a discussion of Islamic influence into the study of French architecture, Leçons professées à l´Ecole du Louvre 1887-1896, Paris 1899, and defended the stance of Longpérier before him, who had been accused of lowering the status of French art by suggesting foreign influences, but Courajod's ideas were regarded askance until after the first world war. The main writings with references to Islamic influence, after those already quoted, have been A.K. Porter, Romanesque Sculpture of the Pilgrimage Roads, Boston 1924; Puig y Cadafalch, Le Premier Art Roman, Paris 1928 (e.g. p. 33), `Decorative Forms of the First Romanesque Style. Their Diffusion by Moslem Art´, Art Studies 1926, and `More Decorative Forms..´ Art Studies 1934 and `La frontière septentrionale de l´art mozarabe´, CRAcIBL 1943; W.W. Cook, `Stucco Altar Frontals of Catalonia´ AS 1924 stressed the high standard of stucco carving in Andalusia, derived from Coptic example, evoked Islamic influence in Romanesque representations of heraldic eagle and lion passant, slender columns and a split palmette as an isolated unit; J.R.Colle, `Essai sur les influences mozarabes dans l´art roman du Sud-Ouest´ Revue de Saintonge et de l´Aunis 1956 cited Mozarab influence in quatrefoil columns, octagonal belfry, façade friezes, doorway massif. For articles on lobed arches see note 27, Chapter IV.

4.   K.Conant, <u>CRA</u> 1966, e.g. p.105; p.175, "oriental spice". On p.143 the possibility of fine craftsmen from Muslim Spain is entertained as one among several explanations for the fine earlier acanthus foliage at Cluny III, and the "exceptional delicacy and classical character of the earlier moulding profiles". Conant also comments on "Moorish" features at Le Puy and at the great west door at Cluny. (pp.104-5).

5.   H. Focillon, <u>L´Art des sculpteurs romans</u>, Paris 1931 and 1964; <u>La vie des formes</u>, Paris,5th ed. 1970; <u>Art d´Occident</u>, Paris 1938; <u>Moyen Age: survivance et réveils</u>, Paris 1945; `Recherches récentes sur la sculpture romane en France au XIe siècle´ <u>BM</u> 1938.

6.   <u>CA</u> 1976. see Chapter IV.

7.   see. Chapter IV, note 27.

8.   M. Gomez Moreno, <u>Ars Hispaniae III, Madrid 1951</u> (henceforth <u>AH III</u>); L. Torres Balbás, <u>Historia de España V</u>, Madrid 1957 (henceforth <u>LTB 1957</u>). The illustrations in these two works will be constantly referred to throughout this book.

9.   M. Durliat gives more notice to possible Andalusian "currents" than the majority of the French "establishment", but in <u>CA</u> 1976 the "mirage oriental" is attacked for the "flou de la pensée" (p. 17) with some spirit, and in <u>CSMC</u> 1978 the sequels to the Ripoll capitals of Cordoban inspiration (F. Hernandez, `Un aspecto de la influencia del arte califal en Cataluña´ <u>AEAyA</u> 1930; G. Gaillard, <u>Premiers essais</u>..Paris 1938) are described as having a style with origins which may be "Visigothic, Muslim or more generally Mediterranean"; P. Verdier, `La sculpture du clocher-porche de Saint-Benoît-sur-Loire dans ses rapports avec l´Espagne califale et mozarabe´, <u>Etudes ligériennes</u> 1975, revived Romo´s thesis in connexion with Saint-Benoît capitals, and was scathingly dismissed in a review by Erlande-Brandeburg (<u>BM</u> 1975, p. 328). The sculpture of Saint-Benoît is now authoritatively published by E. Vergnolles, Saint-Benoît-sur-Loire et la sculpture du XIe <u>siècle</u>, Paris 1985.

10.   D. Jalabert, <u>La flore sculptée des monuments du moyen âge en France</u>, Paris 1965, e.g.p.45; for the "lintels", <u>Roussillon roman</u> figs 20,21.

11.   E. Lévi-Provençal, <u>Histoire de l´Espagne musulmane</u>, Paris 1950; <u>LTB 1957</u>; H. Terrasse, <u>op. cit.</u>; A. Grabar, <u>art. cit.</u> (<u>CA</u> 1954) see note 1, regards Germigny as a witness to a more widespread liking for, or taste shared with, Andalusian art in the Carolingian period.

12.   M. Defourneaux, <u>Les français en Espagne aux XIe et XIIe siècles</u>, Paris 1949. In Aragón, where Pierre de Rodez (Pedro de Roda), Rotrou du Perche and Gaston de Béarn were of the close royal entourage, the king´s son and other no-

bles habitually signed their names in Arabic, and had probably been educated in Muslim Huesca: R. Menendez Pidal, La
España del Cid, 7th ed. 1969, p. 572; A. Duran Gudiol, `La
Iglesia de Aragon...´ Anthologica Annua 9, Rome 1961 presents a number of such documents.

13.   P. Wolff, The Awakening of Europe, London 1972 and
Histoire de Toulouse, Toulouse 1965; C. Verlinden, `The
Rise of Spanish Trade in the Middle Ages´ IHR 1940,
(p.44ff. on Conques); L´Esclavage dans l´Europe médiévale,
Bruges 1955; W.G. East, An Historical Geography of Europe,
London 1966; A.R.Lewis, The development of Southern French
and Catalan Society, Texas 1965, id., The Sea and Mediaeval
Civilizations, London 1978; J.-M. Lacarra, `Aspectos eco-
nómicos de la sumición de los reinos de taifas´, Hom. J.
Vicens Vives 1965; id., Un arancal de aduanas del siglo XI,
Zaragoza 1950; id.,`Colonisation `franca´ en Navarre et
Aragón´ AduM 1953,p. 333; id., `Desarrollo urbano de Jaca
en la Edad Media´, Est..Corona de Aragon 1953, etc. M.
Durliat, `Premiers essais..´GBA 1966 points the correspon-
dence of activity of the marble ateliers and the growth of
the suburbs of Narbonne, Carcassonne and Toulouse with circulation of gold from Andalusia (with further bibliography). Customs houses had to be expanded in Barcelona in
1029, 1050 and 1058: J.W. Thompson, Economic and Social
History of the Middle Ages, London 1948.

14.   Sir H. Gibb, `The Influence of Islamic Culture on
Mediaeval Europe´, Bull. John Rylands Library 38 (1955); A.
Grabar, `Le succès des arts sécularisés à la cour byzantine
sous les macédoines´, L´Art de la fin de l´Antiquité et du
Moyen Age, Paris 1968, vol.1,also defines three degrees of
influence: transfer, adoption and integration, of which the
most far-reaching is integration, where secondary or limi-
nal features take on new significance in a new setting.

15.   L. Torres Balbás, `Los Modillones de Lobulos´,
AEAyA 1936 (I. Jan.-Apr.;II, May-Aug.): the French material
is mostly extracted from CA; R. Crozet, Art roman en Berry,
p. 225, n.1; E. Lambert, `L´Art hispano-mauresque et l´art
roman´, Hespéris 1933; M. Deshoulières, `Les corniches ro-
manes´, BM 1920.

16.   Not only in Cordoba, as is usually implied since
Mâle´s poetic evocations; M. Delcor, `Problêmes posés par
l´église de Saint-Michel-de-Cuxa..´ CSMC 1977, p. 50 refers
to Mozarab traits as the work of "a Christian from these
parts who had seen the Muslim and Christian buildings of
Cordoba on the occasion of some journey and who, returning
north of the Pyrenees, has tried to imitate them". Even in
the 10th century other Andalusian cities, on the east coast
and northern Marches, were to be seen, and they expanded
even more in the 11th.

17. The consensus of meetings at Saint-Michel de Cuxa has
already put there Jaca, Saint-Sernin in Toulouse, Conques,
Santiago, Frómista, Arlanza, Loarre, the Panteón in León,

Saint-Sever, La Sauve-Majeure and many more...It was even recently proposed for the porch of Saint-Benoît-sur-Loire, with Selles-sur-Cher, Saint-Outrille, Méobecq and Issoudun (M. Schmitt, `Traveling carvers in the Romanesque´ <u>AB</u> LXIII,1, 1981). A wider, more convincing chronology is now established for many of these in the masterly work of E. Vergnolle, <u>Saint-Benoît-sur-Loire</u>...

Iguácel is an example of the problem. The inscription date of 1072 is questioned by most authorities because the sculpture is precocious in comparison with what has been decided, on stylistic grounds, is the date of San Pedro in Jaca. But Iguácel had many contemporaries of which only Nogal (in ruins) and Frómista survive, including great royal foundations: Nájera, Cogolla, Astorga, León cathedral, Oña and Burgos were finished or in construction by 1075, Valladolid, Arlanza and Sahagún not much later. The Panteón in León too may follow very soon after the establishment of Alfonso VI in Leon in 1072 (J. Williams, <u>AB</u> 1973). Accepting the recorded dates as a working hypothesis, the plant scrolls of the capitals of Nogal (1063) and Frómista (1066) illustrate how sculptors in North Spain in about 1070 had already assimilated Andalusian motifs into their repertoire before the wholesale occupation of cities that began with Toledo in 1085. The figured capitals in the earliest parts of Santiago in Compostela show this was not the only tradition; the technique of carving at Nogal makes clear the connexion with woodworking which it will be contended was one of the main modes of transmission of Andalusian decoration.

CHAPTER II

THE GREAT MOSQUE OF CORDOBA
ITS PLACE IN ANDALUSIAN ARCHITECTURE

The Great Mosque of Córdoba (commonly called The Mezquita) is the only complete building to survive, for the most part unchanged, from the period of Umayyad rule in Spain (750-1010)(1). Fortunately, as the chief mosque of the capital city throughout the years of the emirate (750-929) and caliphate (929-1010) of Andalusia, it can confidently be regarded as the pioneer of structural and decorative innovation (2) throughout the centuries of Umayyad rule, and as the source of developments for some two centuries more in western Islam. This supreme, and most representative example possible of religious architecture is complemented by the vestiges of secular building of the 10th and 11th centuries, notably the remains excavated (3) at Madīnat az-Zahrā´, together with a few fragments in Toledo, Granada, Malaga, Segovia and Zaragoza. All the evidence points to the absolute dominance of the Cordoban style, and the Mezquita and its decoration can be regarded as the authoritative model for deducing the character of the buildings in the towns and cities such as Toledo, Huesca, Barbastro, Lérida, Valencia, Tudela or Zaragoza that lay nearer to France, were known to have been frequented by many classes of French, and were in more direct and continuous contact than Córdoba itself with the centres of Romanesque building in France.

The most cursory comparisons show that it is the traditional Cordoban elements of the 9th and 10th centuries that find greater affinity with Romanesque decoration than the 11th century style of architectural decoration, surviving only in secular buildings, which was evolving in Andalusia at the same time as Romanesque sculpture was beginning to develop further north. A summary of the history of the Mezquita and a short description of the other surviving Andalusian monuments is thus necessary as a context for distinguishing the features which show analogies or consequences in Romanesque decoration. Some of these features will receive short comment as they arise in this summary, whereas Kufic writing, lobed arches and roll corbels, with associated features, will be discussed in separate chapters.

One stumbling-block to a readier recognition of the affinities between Andalusian and Romanesque decoration must be the horseshoe arch. Though not an invention of Andalusian architects (4), its wholesale adoption and consistent treatment in caliphal art (5) has stamped it irrevocably as Andalusian, for Romanesque designers and modern art historians alike, and its highly distinctive aspect, which found virtually no response in Romanesque architecture, may well explain the prevalent absence of further scrutiny of Andalusian work from the point of view of its influence on Romanesque. In fact the lack of response to this feature in Romanesque architecture, beyond occurrences which may well be accidental, demonstrates rather the nature of borrowings from Andalusia than their absence.It will be argued here that Andalusia was drawn upon either consciously or intuitively for ideas of all kinds, although there was virtually never any attempt to reproduce an Andalusian-looking monument. The horseshoe arch will receive no comment in the following discussions of Andalusian design. Very occasionally the shape seems deliberate: at Châteaumeillant and La Celle-Bruère in the Berry and the Porte Miègeville of Saint-Sernin in Toulouse, for example, and especially at Déols and Vigeois (Chap.IV), Andalusian inspiration suggests itself.

Building Campaigns in the Mezquita

The plans and reconstructions published by Gomez-Moreno and Torres-Balbás (fig.1)(6) show four successive states of the building from AD 786 to 987 as it was enlarged to accommodate a growing population. Although the second extension under al-Ḥakam II during the years 961-965 is in some ways best regarded as a separate "mosque within a mosque" (7), the unity of the building was maintained throughout the extensions and the character of the original design was respected in its essentials and in many details.

The First Mosque

The first mosque contained (8) a sanctuary of ten arcades on columns; each arcade consists of eleven horseshoe arches bearing pilasters which carry round-headed arches. The arcades run north to south and form eleven aisles twelve bays in length, the central one wider and the outermost narrower than the rest (9). The arches are built of voussoirs of white stone alternating with five narrow bricks. The columns and capitals were all reused from Roman or Visigothic sites. Above these the system of support for the roof is entirely new. It uses several stages of corbelling to carry a wider upper order of arches and a wall (fig.2); though never apparently repeated outside the Mezquita, many aspects of it were "copied" in the mediaeval sense of "selective transfer"(10). The distinctive lobed "roll" corbel that initiates the gradual widening of support from the impost imposed its shape on every type of supporting member in Andalusian architecture after the 9th century, making lobing a characteristic Andalusian motif. Its effect on Romanesque decoration will be traced in Chapter IV. This system of corbels and pilasters in the Mezquita is a first manifestation of the Andalusian tendency to carry the emphasis, not only of structural but of decorative weight, upwards; the horseshoe arch form also contributes to this sometimes top-heavy effect (F5).

The sanctuary, and a patio with rows of trees planted to continue the lines of the arcades of the sanctuary, were all surrounded by a wall of solid Flemish-bond masonry. This was reinforced by rectangular buttresses at intervals (11) and crowned by stepped merlons (12).

There were two doors each on east and west, one into the sanctuary and one into the patio, and a central gate on the north. The whole east façade has disappeared, but the west door leading into the sanctuary, perhaps redesigned in part in the 10th century, survives. This door is known as the San Esteban door (Puerta San Esteban). It is crucial to subsequent design in several respects, to be discussed below.(fig.3).

A minaret was built by ´Abd ar-Raḥmān I´s son Hishām (788-822), to whom was left the task of putting the finishing touches to the mosque building.

Three characteristic elements of Romanesque church building are thus already found at Cordoba in the 9th century: a tall tower, a monumental doorway, and a cloister.

The First Extension

´Abd ar-Raḥmān II (822-852) extended the sanctuary southward by demolishing the south wall, leaving piers the thickness of the arcades and the depth of the wall, so that the rhythm of the arcades continued virtually unbroken; he added eight columns to each arcade and a new qibla wall with a mihrab projecting outside it (in the manner of a Roman apse), and he extended the side walls, reinforced with the same rectangular buttresses as before. Some of the material was re-used but a number of capitals were new; they are sophisticated copies of various types of Roman and sub-Roman designs. There is no standard shape; there are either one or two rows of acanthus leaves with the heavy outcurving points already favoured in Visigothic and Merovingian sculpture and destined to be characteristic of Mozarabic acanthus capitals. These leaves are common on the capitals of Spanish and south-west French Romanesque churches (F3). The drill was used in the carving, on the whole sparingly (13). The four capitals that flanked the mihrab show the mastery of the sculptor at his best (fig.4); diversity is plainly sought after, one of each pair has a round rosette on the console, the other a rectangular. The looped stems of the inside capitals constitute a motif frequent in both Andalusian and Romanesque decoration (D1). These capitals, with their paired columns, one dark green one red each side, were so highly prized that they were moved to the same place of honour in the new extension (14).

´Abd ar-Raḥmān II, like his grandfather, left his work to be finished by his son; Muḥammad (852-888) celebrated the completion of this assignment in an inscription on the San Esteban door (F2). It is carved on a stone fillet across the diameter of the tympanum and round its edge, in relief as is usual for inscriptions in Andalusia (fig. 5)(15); it is dated 241/855. Relief inscriptions on French Romanesque buildings are rare; there are two examples in southern France, in Roman lettering, at Marcilhac (Lot) and Saint-Sernin in Toulouse (figs 6,7); in both cases other indications of connexions with Spain, if not with Andalusia are to be found (Chap. III). The same relief technique is used for the four ornamental applications of Arabic script on Romanesque buildings (see Chapter III).

The Puerta San Esteban (Bāb al-Wuzara´), Pioneer of Mediaeval Doorways

This doorway is the forerunner of many aspects of later design in Andalusian and Maghrebi architecture; many features of Romanesque doorway design and Romanesque decoration also can be traced to its inspiration. It occupies the central of the three bays contained between buttresses on the west façade of the original oratory. Parts of it are badly weathered and others restored (16). There has been much patching, but the authenticity of the inscription surrounding the tympanum has never been questioned.

It has not been observed hitherto that this doorway complex is unprecedented, as the entrance to a religious building, in the Near East or the West: religious entrances in earlier architecture are disguised behind porticoes or are modest and purely functional. Here the entrance, projecting at the roof line, is the focal point of the whole façade and announces to the outer world the essential features of the interior: the double arcades, a mihrab framed in a rectangular moulding (alfiz), even the roll corbels supporting the arches. Quite apart from the details of design and decoration yet to be discussed, in itself this new declamatory function of the doorway makes the San Esteban door the earliest expression of, and indeed the ancestor to, the great tradition of mediaeval church doorways throughout western Europe. That this is so is verified by the details of structure and decoration that were adopted from it into Romanesque doorway design. India is (fig.8) the nearest region where monumental entrances to religious buildings are found earlier than this one. The following features distinguish the San Esteban doorway:

Tripartite design: a central entrance section with arcading above the door projects from the roof line and is wider than the sections to either side. These latter sections contain blind niches on the level of the discharging arch of the door opening. Roman triumphal arches and the Golden Gate into the palace city of Diocletian at Split, and more immediately the palace gateways of the early Umayyads in Syria (17) provide models of flanking niches or of arcades above a doorway, but their implications of force and defence are replaced here by splendour of colour and carving for display. The many 12th

12

century façades of western France exhibiting similar design and intent show the potency of this example, launched perhaps at Cluny (Chap.VI). Each section of the doorway is also divided into three horizontally; the central section especially concentrates interest and decoration in the upper part (F5), with cornice, arcades, decorated mouldings, and decorated voussoirs.

The articulation of the façade does not correspond in any way with the interior to which the door gives access. Far from being placed opposite an arch, the door opens onto a column of the nearest aisle arcade, and is not even exactly centred on it (18). The Romanesque façades of churches in the Angoûmois and Saintonge often do not correspond to the interior plan: single nave churches have tripartite façades, or façades imply non-existent tribune galleries. In each case it is the sanctuary, mihrab or apse with altar, that is announced: the interior architectural disposition is not the reference.

The door opening is recessed, as are almost all Romanesque door openings.

The opening has a voussoired lintel, and a tympanum with a discharging arch above. The decoration of the tympanum has not survived. Later Mezquita doorways modelled on this one have tympana of stone with inlaid brick patterns.

Like the arches of the interior arcades, the discharging arch over the tympanum is composed of alternate stone and composite brick voussoirs (Fl3); here the stone voussoirs are carved with stylized plant scrolls, and project slightly beyond the plane of the brick ones. Each stone voussoir is bordered in some way (Fl4), several with a fine ribbon motif of two strands that occasionally cross each other (19). Many of the enriched blocks of the blind arcading and flanking niches are similarly edged with foliage motifs.

The extrados is marked by a projecting enriched cavetto moulding (Fl5).

The same moulding forms a rectangular frame (Fl2) (alfiz), across the top and down the sides of the arch. Projecting chamfered blocks connect the lower ends of this frame with the bottom of the extrados. Though it may be tempting to attribute the uncarved state of these blocks to later restoration (20) it is to be noted that there is no example in Andalusia until after the 11th century of an alfiz turning into the extrados.

Above the alfiz ran a triple arcade, (Fl7) with shallow blind niches, and pilasters enriched with plant scrolls. Two courses above these arches runs a salient fillet moulding; it suggests the upper line of a wide alfiz that may originally have framed the triple arcade.

Above this again runs a <u>projecting cornice</u> supported on nine close-set <u>roll corbels</u> (Fl).

The top of the wall is crowned all round the roof line by <u>stepped merlons</u>. These follow the projection of the roof line at the central section of the doorway in the same way as they follow the projections of the buttresses, with angled merlons at the corners.

The <u>recessed niches</u> (<u>fig.9</u>) flanking the door, though much weathered and patched, can be seen to have been covered with carved decoration. Most of the scrolls are in a style different from that of the voussoirs of the discharging arch, and more similar to that of the fragments of niches found under the floor of the east end of the Mezquita, now propped against one of the pillars (21).

The edges of the blocks are carved with <u>border motifs</u>. This edging is now inconsistent, but the general <u>shape of the niches</u> was clearly always <u>rectangular</u>, with a <u>stepped lintel</u> echoing the shape of the merlons above (Fl9). Below this lintel and its corbels runs a scotia moulding; Torres Balbás thought it may have been the extrados of a voussoired lintel.

The two corbel blocks of each niche are edged with a stepped plain fillet while the upper lintel blocks were bordered with a little trefoil motif (22). The stepped lintel rests on what appear to be simulated <u>roll corbels carved with scrolls</u>.

The upper block of the southern niche lintel is carved with a <u>crossed looped stem</u>, and the northern one was doubtless the same. This motif (Dl), and the related crossed stems on the inner mihrab capitals, persist through the 10th and 11th centuries into the Romanesque repertoire.

The spandrels of the niches were decorated with volute bosses (Fl9). <u>Motifs set in the spandrels</u> between arch and <u>alfiz</u> are characteristic of subsequent Andalusian decoration. On the 10th century mihrab the boss becomes a plant scroll; in the 11th century at Zaragoza (<u>figs</u> 10,51) it adopts the form of a <u>hollow rosette</u> (Dl5), like the great arch spandrels under the dome in the 9th century Great Mosque of Qairawan . The great play made with spandrel decoration in Spanish Romanesque architecture can be attributed to the precedent set in Andalusian design, and in France there was some response to the same inspiration. In 10th century Andalusia the rosette appears both as a small relief medallion and to decorate the ceiling of domes with large coupolettes (<u>fig.11</u>). Spandrel motif and hollow rosette, though not combined, both figure in Romanesque decoration.

Over each niche are traces of a <u>shallow blind arch</u>

hollowed in the masonry. This probably rested on colonnettes, like the niches flanking subsequent doorways (F10);
the surviving carved blocks formed the jambs.

Inserted into each of these arcades, or framed by them
from the beginning, is a pierced marble grille (23). This
grille is standard on subsequent doorways, pierced with
various geometric patterns.

Further Features of 9th century Andalusian Architecture

By the mid-9th century at latest the interior arcades
and west door were in all important respects as they are
now (see n.6), with the interior arcades consisting of the
unique double tiers of arches, the lower of round horseshoe
form, the upper semi-circular. The double tier of arches is
a theme reflected in the arcading (F17) over doorways and
mihrabs, not only in the Mezquita but in all subsequent Andalusian architecture, and it affected Romanesque doorway
design. In the mosque of al-Hakam II the pilasters of the
upper order are sometimes replaced by engaged columns: the
arcades of San Pedro de Roda have superposed columns; two
registers of columns buttress the chevet at Saint-Sernin in
Toulouse (fig. 13) and at Sainte-Foy in Conques ; the apse
at the Ile de Ré is similarly supported (F9).

The extrados of the upper arches is edged with a line
of saw-tooth moulding of small bricks between brick fillets. This ornament, indigenous to the brick architecture
of Mesopotamia, is not uncommon in stone on First Romanesque buildings (for example at Saint-Guilhem-le-désert)
nor in painted representations of architecture, and it occasionally enters Romanesque architecture (24).

The ceiling is likely to have consisted of wooden panels laid flat on transverse beams between the arcades.
Those that survive are from the second extension and will
be described in that context. Al-Idrīsī described the ceiling in the late 12th century, but he does not distinguish
different areas; it is likely that the early parts had
carved and painted decoration like the later, but the style
of decoration is not known.

Torre San Juan

From the 9th century, in addition to 'Abd ar-Raḥmān's
extension to the Mezquita, there survives though in bad repair a small minaret, now the bell tower of the church of
San Juan in Cordoba. On each face is a recess: on one side
it is pierced with twin windows (ajimez,F11), on the others
there are twin blind niches divided by a slender column
(F8) with a capital. Above these ran a frieze of arcading
on marble colonnettes (F17), seven to each side. The twin
window or niche, not yet seen in the Mezquita, became one
of the characteristics of 10th century style, both on Andalusian and Mozarab monuments. It was later adopted in

Catalunya and France (fig.14).

The Sources of these Andalusian Features. Western Character of Andalusian Art

The Mezquita at the end of the second campaign, in 855, was a new type of building in the west of Europe. While it was intended to reproduce the ancestral Syrian monuments of the Umayyad dynasty and to assert the identity of the ruling house (26), the methods and details of its structure and decoration link directly with the pre-Islamic building practices of the peninsula, so that the result is an Iberian, Western interpretation of the Syrian models.

In the reign of ʿAbd ar-Rahmān II (822-850) the fashions of the Abbasid court at Baghdad, its taste for exotic luxuries, its manners and protocol, dominated the palace and high society of Cordoba under the tutelage of the singer Ziryāb (27); secular architecture is likely to have been strongly affected by this influence, but none survives. It is surprising how little the religious building reflects the styles of contemporary Mesopotamia. The architects and designers working in the Mezquita appear to have maintained a vigorous independence: the forms new to the West, dictated by Islamic tradition, evoked responses evolved from features rooted in the local traditions: the clearest example of this is the way the multiple aisle arcades are interpreted with corbels and stabilizing arches instead of the usual Islamic tie beams. The masonry system, buttresses, alternating brick and stone in the arches, horseshoe shape and double tiers of arches, roll corbels and the completely new departure in doorway design, in short every detail except the merlons cresting the eaves, continue ideas inherent in the Roman monuments of the West, many of which still stood in southern Spain itself (28).

It has been usual among art historians of the Romanesque to refer, if at all, to Cordoban features and influences in France as "oriental" (29). In this they take insufficient account of the fact that even at its beginnings the architecture of the Muslim conqueror in Spain, and its decoration, is only to a limited extent a foreign implantation, but is primarily an early Western response, after the inertia of the Migration period, to a revived stimulus from the East, corresponding to the contemporary Carolingian responses to Byzantium (30). It shares features and tastes with Carolingian architecture. The use of polychrome masonry common to both Andalusian and Carol-ingian is an obvious example, but much more generally, Andalusian art is best regarded as one of the richest aspects of the western revival represented further north by Carolingian art.

The 10th Century

In the 10th century the same independence in the choice and treatment of available motifs becomes even more apparent. During the later 9th century Cordoban hegemony was challenged by the emergence of several strong provincial Muslim powers. Toledo and Zaragoza were among the number of quasi-independent regions. The Christian kingdom of Asturias naturally joined in the resistance to Cordoban supremacy and in Andalusia this provoked persecutions of the Mozarab population by the sorely threatened central power. These persecutions in turn provoked the emigration of Mozarabs to the north; they came bringing with them much of Andalusian culture (31). The list of Mozarab buildings begins with San Juan de la Peña in 850 and Valdedios in 893, and grows longest in the first half of the 10th century (32). The legacy of Mozarabic art to Romanesque decoration is most apparent in the ivory and metal workshops of León and Cogolla and in the capitals of San Miguel de Escalada, but Mozarabic buildings with stone corbels, ribbed domes, the use of twin windows and the alfiz also show Andalusian features in the Christian context.

The survival of Mozarab monuments does a little to fill the gap created by the disappearance (33) of all Andalusian buildings of the period between 855 in the reign of Muhammad, when the extension of ʿAbd ar-Raḥmān II was completed, and the time when ʿAbd ar-Raḥmān III succeeded in re-consolidating Cordoban rule and was ready to celebrate his success (34). This he did in 929 by declaring himself Caliph, thereby asserting his equality of status with the rulers of Baghdad, Qairawān and Constantinople (35). This new position required suitably magnificent buildings. Most of ʿAbd ar-Raḥmān's building energy and resources were devoted to his new palace-city of Madīnat az-Zahrāʾ on the outskirts of Cordoba; work began in 935 under the personal supervision of his son, later the caliph al-Ḥakam II. The whole complex was ransacked and obliterated early in the 11th century, but vast quantities of carved stone and building fragments have been recovered in excavations during the present century (3).

In Cordoba itself nothing remains of ʿAbd ar-Raḥmān III's palace buildings, which were extensive. In the Mezquita he enlarged the patio northward and added porticoes on its three sides. These were rebuilt early in the 16th century but the original order was preserved, with three arches on columns separating masonry piers with engaged half columns; this articulation is the Byzantine and Syrian arrangement, adopted by the builders of the patios of the Umayyad mosques of Damascus, Rusafa and Hama (36). The cloisters of Silos and Moissac are early examples of a similar disposition of supports for a cloister gallery.

17

The Minaret

`Abd ar-Rahmān´s new minaret contained two inner staircases which only met at the high outer gallery of the tower. The division was marked on the outside by the two pairs of twin windows lighting the two staircases on the south and north faces. The dual structure is echoed, and now with no justification from the internal structure, in the exterior design of some Catalan belfries, for example San Miguel de Fluviá, Saint Michel de Cuxa, Ripoll, San Pere de Roda. Hernandez believes such dual designs show an influence from the Cordoban minaret, and he traces the influence further into Italy, Germany and France (37).

The windows of the new minaret all consisted of a thick springer block and three voussoirs, but the arch was faced with limestone and plastered in simulation of multiple voussoirs, with an extrados centred well above the centre of the soffit (F16). These simulated voussoirs are white stone alternating with red stucco (F13), on a plane projecting about 20 mm beyond the red. The heads of the voussoirs are given contrasting ends, the white stone a recessed red, and the red "brick" a raised white end, and the join is shaped in a double lobe. The device of decorating the extrados with diminutive lobes was widely adopted in later Andalusian and North African architecture, and will be seen to have had some repercussions in Romanesque also .

In 958 the north wall of the sanctuary of the Mezquita was reinforced with an additional façade, doubling the original transverse arcade which was leaning from the thrust of the internal arcades, not surprisingly after two centuries. These arches, like those of the minaret, are drawn with a higher centre (but only slightly) for the extrados (F16), a device henceforth constant and increasingly exaggerated in Andalusian architecture until the end of the 11th century. The extrados of these arches is simulated by a stucco moulding (F15) which also frames the intermediary panels. It is likely that the arch face was also originally given simulated voussoirs down to the impost by means of a stucco facing. The eaves of the additional roofing rest on horizontal stone slabs supported on roll corbels (F1) decorated with a variety of engraved motifs (<u>AHIII</u>, fig.96).

The Second Extension. The Climax of Caliphal Decoration

In 961 al-Ḥakam II succeeded his father as caliph and immediately initiated a new extension to the Mezquita, already planned in the time of his father. The architects and builders who had been enlisted at Madīnat az-Zahrā´,some from as far afield as Constantinople and Baghdad (38), now transferred temporarily to the capital before returning to resume work at the Madinat.

This second extension to the Mezquita is very different from the simple and sober building which it enlarged

(39). The exterior walls were continued as before, with minor modifications in the masonry bonding (40), with the same rectangular buttresses; monumental doorways on the model of the San Esteban door were inserted between them where previously a single public door had sufficed on either side. The central of the three new main doorways stands forward slightly from the wall line, like the central tract of its model, but little else can now be ascertained about it: all three doors are so much restored that many details must be discounted (41). The previous south wall was pierced by eleven large double arches, those into the extension of the central nave and flanking aisles being richly carved and decorated.

The Villaviciosa Chapel (AHIII figs 146-152)

The first three central bays of the nave extension are roofed with a dome. The arcades are stabilized by a net of superposed intercrossing lobed arches (F20,21,Chap.IV). The south side of the dome rests on four columns at each corner, with two intermediary columns supporting a complex system of lobed and intercrossing blind and open arches under a 13-lobed blind arch spanning the whole width. The dome is formed by eight thick semi-circular arches of cut stone (F22), leaving a square in the centre, with long voussoirs that rise behind the filling web between them (42). These spring directly from the cornice set above the various arches defining the tract. The web between the ribs is carved with miniature domes (D15), three of those in the corners with a pattern of ribs similar to the main domes, but lobed and forming hexagons, not squares; the fourth is fluted, with six wide and six narrow undulations, and contained in a hexagon. The other spaces contain hollow rosettes and small medallions in relief (F4) with geometric devices, or stars (13). In the centre is an octogon containing an evenly-fluted little dome with twelve undulations .

The Miḥrāb and Maqsura Tract (AHIII figs 153-191)

The central nave has pilasters decorated with geometric motifs in carved plaster (figs 37,38) resting on the roll corbels (many of these with a double fillet). It leads from this dome tract to the central of three domes which are raised on double columns (F6 figs 18,16) in front of the new mihrab and its flanking bays, to form a kind of transept. The domes here are again carried on thick rectangular-section intersecting arches (F20), leaving a central space. The mihrab tract dome is faced with mosaic (43); a fluted cupola, one wide undulation between two narrow ones, rests on an impost cornice faced with glazed ceramic. The surviving flanking dome on the west is like the entrance dome, carved with hollow shells, stars and rosettes, and relief medallions.

In these domes the ribs do not fall directly onto the walls as they do at the entrance, but on colonnettes whose bases overhang a cornice. Lobed squinches, their arches framed in an alfiz, create an octagonal drum. Trilobed arches alternate with the squinches (figs 11,14).

Lambert and Torres-Balbás (44) believed these domes to be ancestral to Gothic ribbed vaults; they fulfil the same mechanical and structural function. From the point of view of decoration their influence is evident, first in Toledo at Bab al-Mardum (Cristo de la Luz), then in Spain in the Castilian Mozarab domes of San Millán de Suso (Cogolla) and San Baudelio de Berlanga; in the later Romanesque at Almazán and Torres del Río. In France in the 12th century they were directly reproduced at the Hôpital Saint-Blaise (Landes) and in Sainte-Marie in Oloron (figs 12, 15-17).These two close imitations of Cordoban domes represent the height of a tradition that earlier had given rise to a number of humbler Romanesque domes and vaults with heavy ribs of rectangular section, often springing from the sides as well as, or instead of, the corners of supporting walls, for example at Aubiac, Mouchan, Bessuéjouls, Saint-Pierre Toirac, Saint-Hilaire in Poitiers, Comminges, or the tower porches of Moissac, Corméry and Saint-Ours in Loches.

The domed maqsura tract, separated from the congregation by low pierced screens below and intercrossing arches above (45)(F20), is given increasingly sumptuous decoration round the mihrab and into the domes. Here was concentrated the greatest wealth of materials and forms: marble, glass, ceramic, carved and painted plaster, brick and stone; almost every surface was carved, with much use of painting and gilding. The scrolls were painted with red grounds, and inscriptions with blue (46). Capitals were gilded.
All the columns were new, alternately dark mottled green marble bearing Corinthian-type capitals, and pink breccia under composite. In the central nave the decorated pilasters also hold alternately Corinthian and composite capitals. The alternation of types, particularly of the columns, offers a model for the alternation of supports in some early Romanesque churches, for example, Jumièges, Saint-Hilaire in Poitiers, Conques, Jaca, Santiago de Compostela, Notre-Dame-du-Pré in Le Mans, and the differing rhythms of ribs and engaged columns in the naves of the great Auvergnat churches.

The Mihrab (fig.18)

The analogy of al-Hakam´s mihrab with a doorway is evident. To what extent it follows the previous mihrab is not known, except that the columns of the entrance were moved thence. It perpetuates, with elaborations, many of the features of the San Esteban door: the entrance is recessed, its arch is contained in an alfiz, it is surmounted by arcading, the flanking bays contain secondary mihrabs (niches) surmounted by grille windows, the mosaic decoration, before restoration, alternated light and dark scrolls on a contrasting ground on the "voussoirs". As elaborations we find the entrance arch is now supported on twin columns (47), the alfiz is composite, the arcading above it is trilobed. The increase of decoration towards the roof is enhanced not only by the widened horizontal band of the alfiz but by the design of the main arch and the arches of the arcades, all of which have the centre of the circle of the extrados raised relative to the intrados.

The roll corbels carved in the marble panels beneath the extrados moulding and the alfiz are also elaborated: their concave profile is filled with a down-turned leaf (D16, fig.19), a motif which also decorates some of the corbels of the nave (LTB 1957, fig.364). This wholly unclassical notion occurs in very similar guise, not on corbels but on capitals in Romanesque sculpture, starting at Ripoll in Catalunya and later at Moissac in the cloister, and at Conques, Loarre or Mourens (figs 20-26).

In the recessed spandrels of the mihrab large circular medallions like buds (F19), in various depths of carving but everywhere comparatively deep, sprout from stems, as a variant on more conventional spandrel bosses and hollowed rosettes. These innovations will be seen reflected on later doorways.

The Chocolate Door (AHIII, figs 192,193)

The only surviving doorway of al-Hakam´s east façade is a clear imitation of the mihrab; the spandrels repeat the bud medallion, the alfiz is composite; a two-fold recession of corbels, with down-turned leaf filling the profile, supports archivolt and extrados. The intersecting arches of the dome tracts are acknowledged in the intersecting arches of the arcading above.

The Third Extension

The final and largest extension was carried out by Almanzor (48), chief minister of al-Ḥakam II´s son Hisham II, and de facto ruler (978/9-1002). It was begun in 987/8 (49). Al-Ḥakam´s extension had already come so close to the river bank that a platform had had to be built to support the south wall. Almanzor therefore enlarged the mosque eastwards, since the river blocked further extension southward and the palace stood on the west. He added eight aisles along its whole length. The interior is austere: Almanzor, at pains to secure the backing of the Malikite clergy, cultivated an image of piety and humility to compensate for his usurpation of caliphal power. He forbad any inscriptions bearing his name, and equally any mention of the legitimate caliph for whom he was regent (50). For the first time however some columns bear the engraved signatures of masons.(51)

21

Al-Ḥakam´s mihrab and maqsura were retained, and all the earlier arrangements were respected: the arcades repeat the previous model; the arches are in fact of stone throughout, but are painted to simulate alternate brick and stone. Capitals have no decorative carving, but the corbels are carved with curls at the sides; a number have shell or leaf motifs filling the profile, and there are traces of paint (F1, D16).

The arches piercing the previous east wall have been encased in later centuries, but a small section of two of them has been recently uncovered, revealing in one case the impost and spring of a round horseshoe arch, and in the other a convex-lobed arch (fig.27).

Along the new eastern façade were placed seven spectacular doorways (AHIII, figs 216-223, LTB 1957, figs 382-391), now heavily restored. These faithfully reflected the model of the San Esteban doorway with the addition of pious references to the mihrab and other enrichments of Almanzor´s predecessors. Each entrance was flanked by twin niches (F11) and the columns were supported on roll corbels with a central downturned leaf or projecting rectangular fillet; in one case at least the arches over the window grilles to each side of the door were lobed (52).

The Anomaly of the Eleventh Bay

The curl motif prevalent since its use on the roll corbels of the first mosque finds a rather baroque exploitation in the design of one arch (C-D and G-H on plan fig.28) of the transverse arcade in the 11th bay of al-Ḥakam´s extension. Curls are carved and painted on the face of the only undisguised pointed arch in the building, whose soffit is formed of 44 convex lobes (fig.29). The authenticity of this arch as part of al-Ḥakam´s design is questionable on several counts, although Brisch (53) maintains that the arcade continuing the line of the maqsura to the east and west walls is original. This he argues less on grounds of the style of the carving of the pierced grilles and their positioning, which is anomalous, than for structural reasons: the stone beam that runs along the transverse arcade above the level of the arches is necessary to buttress the thrust of the domes. An inscription painted in plaster on the northern face of this beam in the westernmost aisle is in a style of lettering consistent with a caliphal date and has convinced him of the originality of the whole arcade in spite of its irregularities.

Doubt must surely arise however when it is observed that the final arches both to east and west are designed to coincide with a doorway, that is certainly original, in the outer wall. The impost of the final arch to the west is inserted off centre into the masonry tympanum to rest on the voussoired lintel (fig.30). The corresponding east doorway, where Almanzor cut through al-Ḥakam´s wall for his extension, is walled in, and the transverse arch is supported on a medley of masonry, one piece of which bears two mason´s marks identical with marks that occur several times on columns in Almanzor´s extension. This piece is similar in size and shape to the impost blocks above the short columns that lined the openings made by Almanzor in al-Ḥakam´s east wall. M.-L. Arscott has argued for a date if not in the 13th century at any rate at a date after the east wall doorway aperture had been filled and smoothed by Almanzor´s campaign in 987 (54).

Stylistically the three outer arches of the transverse arcade on each side, and the grilles in their spandrels, are out of keeping with the rest of al-Ḥakam´s extension. On the unrestored west side, the pointed arch flanking the maqsura and the two flattened horseshoe arches further west have concentric intrados and extrados, whereas the centre of the extrados is elsewhere raised well above that of the intrados,with the aim of heightening the efffect of the arch. The arcade bounding the north of the Gothic nave created by Bishop Iñigo Manrique in 1489, westward from the Villaviciosa chapel, is the least altered part of the junction of the second extension with the first, and provides an example of what are certainly al-Ḥakam´s original east-west arches (fig.31). These resemble the arches of `Abd ar-Raḥmān III´s façade on the north front, with a raised centre for the extrados; they are quite unlike the arches of the 11th bay transverse arcade. Furthermore the arch 11C-D with curl voussoirs is the only one with arms narrower than the platform provided by the corbel supporting it (figs 32-34).

There is thus an accumulation of details for questioning the present arrangement. What structure preceded it, and how far the buttressing of the domes was spread laterally in the first instance, is open to debate. The application of the curl motif to elements other than corbels, particularly to arches, is well attested for the 11th century, in the Aljafería in Zaragoza and in North Africa in Merinid Sedrata (55). Already the curl was exploited in a variety of ways at Madīnat az-Zahra´ and a fragment of carved stucco of the 10th century also survives from Granada: it is part of an arch with a smooth soffit edged with curls in deep relief, as on one side of a fillet corbel (AHIII,fig.317).

Cristo de la Luz, Toledo

The only surviving Andalusian structure of the 10th century outside Cordoba is the oratory of a small mosque which stood at the gateway called Bab al-Mardum in Toledo. The mihrab and all surface decoration has gone; an apse was added on the north-east in the 12th century when the mosque was converted into a church named Cristo de la Luz. A relief inscription in brickwork on the south-west façade dates the building to Muharram 390 (December 999) and gives

23

the name of the private founder (56). Nine miniature dome bays create a central plan unique in Andalusia (AHIII, figs 259-263)(57). Each dome is different; all have thick rect-angular section ribs (F22) forming patterns, devoutly if crudely imitating the domes of the Mezquita. The ribs rest on a cornice cresting the walls of each bay and overhang it. The inscription on the exterior runs right across the façade and is set above a band of lattice work and a row of interlaced arcading in relief (F20) resting on trapezoidal imposts. The three entrances beneath are disparate, the westernmost five-lobed and two-centred, the central round-headed with raised extrados, and the southernmost, nearest the mihrab, a round horseshoe. Inside on a level between the arcades and the domes are walls pierced with one or two openings, complemented by niches on the outer walls; many of these openings and niches are trilobed, and over the mihrab was set an arcade with intersecting trilobe and horseshoe arches (fig.35)(58).

Ewert's examination and analysis of the building has led him to the conclusion that not only the decorative patterning of the dome ribs, but every essential part of the building pays tribute to the Mezquita (59). It is from buildings such as this, which followed either the religious or secular traditions of caliphal design, that will have come the greatest impact from Andalusia on Romanesque architectural decoration.

Caliphal Decorative Motifs

A review of the basic decorative repertoire es-tablished by the end of the caliphal period will clarify later developments.

The usual comment evoked by the richness of Andalusian decoration is that it is "dense, compact, covering all the surface like a textile"(61). An equally valid comment, rarely made, is that Andalusian decoration also carefully articulates the architecture: openings, arches and niches and often their components, are outlined with bands and plain fillets, walls are divided into dadoes and panels, imposts and lintels picked out, different planes emphasized or suggested. The integration of decoration to structure, with its marked tendency to concentrate decorative weight upwards, is different from the Romanesque approach, but it is not absent. While plant motifs predominate, and evoked the greatest inventiveness among Andalusian designers, some aspects of the linear and geometric patterns, minor in the 10th century but which were later to become insistent in Islamic decoration, both western and in the East, also found repercussions in Romanesque.

Linear and Geometric Motifs

Intersecting arches (F20). Relief decorative arcading with intersecting arches on the exterior façades of some of

al-Hakam II´s and Almanzor´s doorways into the Mezquita,
and in Toledo at Cristo de la Luz provides a precedent for
this motif in Norman England and Romanesque Sicily. It is
seen occasionally in Normandy itself, at Graville Sainte-
Honorine and a few other places, perhaps influenced from
England (61), and introduced independently of the roll corbel, which appears early at Jumièges and Caen.

Polychrome inlay executed in brick or terra cotta into
stone is confined to motifs in straight lines; the earliest
examples are inside the minaret of `Abd ar-Rahman III, on
walls and in the vaults over the staircases. At Madinat az-
Zahra´ it is used for pavings and for dadoes, and in the
last two extensions of the Mezquita for many vertical surfaces: voussoirs, alfiz bands, tympana, niches. The same
simple rectilinear zig-zag and key patterns, swastikas,
lozenges, are used to decorate the facetted pilasters of
al-Hakam II´s central nave, moulded in plaster, and the
pierced marble grilles assume them as well as rounded plant
forms and circular interlace (62).

There are instances of this inlay technique in the
Rhône valley: coloured cement is incrusted in stone at
Saint-Maurice in Vienne and Saint-Apollinaire in Valence,
terra cotta on the tympanum of Saint-Pierre in Vienne (63).
In Languedoc a number of churches have simple designs inlaid in basalt. These include Saint-Pierre-de-Rhèdes, which
has the lintel with a mock-Kufic inscription (Chap.III).
The polychrome stone mosaic on the façade of Le Monastier
in the Velay and on many later Auvergnat church exteriors
has been claimed as inspired by Islamic exterior decoration
(fig.36). The pilasters of arcades, some fluted as in the
Mezquita,and at Cluny III, on the apse and choir of Saint-
Etienne in Nevers and those of La-Charité-sur-Loire
(fig.37) and other exteriors, particularly in the Berry
(fig.38) (many responding to the radiation of influence
from these) and in the Saintonge, are carved with geometric
designs to produce a similar effect to the pilasters in al-
Hakam II´s nave.
The mihrab mosaics are of course in a different category;
they share motifs with other media of decoration, as painting and relief carving. Mosaic flooring coming to light in
Gascony, at Saint-Sever, Sordes, Layrac or Lescar suggests
a continuing and shared tradition, but the connecting links
are hard to find (64).

Smaller plant and border motifs. Many of these de-
ployed in the mosaic and carved decoration at Madinat az-
Zahra´ and in the Mezquita have a place in Romanesque decoration. The themes are nearly all common to the different
media employed, both in buildings and for luxury objects,
but woodworkers and ivory carvers show certain preferences
more peculiar to their own craft traditions.

These motifs are nearly all versions of a wide-ranging
Mediterranean repertoire; some which are to be found in Ro-

manesque and in which a Cordoban influence is to be discerned are listed in Appendix I with comments. A few of the most obvious may be touched on here. The down-turned leaf (Dl6) will be discussed in connexion with corbels. Asymmetrical plant scrolls and meanders (D8) often appear on voussoirs as a consequence of the shape dictated by simulated jointing systems (AHIII,figs 182,193)(65). They are repeated with a stronger suggestion of Kufic lettering in the spandrels of the lobes of some of the earlier carved marble altar tables from the Pyrenean and Narbonne workshops, for example those of Quarante, Gerona and Rodez, and on imposts at Roda (66).

Round the outer border of the mihrab alfiz a relatively naturalistic acanthus stem flows entwined with curling indented leaves (D9). It is reproduced almost exactly on the façade of Saint-Pierre in Angoulême (67) and other buildings in the area (fig.39(68).

The square composite flower- or leaf-cross Dl0, given prominence on the marble mihrab panels (fig.19), is also the main motif on the relief studs decorating the Villaviciosa and maqsura domes and their walls. It has close affinities with the rosette that dominates the dome decoration in the form of hollowed coupolettes, as is manifest in the eaves panels of Madinat az-Zahra´(fig.20) where the composite flower is framed in a medallion shaped like these coupolettes. It occurs on corbel B-1 at Tudela (69) and it reappears on the wooden doors of Chamalières and Lavoûte-Chilhac (figs 77,78).

The little florets D3 that accompany the composite flower in the Mezquita, at Madīnat az-Zahra´ and on corbel B-1 at Tudela also persisted in the woodworking repertoire particularly in connexion with ceiling decoration, at Toledo, Malaga, Granada, Segovia and finally on the wooden doors of Le Puy. Plaster ceiling members in the Aljafería are also bordered with them. (AHIII figs 151, 113, 178, 307, 316,290-292).

On some caliphal capitals acanthus stems are entwined or more rarely twisted into spirals (LTB 1957, figs 475,487, 499, 503). Spiral stems are more frequent in the 11th century in the Aljafería (fig.40). The spiral "column" among acanthus was exploited on Mozarabic capitals and is one of the diagnostics used by Garcia-Romo (70) to trace a Mozarabic influence on early sculpture in the Loire region, for example at Saint-Benoît, (fig 91 and Vergnolle, Saint-Benoît-sur-Loire nos 44b,51b,31a tower r.-de-ch), Cormery, Saint-Hilaire in Poitiers and Méobecq.

The hollow rosettes or coupolettes of the Cordoban domes were regarded by Mâle as ancestral to the rosettes in the soffits of Auvergnat corbel tables. Similar rosettes decorate some of the miniature stud medallions in the maqsura. The affection of Andalusian designers for many forms of rosette was shared by Romanesque artists; in addition to the Auvergnat hollow rosette (anticipated on soffits at Madinat az-Zahra´ with an intermediary suggested by the wooden ceiling in Segovia fig 46), the great rosettes of the Moissac and Thézels lintels and an altar panel from Cluny (71), or of the eaves soffits and metopes of Jaca, Moirax and the Porte Miègeville of Saint-Sernin in Toulouse, have Andalusian precursors in plenty in architectural decoration and in the lobed medallions of applied art. The mihrab of the Aljafería mosque chapel has particularly fine examples in the spandrels of the arch (fig.10).

Motifs used in Woodwork: the Ceiling of the Mezquita

The decoration of the wooden ceilings in the Mezquita introduces elements not found in stone or plaster carving (LTB 1957, ˙ figs 343-351 and col.pl.opp.p.544)(72). Colour is more varied, adding green,black, white and brown to the blue, red and gold of the stone and plaster carving (73). The variety of combinations of straight line, angle and curve produces cartouches and medallions of ever different shapes; they run along the separate planks of the ceiling to create frames, executed in gold dots along a black band, within which other carved or painted panels were nailed. None of these panels survives. The beams, underneath and on the sides, were carved with formal plant motifs, specially running palmette scrolls (fig 41)(LTB 1957, figs 346-351, 393).

The legacy of this wood workshop is seen persisting in the 11th century and still operative in mudéjar work in Spain into the 14th (AH III fig.278a, 13th century) (74). There were signs of trans-Pyrenean ramifications too in the Romanesque period: the double half-palmette (D7) meander is repeated almost exactly on wood in the Velay, in associa- tion with the flower cross, florets and split palmette mo- tifs of caliphal marble decoration, and it reappears in the same woodworkers´ technique of low two-plane flat relief on some distinctive stone imposts, not only in 11th century Spain at Jaca, Nogál (fig.43) and León, but in the Vendée at Maillezais (fig.42) in the mid-11th century, a few decades later at Saint-Outrille in the Berry, slightly grooved (Berry roman, fig. 16), and then at Villesalem in Poitou.

The Fez Mimbar

Another rare survival of caliphal wood carving is a panel from the mimbar of the Andalusians´ Mosque in Fez (75). A relief inscription (fig.44) containing the names of Hisham II and al-Mansur ibn Abi `Amir (Almanzor) surrounds and bisects it, dating it to the late 10th century. It mer- its a detailed description since the carved decoration adds a number of motifs to the repertoire of caliphal adoptions into Romanesque. A mihrab, a trilobe arcade on columns, oc-

cupies the vertical panel of the top arched section. The
arch is a plain fillet from which rise at the top two divergent half-palmettes held with two binders (D6). The
niche contains three leaf scrolls in a form which also decorates a border inside the upper inscription band of foliated Kufic. This consists of a circle divided by an S-curve
(D14), shaped by a pear-shaped pine cone (D2) occupying one
half of the circle, the other part of which is filled with
a half-palmette. A similar motif occurs on Mozarab chancel
panels, and it is little changed as impost decoration in
Moissac cloister. Circular floral medallions (D15) containing leaf bosses, with an outer ring of petals holding florets (D3), are set either side and below the central section of the panel. The lower rosette is flanked by geometric medallions with rosettes in the interstices (D13), made
of grooved lines. The columns of the representations of the
mihrab are also grooved, as are the outlines of the
rosettes and inner borders (D12). The inscription and all
the edging of the lower section is a plain fillet. The centre of the lower section is occupied by a succession of
stepped "mihrabs" (F19) containing half-palmette scrolls,
on either side is a rosette in a square over a horizontal
panel containing mock Kufic. The letters of the inscription
round three sides of this section are angular, while those
of the upper one are rounded. Both are partly foliated,
with half-palmette terminals. There are no fleurons over
the small letters and they are rounded, but some triangular
forms might suggest to a non-Arabist a triangular mim such
as appears on the Le Puy door (Chap.III).

The details of the decoration on this panel exemplify
a tradition which can without difficulty include the non-
figural decoration of all four wooden doors in the Velay to
be discussed in Chapter III, and indeed the general composition of the Fez panel has many analogies with that of the
other three doors in the neighbourhood of Le Puy.

Architectural Decoration in 11th Century Andalusia

Nothing comparable to the Mezquita remains for the
post-caliphal period. In Toledo the chapels of N.S. de Be-
len in Santa Fe, and of San Lorenzo in the parish church of
that name, are quoted or illustrated by Gomez-Moreno (AH
III, pp. 207 ff.) together with details from San salvador
and Las Tornerías, as examples of the continuation of the
Cordoban tradition through the 11th into the 12th and 13th
centuries. Corbels from Tudela (fig.45) and an 11th century
wooden ceiling from Segovia (fig.46) are other such examples to be examined.

With the death of Almanzor in 1002 began the fragmen-
tation of Andalusia into the taifa kingdoms. The accumu-
lated wealth of the caliphate was now dispersed among a variety of city states, and added to the revenues from their
ever-thriving industries and trade (76). Every large city
became a capital with a royal court, yet of all the palaces

built during the 11th century only rare traces remain standing; these are primarily in Malaga and Zaragoza.

The style of decoration, especially in stone and plaster, surviving on these fragments and on finds elsewhere such as those in Granada and Almería, is consistent enough to allow of the generalization that Andalusian architectural decoration had entered a "baroque" phase. The model was still Cordoban, its idiosyncracies like lobed and intersecting arches, the top-heavy loading of columns, voussoir decoration or palm-leaf arabesques are all heightened and exaggerated so that surface decoration becomes progressively more elaborated and unstructural (AH III, figs 305, 2286, 295). The approach was thus alien to the organic and architectural character of the contemporary experiments in Christian decoration (77). Even so some of the motifs and methods were adopted by Romanesque designers.

Malaga (AHIII, figs 305-309)

In Malaga a few pavilion arcades are attributed to the reign of Yahya (1023-1035).Intersecting arches (F20) are supported on slender columns (F8); the decentralisation of the extrados (F16) is higher than in caliphal arches and the contrast thus more marked between the heavy arch and its slender supports. The alternation of carved and plain voussoirs (F14) is echoed in the extrados which consists of a broad, plain-grooved moulding inside a band of carving. The decoration makes much of the geometricized and stylized plant interlace and the elongated fern-like palm leaf that had already begun to make its appearance at Madinat az-Zahra´ (78) and on the Chocolate Door (AHIII, fig.193). This is an aulic "baroque" style suited to plaster carving and doubtless developed by plasterers.

A different style is however apparent in the decoration of the wooden beams of the same building, now in the museum (AHIII, fig.307) with inscriptions and corbels carved with bands of little isolated florets (D3) or rings in flat two-plane relief. The ends of the corbels are shaped as a down-turned leaf (D16), and the heart-and-dart (D11) is taken from the mihrab panels or its imitation at Madinat az-Zahra´ (79).

Granada (AHIII, figs 316, 326)

In Granada the lions of the fountain court (D17h) and some fragments in the museum belong to the Zirid period (1012-1090)(80). There is also the Bañuelo, a baths building next to the arch of the Islamic city wall across the Darro, near the Alhambra. It contains a series of capitals (AHIII, figs 313-315), some of which show development of the same type as the early capitals of Ripoll (81). The volute stems of the Granada capital are plain and rise vertically, like early Romanesque capitals at Tournus, Frómista

29

or Iguácel (see Frómista, Chap.III).

Roof members of wood in the museum are carved in the same way as those of Malaga, some with a little more attempt at the kind of relief achieved in plaster work, but with the same border bands and motifs, downturned leaf and scrolls. Among plaster fragments is the arch with curl border already quoted, and a heavy acanthus leaf-point from a capital. Scroll carving introduces many little rings or curls, both where stems branch, and at the ends of folioles, in contrast to Cordoban leaves which tended to have similar rings or eyelets between the folioles.

Toledo

Fragments of carved marble plaques and a few capitals are all that is left of the famous Galiana palaces in Toledo, built by the Dhu-n-Nunids Isma´il az-Zafir (1028-1043) and Yaḥya al-Ma´mūn (1043-1075) (AHIII, figs 270-278) (82). Their public works will be discussed in the section below on marble carving.

Tudela (fig. 45)

A simpler form of the circular half-palmette type of branching scroll than on the Toledan fragments is applies as a half-palmette in a number of versions in low relief on the stone corbels that survive from the mosque of Tudela (83). These will be compared in Chapter III with scrolls on the 12th century wooden doors of the Velay. Once again we find roof elements, albeit this time of stone, approximating to the flat style of all surviving Andalusian woodwork, described above in connexion with Malaga and Granada. Some stem branchings on these Tudela corbel scrolls are held in a double band, similar to the characteristic triple-V bands of Romanesque capital scrolls, such as at Toulouse.

San Millán de Segovia (fig.46)

Strong evidence for the rôle of roof and ceiling work in the transmission of Andalusian motifs into Romanesque comes from Segovia(84). Remains of a wooden ceiling discovered behind the 17th century vaulting of the church of San Millan are parts of the ceiling of the church built during the repopulation of the city after its occupation by Christian forces in 1088. The ceiling is constructed in the same manner as the ceiling of the Mezquita, and carved in the same style, and there is even a Kufic inscription on the architrave panels: "al-mulk lillah" "The kingdom is Allah´s". This is the same, very common, phrase as is inscribed on the doors of Le Puy, and on the ceiling panels of the 11th century in the Great Mosque of Qairawan. "There are four-lobed coupolettes [i.e. hollow rosettes, D15] on the soffits of the San Millan ceiling, just like those of the cornice at Ebreuil"(85), which is to say like all the typical Auvergnat cornices. The corbels at Segovia are ei-

ther fillet-roll corbels or "prow-shaped" with a down-
turned leaf (D16); they and the accompanying panels are
carved with little florets (D3), detached or in circles,
palmettes in hearts (D11) or coiling scrolls (D7), all in
two-plane relief, and bordered with plain rectangular-section fillets "exactly like the woodwork from Malaga,
Granada, the ceiling members of the Mezquita and indeed of
the Great Mosques of Qairawan and Tlemcen" (86).

The Aljafería, Zaragoza (AHIII, figs 279-299)

Restorations in the Aljafería and excavations at Balaguer (87) have revealed a small part of the achievements
of a mid-11th century workshop in the northern marches,
working for two rival members of the same princely family.

The interlacing arcades of the Aljafería were removed
to the museums of Madrid and Zaragoza in 1866 (AHIII, figs
295-298). The oratory and mihrab are preserved in situ and
now restored. The surrounding wall and defensive tower,
probably an earlier construction, are of stone; the internal work is all of brick and plaster. The arcades of the
porticoes, which stood at either end of a large court, simulate with a bewildering complexity of interlacing arches
and columns a series of five-lobed arcades, all rendered
with outlines of a broad composite plaster moulding against
a lattice of foliage. The same 5-lobed and mixtilinear
arches that surround the oratory on two registers are here
jumbled with their columns tossed at all angles on a screen
that spanned the width of the patio; Romanesque wheel rose
windows, such as that at Balaguer, on a small church on the
very site of the ruined palace (fig.47), exemplify a simpler stricter discipline imposed on this composition (88).

The mihrab arch of the Aljafería has deep coupolettes
in the spandrels, similar to the rosettes in the mihrab
tract of the Great Mosque of Qairawan. They correspond to
the incrusted bacini popular in Romanesque Italy. In
France, a rare example of the use of bacini survives at
Saint-Antonin (Lot) (figs 48,49) where the incrusted bowls
are Fatimid of the 11th century, whether imported from
Egypt direct or via Spain is unknown (89). St Antonin also
has lobed arches.

The process first seen in ´Abd ar-Raḥmān III´s minaret
and developed in al-Hakam II´s mosque (fig. 50) of marking
extra lobing at the head of each or alternate voussoir to
give a filigree or fishtail effect is taken further on the
intrados of arches in the Aljafería, with secondary lobing:
this marks a stage towards the lambrequin profiles of Almoravid arches. It provides a possible source for the fish-
tail and voluted voussoirs of the group of lobed arches
connected with the Cahors south door (Chapter IV).

The capitals of the Aljafería belong to the same type
as those noted at Granada, represented also in the early

churches at Ripoll and Cornella, in the tradition of the caliphal models of the later 10th century (fig.21). The larger Aljafería capitals have heavy projecting acanthus leaf points (F3) (figs 40) and the decoration is profuse. It includes twisted columns between the acanthus leaves and the Cordoban crossed stem (D1) under the console (which itself has almost or entirely vanished) .

The plant decoration carved in plaster in the Aljafería and at Balaguer is everywhere restricted to single-foliole palm leaves of baroque aspect; the carving on the members in and supporting the dome (fig.52) at Zaragoza however comes closer to the style found on the roof members described above from Tudela and Segovia than the decoration in the rest of the palace: the two-plane relief is dominant, the soffit and metope panels are bordered with separate small florets (D3), both features constant on wooden ceiling work at Malaga and Granada as well as Segovia. The downturned leaf (D16) is much exploited on the corbels, as will be seen in Chapter V..

Non-Architectural Secular Decoration, Caliphal and 11th Century: Marble and Ivory

What survives of marble and ivory carving must represent all that is lost from the palaces of Andalusia. There are many recorded buildings which do not survive, the Alcazaba of Malaga, for example, rebuilt by Badīs of Granada (1057-1063), and a large palace built by Jarrán (1012-1028) in Almería, as well as baths and fortifications; many records are still unexamined. Baths were often decorated, and the roofs pierced with patterned openings. They were much frequented: Ibn `Idhārī reports that there were 300 baths in Cordoba alone in the 10th century (90). Animate themes and the peculiarities of design in the Aljafería show secular architecture following the lead of ideas initiated in the precious materials. Two new features stand out, both testimony to the western complexion of Andalusian artists´ aspirations.

It is highly appropriate that it was in western Islam, among the ivory carvers of Cordoba, that animate themes, hitherto only countenanced on textiles and ceramics, should be adapted to sculpture. Andalusia was here a pioneer in the formation of the "general Mediterranean style", and with themes particularly relevant for Romanesque decoration. The second innovation initiated by these artists is the new prominence given to a device used only occasionally in the Byzantine tradition: the inclusion of borders in the field of design by interlacing them with the outlines of the larger elements, such as medallions, cartouches or arches, as well as linking the medallions themselves in the more usual Byzantine manner (91). This device brings added movement to the whole pattern. It was little cultivated by the architectural decorators in Andalusia until the 11th century, when it was exploited with some panache in parts

of the pavilion in the Malaga Alcazaba and in the Aljafería
(92). There not only are medallions created by twisting the
frame of a frieze (a similar border is carved on the wooden
door of Blesle in the Velay), but arch mouldings themselves
link with medallions, cartouches, alfiz or framing architrave; the loops between are dotted with florets or interlace studs.

Marble

Marble troughs and basins (93) illustrate a repertoire
of animate motifs in decoration which are vouched for in
Andalusian literature (94) but little known in surviving
buildings. Discoveries at Madīnat az-Zahra` since the war
(95) have included many vestiges of Roman sarcophagi,
deemed to be evidence of al-Ḥakam II´s famous enthusiasm
for collecting antiquities. These might encourage Andalusian sculptors to attempt other than plant decoration even
in architecture; the carved limestone facings of the halls
and pavilions of the palace built during his reign include
a few fragmentary animate motifs such as birds in foliage.

The plant decoration of the basins on the whole differs little from that of the architecture. Some fragments
of panels (AHIII,figs 242;243), probably from basins, show
a greater exploitation than is found in the Mezquita of
large rosettes (D15), like those on early Islamic architecture in the East, as at Mshatta (96), but equally like the
dished circles on some Roman sarcophagi. They are framed in
plain stem medallions or in arcading. The use made of this
large rosette motif in Romanesque decoration, among other
examples at Cluny, Vienne, Valence and Lyon, and on the
lintels of Moissac, Beaulieu and Thézels, is strikingly
similar in effect (97).

As to animal motifs, two capitals and the volute of
another are the only known architectural pieces, apart from
wall facings, with animals carved on them (AHIII, fig.245,
LTB 1957, fig.502). One capital, from the site of a palace
west of Madīnat az-Zahra` has consoles carved alternately
with animal attack (two lions attacking a gazelle) and confronted basilisks (D17e); the volute fragment is from the
same site and consists of a lion head (D17f) or moustached
mask without a jaw, spitting a foliage scroll, and little
birds in procession round the sides. The other capital, of
unspecified provenance and location, has a geometricized
lion head replacing the volute of a cylindrical composite-
type capital. Torres-Balbás groups it with Corinthians of
the period of al-Ḥakam II, without commenting on the volute
form (98).

The figure decoration of the basins is much more
prominent. It is based on a standard composition. None is
dated earlier than Almanzor, and the whole series is generally attributed to 987 and after, as furnishings for Alman-

zor´s vanished palace of Madīnat al-Zahīra (99). The animal
repertoire of the main decoration is restricted, on the series of basins with vertical sides, to lions attacking
gazelles, and the triumphant spread- or half-spread eagle
with ancillary creatures at its feet or on its wings, or
both, mostly felines or griffins (fig.55)(D17d,e). There
are suggestions here for the piled animals of the Moissac
trumeau (D17g, cf. AHIII,figs 246-7) and a precedent for
the long necks of Romanesque beasts in Poitou and Angoûmois. Several basins are bordered with a band of small
birds and fish, and these motifs, the birds more specifi-
cally ducks, are used as a main motif on the other series
of basins with flaring sides, designed to stand on
pedestals (D17b,c).

The tails of all the lions on these Cordoban basins
are tufted. and leaf-shaped, a detail, like the stilts under the feet, repeated on the lions of the Christian font
in León discussed in the next paragraph (100). An
abbreviated reference to the animal attack theme is used on
two of the shallower type of basin where the heads of lions
and their prey, antelope and other horned heads are framed
alternately in a line of V-shaped leaf motifs (AHIII,
fig.252). The lion heads, like that on the volute just
described, have moustaches and are without a lower jaw.
This composition, most usually with a lion head framed in
the V, and the lion head or mask spitting foliage, had
widespread appeal in Romanesque sculpture (figs 53-
54)(101). Part of the leaf motif adapted on this basin to
the upper border is repeated on capitals at Zaragoza
(AHIII,fig.280) and comes strangely close to the horn
volutes on certain early capitals with ram heads at La
Trinité in Caen (102).

The Stilt Motif (figs 55, 56)

The Alhambra basin depicts both the predatory lions
and their prey with their feet perched on trangular
"stilts". The origin of this curious and very rare device
is puzzling. The fact that the lions´ feet have added
"heels" on the sudarium of Ste Colombe and St Loup in Sens
cathedral suggests that the sculptor had misread a oriental
textile design (the "heels" in the textile can perhaps be
interpreted as claws), but some contact is implied between
Cordoba where the design originated, and similar occurrences in Tuscania and León. At Sa Maria Maggiore in Tuscania (103), over the blocked 9th century doorway in the
south aisle, above twin colonnettes (F6) with crude palmette and volute capitals, is carved a man holding his arms
to about the height of his ears, and possibly involved with
a lion now destroyed; his toes are supported on discs. At
León a font (fig.56) with crudely represented Christian
themes on two sides is equally crudely carved on the third
with confronted lions perched on "stilts" similar to those
of the Alhambra basin lions. It can hardly be that this
same device was taken unthinkingly from a textile motif

into sculpture in three separate places quite independently. In the Silos Beatus manuscript (104) jongleurs are represented with fantastical triangular heels, providing another example of "lifts", but this does not suggest a solution as to why animals be portrayed with them; the transference of this curious motif to animals by Spanish sculptors remains obscure without further documentation. On the St Martin capital in the tower-porch of Saint-Benoît (fig.57) the saint's attendant angels stand on jawless lion heads(Dl7f). This suggests that the saint, posed frontally, is intended to stand on a footstool rather than on stilts? The corner figures also are curiously raised (Val de Loire roman, fig.23). A stucco panel of a peacock from Ctesiphon (105) has claws so exaggerated as to become almost stilts; the connecting thread is elusive.

A scaley tail coiled near the feet of the lion's prey on one of the fragments of a tall vertical-sided basin found in the Alhambra introduces the snake (Dl7k) as another subject in the caliphal repertoire of animals (106) (AHIII,fig.248 [drawing], (LTB1957, fig.562 [photograph, not very clear]; this corresponds with a lively tradition in Romanesque iconography, particularly in Spain.

The 11th Century: the Játiva Basin (107)

In the decoration of the basin preserved at Játiva the caliphal repertoire is extended to include more themes with human figures (AHIII, figs 320,330). Baer has found that all but three of the subjects derive from earlier Islamic treatments of ancient oriental motifs. Of these three exceptions, two are purely classical: the atlantes and the woman lactans ("from a Hellenistic Gaea"), while the beard-pulling old men (fig.58) are equated by her with the mimus calvus of late classical theatre, set in an Islamic type of wrestlers' pose such as is seen on the al-Mughira casket in the Louvre (108). There is no reason to dispute her conclusion, already arrived at by Gomez-Moreno, that these lively carvings express the mixed urban society of 11th century Spain.

The influence of Roman and early Christian sarcophagi has not been commented on by these scholars in relation to the composition of this piece. The plain frames and ground of the slightly hollowed medallions and their spacing between frieze-like scenes derives more directly from such a source than from the elaborated floral medallions of the Cordoban ivory caskets quoted as parallels by Baer. Though the precise model for the Játiva basin is not immediately apparent among sarcophagi illustrated in current publications (109), analogies in gesture and composition can be seen at a cursory examination of such sarcophagi as those preserved at Huesca, Ager, Gerona, Covarrubias, Ampurias and Zaragoza, illustrated in Ars Hispaniae II (110).

The beard pullers, tilting knights, atlantes and pea-

cocks with entwined necks, the animal attack, the eagles
and the musicians of the Játiva basin are all motifs found
in Romanesque sculpture. The depiction of fiesta scenes on
the Játiva basin is paralleled in the Romanesque of north
Spain by the introduction of fairground or circus themes in
capital and corbel sculpture: monkeys, bear-tamers, acro-
bats, at Santiago, Frómista, Jaca and León. This same topic
of entertainments took hold in Poitou and Middle Loire
(111). Andalusia provides no examples of sculpture with
performing animals, though the traditional animal attack
possibly carried a reference to contemporary circuses, appearing as it does among scenes of court pleasures on the
ivory caskets and the Játiva basin. At the Muslim palace of
Qusair `Amra in Syria a mural painting of a bear playing a
musical instrument (112) is a rare parallel in eastern Islam.

The bald-headed beard-pulling wrestlers appear in the
margins of the Saint-Sever Beatus and on a number of Romanesque capitals and reliefs (figs 59-61)(113). The tail
of the peacock of the Játiva basin is reproduced exactly on
the capital of the portico of the little 11th century Romanesque church of San Esteban de Gormáz in Castile, situated near the Muslim-built castle (fig.62); nothing else in
these rough capitals shows any close connexion with Andalusian themes apart from one corbel with a beard-puller, and
he is reminiscent of a capital on the serpentine basin from
the cloister in Conques (figs 63,64).

There are no surviving illuminated Muslim manuscripts
from Andalusia with which to compare the treatment of drapery on the Jativa basin. Its stripes and spirals are not
unlike some Mozarab drawings (fig.65) where the turban is
also relevant for Romanesque parallels; the closest resemblances in sculpture are with the lintel figures of Saint-
André-de-Sorède (Roussillon roman figs 20, 21) and capitals
of La Sauve Majeure (fig..67)(113), rather than with
caliphal figures, known only on ivories.

The Játiva Atlas Figures and Related Compositions

The atlas figures of the corners approximate in their
relaxed stance to many figures of the caliphal ivories,
with something of a dancer´s gait. They wear the same short
tunic as is always found on beard-pullers, wrestlers and
other figures of this kind, the shared head and the leg position also connects them with a distinct type of Romanesque design associated with the beard-pulling theme
(figs 68-70).

The powerful version on a capital of the Puerta de las
Vírgenes at Silos (fig 61) is echoed at Chauvigny in
Poitou, where a veritable circus is portrayed, all on a
similar symmetrical pattern. This composition had
repercussions in the Saintonge, for example at the Abbaye
des Dames in Saintes for a "Gilgamesh" with birds, or at

36

Colombiers (Saintonge romane, figs 24, 131-136). At Avy, the figures on the doorway, copying Chauvigny but with thin legs crossed, have the short tunics and beards harking back to Silos. At Marignac, the capital sculptor treats the Saintes Gilgamesh subject in a style closer to Silos, as a corner figure with thin legs, gathered cuffs and "turban" hair (114). At Blesle the composition follows the version copied on capitals at San Juan de las Abadesas from the Silos model, but there are no beard-pullers. Figures on the porch capitals of Saint-Benoît show an early stylistic stage in this type of composition: adjacent capitals upstairs in the tower-porch show a beard-puller who provides a model for those in the Saintonge, and a rudimentary figure composition of this symmetrical type, with short-belted tunics. Furthermore, the lion-rider resembles the Silos beard-puller with thin legs, gathered close-fitting cuffs, braided headgear and wide sleeves.

Turban Hair Style

The headgear of the "stave dancers" and peasants (115) on the Játiva basin raises the topic of "turban" hair style in Romanesque figures: the shepherds of capital 61 in Moissac cloister and the figures of several other capitals belong in a series that needs investigation for its associations. A provisional list includes the Silos beard-puller capital, examples on the Silos reliefs, the Risen Christ capital at Bayeux, the Saint-Benoît lion-rider and the Marignac Gilgamesh just mentioned; an acrobat on an early capital from La Daurade, Toulouse, the St Peter on the Porte Miègeville at Saint-Sernin in Toulouse and the similar figures on the Lamb doorway at San Isidoro, León; the Christ healing the Leper in the Panteón in León, a capital at Varen (Lot), the Lavaur altar (116) and one of the wrestlers on the façade of Notre-Dame-la-Grande in Poitiers (figs 124, 261, 93).

Carved Marble in Toledo

Well-heads set up by the civic munificence of the Dhu-n-Nunid emirs, together with inscribed tombstones and steles both Jewish and Muslim are preserved in the Santa Cruz Museum. The well-head set up in Toledo in 1032 (fig.71)(118) has an idiosyncracy in the form of writing of the inscription which relates it closely with the "Kufic" inscribed on an impost in Moissac cloister. This will be discussed in greater detail in that context (Chapter III). The decoration, with plait interlace and notched border motifs, has affinities with ivory carving. The distinctive split form of the letters is first seen in caliphal ivory carving (119). The plain rectangular-section fillets separating the registers and the shallow relief standing out in one plane are close to the examples of wood-carving style already noted. This is even more apparent on an inscribed brick tomb slab in Toledo not listed by Lévi-Provençal (AHIII,fig.274).

37

It will be shown in Chapter III that the type of lettering on impost 50 in Moissac cloister must derive from Toledo. For this reason the scrolls carved on the marble fragments from the Galiana palace in Toledo museum merit special scrutiny as a likely source for the distinctive type of scroll associated with this impost. On one such fragment ((AHIII, fig.272a) an axial stem tends to proliferate at intervals or form a bud or knot. On fig. 272b are confronted birds. Fig. 272c introduces a six-point star rosette and the double stem axis finishes at the top with crossed leaves. The emphatically circular coils of grooved stem, with palm-leaf folioles extending beyond (in 272a behind) this circle, the curl of the inner foliole creating a circle in 273c, are all features of the scroll at Moissac, even though the fronded palm leaf of the Toledan models, which is totally characteristic of Andalusian ivories and architectural decoration ever since Madinat az-Zahra`, is rejected at Moissac; as with the horseshoe arch form the Romanesque designer has avoided the most distinctive and characteristic elements of his Islamic model.

Ivory

The earliest examples of animate motifs in Andalusian art are the series of ivory carvings. The workshop began a little before 960: the earliest pieces are those inscribed for the daughter of `Abd ar-Raḥmān III, one before and one after his death in 961 (121); the majority of surviving pieces were produced in the following decade. There is no evidence of earlier ivory carving in the peninsula, but the work begins with no sign of hesitation in the style of its plant scroll carving. It is a mature stage of development from the fusion of disparate elements that began, as far as can be deduced from the evidence, in the decoration of the state rooms of ´Abd ar-Raḥmān III at Madīnat az-Zahra` from 1035 onwards (122) and went on to the end of the reign of al-Hakam II with a break while the same sculptors were seconded to the Mezquita. The plant repertoire of this carving in stone, stucco and marble is interpreted on the ivories in higher relief, relative to scale, with more modelling and more sensitivity of movement as befits the precious material, and matched by particular care and subtlety of detail. The incurled hollow leaf D4 comes into its own with deeper relief. The attention to relief and modelling as well as the introduction of animate motifs makes the ivory caskets particularly relevant to Romanesque sculpture (figs 301 a - d).

Like the carved decoration of the Mezquita, the carved ivory was not left uncoloured, but was given the same red ground and blue relief as the wall facings, with the addition of gilding on occasion (123). Many of the animate motifs on the ivories are those familiar from oriental ceramics and textiles (124). Just as the effect of rich hangings was that aimed at on the carved and painted wall facings, the silks which provided models for the designs and often lining or wrapping for the objects, were imitated with all their lustre and colour on the ivories themselves.

Inscriptions on the caskets form part of the whole composition, and the calligraphy is varied subtly to match the style of the designs (125). The animate themes in general relate to courtly pleasures of Iranian tradition; many of the subjects are found in Romanesque iconography also, among them elephant, animals and birds with crossed or intertwined necks tails or bodies, wrestlers, confronted dancers or riders, lion vanquishers, hawkers (Dl7o,a,h,s,t, u.v).

The creation of major patterns, not only with plant stems (as on the Hispanic Society casket, AHIII,fig.356), but with symmetrical figures (as with the dancers on the Metropolitan Museum plaque AHIII fig.359) and the Zamora box, AHIII fig.355)or, if in festooned medallions (as on al-Mughira's casket in the Louvre, [AHIII fig.361] and the caskets of al-Ḥakam II and ibn Aflaḥ in the Victoria and Albert Museum [126]) against a sinuous interplay of foliage, is however not an art acquired from textiles or other media but an innovation comparable to the inhabited scrolls of Christian art (127).

Some familiarity with ivory figure-carving in Christian Europe, particularly the late Metz school (128) is implied in the treatment of drapery and hair on the al-Mughira and ibn Aflah caskets, but in the Christian designs the concept of frame or background is static, and all energy and life is concentrated in the figures. Ottonian plaques and book covers tend to be surrounded with repeated acanthus, or studded with closed-form scrolls (129). These are the same Byzantine-inspired scrolls that decorate the panels of the mihrab in the Great Mosque of Qairawan though on the Qairawan mihrab the motifs are used not as borders but in statically juxtaposed groups. It is, nonetheless, the same repertoire that was disseminated all round the Mediterranean. In Cordoban decoration these same abstract plant forms are combined into flowing patterns. Asymmetry and dynamic interlace are introduced, albeit with the restraint befitting the most refined and civilized court in Europe (130). The naturalistic plant forms of Roman capitals and friezes are one factor that might inspire such organic development out of the universal static medallion scroll; Kufic lettering is another that would tend to a cultivation of asymmetry and movement. But underlying these currents there is a pressure to fuse the assembled elements into a new style where motif and border share the same energy. This pressure is best explained by affinity with Celtic and Nordic art with their even greater drive to all-

over movement, to intertwine the energy of motif and border
(131). It may be deemed to be the contribution of the
indigenous Celtic sub-stratum of the population from which
Romanesque art must also have derived some part of its
character.

1.   see Glossary: "Andalusia". The Great Mosque of Cordoba is referred to consistently in Spanish as "La Mezquita" and will be referred to hereafter as "the Mezquita". The different parts will be named according to their building patrons, or as first mosque, and first, second and third extensions. In this chapter references to illustrations in the two standard works AHIII and LTB 1957 (see Chapter I, note 8) will be made in the text, to supplement those presented here.

2.   The decoration of the façade and the ribbing in the nine-domed bays of the small mosque at Bab al-Mardum, now Cristo de la Luz, in Toledo, dated by inscription (completed Muharram 390/December 999), shows how strongly the Mezquita influenced Andalusian architecture, even the most modest. C. Ewert, `Die Moschee am Bab al-Mardum, eine "Kopie" der Moschee von Cordoba´, Madr.Mitt.18.1977, pp287-354, refers  p.290 to  R. Krautheimer,  `Introduction to an "Iconography" of Mediaeval Architecture´, JWCI V, 1942 (n.11,p.2ff) and G. Bandmann, Mittelalterliche Architektur als Bedeutungsträger, Berlin 1951; id., `Ikonologie für Architektur´, Jhrb. f. Ästhetik u. allg. Kunstwissensch. 1951, and other subsequent writers for discussion of the mediaeval concept of a copy.

3.   LTB 1957, pp 423-463,(p. 439, n.88, for further bibliography); R. Castejón, `Nuevas Excavaciones en Madinat al-Zahra´´, al-And  x, 1945,  pp 147-154;  M Ocana Jimenez, `Inscripciones arabes descubiertas en Madinat az-Zahra´ en 1944´ al-And x, 1945; L. Golvin, `Note sur  un décor  de marbre  trouvé  à  MaZ´,  al-And  xxv,  1960;  B.  Pavon Maldonado, Memoria  de la Excavación de la Mezquita de MaZ, Madrid 1966;  id.,  `Influjos occidentales en el arte del Califato de Cordoba´, al-And xxiii, 1968. The workforce numbered 10,000 labourers and slaves with 1.500 skilled tradesmen; they employed 400 camels belonging to the Caliph and 1,000 mules; 6000 blocks were laid daily apart from floors, foundations and bricks, and 1.100 loads of lime were delivered every three days; 4,313 columns were used of which 1.013 came from North Africa, some from Rome, 19 from the region of the "Francos". The "King of Rum" (Emperor of Byzantium) sent 140, others were turned from the marble of Taragona, Almeria and the veined onyx of Reyyo in Malaga. Some green and pink columns came from a church in Sfax. The number of door valves, lined with iron or bronze, was 15,000. The mosque was built in 48 days with 300 masons, 200 carpenters and 500 labourers (LTB 1957, p. 433-435).

4.   LTB 1957 pp 364-5, quotes earlier horseshoe arches in Visigothic Spain, Italy, Portugal, Syria, Cappadocia, Armenia, Sasanian Persia. See also M. Gomez-Moreno, `Excurción a través del arco de herradura´, Cultura Española, 1906.

5.   Standardized at about 1/3 of the diameter below the semi-circle. The separation of the jambs is always as wide as the diameter of the arch, with a scotia curve from the impost. E. Camps Cazorla, Modulo, Proporción y Composición en la Arquitectura Califal Cordobesa, Madrid 1953, analyses many examples; P. Ponsich, `L´Architecture pré-romane de Saint-Michel de Cuxa et sa véritable signification´, CSMC, 1971.

6.   These are based on the plan drawn up by R.H. Carpenter, `The Mosque Cathedrals of Cordoba and Seville´, Trans. R.I.B.A. XXXIII,1883, from a Spanish Government plan of 1859. Working under my supervision M.-L. Arscott, in The Transverse Arcade in al-Hakam II´s Extension to the Great Mosque of Cordoba, Fifth Year General Studies Thesis, Architectural Association, London 1976 (unpub.thesis) pp 37-39 gives a list of plans and publications of the Mezquita, reproduced here as an Appendix to the Bibliography. I am much indebted to her for her co-operation and for permission to use her findings. Full documentary details of the second extension are given in the notes of E. Lévi-Provençal (henceforth ELP), L´Espagne musulmane au Xe siècle, Paris 1932.

7   A dome marks the entrance to the new nave, and each aisle of the new extension was entered through a transverse arch. Along the sides were monumental doorways, the central one distinguished from the rest by a raised roof line.

8.   There are discrepancies in the chroniclers concerning the chronology and stages of the building, even though they all derive more or less directly from a single source, but not a contemporary one: the lost annals of al-Razi (+955). Al-Maqqari, though the latest, is the most detailed and considered by Torres Balbás to be the most faithful to the common source. Creswell also follows al-Maqqari (EMA short, p. 214); his account is followed here. ELP III p.389 gives an interpretation of various statements culled from chroniclers of the 10th century onwards: according to some, `Abd ar-Rahman II both widened and lengthened the building.

9.   Some texts, notably those purporting to quote al-Razi (the most important are al-Maqqari and ibn Hayyan (cf ELP I n.1, p. 262), give two dates for work on the first extension: 833 and 848. From this Lévi-Provençal deduced that an original mosque of nine aisles was widened by two aisles in 833 and the whole width extended southward by eight bays in 848. This in no way tallies with the findings of the excavations carried out by F. Hernandez (cf. for references, LTB 1957, p. 390). The foundations of the first mosque are laid out for eleven aisles, the qibla wall runs without a break across them to join the north-south walls. There is no trace at all of wall foundations corresponding to a nine-aisled building, only the flimsy separate column foundations. Al-Himyari and al-Maqqari both state the number of aisles of the first mosque was eleven.

(EMA short, p. 214). Lévi-Provençal´s interpretation would mean that the San Esteban doorway was not built until 833, and that twenty years later it was already needing repair, which is unlikely. There is an anomaly in the form of the corbels in the arcades of the first two campaigns: in the two outermost aisles of the first mosque and in all the arcades of the first extension the corbels supporting the pilasters of the upper arches have a convex profile. The eight inner arcades of the first mosque and all arcades of subsequent extensions after the first have corbels of concave profile with a lobed outline (roll corbels, Chapter V). The addition of two aisles at the time of the first extension would explain this, but cannot be allowed, as has been shown. E. Lambert, `Las tres primeras etapas..´ al-And. 1935) proposed that the upper rows of arches were not added to heighten the roof until `Abd ar-Rahman II´s extension of 833. This however is no solution to the anomaly of the different types of corbel and their location. Al-Sayyid Salim, `Cronología de la mezquita mayor...´, al-And. 1945, suggested that `Abd ar-Rahman I´s arcades all had plain convex corbels like the outer aisles, and that Muhammad I had the convex corbels of the nine inner aisles carved into concave roll form. This he justified by interpreting Ibn `Idhari´s statement that Muhammad "perfected the tirar" as "perfected the curls", a possible alternative reading to the more usual "decoration" preferred by Lambert, Lévi-Provençal, Torres Balbás and most others. The anomaly remains of the variant corbel form in the outer aisles of the first mosque and all the aisles of the extension, so little is gained. The least unconvincing hypothesis (Gomez-Moreno, Torres Balbás and Castejón) is that the outer aisles of the first mosque were partitioned off, probably for women´s prayer. It is now generally accepted that the roll corbels of the first mosque are original, and so is the west wall containing the San Esteban door. For a design in the arrangement of spoil and new capitals in the first extension: P. Cressier, `Les chapiteaux de la Grande Mosquée de Cordoue (oratoires d´`Abd ar-Rahman I et d´`Abd ar-Rahman II) et la sculpture de chapiteaux à l´époque émirale´, Madr. Mitt. 1984/85. C. Ewert, `The Almohad Mosque of Tinmal..´ Proc.Br.Acad. LXXII, 1986, Oxford 1987, elaborates on how a ".. ground plan..is realized..on two levels".

10. The upper arches are corbelled out by an impost bearing pilasters which are themselves thickened just below the springing of the upper arches. The imposts are cruciform blocks comprising the springer of the lower arches on the two other arms. The columns, with a diameter of about 20 cm, standing on small separate foundations, carry walls over a metre thick. These walls carry wide stone gutters which, running along the axis of the arcades, take water from double-pitched roofs spanning the aisles. Inside was a flat ceiling of planks on transverse beams, carved and painted. see note 73.

11. "Emplecton" or Flemish bond. The thickness of the wall is that of the length of the blocks (1.07-1.15 m.) and it is thus composed entirely of masonry, bonded with lime-and-sand mortar. The buttresses, of course, bear no relation to any interior structure, since the arcades run parallel to the north-south walls, and there were no transverse arcades except along the north façade. The excavations showed no trace of buttresses on the qibla wall. Each column has a separate foundation of no great strength; the walls are solidly based (AHIII,p.30).

12. Merlons are the only completely exotic feature of the building. They are close imitations of those crowning the walls of the Great Mosque of Damascus, and that of Medina, and of the Umayyad palace of Khirbat al-Mafjar (LTB 1957, pp 367-8 and n.84).

13. A series of capitals is illustrated in AHIII, figs 51-65, most with little drilling, but 57 and 60 have all-over drill work. The use of the drill is mainly characteristic of the later caliphal capital sculpture. It became almost excessive in the later 10th century, e.g. AHIII, figs 182, 183, 188, 211; LTB 1957, figs 484-502, who refers p. 680 to "abuse of the drill", but it was known in pre-Islamic Spain as early as the 7th century. Torres Balbás p.400 quotes examples in San Fructuoso de Montelius in Portugal c.660 AD and others of similar date re-used in Toledo and Cordoba.

14. Ibn `Idhari, qu. LTB 1957, p.394 n.62 (Bayan II,pp 253-254; trans. pp 392-393). No known trace of `Abd ar-Rahman II´s mihrab survives apart from these columns with their capitals.

15. ELP, Inscriptions arabes d´Espagne, Leyden/Paris 1931, passim. The San Esteban door inscription is No. 1, pp 1-2. A passage by Ibn Mufarrij (pub.id., Arabica I, 1954, p. 92) states that the original mosque built by `Abd ar-Rahman ibn Mu´awiya (the Emigré, i.e. `Abd ar-Rahman I who fled after the defeat of the Umayyads to Ifriqiya [the Muslim province of North Africa] and thence to Spain in 750), which now formed the rear of the sanctuary, "was ageing in some parts and in need of repair because of the long time that had elapsed since its construction. Muhammad repaired it and did everything possible to make it perfect, restoring it to its original condition". The inscription is accepted as signifying that the works here referred to were complete when the door was finished and inscribed. Muhammad succeeded `Abd ar-Rahman II in 852 and proceeded to complete the works undertaken by his father. The doorway has been studied in detail by Gomez-Moreno AHIII pp 41-43 and 58-59; LTB, al-And X 1947, pp 139-144 and 1957 pp 356-358, 367 and 404-413; K. Brisch, `Zum Bāb al-Wuzarā´´, in Essays in hon. K.A.C. Creswell, 1965. All agree on the originality of the doorway as a monumental entrance and differ only on the dating of some of the elements: Torres Balbás and Brisch conclude that in essentials - door

opening, tympanum, blind arcading, cresting, windows and flanking niches - it is to be taken as a unit that has survived unaltered from the 9th century to the present. Obvious restorations include the stonework below the impost level, now plain ashlar. Gomez-Moreno thought the corbel table was added to support the wall cresting in the 10th century and that some of the scroll carving is 12th century. H. Terrasse, L´Art hispano-moresque, Paris 1932 (hereafter HT1932) p.67, n.2, considered the carving of the voussoirs of the discharging arch over the door lintel to be modern and the marble grilles "discordantly placed over the old decoration" also. Castejón (R. Castejón, `La Portada de Mohamed I en la gran Mezquita de Córdoba´, Bol.Rel Acad.de Ciencias, Bellas Letras y Nobles Artes de Cordoba, XV, 1944, qu. LTB 1957, p. 407 n.80, an article I have been unable to trace) attributed the voussoirs to the restorations carried out by de Luque about 1860. Gomez-Moreno and LTB, though they agree that the jambs and lintel are restored, perhaps in the 17th century (LTB, al-And.1947, pp 133-4) consider the voussoirs of the arch original from 855. The decoration of the tympanum and all the aspect of the lower parts below the imposts of the arch and the niches is lost, but it is now accepted that the scheme and style of the whole is original. This conclusion is verified by the way in which all entrances on subsequent extensions follow the same scheme, and by the similarity of this design to that of the mihrab.

16. AHIII p.36-38; LTB 1957 p.407 reviews the record of restorations: in 1602 Martin Ordoñez, the cathedral overseer of works, replaced the jamb masonry and the splay of the door. It was not an extensive operation and was scheduled to take one month and to cost only 500 reáls (E. Romero de Torres, `Restoraciones desconocidas en la mezquita aljama de Córdoba, la puerta de la primitiva mezquita, que fundó `Abderraman I, fue restaurada a princípios del siglo XVII´, Actas y Memórias de la Soc. Esp. de Antropologia, Etnografía y Prehistoria, Madrid 1948, pp 83-88). In c1860 the municipal architect Rafael de Luque restored the door (R. Castejón, op.cit, p.496). In 1895, when R. Velazquez was directing architect of the Mezquita, he engaged the sculptor Mateo Inurria to restore the jambs of the discharging arch, substituting new worked stone for old patches of brick and perished stone, and also the "lower small horizontal parts of the alfiz and the parts next to it and to the archivolt". Old photographs taken between 1875 and 1880, published by Torres Balbás(art.cit. note 15, p. 496), show that the decoration has not changed since then. Torres Balbás therefore agrees with Gomez-Moreno that the decoration of the arch is authentic and that the difference in preservation is due to the better quality of stone used in some parts. "A detailed examination of the arch, inside and out, of its alfiz, archivolt and spandrels, and of its inscription, all worked in finely jointed ashlar, gives not the slightest

indication that anything has been moved since it was constructed" (pp 408-9).

17. Brisch, op.cit. n.15 above, regards this doorway as the transposition of a palace entrance, quoting particularly those of Qasr al-Hayr al-Sharqi. The absence of a model in religious architecture is noted by him, and the originality of this door, but the pioneering significance of its monumentality in this context is not brought out.

18. The fact that there is an upper register of arches above the door here cannot therefore be taken as evidence that there already existed an upper row of arches in the interior arcades (Lambert suggested that the upper arches were added in 833, see n.9). However, it is most likely that the arcade arches were there, and that the door is designed to "copy" them.

19. This motif is quoted by LTB as the only importation from Samarra, in the 9th century, and that not necessarily transmitted directly or through architectural examples. It appears in the mosque of Ibn Tulun in Cairo at about the same date (LTB 1957, p.409).

20. LTB 1957, p.404 mistakenly describes the alfiz as "prolonging the extrados" and Marçais, Architecture musulmane d´Occident (hereafter AMO), fig. 102,p. 166, draws it thus. The vital pieces are restored (see n. 16) but probably faithfully so. The niche of uncertain date in the Dome of the Rock has the alfiz joined to the extrados (Creswell, EMA I, fig. 139, p. 100: "We have here the oldest mihrab in Islam from the days before the concave mihrab was introduced.") This passage is omitted in the second edition. If this niche is of the 7th century, as Dr Fehérvari argues from its reproduction on 7th century coins, it provides the earliest example of an alfiz and spandrel bosses.

21. AHIII, fig. 39. Gomez-Moreno implies that these are Visigothic and regards them as proving the early date of the niches, which he puts in the first campaign. LTB however suggests they may be contemporary with `Abd ar-Rahman II (p. 358); possibly they formed part of his mihrab which excavations have found did not project beyond the line of the south wall (AHIII, p.42). The plant scrolls carved on niches, arcades and the central door are of two types: it would be convenient to ascribe them to the two building campaigns. THe first is a full rounded, broadly-drawn style such as occurs on the aisle arcade corbels of the first mosque (AHIII, figs 39-41). The second is a drier and sharper chip carving, with a groove along the stems and hollowed leaves. This style Terrasse finds difficulty in accepting as 9th century.

22. The corbel on the right of the southern niche is closer in style to the door voussoirs, which Terrasse (1932) preferred to date

to the 10th century. Gomez-Moreno quotes a fillet roll corbel in this style from Tudela which he attributes to the mosque built by Musa II of the Beni Qasi in the 9th century (AHIII, figs 72-74). Similarities with work at Madinat az-Zahra´ lead Maldonado (Tudela, Ciudad Medieval: Arte Islamico y Mudéjar, Madrid 1978; hereafter Tudela) to date these corbels and allied fragments to the 10th. LTB says there are similar carvings in the mosque at Tunis, also 9th century (1957, p.411). The capital illustrated by Gomez-Moreno (fig.62) "of the time of `Abd ar-Rahman II" has a tree of life motif in this voussoir technique; it differs from most of the other examples he illustrates for this period; they do not have hollowed leaves. There is thus a strong suspicion that this capital, the voussoirs of the San Esteban doorway and the Tudela corbel are all of the 10th century, and equally the lintel fragment of the niche.

23. The date of the grilles themselves is uncertain. LTB thinks they may be re-used Roman ones. Al-Hakam II and Almanzor both continued the practice of setting a grille on either side of a door, and these were made to the same dimensions as those of the San Esteban doorway. Creswell and Terrasse described them as inserted. Brisch considers them part of the original scheme (`Die Fenstergitter..´ Madr.Forschungen III, Berlin 1966; id., `Zum Bab al-Wuzara´..[op.cit. in n.15], p. 38, n.2).

2 . At Raqqa, AMO, fig.56; it was often imitated in wall paintings in Catalunya and France: O. Demus, Romanesque Mural Painting, London 1970, pls 107 (St Chef), 154 (Brinay), 160 (Tavant), 192 (Bohí), 193 (Pedret), 207 (Estahón, where is also a mock-Kufic border), 206 (Taüll), 211 (Maderuelo); BM 1925, p,233 (Corneilha de Conflent), Aragon roman, pl.22 (Obarra).

25. AHIII, fig. 64; F. Hernandez Gimenez, El Alminar de `Abd al-Rahman III en la Mezquita Mayor de Cordoba, Granada 1975, illustrates a stepped merlon found buried close to the tower (fig.34) and gives full descriptions and discussion of the San Juan minaret pp 134-153. He dates it to the very end of the 9th or very early 10th century.

26. LTB 1957, p. 343.

27. ELP I, pp 268ff, with references. A pupil of the court singer of Harun al-Rashid, he was called before that caliph and was so much praised that he feared the jealousy of his master and fled to the West. He stayed for a time with Ziyadat Allah in Qairawan and then was persuaded to visit Andalusia. Here he was so well received that he settled for life and founded a conservatoire. He became the arbiter of fashion and revolutionized the court life, dictating new manners, music, clothes, cooking and table manners, beauty culture, furniture and diversions. His introduction of the use of leather table coverings, instead of eating off plain wood, gave an impetus to the already famous leather

industry of Cordoba.

28. i. Masonry of Flemish bond is used on the Roman bridge at Cordoba, and the Roman city gate, Puerta de Sevilla. ii. Rectangular buttresses are frequently found on the interior of military and engineering works in Spain and North Africa (LTB 1957, p.362); the aqueduct at Mérida is also provided with them, and this great monument supplies as well a model for iii. the superposed arches of the Mezquita, the lower ones bonded in exactly the same way in both structures, and for iv. the alternation of brick and stone, found frequently in late Roman building and adopted widely in Byzantine and Carolingian architecture. LTB 1957 p. 366 quotes a Roman vaulted underground gallery in Cordoba with this alternation of material. v. The horseshoe arch was common in Visigothic Spain, e.g., relief niches, AHII, figs 262,263,287; apse arcades: Quintanilla de las Viñas. 319, 320; Baño, fig.291; San Pedro de la Nave, fig. 112. Its adoption in Romanesque was minimal. Precursors for vi. roll corbels include Visigothic corbels with a large single roll. The design of doorways, vii, is complex and owes much to Roman gateways. San Miguel de Liño and Valdedios in Asturias have 9th century examples of viii. twin windows.

29. "Orientalism" is even on occasion explained by a location on the route to Compostela in the far west, e.g., Angoûmois roman, p. 19.

30. A. Grabar has in many of his writings demonstrated the frequent interchange of ideas and motifs between Islam and Byzantium, e.g., `La décoration architecturale de l´église de la Vierge à Saint-Luc-en-Phocide et les débuts des influences islamiques´, CRAcIBL, 1971; and Byzantium, London, 1966.

31. M. Gomez-Moreno, Iglesias Mozarabes, Madrid, 1919 (henceforth Ig.Moz.) gives in Chapter I a full account of the effects of the migration into León and Castile, with lists of Arabic names, words and customs taken into common use: they reflect a profound enrichment of techniques, institutions, trade and industry, and the conveniences of everyday life. A. Sanchez Albornoz, Estampas de la Vida de León durante el siglo X, 3rd ed., Madrid, 1934, shows the effect of Andalusian culture on the life of the capital city of León.

32. Ig.Moz., p. XVII.

33. LTB 1957, p. 413 ff, reviews the building works reported for these years. Cities were built and fortified and provided with mosques, in some cases renewing old foundations, among them Ubeda, Madrid, Talamanca, Calatrava, Catalayúd, Lérida, Daroca, Badajóz, Pechina, Bobastro. Mosques of special importance and splendour were those of Lérida, Badajóz and Pechina. The latter port developed enormously with the active trade with North

Africa, and was much frequented by Mozarabs and Muladíes. Some of its prosperity was due to the slave trade and the supply of eunuchs to the East. Building and repair of mosques is recorded also at Medina Sidonia and Ecija, the mosques of Elvira near Granada and of Zaragoza were enlarged.

34. The entire volume III of ELP, Histoire de l'Espagne musulmane, Paris 1967, is devoted to a description of the period of the Cordoban caliphate, the active economic life under a strong central administration, extensive trade, industry, urban development and social life, as well as agriculture, horticulture, stock-raising and the exploitation of natural resources in the countryside. By the end of the reign of `Abd ar-Rahman III the capital "begins to rival Baghdad for its industries and luxury trade" (p. 309). The Christian principalities of northern Spain already provided an important outlet for these industries and for imports from the east acquired through the caliphal capital. J.Gautier-Dalché, `L'Histoire monétaire de l'Espagne septentrionale et centre du IX au XII siècle´, An. Est. Med. 6, 1969; C. Verlinden, `The Rise of Spanish Trade in the Middle Ages´, EHR 1940.

35. ELP op.cit. above pp 111-117, stresses the internal political reasons for this decision.

36. LTB 1957, p. 476.

37. F. Hernandez Gimenez, El Alminar.. (as note 25)., pp 227-263; figs 7 and 8, the reconstructed façades; figs 16-18, the windows.

38. Ibn Khaldun, qu. LTB 1957, p. 432 n.56. The same names appear in inscriptions on both monuments.

39. Each aisle arcade was prolonged by twelve columns southwards, the southernmost bay being hidden behind the qibla wall: to the west of the new mihrab a passage with a series of doors led to a new bridge (destroyed in the 17th century) over the street to the palace, and the earlier bridge was removed. To the east of the mihrab ran a series of rooms for the Treasury and for cult furniture, entered by a single door from the sanctuary. An upper storey of interconnecting rooms was built on both sides with windows looking inside and out through pierced marble grilles similar to those on the façades. The outermost room on the east gave onto the street by the only door now surviving on al-Hakam II´s east façade, called the "Chocolate Door" in modern times: AH III, figs 192, 193.

40. The blocks are 1.60m. long by 64 and 38 cm., with two or three headers between each stretcher, bonded with lime mortar (AHIII, p. 92).

41.Compare AHIII, figs 199 and 200 to see the extent of the

"restorations".

42. Roman vaults sometimes were constructed on a skeleton of brick arches, but these did not show below the filling (LTB 1957, p. 518), and there is no intermediate example in time. LTB describes the ribs as "no more than an ingenious extension of the system of intersecting arches, admirably adapting the flat vertical planes to a three-dimensional space".

43. A master mosaicist, together with 320 quintals of mosaic, was sent as a gift from the Emperor of Constantinople, Nicephoros Phocas, and a number of slaves were set to work with him and soon equalled him in skill (AMO, p.140). X. Barral i Altet, `Les débuts de la mosaïque de pavement romane dans le Sud de la France et en Catalogne´, CSMC 1972, attributes the source of all south French Romanesque examples to Italy, which "was half a century ahead".   Such conclusions are likely to be premature: A. Grabar, Cah.Arch 1954 p.171ff, on Germigny´s Islamic component, and see note 65.

44. LTB 1957, p. 528; E. Lambert, GBA,1925, pp 141-161.

45. C. Ewert, `Die Moschee am Bab al-Mardum..´ p. 352 n.198 and fig. 13, has followed the measurements given in al-Maqqari´s quotation from Ibn Bashkuwwal for the dimensions of the maqsura and concludes that the congregation was kept further away from the focal area: the screen was placed a bay further north than the dome tracts and one aisle further east and west. The effect of the interlaced arches in marking the area would be even more felt.

46. C. Ewert, `Spanisch-Islamische Systeme sich kreuzender Bögen´, Madr.Mitt.7,1966, p. 250, has observed traces of plant scrolls painted in gold on alternately red and blue grounds in the wide bays of the maqsura, on the stucco "voussoirs" of the intercrossing arches overlying the true stone arches.

47. Double columns were used in North Africa in 4th-7th century buildings (W. Kronig, 19th Congr. Hist. Art, 1958), no doubt, as argued by LTB (AEA, 1946, p. 274) under Byzantine influence. Their use at Santa Combe de Bande, Naranco, Sa Cristina de Leña, Melque (AHII, figs 361, 362, 386, 388) shows them implanted in the peninsula before `Abd ar-Rahman II endowed them with the additional prestige of flanking the mihrab. They are used in the colonnades of the Aljaferia, at the entrance to the chapel of San Millán de Suso at Cogolla (AD 984), and in the series of small churches in Upper Aragon, where they are ubiquitous on walls and large arcades, (fig 99) but not for doorways. At Nant in Rouergue, as at Saint-Pierre-de-Rhèdes (fig 16) and neighbouring churches, they are used in the same way. Twin columns flank the entrance at Jumièges, and are not

uncommon in French Romanesque cloisters and tribunes (Moissac cloister, Conques tribunes, Saint-Sernin tribunes).

48. This is the Spanish rendering of the title assumed by al-Mansur ibn Abi `Amir, and the name by which he is known in the West.

49. ELP 1957, p. 394.

50. LTB 1957, p. 573: this is reported along with other legends, but is confirmed by the absence of any such inscriptions.

51. Before this the names of supervisors, sculptors and marble workers appear in the relief inscriptions of al-Hakam II´s mosque and Madinat az-Zahra´, on friezes, bases and capitals, but there are no signatures. LTB 1957, for inscribed capitals of `Abd ar-Rahman II: p. 397; for MaZ inscriptions: p. 457 ff and n.95 with further references. Those named are important people connected with the building; mihrab inscription: p. 478; on side "mihrabs": p. 532, p. 534, p. 537 n. 83; engraved on ceiling panels: p. 549.

52. The later history of the Mezquita can be briefly summarized from LTB, La Mezquita de Cordoba y las ruinas de Madinat az-Zahra´, Madrid 1952, pp 100-106: after the Christian conquest of Cordoba in 1236, mudéjar masons were kept working regularly on maintenance, and the Capilla Reál was decorated in mudéjar style. (The Capilla Reál adjoins the Villaviciosa chapel on the east and is now included in the Cathedral complex). In the next century an austere hall church was inserted in the three aisles west of the Villaviciosa chapel, vaulted across three bays. Finally in 1523 work began on the cathedral. It was finished in 1607. Chapels have been inserted all round the walls of the sanctuary at various times, and restorations are recorded as carried out on the San Esteban doorway in 1602, 1860 and 1895. Other doorways have been restored in this century. The minaret, the description of which by Ibn Bashkuwwal in the 12th century is transmitted by al-Maqqari, lost its crown of gold and silver fruit and lilies in a storm in 1589; it was replaced with a Renaissance top designed by Hernan Ruíz between 1593 and 1618, and was encased in a new tower because it was crumbling, in 1664. It has been excavated by F. Hernandez, El Alminar..1975; cf. also K. Creswell EMA (short), p. 216.

53. K. Brisch, `Die Fenstergitter...´, 1966 (Spanish translation, `Las celosías de las fachadas de la gran Mezquita de Córdoba´, al-And XXVI, 1961 (ii); id., `Una nota marginal a la epigrafia arabe de la Mezquita de Córdoba´, al-And, 1959, pp 183-9.

54. M.-L. Arscott, The Transverse Arcade.., op.cit.in note
6, p. 28. The doorway on the east was filled and smoothed
during the changes involved in Almanzor´s extension of 987.
The supportive solution for the eastern arm of the final
arch of the transverse arcade takes this into account, and
differs consequently from that for the western arm of the
final arch on the west. The conclusion must be that the
east wall had been filled and smoothed before the eastern
arch was constructed, and therefore the arch must be dated
after 987. Arscott suggests a date in the 13th century by
analogy with an arch in San Román, Toledo, illustrated in
B.P. Maldonado, Arte Toledano, Madrid 1973, pl. XXIX.
Concentric archivolts were again current in the 11th
century however, and so were pointed arches, and this may
have been the time when the transverse arcade was carried
to the outer walls. The inscription running along the
horizontal beam is painted in the same red paint as the
outline of the keystone that projects above the extrados to
touch the beam; it has been renovated more than once
(Brisch, `Una nota..´ al-And. 1959, p. 188) and Brisch
admits that the details of the epigraphy are not conclusive
for the 10th century. Archaism is always to be expected in
a religious context of this sort, and other anomalies such
as the rectangular fillets in angles of the imposts and
above (fig.33) which have no explanation in the present
arrangement suggest there were alterations to the arcade
subsequent to the 10th century.

55. AHIII, fig. 293; M. van Berchem, `Sedrata. Un chapitre
nouveau de l´histoire de l´art musulman. Campagnes de 1951
et 1952´, Ars Islamica II, 1957. Also in Egypt, MAE, pl.44:
m5, m7; pl. 64 etc.

56. M. Ocaña Jimenez, `La inscripción fundacional de la
mezquita de Bib al-Mardum in Toledo´, al-And, 14, 1949, pp
175-183.

57. G. King, The Mosque Bab Mardum, M. Phil. Thesis,
London 1972; id., `The Mosque Bab Mardum in Toledo and the
Influences Acting Upon It´, AARP 1972, pp 29-40. C. Ewert,
`Die Moschee..´ (see note 2).

58. The trilobes all have larger side than top lobes
(Ewert, op.cit above, figs 5-9, pls 56 and 57), possibly to
increase an illusion of height.

59. A nave and transept are implied in the arrangement of
decoration: a double register of niches inside and on the
two façades; an entrance on the northern side for the
public and on the west for the patron; this (south)west
façade can be read as a series of quotations from the
Mezquita. Applied negatively the "copy" theory (see n.2)
might be used to help solve the paradox that troubled Mâle:
how could the great abbots of Cluny, the champions of
Christendom against Islam, borrow decoration from a mosque

to adorn their church? The answer would be that they were not "copying" in the mediaeval sense of the term.

60. LTB 1957, p. 691.

61. Normandie romane II, 1974, p. 22: Graville Saint-Honorine, Broglie, Sainte-Marie-sur-Mer, Pont Audemer (Saint-Ouen). In England, Castle Acre, Wenlock Abbey, Malmesbury Abbey, Canterbury etc.

62. K. Brisch, `Die Fenstergitter..´ illustrates every grille.

63. J. Vallery-Radot, `Saint-Maurice de Vienne´, BM CX, 1952, p. 355 ff; `Saint-Pierre de Vienne´, CA 16, 1923.

64. H. Stern, `Mosaïques de pavement préromanes et romanes en France´, CCM 1962; `Notes sur quelques mosaïques de pavement romanes´, Cah.Arch 1966, dates the mosaics of Saint-Sever and Sorde to the third quarter of the 11th century; in the latter article Stern illustrates a mosaic in Die (Drôme), which has the Four Rivers represented as jawless horned monster faces with ear-caps; `Une mosaïque de pavement romane: Layrac (Lot et Garonne)´, Cah.Arch 1960, `before 1085´; J. Lauffray, `Les chevet-martyria de Saint-Sever sur l´Adour et de Sorde l´Abbaye (Landes)´ Cah.Arch 1966, fig. 26a shows a dog and a very Islamic hare (p. 108, n.8: a bibliography for Saint-Sever). The same Kufic-derived border motif as is used round some Saint-Sever Apocalypse illuminations (Bib.Nat.lat.8878) is on one of the interlocking large circles of the mosaic; another is edged with saw-tooth. H. Stern, `La mosaïque de l´église Saint-Genès de Thiers (P.deD.), Cah.Arch 1954-1955, comments on the Mozarab associations (Ripoll, Berlanga, the Gerona tapestry) of the mosaics of Thiers, Cruas and Lescar. A. Grabar, `Les mosaïques de Germigny-des-Près´, Cah.Arch 1954-1955, pp. 171 ff gives the Andalusian connexion an earlier history . In CCM 1962 Stern refers to the use in mosaic of the "vermiculé" motif. This M.-M. Gauthier (CCM 1961) has described as Islamic, but dates much later on enamels than these mosaics.

65. Many Andalusian arches are shaped in the wall to well above the diameter of the soffit, and only voussoired over the upper part. The simulated jointing of the total arch may be radial, centred on the impost, or follow a descending vertical below the impost.

66. M. Durliat, `Tables d´autel à lobes de la province ecclésiastique de Narbonne, IX-XIe siècles´, Cah.Arch 16, 1966, pp 31-75 gives plentiful illustrations. Gerona altar: Palol and Hirmer, p. 54.

67. P.Dubourg-Noves, Iconographie de la Cathédrale d´Angoulême, Angoulême 1973, pls LV-LXV.

68. For example, La Couronne _fig_. 39, Genouillé; a coarser version is at Sainte-Marie in Saintes and, derived from there, at Marignac.

69. _Tudela_, pl. XXXVII. On corbel B-12, pl. XLIV, the rolls are each carved with the single unit of this motif. These can be compared with the MaZ pilaster of pl.XXVII, with the full motif above in a lozenge frame and single units below enclosing florets. The association of all these elements can be appreciated by perusing the details of Maldonado´s drawings, figs 17 and 18. The floret appears on an early capital in Saint-Sernin(_fig_.97) associated with the "heart-and-dart" motif that often suggests Kufic lettering.

70. F. García Romo, _La Escultura del siglo XI (Francia-España)_ y sus precedentes hispánicos, Barcelona 1973. This volume contains the articles written from 1953 to 1962; see especially `Un taller escultorico de influjo hispano-musulmán en el Loire medio (antes de 1030-1050)´ _al-And_ 1960.

71. K.J. Conant, _Cluny. Les Eglises_....1968, pl. 180: altar of 1130.

72. F. Hernandez, `Arte Musulman: La Techumbre de la Gran Mezquita de Cordoba´, _AEAyA_, 1928, pp 191-225; _LTB 1957_, pp 538-551.

73. _LTB 1957_, p. 544 and n. 100 quoting Idrisi´s description. R. Amador de los Rios y Villalta, `Fragmentos de la techumbre de la mezquita aljama de Córdoba que se conservan en el Museo Arqueolgico Nacional´ _Museo Español de Antiguedades_, VIII, 1877, pp 89-114.

74. B. Pavon Maldonado, _Arte Toledano_, fig.50, p. 151; D. Jalabert, _La Flore sculptée_, pl. 40c.

75. H. Terrasse, _La Mosquée des andalous à Fez_, Paris,n.d. pls LV,LVI.

76. M. Defourneaux, _Les Français en Espagne_, Paris 1949, p.6; L.G. de Valdeavellano, _Historia de España_ I,2, Madrid 1973, pp 613-618; A. Prieto Vives, _Los Reyes de Taifas_, Estudio historico-numismático de los Musulmanes españoles en el siglo V de la Hegira (XI de J.C.), Madrid 1926; for an analysis of the "intima conviviencia" of Muslims and Christians during the taifa period, R. Menendez Pidal, _España del Cid_, pp 72-83.

77. H. Focillon, _L´Art des sculpteurs romans_, Paris 1931, first formulated this essential character of Romanesque sculpture.

78. The motif can be seen developing from the classical three-foliole border motif of the early niche panels

preserved in the Mezquita (the first mihrab? AHIII fig.39), for examples on spandrels on the mihrab arch (AHIII fig.179, and at MaZ, fig.209).

79. These carved beams can be compared with the imposts on the capitals of the ambulatory of Saint-Sernin in Toulouse (Haut-Languedoc roman fig.11): the earliest campaign, c.1080.

80. F. Bargebuhr, `The Alhambra Palace of the 11th century´, JWCI, 1956, pp 192 ff.; id., The Alhambra, Berlin 1968.

81. F. Hernandez, `Un aspecto...´ AEAyA XVI/4, 1930, pp 21-49; compare AHIII, figs 313-315, with figs 426 and 427.

82. AHIII, figs 275-278 show the persistence of the caliphal woodworking style and motifs into the 12th century. It was in the Galiana palace that Alfonso VI of León found refuge during the conflict with his brothers before his reign was established in 1072. Such assistance was expected under the paría system. Alfonso was helpless, but was an honoured guest. After his coronation he remained Yahya´s ally and protector (R.M. Pidal, España del Cid, pp 176 ff). J.M. Lacarra, `Aspectos económicos de la sumición de los Reinos de Taifas (1010-1102), Homenaje a Jaime Vicens Vives, Barcelona 1965, discusses the rise and fall and implications of the paría system, one of which latter was close social and cultural exchanges between Muslim and Christian courts.

83. Tudela (see note 22); AHIII fig.331 also for later 11th century wood carving, probably from Almería. Tudela, founded in the late 8th century, became important under the Banu Qasi in the 9th (J. Oliver Asín, `Origines de Tudela´, Hom. D. Jose Estaban Urranga, Madrid 1971; LTB, Ciudades Hispanomusulmanes I, Madrid 1970, p. 78). In 929 these rulers were superceded by the Banu Tuyubi, much in favour with the new caliph `Abd ar-Rahman III. Gomez-Moreno attributed the mosque, from which came the pieces now re-used in the late 12th century cathedral of Santa Maria la Mayor, to Musa II of the Banu Qasi who also enlarged the White Mosque of Zaragoza in 856 (AHIII, pp 69 ff; id., `La Mezquita Mayor de Tudela´, Principe de Viana 1945); LTB postulated a Mozarabic church of the 10th century. Recent finds at MaZ (Maldonado Memoria..) accumulate support for a dating of the Tudelan material in the wake of stylistic developments initiated there in the later 10th century. The city was taken by Alfonso I of Aragon in 1119, and the Chief Mosque was consecrated as the church of Santa María la Mayor probably in 1121. Another building, possibly a Mozarabic church, was given to the Bishop of Pamplona in recognition of his help at the sieges of Zaragoza, Tudela and Pamplona (J.M. Lacarra, Documentos para el estudio de la Reconquista, 3rd series, Doc. No 303, p. 530; id., `La iglesia de Tudela entre Tarazona y Pamplona´ E.E.M.C.A.

V,1952, p. 419). The alabaster corbels and other carved fragments from Tudela illustrate the kind of decoration that will have been prevalent in such other important cities of the Marches as Zaragoza, Toledo, Huesca, Barbastro, Lérida or Balaguer, at the time they were occupied by the forces of the Reconquista, in the late 11th and early 12th century.

84. "TB" (=LTB), `Restos de una techumbre de carpintería musulmana en la iglesia de San Millán de Segovia´, al-And III, 1935, p. 426.

85. A drawing published in Tudela, p. 51, verifies this.

86. LTB, as note 84, p. 431: this gives a range of almost two centuries, if we include the carved stone corbels of the mosque at MaZ: Tudela, figs 5, 32 and pls XIX,XX, XXIXc.

87.C. Ewert, Balaguer, Madr. Forsch. 1971; no full report of the Aljafería has yet appeared. AHIII pp 221-243 gives the best account.

88.H. Franz, `Das Medallion als Bauornament in der Kunst der Omayyadenzeit´, Ztschr. d. Deutschen Palastinavereins 72, 1956, pp 83-98; `Les fenêtres circulaires de la cathédrale de Cefalú et le problême de l´origine de la rose au moyen âge´, Cah.Arch IX, 1957, pp 253-270; `Die Fensterrose, ihre Vorgeschichte in der islamischen Baukunst´, Ztschr.f. Kunstwissenschaft X, 1956, pp 1-22; `Das Medallion als architektonisches Schmuckmotif in der italienischen Romanik, zur problem des islamischen Einflusses auf der abendländischen Baukunst´ Forschungen u. Fortschritte XXXI, 1957. H. Dow, `The Rose Window´, JWCI XX, 1957 pp 248-297 also stresses the Spanish and Islamic element.

89. I have to thank Dr Oliver Watson of the Victoria and Albert Museum for identifying the pot fragments. A. Nicolai le Vallauri, `A propos des céramiques ornementales sur les édifices médiévaux du sud de la France´, Archéologie du Midi médiéval, 1986/4 p. 103 ff., lists the Saint-Antonin dishes as "Malaga". He reports bacini or traces of them at Peilles (Alpes Mar.), Pont St Esprit (south Spain derivation), Claps near Aix en Provence, Silvacane, St Veian d´Utelle (Alpes Mar.). The Pisan examples he attributes to the Mahgreb or Sicily.

90. LTB 1957, p. 617. In Barcelona, a Jew was licensed by Raymond Berenguer to build a public bath and keep one third of the income. Y. Baer, A History of the Jews in Spain, Philadelphia 1961.

91. Earlier uses include a panel at Ravenna, A. Grabar, Byzantium, 1966, pl. 315, and at Bawit, ibid., pl. 303. The Bawit relief between two columns, in Berlin, has a cross

with flaring arms in the centre. The interlacing 3-strand ribbons prefigure the jumbled arches of the Aljafería screens. The device is not common in Byzantine art before the 10th century however, and less flamboyant than in Andalusia.

92. C. Ewert, Madr. Mitt. 7, 1966, pls 76-79, 85.

93. The two earliest datable basins known are a twelve-sided one from the excavations of `Abd ar-Rahman III´s hall at MaZ (Maldonado, `Influjos occidentales..´ al-And XXXIII, pl.10) and an eight-lobed one (AHIII, fig.251) in Granada Museum with an inscription on the border dating it to 360H/970-1 (ELP Inscriptions.. No 215) The former is decorated in a style similar to the undersurface of the Corneilhan altar and the Saint-Martin-de-Bize altar support (M. Durliat, `Tables d´autel..´, Cah.Arch 1966, figs 21, 23). Also AHIII, fig. 328: three 11th century fragments, with a seated figure, a horseman and attendant, and a human head console in deep relief. Except for Kufic round the border, the latter two would pass as Romanesque. Apart from these there are two series: one type is large, oblong and deep with vertical sides; the other smaller, near square and shallow, either with sloping sides, or vertical and rounded at the base. Seven are known in the first series:

i. National Museum, Madrid. Inscribed with the name of Almanzor, who ordered it for Madinat az-Zahira in 377H/AD987-988 (ELP Inscr No 216). It was found in Seville, incomplete. On one side three arcades on columns and plant decoration, on the other lions attacking horned prey; a border of ducks and fish; on a short side eagles with felines and griffons (AHIII, figs 246a; 247b,d; 249) 1.05m.x 0.78m.x 0.68m. high.

ii. Found in the madrasah of Ibn Yusuf, Marrakesh, mutilated. Inscribed "made for al-Malik, son of Almanzor" (reigned 1002-1008) ELP Inscr No 217. The only remaining figure sculpture is a short side with half-spread eagles and griffons. A fragment of border with wave stem enclosing six-petal florets and other plant motifs (AHIII, fig.246b). 1.55m.x 82cm x 70 cm high.

iii. Alhambra. Inscription added in 14th century (ELP Inscr No 220). Both sides with lions attacking gazelles. Border of ducks and fish with toad on one side (AHIII, fig. 247a). 1.46m. x 89cm x 61cm high.

iv. Fragments of another basin in Granada Museum. Lion attack and inscribed border. Snake among prey´s legs. (AHIII, fig. 248 [drawing]; LTB 1957, fig.562). Also, arcade with bird, and shell.

v. Fragment of short side of similar basin, Cordoba Museum. Lions attacking horned prey (AHIII, fig.247c).

vi. Seville Museum. A border with ducks and fish (AHIII, fig. 245e) and rosettes; from Moroquil.

vii. Cordoba Museum. Fragment of a similar basin (?) found at Moroquil (probably on the site of Almanzor´s Alamiriya). Confronted simurgh heads, scroll between, cording and inscription above (AHIII, fig. 245c).

The second series has eight examples:

i.   Seville Archaeological Museum. Vertical sides, curved at base. Ducks and tortoise, flanked by fish. Foliage probably unfinished (AHIII, fig. 251c); The Arts of Islam, Arts Council Exhibition, 1976, No 489.

ii. Instituto de Valencia de Don Juan, Madrid. Sloping sides, inscribed border, foliage decoration (AHIII, fig. 251b), 59 x 52 cm.

iii. Hispanic Society of America, New York. Sloping sides, inscribed border, relief decoration below it modern (M. Gomez-Moreno, A Hispano-Moresque marble basin in the collection of the Hispanic Society of America, New York, 1928: qu. LTB 1957, p. 725, note 51; work not consulted).

iv. Madrid, private collection. Sloping sides, decoration inside: ducks pecking fish, crossed fish between ducks; outside, a dromedary, engraved (AHIII, fig. 250 and 255).

v.   Cordoba Museum. Find-place unspecified, probably Moroquil. Sloping sides; plain acanthus alternating with V-shaped leaf pair framing horned heads; between them jawless lion masks; upper border of similar curled leaves like rams´ horns; at the corners, addorsed lions looking back, tails meeting at corners (AHIII, fig. 252b).

vi. Fragment, Malaga, with similar leaves rising from sheath (AHIII, fig. 252c).

vii. Cordoba, private collection. Vertical sides, rounded at base; plain acanthus leaves alternating with little trefoil motif; jawless lion mask over aperture for water spout. (LTB 1957, fig. 564, drawing). 105cm x 67cm, 30 cm high.

viii.Cordoba, (?)found in Moroquil. Vertical sides, rounded at base; plain acanthus, alternating with curled V-shaped leaf pair rising from sheath, framing alternate horned head and jawless lion head. (AHIII, fig. 252a).

94. ELP II, pp. 148-149, gives the following extract from Ibn Hayyan in the Analects of al-Maqqari (also in F. Bargebuhr, El Palacio de la Alhambra en el siglo XI, Granada 1966):

As for the carved and gilt basin, admirably formed and of great price, it was procured for the caliph by Ahmad al-Yunani ["the Greek"], who brought it him when he returned from Constantinople in company with Bishop Rabi´ who was returning from Jerusalem. The little carved green basin, with its bas-reliefs representing human figures, was brought by Ahmad from Syria, or, it is said, from Constantinople, when he came back with Rabi´ the Bishop. It is said to have been of incomparable value, decorative richness and beauty. This basin was brought from place to place to the sea. Al-Nasir placed it in the bedroom of the eastern great hall (majlis) called al-munis. He had twelve gold statues of red gold incrusted with precious stones set over it; these were made in the royal workshops (dar al-sina`a) of Cordoba. There was a lion flanked by a gazelle and a crocodile; opposite, a dragon with an eagle and an elephant; on two sides, two groups, respectively a dove, a falcon and a peacock, a hen, a cock and a vulture... All these were of gold encrusted with gems and water came from their mouths.

Rabi´ ibn Zaïd, also known as Recemundo, was a Mozarabic cleric. He was promoted Bishop of Elvira when sent on a mission to Otto I in 955 while Otto´s envoy, John of Gorze, remained in Cordoba. At Frankfurt Recemundo met Liutprand and persuaded him to write his Antapodosis, which Liutprand dedicated to Recemundo. The latter returned to Cordoba with Dudo of Verdun whose briefing under Recemundo´s advice solved the protocol deadlock that had arisen previously and occasioned Recemundo´s mission to Otto; a magnificent reception then took place for John at MaZ.

Statues stood over the gates of Cordoba and Pechina (ELP II, p. 135-6); over the entrance gate to MaZ stood a statue of Zahra´ herself.

The lions of the Alhambra fountain are thought to be of the 11th century. A single lion stood at the end of the aqueduct into Cordoba, spitting water; it had gems for eyes. F. Bargebuhr, The Alhambra, A Cycle of Studies on the Eleventh Century in Moorish Spain, Berlin 1968, and op.cit. above, attributes an 11th century palace within the Alhambra precinct to Samuel and then Yehoseph ibn Naghrall: two Jewish chancellors; the latter was killed in 1066 in an uprising against him. Bargebuhr also discusses the lion as a Jewish symbol, taken over by the Muslims (as by the Christians, cf. Jaca tympanum). The "statue of the Caliph" at Khirbat al-Mafjar rests on two lions, and the lion figures widely in Andalusian iconography. cf. also LTB 1957, pp 424 and 436.

95. Maldonado, Mem.Mez. The material known before these discoveries is shown in AHIII pp 185-190 and fig. 252.

96.   Oriental examples: the famous rosettes on the façades of Mschatta (Berlin Museum); the stucco medallion of Khirbat al-Mafjar; the façade of the court of the mosque of Ibn Tulun in Cairo.

97. J. Vallery-Radot, `Les limites..´ BM 1936, p. 110; J. Evans, Cluniac Art of the Romanesque Period, pls 64, 66. For the Thézels lintel, now in Cahors Museum, D. Fossard, `A propos des linteaux de Moissac et de Saint-Sernin de Thézels´, Synthronon, Recueil d´Etudes..A. Grabar, Paris 1968, pp 209-224.

98.   Excavated at what was thought to be the site of al-Alamiriyya, Moroquil, near Cordoba, a little to the west of MaZ; but al-Maqqari (Anal.I, p. 383) described this residence as "close to the right bank of the Guadalquivir", not at the foot of the sierra, cf. ELP II, p. 220. The second capital, LTB´s fig. 502, is mentioned on his p. 676.

99. ELP III, p. 220.

100. This shape of tuft is of course not peculiar to these pieces, but it is a distinctive feature they share.

101. The motif is noted in F. Henry and G. Zarnecki, `Romanesque arches decorated with human and animal heads´ in G. Zarnecki, Studies in Romanesque Sculpture, London 1979, Chap. vi, p. 16 and fig. 6 as appearing in Poitou, where it "may have some connexion with Moslem carvings". The absence of a lower jaw links this mask motif with the tao tieh (fig 72) and kirtimukha monster masks of East and South Asia, whose monstrous, horned aspect is assumed more than once at Moissac, spitting the border of the doorway archivolt (fig. 73) and in a vertical series on the marble panels at the porch entrance (fig. 74). There are no intermediary examples to be quoted in Andalusia however, of monstrous aspect. For South Asian examples: in the British Museum,1880.5, Jain Tvirthankara Parsvanantha, 10th century, mask atop the arch with foliage; 1880.20, base of pillar, West India Gujarat, 11th century: masks spitting foliage; 1887.15, terra cotta panel, Mathura 6th-7th century, sea monster; 1880.14, stone panel with makara, East India, 7th-8th century; 1880.7, monster on back of panel with Buddha preaching, 5th-6th century, Gupta; etc. The Roman motif of swags and bucrania coincides with one aspect of the oriental development, cf. K. Batsford, The Green Man; F.D.F. Bosch, The Golden Germ, `s Gravenhage 1960; and S. Cammann, `Tibetan Monster Masks´, Jrnl West China Border Research Society XII, 1940, Section A, pp 9-24. It seems impossible that the parallel evolution should not have some cross-connexions. At Bari (figs 53,54), the sloping backs of birds frame the head on one capital. On the other, the lions with heads shared on two corners alternate with ram or gazelle heads on the others. On Islamic influence in Apulia: T. Garten, `Islamic Elements

in Early Romanesque Sculpture in Apulia´, <u>AARP</u> 1973, iv, p. 100 ff.

102. M. Baylé, <u>La Trinité de Caen</u>, Paris 1970, figs 105, 106, 107.

103. I have to thank Professor Zarnecki for this reference: photographs in the Conway Library, "Toscanella", Lazio. The <u>sudarium</u> is illustrated in J. Ebersolt, <u>Orient et Occident I</u>, Paris 1928, pl.XI.

104. M. Schapiro, `From Mozarabic to Romanesque in Silos´, <u>AB</u>, XXI, 1939 (repr. <u>Romanesque Art</u>, 1977), fig. 9.

105. R. Ghirshman, <u>Iran</u>, London 1962, pl. 240: in the Berlin Museum.

106. Series 1, iv (see note 93). This serpent is notable in connexion with the frequency of snakes in the iconography of Spanish Romanesque capitals (Santiago, León, Jaca especially). F. Iñiguez, `La Escatalogia Musulmana en las Capiteles Romanicos´, <u>Principe de Viana</u> 1967, quotes punishment with serpents for the impious, for misers, adulterers and bad mothers rehearsed by Algaceb, and in Samarkandi´s descriptions of the Muslim afterlife, among a number of other torments described in Muslim eschatology that find illustration, deliberate or unwitting, in Romanesque sculpture. The common ground of Islamic and Christian imagery may be sufficient to explain the "coincidences": this is the view held by M. Durliat, J. Williams and most recent writers on the subject, but "co-incidence" creates a climate conducive to cross-influences. A belt-clasp from a Visigothic burial at Estables (Guadalajara) shows a long ancestry for the motif (<u>Palol and Hirmer</u>, pl.22).

107. E. Baer, `The "Pila" of Játiva, a document of secular urban art in western Islam´, <u>Kunst des Orients</u>, VII/2, pp 142-166. The basin is dated to the 11th century by Baer, as by Gomez-Moreno (<u>AHIII</u>). Baer discusses other dates proposed previously.

108. <u>EK Elf</u>. No 27; <u>JBCC</u>, pl. 7. Closely similar on the façade of Notre-Dame-La-Grande in Poitiers. <u>AHIII</u>, p. 278.

109. S. Moralejo Alvarez, on the other hand, discovered the very work that served as a model for the sculptor in north Spain who carved capitals at Frómista and Jaca: `Sobre la formación del estilo escultórico de Frómista y Jaca´, <u>Actas XXIII Congreso Intl. Hist. Arte</u>, Granada,1976, I, pp 427-433. Roman remains were thus a continuous influence, from the 10th century on the sculptors of caliphal basins, through the 11th century (Játiva) in Andalusia, into the Romanesque.

110. Medallion: e.g. AHII, fig.111 (Huesca); fig. 110 (Ager); for the Good Shepherd who figures in the "procession of peasants" on the Játiva basin, AHII, fig. 194 (as Atlantes on the Gerona sarcophagus); fig. 208 (Covarrúbias) and also the medallion; for an Atlas, Fig. 205. Al-Hakam II´s collection of antique sarcophagi is likely to have influenced the compositional layout of the caliphal basins also, e.g., the arcades on the non-figurative panels. H. Pérès, La poésie andalouse, Paris 1966, quotes a poem referring to a nursing mother with a serpent threatening the infant at her feet ; the literary elements on the Játiva basin have not been studied.

111. E. Vergnolle, `Les chapiteaux de La Berthenoux´, GBA 1972 for the Berry; GG 1938: León, Panteón, Nos 25,26; San Isidro, 16,28-30, 35; Jaca, Nos 23,24; Frómista, Nos 12, 13, 18,(capitals) and 1 (corbel); Santiago, Nos 20-22. If snake, lion tamers and drama scenes be included, there are many more. .

112. A. Papadopoulo, Islam et l´art musulman, Paris 1976, col. pl. 18.

113. For Beatus illustration: E. Mâle, L´Art religieux au XIIe siècle, p. 15, fig.9. On the famous capital in Poitiers Museum the disputants are again bald. They wear short tunics. Their heads are shaved back to front, but the remaining hair is not in a tuft as at Játiva. The reliefs of La Celle Bruère (Berry roman, figs 82, 85) inscribed Frotoardus, show the disputants in one case seizing one the other´s neck, the other his opponent´s hair. This is cut away from the brow. A group probably originating at Anzy-le-Duc, including Saint-Pierre-le-Moutier, Saint-Sauveur in Nevers, Bois-Sainte-Marie, Saint-Révérien, is connected with the Poitiers composition. La Revue française, suppl. to no 152, May 1963, entitled `Sculptures romanes et modernes...Poitiers´, has large-scale illustrations of the Poitiers capital. The eye drilled in the wrong place suggests that the carving was originally painted and the drilled eye disguised. The drilling would not be original.

114. see also Roussillon roman, figs 19-20 (Saint-Genis des Fontaines) and 26 (Arles window: the dished rosettes); Guyenne romane, figs 89,90 (La Sauve).

115. Saintonge romane, figs 24, 131, 136, 153. The hair style of many of these figures is that of the figures on the Pamplona casket, EK Elf. No 35; the lion mask of fig. 153 recalls the footstools of the angels on the St Martin capital at Saint-Benoît (fig 57).

116. Baer, op. cit., fig. 6.

117. Haut-Languedoc roman, figs 132, 138.

118. AHIII, fig. 273; ELP Insc. No 57.

119. EK Elf., No 34; JBCC, pl. 26.

120. E. Kühnel, Die Islamische Elfenbeinskulpturen, VIII-XIII Jahrhundert, Berlin 1971 (EK Elf) is the standard, most comprehensive work, superceding J. Ferrandis, Marfiles Arabes de Occidente,I, Madrid 1935. J. Beckwith, Caskets from Cordoba, London 1960,(JBCC) gives an account of the series in English.

121. EK Elf, Nos 19, 20; JBCC, p. 6, pl. l and pls 2-4.

122. A comparison of different styles is shown in LTB 1957, figs 512-120.

123. LTB 1957, p. 734.

124. EK Elf, No 32, JBCC, figs 18-20, 22.

125. H. Focillon, Art des sculpteurs romans, p. 95, makes an illuminating equation of Islamic calligraphy with Romanesque figure composition.

126. EK Elf, Nos 22, 27, 31, 32, 35-37, 39; JBCC, pls 5-7, 14-30.

127. J.M.C. Toynbee and J. Ward Perkins,`Peopled Scrolls..´ Papers of the British School at Rome, XVIII (n.s., vol.V), 1950, pp. 1-43. It is notable that in Islamic art there is far less tendency to entwine the figures with stems than in Christian.

128. e.g., compare P. Lasko, Ars Sacra, pls 67-70 with the drapery of JBCC, pl. 16 or 20; The Milan and Basilewski situlae (Lasko, pls 83 and 86) are a decade later than the Cordoba caskets (968 and 969-970 AD as against 983); the hair is different, but the drapery and stance are very similar.

129. e.g. the Tuotilo book cover, Lasko, pl. 64: Aribert´s book cover, pl. 76, and especially the enamels on the Sion cathedral book cover, pl. 77 and Echternach cover pl. 92 which are more nearly contemporary. Painted decoration at Qairawan is looser than the carving, as seen on the dome ceiling (AMO, fig. 26), but it is relatively simple and incoherent; it is in Cordoba that the more mobile scroll style develops further.

130. JBCC, lower spandrels of medallion, and tree branches, pl. 17.

131. M. Rickert, Painting in Britain; the Middle Ages, Harmondsworth 1954, p. 19, describes an early page illuminated at Canterbury, pl. 10b, as "an almost unique example of the well balanced blending of the two antipodal styles, Hiberno-Saxon and Mediterranean". The combination

of figures and plant decoration on this page is among the nearest in Christian illuminations to the Cordoban decorators´ way of manipulating these motifs together. The special flavour of Andalusian caliphal ivory carving may be attributed to a similar blending of Mediterranean and, in this case, Celtic styles.

CHAPTER III

ARABIC SCRIPT AND ITS IMITATIONS

Though the Islamic origin of a rendering of Arabic script on Romanesque monuments is beyond doubt, it is an influence that may be of the most indirect kind, through imitations of textiles or portable objects bearing inscriptions; the models may have passed through many hands. This seems particularly the case with enamels, for instance. The examples surviving on architecture however share a technical similarity, and a similarity of style, with Andalusian models and between each other which argues for a common tradition alive in southern France in the decades either side of the year 1100.

There are only four explicit examples of Arabic (Kufic) writing (1) in the carved decoration of French Romanesque buildings; two are on wood and two on stone. The former are in the Velay: they are doors, and belong to a larger local group with a clear workshop tradition. One of the two pairs of Romanesque carved wooden doors in the cathedral of Le Puy is inscribed with a Kufic border, and the single valve of another such door at Lavoûte-Chilhac is decorated with a band of conventional repetitive mock-Kufic (2). There is a similar contrast in the two stone examples: the decoration is varied, as though imitating a text, on the impost of capital 50 on the north gallery in Moissac cloister (3), whereas the carved lintel at Saint-Pierre-de-Rhèdes north of Béziers is carved with the conventional repeat. There is one further example in Spain. The small church at the foot of the castle of Atienza in the long-disputed frontier zone between Castile and Andalusia has a north door, now blocked, of which the archivolt bears a Latin inscription incised in the limestone, doubled by a Kufic `inscription´ in flat relief which is possibly a garbled version of a repeated al-mulk lillah (fig.75). Recent pointing has made the Latin illegible but it was read by Serrano in 1945 to give the date 1112 and the name of Alfonso I (4).

Common to all these examples is the two-plane relief in which the inscriptions are carved. As noted in Chapter II this is the standard technique of Andalusian epigraphy on stone, marble and wood and less exclusively on ivory. The choice of this relief technique is particularly notable at Atienza, where in contrast the associated Latin inscription is incised, and the scroll decoration outside both is rounded and modelled.

The Wooden Doors of the Velay (figs 76-80): Le Puy, Lavoûte-Chilhac, Chamalières, Blesle.

The wooden doors of Le Puy are distinct from the similar doors at Lavoûte, Chamalières and Blesle by virtue both of the composition of the decoration and their simpler structure. On the other hand the decorative motifs, the carving and the colouring technique are the same.

Le Puy

The inscription framing the scenes of the Infancy of Christ on the doors of St Gilles´ chapel was definitively interpreted by Marçais (5) as a rendering of the phrase al-mulk lillah [the kingdom is God´s], sufficiently correct to establish that the sculptor had under his eyes either the exact drawing of the model, or an object of wood, perhaps a chest, or a door valve, from an Islamic country. For Fikry this means that "only in an Islamic country could the artist have found his model and learnt its secret" (6); he quotes analogies of style in inscriptions at Madinat az-Zahra´. Marçais gives analogies of detail with Fatimid inscriptions and scroll decoration of the 11th century and rejects Fikry´s attribution in favour of a source for the decoration in Tunisia or Sicily. In particular the triangular form of the letter mim with a fleuron above it speaks for a source in Ifriqiya (North Africa). Like Marçais, Cahn points out traces of contact with Italy and the Rhône valley in a number of features of the architecture of Le Puy, but "given the diffuse but persistent current of Islamic influence in Velay our sculptors need not have displaced themselves afar" (7).

The division of the ground into scenes in panels is that of doors on the Byzantine model surviving in Germany and above all in Italy (8), and speaks for an influence from beyond the Rhône. This connexion however does not exclude the possibility of Andalusian elements in the decoration of the doors also, transmitted either via Italy or direct. Not only the Kufic but a number of associated features and decorative motifs on these and the other Romanesque doors in the region of Le Puy have striking similarities of detail with near-contemporary woodwork in Spain, notably the ceiling, totally Andalusian in tradition, of San Millán in Segovia, which was examined in the foregoing chapter (fig. 46).

The Inscription on the Nativity Doors   The letters of the inscription are foliated, the size of the half-palmette terminals being varied, it may be deliberately, so that the impression of repetition along the borders is reduced.

The space-filling fleuron over the mim inside the lam-aliph part of the character,(or, interpreted by Marçais as "al-mulk", the lam-mim-lam), appears in the same conjunction in the inscription panels at Segovia, on the Silos ivory casket (AHIII, figs 367-8), on the mock inscriptions of the Oviedo Arca Santa (fig. 81), round the page of the Saint-Sever Beatus, on the Fez mimbar panel (fig.44), bordering the apse-painting at Santa Maria in Taüll (fig.94) (9), and indeed in the Mezquita itself, in the mosaic inscriptions of the mihrab and on doorways (AHIII, figs 163-5, 193). In many of these cases the mim is not triangular, but other angular forms might easily be transferred, by a sculptor not wholly literate in Arabic, to this position between shafts, for example in the floriation of shafts seen on the Fez panel, the Toledo inscribed well heads, the Pamplona casket (AHIII, fig. 363), the Arca Santa, or the tombstone of the Princess Badr from Cordoba, dated 1103 (10), where other letters are written with just such triangles.

Plant Motifs Within the panels various versions of trefoil, palmette or half-palmette and composite rosette are used to fill spaces, especially along the register illustrating the Journey of the Kings: the stems form hearts or arches of interlacing half-circles, stiff "fir trees" or irregular branches.(D10,F20,D12a). All of these are matched in Andalusian wood carving (fig. 82) (11).

Eight-point star florets (D3) simulate decorative nails. They are set exactly as on Andalusian examples, between plain rectangular-section fillets (12).

Down the vertical batten is a Latin inscription including the words GAUZFREDUS FECIT (13). It begins at the top with an interlaced palmette scroll, like examples on the beams of the Mezquita and Segovia alike. The motif itself would scarcely call for comment, so ubiquitous is it; it is current for example in pre-Romanesque manuscript illumination, and it might be reinvented at any time where the undulating half-palmette scroll was employed (14). It is however one more motif shared with much of the low relief wood sculpture in Andalusia, and we have found the technique of its execution perpetuated when it is adopted (rarely) into Romanesque stone carving (figs 42,43).

The oblique side of the batten has the same truncated border motif of trefoil and arch as along the edges of some Segovia panels, outside the fillet border; it is inherited from the beams of the Mezquita (LTB 1957, fig.347)(15); it recurs on the cornice of the façade of Le Monastier (CA 1976, fig. 5).

Colour Traces of colour (two reds, brown, dark green, blue and white) show that these Le Puy doors were primed and painted in the same ways as the ceilings of the Mezquita (16), allowing a Spanish source, though not of course necessitating it.

Interlace On the corresponding set of doors, for St Martin's chapel in the cathedral, with scenes of the Passion, a "bretzel" or fan-shaped interlace scroll takes the place of the Kufic of the Infancy doors. The disappearance of this scroll in stone carving soon after 1100 (17) gives reason for dating the series soon after 1100 if not before. While the woodworking tradition has shown a consistency and conservatism that warns against making hasty analogies of fashion with the more recently established craft of stone carving, a detail of political history offers justification for this chronology in a suitable context for the Fatimid influence postulated by Marçais. This is the marriage in 1086 of the young count of Auvergne to Emma, daughter of the future King Roger II of Sicily and sister-in-law to Raymond de Saint-Gilles (18).

The Lavoûte-Chilhac Door

The Inscription   At the church of Sainte-Croix at Lavoûte-Chilhac only a single door valve survives (19). The foliated lam and aliph of the repetitive mock-inscription are linked by a small letter (mim, `ain or sad) of the usual Spanish semi-circular form, with a trefoil above it like that above the triangular mim of the Le Puy door, and similarly in the inscription on the vertical panels of the ceiling of San Millán in Segovia.

The Cross   A large cross with flaring arms occupies the upper section of the door: a clear reference to the dedication of the church to the Holy Cross (20). It is edged with cording and has large ringed bosses and interlace knots on each arm and a large boss at the centre. The bosses and knots play a similar decorative rôle to the rosettes and geometric medallions on the Fez mimbar panel. Parallels approaching in time are the bosses in rings on capitals at San Pere de Roda (figs 83-89), sometimes associated with a corded astragal (fig. 84), and the well head at Toledo of 1032 (fig. 71)(21), which for half the circumference fills a narrow band with nail head disc bosses. The other half has only cording.

The Latin Inscription   Below the great cross is an inscription in low flat relief with Latin verses naming Odilo as founder of the church. The reference is to the celebrated abbot of Cluny, a member of the leading local family, the Mercoeur. The church belonged to a priory founded by Odilo close to the family castle where he was born. It may not be fortuitous that the Mercoeur were closely concerned not only with Lavoûte, but with Le Puy and Moissac also (22). There is no institutional parallel between the three monuments with their Kufic decoration, but this family connexion links them.

Cording   Corded edging is not found on surviving Andalusian woodwork but it is frequent in marble and often associated there with corbels (23); it borders the arch and alfiz of the mihrab in the Aljafería. The iconographic model for this treatment of the cross however may be the kind of work represented by the Carolingian ivory book cover at Narbonne, where the cross is edged in the same way, as are indeed some of the flared Visigothic crosses such as the Angeles cross in Oviedo (24). Cording in fact was much used in Visigothic stone carving also.

Fan-knot Interlace   The door is bordered by the same "bretzel" fan-knot interlace scroll as that on the Passion doors of Le Puy. This Coptic, then Irish, motif is traced by Bousquet through 9th and 10th century manuscripts and chancel plaques into early Romanesque sculpture (25), where it is most concentrated in the orbit of Aurillac, San Pere de Roda and Conques, before the end of the 11th century. There are also examples on capitals further north, in the Auvergne, at Blesle (where there are a wooden door like that at Lavoûte and roll corbels F1), Saint-Quentin-sur-Sioule, and Glaine-Montaigut, and on an impost at Ebreuil. Glaine Montaigut has roll corbels and Ebreuil has an early example of the classic Auvergnat eaves with hollow rosette (D15) soffits between its roll corbels, like those of Segovia. Pilasters on the apse of Saint-Outrille-en-Graçay in the Berry (26) are carved with this fan interlace, and an impost has the running palmette scroll (D7) of the Le Puy door. No corbels survive there, as the roofing is recent, but the Berry as a whole has the greatest concentration of roll corbels in France, outside the Auvergne (Map 2).

Scrolls   The band of mock inscription (F2) is set between two bands of scroll work. The upper has two rows of split palmettes (D6) as on a corbel at Segovia and those on corbel A-6 at Tudela (27), contained in interlaced rings. Between the rings is a row of imitation nail heads (D3), this time six-petalled florets rather than the stars of the Le Puy door.

The bottom panel has two rows, the lower badly damaged, of oblique crosses formed of pairs of split palmettes radiating from a centre (D10); these are surrounded by stems forming round squares. A palmette in a heart is set obliquely to complete the scroll at the undamaged end. Both these applications of the palmette are current in caliphal decoration, and the roofing association is underlined by the existence at Le Puy of fragments of a stone cornice carved with the same flower cross for a soffit rosette (fig. 90)(28).

Construction   The construction of the Lavoûte door differs from that of the Le Puy doors; it is more complex and skilfully composed, with rebates and mitring. Much of the decoration is carved on thin horizontal panels and nailed to the backing planks (the method used on the Mezquita ceiling), whereas at Le Puy the carving is direct on the vertical planks composing the valves (30). The door at Lavoûte is one of a group of three, with Chamalières and Blesle in the same area, all built in this way. The latter two, decorated and painted according to the same schema, albeit with less explicitly Islamic motifs than at Lavoûte, can be attributed to the Lavoûte workshop (31).

The Chamalières Door

The pair of valves at Chamalières each has a cross like that on the Lavoûte door; the arms do not flare and the cording edging them is double. Interlace knots (D13)

fill the upper spaces outside the arms, the lower spaces
have figures in relief, and more figure motifs consisting
of confronted lions [?] (D17h) and confronted riders with
lances fill a panel above two rows of lattice woodwork
(32).

On a lower register it is just possible to make out on
the left valve a carved interlacing diagonal lattice,
framing split palmettes arranged in fours radiating from a
centre (D10). The corresponding register on the other valve
has a plainer version of the split palmette flower cross,
as on the bottom register of the Lavoûte door.

The border is carved with an elaboration of the interlaced palmette scroll of the vertical batten of Le Puy
(D7); the palmette is here transformed into a pair of entwined stems ending in split palmettes which meet a similar
smaller motif that begins the next pair of stems. Thus each
stem ring is separate from the next (33).

The Blesle Doors

The doors at Blesle repeat the large crosses of
Chamalières with doubled cording. The vertical batten is
carved with the common running half-palmette scroll (D7).
The border brings a new motif to the range of the atelier's
repertoire: the Labours of the Months are framed in the
spaces of a pair of bands that meet in interlace knots at
intervals; this has an analogy in the Aljafería and again
in Egypt in a secular context (34). The lower part of the
door is too weathered to allow any idea of the decoration.

Unlike the Le Puy doors all these latter three examples concentrate the focus of attention in the upper register, with the cross, while the lower part is like a dado or
hanging: this approximates them to Andalusian compositions
(F5)(35).

Discussion of the Workshop   The number of motifs on this
series of doors that are similar to those used on
Andalusian work in the same low relief technique is too
generalized and too integrated into the Romanesque
repertoire to be explained as the result of the influence
of one individual's chance experience (36). The Le Puy door
has a simpler construction than the rest, its composition
differs in being uniformly concentrated in the manner of
bronze doors in Germany and Italy, and the Kufic border
sets it apart. Its main field with figure scenes is subject
to influences outside those held in common by the group,
but the manner of carving and the decorative elements are
the same. It is arguable that it is earlier than the rest,
not that it is their model; the four sets of doors are
better regarded not as the unique product of a single
stimulus, but as among the few examples surviving from work
in an enduring tradition, which will have included not only
many other variants of door decoration with equally
divergent tendencies contributed from different sources,

but many other kinds of furniture. The choir stalls at Ydes (Cantal) (<u>fig</u>.104) illustrate its persistence, probably into post-mediaeval times.

It is the most plausible to envisage the kind of work-shops proposed by Cahn (37): independent of the building sites and manned by the versatile type of craftsmen to whom Theophilus addressed his treatise (38); men not yet specialized in a single trade (39), but working in a range of techniques and materials besides, and complementary to, wood; for example, erecting ceilings, forging the iron for the bars and nails needed for doors and other structures, and also undertaking the finishing in inlay, plating or painting (40); ready also to produce cult objects including images, and furniture (41) and fittings not necessarily ecclesiastical (42).

The group of doors taken as a whole suggests that the low-relief technique involved initiation into an established tradition of basic designs that had continued largely unchanged for centuries and that this tradition, operating in a wide area of the western Mediterranean, embraced southern France and Andalusia, the islands and African coast as well (43).

Parallels in Catalunya

The eastern Pyrenees, described by Durliat as the meeting place "of two milieux where artistic activity had been particularly productive during the immediately pre-Romanesque period", form a nodal point within this area. Barcelona was the focus of traffic both by land and sea (44). The political concerns of the houses of Barcelona and Toulouse to control the coastal cities show them working, on the whole in concert during the half-century hinged on 1100, to maintain a regulated environment necessary for commercial prosperity. Catalunya is a region remarkable for its abundance of images, altar retables and frontals of carved, gessoed and painted wood (45). Like the Massif Central it is largely a highland zone where both objects and traditions survive; moreover it was here that the same two-plane technique was used on the earliest of all Romanesque figure carving on stone, at Saint-Genis-des-Fontaines (San Genís les Fonts) and Saint-André-de-Surède (San Andrés de Sureda), soon after 1020.

At San Pere de Roda the capitals present a combination of wood and marble carving traditions. There are two distinct forms of capital: Corinthians for the vault arches and smaller "plait capitals" for the intermediary axial arcades. It is usual to restrict references to Andalusian influence here solely to the former. San Pere is manifestly a point of contact of two artistic traditions: it is the southernmost location where the northern "bretzel" fan scroll is used in interlace by sculptors, and one of the northernmost where a Madinat az-Zahra´ style of plant decoration is still in full sway, and where the idiosyncracies

71

of Cordoban capital design are undisguised. But the meeting
is an integration, and there is no basis for isolating the
Andalusian elements and limiting the influence to one group
of capitals, as though they were extraneous to the general
activity of the workshop. There is no means of differentiating an "Andalusian" hand from the rest: both types of
capital, and all the imposts, share one style and many details of decoration.

The capitals of Ripoll and Cornelha are unmistakably
derived from Cordoban models. Hernandez (46) shows this in
the form and motifs of decoration; this is validated by
similarities in the profiles of bases. No one however has
observed that the down-turned leaf (D16) used as a volute
on these capitals reproduces exactly the device worked out
on corbels in Andalusian decoration (figs 20-26). Then at
San Pere de Roda a few decades later than the beginnings of
the Ripoll group of capitals (47) Cordoban acanthus and
Carolingian interlace are both subjected, on the different
capitals, to innovations heralding Romanesque treatment of
capital design. The outcome of these experiments is manifest quite early at Saint-Benoît-sur-Loire (fig.91), later
at Rodez, Conques (fig.92), Moissac, and on the acanthus
capitals of Le Puy itself (48).

Script-Scroll Ambiguities

In the same artistic milieu as Roda, some of the altar
tables from the workshops of Narbonne (49) are decorated
between the hollowed lobes of their borders with asymmetrical scrolls (D8); their resemblance to units of Arabic
script may not be wholly fortuitous. This is not to argue
an exclusive derivation or prime inspiration from Kufic for
these motifs; elements handed down over several centuries
or copied from Merovingian sarcophagi and Carolingian
manuscripts indeed may well have been the main source, but
in an area where Andalusia had been providing the chief intellectual stimulus as well as the chief commercial market
for a century and more it is only to be expected that an
awareness of the peculiarities of Kufic script should affect the choice of just these forms from among all the
scrolls available, and influence their handling.

There is an analogous reflection of this device in the
Mezquita, where voussoirs are carved with asymmetrical
branching stems (D10). These scrolls foreshadow the convo-
lutions of later floriated Kufic, (AHIII, figs 124, 180-
182)(50) which often in the 11th century disguise the inscriptions to the point where they are almost beyond recognition as writing (AHIII, figs 279d, 280, 286)(51).

Yet another, perhaps often barely conscious ambiguity,
in addition to more deliberate and patent evocations of
Kufic or pseudo-Kufic lettering occurs for example in Cordoba along the top border of the mihrab plaques, and in
both early and later Romanesque decoration, in the treatment of the line of linked palmettes or "heart-and-dart"

motif (Dll) (figs 19, 85, 94), so that a lam-mim-aliph
seems to lurk behind it. This is a frequent motif on Romanesque imposts in north-west Spain and at Toulouse and
Moissac; its origin was attributed by Gaillard to an Andalusian and especially a Mozarabic reassemblage of acanthus and palmette scrolls, arising from dividing the two
halves of an acanthus leaf and combining them anew (52).

St-Sever   Fez,MaZ   Cordoba   MaZ   Cordoba

Roda   Mourens   Rhèdes

    The imposts of San Pere de Roda include examples of a
relatively neutral version of this motif, but the
neutrality of the motif is belied, for other imposts, and
even in some cases other stretches of one impost bearing
this version, are given over to freer stem motifs executed
in refined chip carving, and the play with hints of Kufic
is given full range as different possibilities are tested,
combined and manipulated almost explicitly. That it was not
unknown for the Christian sculpture of the Mediterranean
area in the 10th century to decorate imposts with mock-
Kufic is shown by the capitals at Hosios Loukos in Phokis;
there also masonry is decorated with occasional carved
Kufic motifs (54). Explicit applications of lam-aliph as a
border motif appear on some 12th century wall paintings in
Catalunya (fig.94).

The Rôle of Roofing
    The carpenters' workshop that left its trace in
Segovia at the end of the 11th century followed a tradition
rooted in the Mezquita and Madinat az-Zahra', both in the
construction and the decoration of the ceiling. Their work
is especially valuable as showing decoration less rich and
elaborate than what was required for the palaces of the
taifa kings, and so more typical of the general run of
workshops. Whereas the stone and plaster decoration of ostentatious palaces at Malaga, Zaragoza and Balaguer does
not suggest a clear sequence leading from caliphal to Romanesque, the scattered remains of roof members in wood and
stone so far discussed (wood from Granada, Malaga and
Zaragoza as well as Segovia, and stone corbels from Tudela
with their curls and flat relief of split palmettes, bosses
and split stems) bear witness to a simpler tradition in
both media; it is aspects of this tradition that we find
adopted into various aspects of Romanesque decoration. The

ceiling at Segovia is evidence that work of this kind had been going on all through the 11th century.

In so far as the Velay doors have affiliations to this tradition, much more is implied than an origin for their own decoration; they are evidence of the likely process of transmission for many of the motifs and features that have presented the problem of the chronological gap between Cordoba and Romanesque. For example a timber workshop involved in ceiling and roofing work as well as, or perhaps even more than, with doors, suggests itself as the most likely agency responsible for the transmission of the roll corbel form from 10th century Andalusia into the Auvergne and Nivernais, at latest early in the 11th century. The chain of evidence is incomplete: there are neither wood nor stone corbels in Catalunya, where the flat low-relief decoration generic to woodwork is exemplified particularly well in stone and marble, but other elements show how the interchange of motifs went on. Corbels are rare in the Velay also. There are no corbels or corbel tables on Le Puy cathedral or any of the buildings in its vicinity which share many of its features, but this is perhaps because they all now date, at least as far as their roofs are concerned, to well towards the mid-12th century or later. Le Puy Museum preserves for example (fig.90) the fragments of a stone corbel table: there are soffits carved with square leaf-crosses, like those enclosed in mixtilinear medallions on soffits at Madinat az-Zahra´ (fig.20)(55) and on the Chamalières door. The corbel is carved with a lion head like those on Cordoban basins; it spits foliage of what at San Pere de Roda is described as type "phase 2" (56). The corbel table must come from late-11th century roofing at Le Puy, and fits well with the wooden doors as regards the style of carving of the soffit and the motif.

At Le Monastier too Bousquet (57) has shown there were changes of design during the late 11th - early 12th century building, and again during the 12th century and later, which have removed the original roofing scheme. The absence of corbels in the Velay remains nonetheless remarkable since in neighbouring Auvergne the corbel table remained standard well into the 12th century.

Flat Relief and Chip Carving

The Andalusian work that has been mainly quoted above in discussing the Velay doors and their associations: wooden ceilings and corbels, the stone corbels of Madinat az-Zahra´ and those reused from the Mosque of Tudela (fig 45), shows flat relief technique used on both wood and stone in Andalusia. The Tudela pieces compare closely with stone and marble work from Madinat az-Zahra´. No example of wood has been found in the palace ruins, but the Mezquita ceiling fragments demonstrate that simplified versions of this stone and marble carving were applied to wood in caliphal building (58).

The corbels at Tudela are decorated, sometimes on the same piece (Bl, B2) with both flat relief and the fine chip-carving so highly developed at Madinat az-Zahra´; the difference is one of degree only. The two methods are found side by side again at San Pere de Roda. Stone carvers on the whole found their greatest scope in the latter style, but two more Romanesque examples of flat relief applied to an explicit Kufic motif survive in France, one at Saint-Pierre-de-Rhèdes and the other at Moissac. The pseudo-Kufic inscriptions of these two monuments will now be examined as further evidence of the Andalusian influence alive in this same workshop tradition.

Saint-Pierre-de-Rhèdes

The monolithic lintel of the south door of Saint-Pierre (figs 96,98)(59) near Lamalou-les-Bains (Hérault) is carved with a repeat lam-mim-aliph motif in shallow relief, similar to.the mock inscription on the Lavoûte door, except that the base of the mim is rectangular, not rounded, and the fleuron over it rises and flares to form an arch over the shafts, thus approximating the motif to a "heart-and-dart" scroll. The foliation is of the same type as on the Lavoûte door. The "inscription" begins with two shafts whereas the motif on the Lavoûte door begins with one. Despite these minor differences the two examples are closely related, and the style of carving is the same.

In addition to this "inscription" two further features, the encrusted decoration in black basalt, and the twin columns of the interior (F6), deserve consideration. They are attributed by the authors of Languedoc roman to the example of Le Puy. Saint-Pierre, they point out, is situated on a cross roads where the route from Arles to Toulouse meets that from Béziers to Cahors via Albi, or to Aurillac via Rodez. These long-distance routes from the coast inland, and their significance as bearers of "influence" is rightly stressed here, but the direction from which these features travelled may be debated.

The basalt is found locally, and is employed to embellish the arches of doors and windows on a number of Romanesque churches round Béziers (60).

Twin columns are not unknown in the vicinity of Saint-Pierre, and are frequent in the Rouergue; the double line of voussoirs round the windows that recurs at Quarante and other buildings in the area makes a link with the group of small churches in the Aragon highlands (61), where openings mostly recessed inside rectangular frames are similarly treated, and where twin columns abound. At one such, San Juan de Busa, the door archivolt decoration even perhaps also makes a reference to Kufic (fig.172).

Another Andalusian feature at Saint-Pierre is the eccentric archivolts of the openings on the south front, including the doorway, again a characteristic of the region, described as "Lombard" (62) and at Saint-Pierre associated with Lombard bands.

All these features, and the rectangular-section ribs of the apse, appearing on a minor monument like Saint-Pierre, built some time during the first half of the 12th century, bear witness to the kind of "broadly shared system of formal conventions" invoked by Cahn; they show Andalusian elements playing an integral part, not only for crafts accessory to architecture, but for the detailing of architecture itself.

<u>Textiles and Woodwork</u>   The long- and medium-distance trade routes that crossed the Languedoc facilitated communication between craftsmen and thus fostered the continuity of traditions within the wide area they spanned, from Andalusia to Auvergne, which manifestly existed already in the 10th century. Textiles, playing a major rôle in establishing and confirming what was acceptable in decoration of all kinds, bulked large in this trade, and the markets and looms of Andalusia (63) continued to supply a considerable share of it. The church treasures of the Auvergne still preserve rich examples of these cloths, and they were copied by image-makers (64) here, as they were in Catalunya. The loin-cloth of the Christ on the wooden Crucifix at Lavoûte, the sleeves of the Virgin of Le Puy, the cushion of the reliquary image of the Virgin at Orcival (65) are each decorated with a border of pseudo-Kufic. These are explicitly copies of textiles, not an "Islamic influence" on the style of the sculptor or painter, but they confirm a familiarity with Kufic motifs as part of the craftsman's stock-in-trade.

The shrine of Bishop Ulger in the Cathedral Treasury at Angers (66) and the throne of the Madonna from Ayl, in Trier Episcopal Museum, are rare survivals of Romanesque woodwork; they are quoted by Cahn (67) to associate with "Gauzfredus' idiosyncratic style". Two further examples can be quoted. The church bench from Taüll in Barcelona Museum <u>figs 100-101</u> bears striking witness to the rôle of woodworking in fusing Andalusian and Christian elements. That it was no exotic singleton is vouched for by the existence of fragments of similar work (<u>fig</u>s 102,103)(68) in the area. At Ydes in the Cantal the decoration of the choir stalls (<u>fig</u>.104), of unknown date but certainly Romanesque tradition, shows this fusion was not just due to the frontier position of Catalunya: these stalls too have slender columns (F8), angle columns, lobed arches (F21), lattice work and rosettes (D15), and even a hint at roll corbels (F1). Slender columns, lobed arches and rosettes are found, carved in stone, at Moissac also, but earlier than the porch and doorway where whey appear is the mock-Kufic inscription in the cloister.

The Mock-Kufic Inscription at Moissac (69)

Capital No 50 in the cloister is a double capital with a single pyramidal zone flaring to the volutes, and in the centre to a thick out-turned acanthus leaf tip (F3) (figs 105-109). The volutes extend from behind this leaf, with a striated support of the volute stem characteristic of a number of capitals in the cloister, and almost exclusive to it (70). The whole bell is decorated with an all-over linked scroll motif ("Moissac scroll type 1"): a curled four-leafed half-palmette (D5) enclosed in an almost circular ring of the stem. This stem branches from a vertical trunk, creating wider circles as the surface expands upwards. The two longer folioles of the palmette leaf entwine the stem from behind to lap over the front of the scroll. The folioles are ridged and grooved along the axis, like the stems, and in addition are hatched obliquely. The same feathery fronds are carved on the walls of the triangular cleft between the twinned capitals. The scroll could be described as a fusion of the palmette scrolls of Saint-Benoît with the more intricate and dynamic scrollwork of Andalusia, such as the wooden corbel fig. 110 in Toledo Museum.

The Impost.

On the impost the scroll is repeated on the oblique faces as an undulating stem from corner to corner, branching to fill each circular undulation with a half-palmette; at the centre it is interlaced with another stem that forms two scrolls flanking the interlace. These separate stems are on the long sides of the impost, on the short the final scrolls of stems leaving the corners are bound together asymmetrically where two and three stems meet. Curled tendrils fill spandrels at the branchings, and above and below the interlace on the long sides, the binding on the short. The tips of these tendrils are finely curled, in a style reminiscent of ivory carving and particularly of the 1063 León Cross of Ferdinand and Sancha (fig.111)(71), and of scrolls on capitals and specially imposts at Santiago (72), which provide a possible stone prototype.

The arrangement of the circular scrolls on the short sides of the capital 50 impost foreshadows the asymmetry of the great rosette scroll on the lintel of Moissac doorway (fig.112). The affiliations of the impost scroll will be traced after a discussion of the vertical faces of the impost.

The Kufic Inscription

Inscriptions in Kufic lettering, generally considered meaningless, are carved on the vertical faces of the impost (73), in a relief similar to the carving on the Velay doors; the "wording" is different on each face.

The south face (fig.108), naturally most weathered since it faces the open court, seems even discounting this weathering to be the least finely treated. Towards either end the monotony of a lam-aliph repeat is broken by a sloping shaft (kaf?), on the right after one pair of shafts, on the left after two, corresponding to the three scrolls of the left-hand stem compared to the two on the right on the oblique face below.

The west face inscription (figs 105-6) is similar, but in addition the fillet below the letters is notched under each pair of shafts. There are eight pairs between the sloping shafts as compared with five on the shorter south face, and again two beyond the "kaf" on the left, two on the right: there is no correspondence with the scrolls, which here are symmetrical.

On the east (fig.107) the characters are less uniformly arranged and look most like a genuine inscription. The notches below are more integrated into the shaping of the letters, the line of the fillet curves up to correspond to them.

On the north face (fig.109) is a broader, more formalized symmetrical arrangement approximating to a leaf border motif, based on a lam-aliph enclosing a mim, `ain or sad (74) between a divergent lam-aliph. The result is very close to the "heart-and-dart" motif used in the Mezquita for a border on the Chocolate Door (AHIII fig.194)(75), pointing the argument for connecting debased Kufic with that motif (AHIII, fig. 193) in less obvious contexts than on this impost.

The Style of Lettering

On all four faces the style of the letters is consistent. They have much in common with the inscription on the Le Puy doors and with Andalusian woodwork inscriptions and carving, but they are not fully foliated: the additional curls at the base of each letter can be interpreted as the Moissac master´s own interpretation of foliation. But this lettering has a peculiarity: the wedge-shaped hollow at the widened top of the shafts, which is highly unusual. There are analogies, rare and precisely confined. There appear to be no examples from Iran, Syria, Egypt or North Africa (76), but there are several in Andalusia.

Andalusian Examples of Wedge-shaped Hollows

The ivory casket EK Elf No 32 (No 368-1880 in the Victoria & Albert Museum) has an inscription with some but not all of the shafts cleft with a line, and occasional shafts with a wedge-shaped hollow at the top (77). The casket in the Bargello Museum in Florence EK Elf 34 (AHIII, fig. 366)(78) is inscribed in relief with letters with a consistent central groove, expanded at the top of shafts to a wedge. The former casket is dated 969/970, the latter, undated, is by analogy with others a few decades later. No monumental epigraphy is known bearing this peculiarity before the appearance of a group of inscriptions in Toledo of

the second third of the 11th century. Examples so far noted
are:

1. A well-head dated 423H/AD 1032 (fig. 71)(79)
2. A well-head dated 429H/AD 1037/38 (fig.113)(80)
3. A brick tomb-slab c.AD 1040 (fig.71a; AHIII, fig. 274)
4. A marble funeral stele 447H/AD 1055 (81)
5. A funeral inscription on brick 465H/AD 1073 (82)

These all in Toledo; also

6. A plaster frieze in the Salón de la Chimenea in the Aljafería (AHIII, fig. 286)
7. ?The dado at Tarifa drawn by Gomez-Moreno (AHIII fig. 309).

Both well-heads were commissioned by the same prince,
the first of the Banu Du´n Nun dynasty of Toledo. The tomb
slab inscription (No 3) is interlaced with a foliage stem
and has a row of beading above. The shafts of the lettering
of the funeral stele are grooved rather than looped into a
wedge at the top. The Zaragoza frieze inscription is likewise interlaced with coiling foliage stems; there are triangular cavities at the top of the shafts, but the style of
epigraphy is finer and less like the Moissac example than
are the Toledo inscriptions on stone and brick. Some knowledge in Moissac of Toledan monuments must be assumed. The
enrolment of the monk Gerald from Moissac by Bernard Archbishop of Toledo in 1096 (83) is the only occasion recorded
of a direct contact between Moissac and Toledo, but the
features that make the cloister capitals (with some from La
Daurade and a few at Saint-Gaudens) unique in Romanesque
sculpture show that artistic relations with Spain were
close.

The Capital 50 Scroll and variants.

That this "Kufic" impost is intimately related to much
of the sculpture in the cloister and cannot be attributed
as a singleton to the contribution of a passing visitor is
manifest by the frequency elsewhere in the cloister of the
associated scroll, and the chain of interconnexions thereby
created, particularly from three other features of the capital: the ribbed volute-stem supports, the hollowed double
flower under the consoles, and the over-all flaring shape;
all of these are prevalent throughout the cloister.

The scroll is used again on the impost of capital 63
(fig.115), an uncompromising figure capital with no additional decoration: there are men blowing horns at the corners, distinctive caulicoles with the snailshell form familiar at Frómista and León (84) but unusual at Moissac,
and beneath them the crossbowmen who also figure at León,
Santiago and Jaca, with the bolts held in their teeth. The
tendrils between the scroll circles are absent but the triangular bud between them remains.

On impost 16 over the Transfiguration and Descent from
the Mountain (fig.116) the scrolls are paired, and the ar-

rangement symmetrical, and between the pairs hangs a leaf
formed of half-palmettes (D6) from either side. On the vertical faces a band of semi-circles is carved in a relief
similar to the lobed arch of capital 17 (fig 194).

A variant of this scroll ("Moissac scroll type 2"),
where the folioles have become the looped stem itself, covers capital 55 in an all-over pattern in the same scheme as
capital 50, created by the stem movements from a central
trunk, but with less clarity of the larger design
(fig.117). The form of the capital, on a single column, is
the same in profile but is facetted with a projecting angle
down the centre of each face, whereas capital 50 is divided
for the two columns and flat. The volute and its stems and
the double flower under the console are the same. The
impost uses the same stem to enclose paired leaves with
deeply excavated centres, a refinement of an impost motif
familiar in Spain, particularly León, where it usually has
a single leaf (85). The tendril and striated bud motif
between the scrolls is identical with that on capital 50.

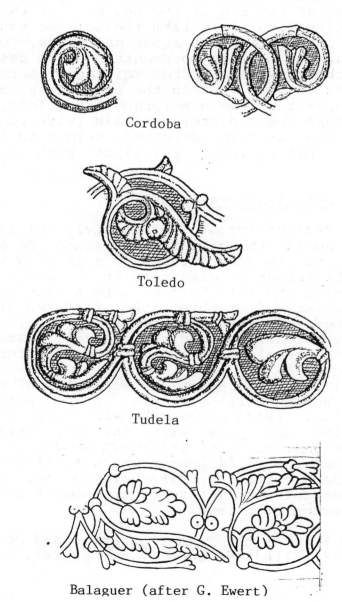

Cordoba

Toledo

Tudela

Balaguer (after G. Ewert)

The version of the scroll executed on capital 55 also decorates the imposts of capitals 28 and 32 (fig.118, 119); the former has a motif of monsters clutching a human head, current since early in the 11th century in the crypt of Saint-Bénigne in Dijon and at Bernay, and well-known at Saint-Sernin in Toulouse from the workshop of the master of the Porte des Comtes (86). On impost 28 the scroll stem is continuous across the face, not in two parts as on capital 50, and between the scrolls the tendrils have disappeared. On impost 32 the tendrils between the scrolls are identical with those on impost 50, but the feathery triangle has gone and the scrolls are arranged symmetrically, meeting at the centre.

Further Comparisons, and Affiliations of the Scroll

The curled leaf unit (D5) of the capital 50 scroll might be thought too elementary a motif to signify any direction of stylistic direction or influence, but it has a recognizable identity and the accumulation of associations surounding its variants has a strong bias towards Spain; this makes it unlikely that all the wealth of decorative scroll work of Andalusia with similar motifs should have played no part in its genesis.

This ancestry may be traced back to the marble panels of the mihrab of Sidi Oqba's mosque in Qairawan which include a section with analogous scrolls with double leaves. A motif even closer to the Moissac scroll is repeated at Qairawan four times round a medallion grille in the courtyard (fig.66) (87) and on window grilles.

At Cordoba the motif makes its illustrious début on the looped stem caulicoles of one of the pairs of capitals flanking the mihrab (fig.4); and on the mihrab plaques the pendant "shell" of the simulated roll corbels is presented as a curled leaf (fig.19). This is emulated at Madinat az-Zahra' (AHIII, fig. 208). A few capitals from Cordoba (88) also have volutes filled with a similar leaf (fig.130).

On the corbels of the Mosque of Tudela the curled leaf motif is transferred from the filling to the rolls themselves (89).

In Andalusian decoration of the 10th century, and of the 11th, no examples survive of this particular leaf enclosed in the many variants of running scrolls; digitated palm fronds or rosettes are preferred (e.g. AHIII, figs 271b,c; 272; 273c,d; 286; 291; 291b,c), but it is a very short step to recombine these elements (half-palmette, split stem, volute, "shell" curled leaf) into the versions of Romanesque running scrolls: the leaves contained in Andalusian corbel rolls or capital volutes are transposed back inside continuous stems; the shell or down-turned leaf of Cordoban volutes is sometimes restored to a half-palmette or more open leaf, as at Nogál (figs 42, 120) and

Frómista (figs 121, 122), Loarre (fig.123), the Agenais (fig.126), Saint-Benoît (127), or Conques (fig.92) with added balls or fruits. At Bayeux the scrolls sprout from the volute stem (fig. 124).

| Corbel MaZ | Panel Toledo | Impost Moissac | Impost Moissac | Impost Conques |

Mozarabic Parallels

Chancel plaques in Mozarabic churches show several aspects of the scroll tradition that culminated in the Moissac cloister capital scrolls. A plaque at Santa Coloma in Navarre (90) with patently Andalusian leaf forms and allied to the woodworking style signifies a stage in the ancestry of the scrolls of Frómista and Nogál; these in turn can be seen as the direct typological precursors of the Moissac scrolls. At San Miguel de Escalada the panel carvings of claustra have another version of the incurled leaf scroll (91). The likelihood of immediate links is strong in this instance since the shape of some Escalada capitals is close to the unusual wide-flaring form of Moissac, and furthermore there are striations on volute stems (92). The tendrils of the animal frieze in the choir (93) are of the same type as those much employed at Santiago on imposts and associated with the Moissac scrolls of capitals 16, 50, 55, and 63, (but not 28).

Spanish Romanesque Scrolls

Simple all-over running scrolls containing single curled leaves decorate capitals at both Nogál and Frómista(94). In each case the leaf is veined and slightly hollowed at the centre, more modelled than Moissac type 1, but certainly related to it.

Frómista. At San Martin these scrolls occur on imposts and once as the main motif on a capital (here very similar to Moissac: the folioles do not overlap but are not wholly inside the circles). The axial-grooved vertical volute stems are of the type shared with Escalada, Tournus, Iguácel, Jaca and Loarre (95). The scrolls are used again as a background for confronted and frontal eagles on the capital with volutes decorated with curls, and there are also cruder versions less relevant to the evolution of the Moissac examples (96).

Nogál. At Nogál only the two capitals of the triumphal arch survive, and both are decorated with the scroll. As at Frómista the folioles are cut off by the surrounding stem, while the Moissac master will bring them round to overlap it in emulation of the Saint-Benoît porch scroll (fig.127).

Veining and hollowing in both cases show the beginnings of emancipation from the two-plane woodworking style.

The "piton d´angle", the horn-shaped protuberance characteristic of Santiago and Jaca, projects under the volutes (97). On the south capital the scroll is the main motif, the impost having a row of circles (fig.120, and cf figs 131 and 22) enclosing seven-petalled rosettes (cap.66) (D15), much in the woodworking style: the circles are square in section, and separated by fleurs-de-lis. The console is framed by little stems swelling into half-palmette leaves in relief like one of the constitutive elements of floriated Kufic (AHIII,fig.145), and constant in Andalusian woodwork (98) or chip carving.

The north Nogál capital also has the "piton", and foliage in relief framing the console on the face; below the console and between the grooved volutes stands a frontal figure. The impost is carved with an interlaced double palmette running scroll (D7). The palmettes are veined like the leaves of the scroll on the capital, and the curl of the first folioles against the stem is excavated with a round drill hole, as are the scrolls on the capital. This is the standard practice in Andalusia, for example in the chip carving of Madinat az-Zahra´ (AHIII, figs 113, 115, 124, 244c) and at San Pere de Roda (99). Though this palmette scroll motif is certainly not exclusive to Andalusia (100), it was current in Andalusian woodwork and the version at Nogál with its rectangular section stem and two-plane relief is strongly suggestive of wood-carving, as a comparison with the motif on the doors of Le Puy and Chamalières can show (101). As an impost motif it is notably rare both in Andalusia and France; examples in a similar style (fig.43)(102) have already been mentioned in Chapter II (p.27)

The Standing Frontal Figure

Distinctive in its stance and robed in looped folds, generally bareheaded, this figure is frequent in early Romanesque sculpture representing Christ, or Daniel, angel, saint or bishop. The Nogál bishop is very like the figure on two capitals at Toulouse: one is in the south transept triforium on a double capital, against a similar scroll pattern in deeper relief than at Nogál. On this capital the volute stems are like those of the Frómista scroll capital fig.121, and snail-shell or corkscrew (103) protuberances project below the volutes. The capital is described by Lyman, Durliat and Moralejo-Alvarez alike (104) as "Spanish". The same figure isolated against an undecorated background is carved on the capital of the central pier of the south transept at Toulouse (105). At Moissac the figure is used to represent Bishop Fructuosus on capital 37 in the cloister, in the Martyrdom of the Three Spanish Saints.

At Loarre there are several versions, but not associated with circular running scrolls (106), which are restricted to one apse capital carved with overall Moissac type 2 (fig.123). The figure is made to serve, among other avatars too weathered to distinguish, as an angel, and is flanked by other frontal figures, by riders or by lions, and one stands on a corner under devouring monsters. The Daniel between lions (fig.133) may be seated and has lost the distinctive looped garment; he remains similar to the rest nonetheless. At Saint-Sever-des-Landes the Daniel on a capital in the intermediary southern chapel has the stance of our motif but the draped folds have gone and a bordered triangular overgarment is substituted (107). At Saint-Eutrope in Saintes the transept capital with a seated Daniel between superposed lions is similar in composition; it has scrolls of circular stems containing incurled leaves D4 at either side (Saintonge Romane, fig.14).

In the tower-porch of Saint-Benoît, St Martin, like the Saint-Sever Daniel, wears a pointed dalmatic, held at the neck with a brooch (fig.57), rather than the uncut chasuble, but the stance is frontal and the folds symmetrical, and the running scroll behind him on the mandorla evokes a comparison with Nogál, especially as it is in two-plane relief. The capital with the Risen Christ from Bayeux cathedral (fig 124) associates the frontal figure, not symmetrically robed, with curled leaf scrolls branching from the volute stems. The technique with flat rectangular-section bands once again evokes woodworking.

An early example of the motif is on capitals at San Miguel de Fluviá in Catalunya (figs.134+6)(109). The imposts have running wave-palmette scrolls very similar to parts of the corbel table cornice on the tower of Saint-Hilaire in Poitiers, and in this location and at this date such a scroll is unlikely to be independent of Andalusian models. The Museum in Zaragoza has recently acquired a plain-leaf capital from excavations in the Seo which is carved on the side with this scroll: it has on the console an interlace cross like those on the Blesle doors. The leaves of the scroll in each of these cases is excavated with triangular and wedge-shaped hollows in the same way as the letters of the Moissac impost inscription and leaves on Roda imposts. The volutes at Fluviá are grooved and rise vertically as at Nogál, Frómista and Loarre; the large leaf sweeping in and down from the volute is also repeated at Loarre (D16)(110). The collarette of acanthus behind which the figure stands has elements of Mozarabic-style foliage in the grooved fleshy tips (F3), and the central veins interpreted as spiral columns are another Andalusian and Mozarab feature (111).

Loarre

At Loarre the capital of the apse arcade with the type 2 Moissac scroll combines it with half-palmette unenclosed

84

leaves (D4) and hollowed leaf scrolls with curled tendrils; the form has flaring fleshy acanthus (F3) in two zones. The chevron bindings are a trait characteristic of the early parts of Saint-Sernin; they also occur at Jaca (112) and are already suggested on the "lintel" of Saint-Genis des Fontaines.

Andalusian decoration provides a source for many of the motifs associated with the second Moissac scroll type on the Loarre capital: the composite rosette (D10), the scrolls on the volute stem (scroll corbels) and the hollowed leaf scroll (D4) of the bottom register. The corbels from the mosque of Tudela in particular provide a number of parallels which are more immediately apparent from their flatter, less modelled technique (closer to woodworking) than fundamentally similar examples from Cordoba, Toledo and Zaragoza (AHIII, figs 109, 110, 208, 209, 270c, 276; 279a,d).

A model for the running scroll itself can be extrapolated from corbels at Tudela (113) (B7, B8, B9): the back-to-back half-palmettes (D6) from B11 or A6; the chevron sequence on B11 is a forerunner of the triple chevron binders whose Romanesque beginnings go back at least to the lintel of Saint-Genis. B1 has a flower-cross rosette (D10) composed of fleurs-de-lis. The emphasis on a vertical axis of the stem and the fleshy acanthus tips of the Loarre capital both are features of capitals in the Aljafería (AHIII, fig. 280).

If Loarre was finished not long after 1080, which the historical record insistently urges (114), this capital is at least contemporary with Toulouse and represents a part of the process of assimilation of Andalusian elements into a developing Romanesque style. Loarre had close relations with Toulouse as its corbels show; other capitals at Loarre show relations with Conques (the angel head motif on imposts), Frómista, Jaca and Iguácel; relations with Muslim and Mozarabic Huesca, some 30 kms down the valley, might well be equally able to explain the Andalusian elements in the sculpture, were any of Huesca´s pre-reconquista monuments remaining (115).

Conques

Investigations into the fabric of the chevet and transepts of Sainte-Foy at Conques made recently by Christopher Bailey, not yet published, give strong evidence that both north and south transept doors (figs 125, 132) belong to the first campaign, begun between 1041 and 1050 (116) and ended not very long after the death of Abbot Odolric in 1065. It has always been agreed that the sandstone capitals of the north transept door belong to that campaign, but the limestone decoration of the south door has until now been dated later. The corbel table, like the arch of the doorway, is masked by the south aisle and must therefore, with the capitals, be part of an earlier campaign. It is unusual in having a decorated cornice; the closest parallel is at Saint-Hilaire in Poitiers. Though restored, some parts remain to vouch for the authenticity of the decoration; the scroll of the metopes (D5) is therefore to be included in the ancestry of the Moissac running scrolls.

The rosette circles of the soffits resemble the impost rosettes of Nogál; the impost of capital 66 at Moissac has similar rosettes. The metope scrolls have something of stiff Mozarabic leaf scrolls, like the Escalada panel (AHIII, fig. 437), but the sharp angles between the leaves are also not unlike the Frómista scrolls and the trefoils at the forks are those of Nogál, Frómista and Tudela (117).

The inner capitals on the doorway have incurled half-palmette leaf scrolls (D7), vey like Moissac type 1, drilled at the inmost curl, placed here and there among the pendant globular fruit under the acanthus tips, and on the impost the same scroll supports the balls known at Saint-Sernin in Toulouse, in Gascony and in Spain. On the adjoining impost, over a capital with a fan-knot interlace, and leaves framed in arches, the balls are reduced to swellings on a foliole. Here are suggestions for both types of Moissac scroll. The type 2 motif later came back to Conques again from Moissac: from Conques cloister the fantastic headless bird motif owes as much to the Moissac refinement of the scroll as to the bird motif itself (fig.135).

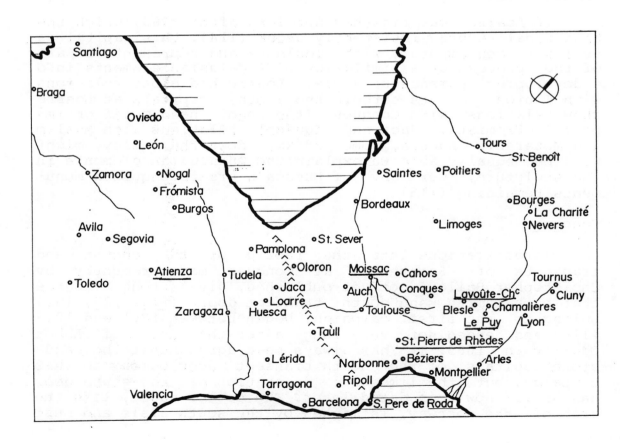

CHAPTER III NOTES

1.   K. Erdmann, `Arabische Schriftszeichen als Ornament in der Abendländischen Kunst des Mittelalters´ Ak. Wiss. Lit. Geistes u. Soz. Wiss. K.9, 1953 (Mainz), for the 11th century lists only the page of the Saint-Sever Apocalypse with a mock-Kufic border (Paris B.N.lat. 8878, fol.1, illustrated by J. Ebersolt, Orient und Occident, Berlin 1928, pl. XXVI and Cahn, Doors, fig. 10) . He does not include the lines of Kufic copied, it would seem from metalwork, by Adhémar de Chabannes in his notebook (University of Leyden Library, Voss 8o 15, illustrated by D. Gaborit-Chopin, La décoration des manuscrits à Saint-Martial de Limoges et en Limousin, Paris/Geneva, 1969; id., `Les dessins  d´Adhémar de  Chabannes´ Bull.Arch. 1967, pp. 213 ff).  Erdmann´s list  for the 12th century includes the Bourges plaque  inscribed round  the border  in what is now thought to `be Armenian, and an impost block "in Toulouse Museum" which is not to be found anywhere in Toulouse and is clearly the item he lists next but does not illustrate: the impost in Moissac cloister. This erroneous attribution is repeated by S.D. Spittle, `Cufic Lettering and Christian Art´, Arch.J. 1954-55, and by W. Cahn in his admirable study The Romanesque Wooden Doors of Auvergne, N.Y. 1974 (hereafter, Doors), leading the latter author to exaggerate the extent of explicit imitation of Kufic on architectural elements (he speaks pp 17-18 of "a true vogue...in Aquitaine and Languedoc").

2.   Both doors are exhaustively studied by W.Cahn, Doors, with full descriptions, illustration and discussion which has stimulated many ideas in this chapter, as will be evident.

3.The Moissac cloister capitals are here numbered according to current practice, anti-clockwise, starting along the south gallery at the modern entrance; cf. M. Schapiro, "The Romanesque Sculpture of Moissac", AB III, 1931; M. Vidal, Quercy roman. This numbering differs from that of E. Rupin, L´Abbaye et les cloîtres de Moissac, 1897, repr.Treignac, 1981, which nonetheless remains the standard monograph.

4.   I am much indebted to Humbert Jacomet, of the Caisse Nationale des Monuments historiques et des Sites, who told me of this doorway and gave me the reference to L. Serrano, Historia de la Villa de Atienza, Madrid 1945.

5.   G. Marçais, "Sur l´inscription arabe de la Cathédrale du Puy", Mélanges...Marçais, 1957: only funeral steles of about 1025 in Qairawan show mim written in this way, and the final ha of the Le Puy inscription is peculiar to the painted ceiling of the Great Mosque of Qairawan: . Marçais discusses the previous interpretations, including that of Fikry, and pronounces for the rendering, by a craftsman probably illiterate in Arabic, of al-mulk lillah (the

kingdom is God´s): "one of the most frequent in the decoration of buildings and portable objects", the <u>kaf</u> having been somewhat deformed and <u>inverted</u>. p. 207.

6. A. Fikry, <u>L´Art roman du Puy</u>, 1934, pp 163-266, fig. 330.

7. The artistic influence of the Rhône valley on Le Puy has lately been emphasized. Where Fikry was prepared to see Le Puy as the model for Tournus, Lyon and Vienne, it is now established that 1) the squinches of Saint-Martin-d´Ainay in Lyon, of about 1102, preceded those of both Tournus and Le Puy, and 2) it was the capitals of the crypt of Tournus, and 3) the incrustations of the façade and belfry of Saint-Martin that influenced Le Puy, not the reverse. A similar receptivity is seen in the neighbouring monastery of Saint-Chaffre at Le Monastier, which had 258 dependencies, nearly all towards the Rhône, and as far as Piedmont (<u>CA</u>, 1976, p. 440 and n. 11).

Le Puy was not only part of the Rhône valley sphere however. It stood on one of the land routes from the far north, either via Lyon or Clermont, to Toulouse, Barcelona and thus, ultimately, to Andalusia. C. Rocher, "Les rapports de l´église du Puy avec Gérone et Bigorre", <u>Tablettes historiques du Velay</u>, 1873, sought to prove that a legendary fraternity between Le Puy and Gerona was based on fact. He used statements of the 17th century Jesuit, Odo de Gissey, and documents of the late-15th century to support the tradition that the fraternity was established by Charlemagne, and that the first bishop of Gerona in the 8th century was a canon of Le Puy. Evidence for the 11th century is confined to two details, small but telling: 1) a visit from Oliba of Vich in about 1035, in connexion with the acquisition of some relics (L. Albaredo, <u>L´Abat Oliba</u>, Montserrat 1972, pp 319 and 329), stands out as one of his rare journeys abroad (his only other distant contact, apart from Rome, was Fleury, but he is not recorded as having paid any visit there), and 2) in 1010 Ermengaud of Urgel made a gift to Le Puy (<u>Gall.X</u>, pp 228-229).

The connexions of Le Puy with more westerly regions of France and Spain were not confined to the oft-cited visits of its bishops, Gotescalc to Santiago in the mid-10th century, and Pierre de Mercoeur to León in 1063 at the festivities surrounding the arrival of the relics of St Isidore from Seville (de Parga, in L.V. de Parga, J.-M. Lacarra and J. Uría, <u>Las Peregrinaciones a Santiago de Compostela</u>, Madrid 1946-1949, p. 47 ff). This latter visit was possibly linked with the presence at Le Puy of Bernard I of Bigorre in 1062, through whose territory Pierre would probably travel to León. Bernard gave a rent in Morlaas currency to one of the altars of Le Puy, and subjugated his county to Le Puy: "a patronage that was still effective in the 13th century, being mentioned in writs of Henry III of England, though no material survives to show whether there was any succession of gifts or whether Le Puy built up any estates in Gascony. In 1062 also Bernard Tumapaler, count of Armagnac, made a gift to Le Puy." (I am most grateful to Dr Rowan Watson for this comment, and for investigating the details and implications of Rocher´s claims).

8.   The Basle and Milan altars, and such pieces as the Oviedo Arca Santa, are examples of other types of model for the composition, with which the wood workshop would be familiar. A comparison is to be made also with the wooden doors of St Mary in Capitol in Cologne. They are dated before 1065 (Ornamenta Ecclesiae, Cologne 1985, Vol.2, No E 98). The relief of the figured panels is much higher and more rounded than on the Le Puy doors and the border has a torus profile. Flat interlace and scroll work, large decorative bosses and bobbin moulding recall the Fez mimbar however. The all-over composition, based probably on a manuscript page, is similar to Le Puy, and its alternation of full and half-width panels creates a series of crosses to compare with the single crosses of Blesle, Chamalières and Lavoûte-Chilhac. The construction, of walnut panels and strips attached to oak vertical planks, differs. The tituli are incised.

9.   Segovia: al-And 1935, pl.15; Silos casket, AHIII, fig. 368; Pamplona casket, EK Elf, No 35, JBCC, pl. 23. The border motif under the two lower medallions on the Fez panel is formed of the same tree shapes, or symmetrical fleurons as the mim of the border of the Saint-Sever Apocalypse page and the Taüll apse-painting border also.

10.   J. Sourdel-Thomine and B. Spuler, Die Kunst des Islam, Berlin 1973, pl. 185. The stone is now in Malaga.

11.   Marçais fig. 3 illustrates a parallel for the branch in Qairawan; the scroll on the ceiling panels in San Millan in Segovia provides one in Spain (al-And 1935, p. 429). G. Zarnecki, Studies 1979, VIII: Payerne capitals 6, 7 and VII with a fir tree motif which he refers to Valdedios and Dijon (there are also hints of D16 downturned leaf, or D2 pine cone, on caps 6,7,III). This tree motif can be added to the links with Spain he postulates for Payerne via Cluny: it is identical on corbels in the Mezquita (LTB 1957, fig. 363) and at Poitiers on the tower corbel table (fig 239).

12.   B.P. Maldonado Memoria.. shows octogon and star borders from the Mosque of Madinat az-Zahra´ dotted with six-petal florets; AHIII: plaster panels of the Aljafería, figs 291, 292; Malaga corbels, fig. 307; Granada, fig. 316. LTB, al-And 1935, p. 432 quotes a corbel in the Archaeological Museum in Madrid of the 12th century and continues "the [florets] frequently met in the same period [late 11th-early 12th century] in the decorations of Andalusian and African monuments ..have six or more petals". Cahn, Doors, fig. 12 illustrates the carved beam

89

from Santa Maria de Tarifa, Cadiz; it has seven-petalled florets surrounded by ring like those down the vertical batten of the Le Puy door. The wooden members from the Alcazaba of Malaga (AHIII, fig. 307) have eight and six respectively.

13. Cahn, Doors, p. 15, gives various readings suggested by different scholars and "the correct and now generally accepted version": GAUZFREDUS ME F[E]CIT; PETRUS EDI[ficavit]. The EDI is convincing but far from clear to see. That Petrus was a bishop is also only a surmise. Weighing the relative likelihood that the donor or builder was Pierre II (1050-1073), Pierre III (1145-1155) or Pierre IV (1159-1189), as is done in all discussions of the date of the doors is thus speculation about a speculation (cf. Cahn, Doors, p. 63). The use of a batten of this kind on a door is common in later Persian and Turkish woodwork, not in Egyptian (I am most grateful to Dr Oliver Watson, V&A Museum, for this information). It is not shown on doors in Mozarabic illustrations of buildings. Some investigation into its appearance in other manuscript illuminations would be worth pursuing.

14. e.g. Corbie Psalter, Amiens, 9th century, D. Jalabert, La flore sculptée.., Paris 1965, pls 40 C,D; also cf. P. Lasko, Ars Sacra, 1972, pp. 102 and 103: drawings of altar crosses of Abbess Mathilde and Duke Otto, Essen, 10th century. Islamic examples: Marçais, AMO, figs 107, 108, 109 (Madinat az-Zahra'); fig. 124, Tangiers; LTB 1957, figs 346, 348 (Cordoba); al-And 1935, p. 430 (Segovia).

15. The underside of the beam fragment of the Cordoban ceiling has a motif identical with this and the Segovia beam just quoted.

16. Cahn, Doors, pp 23-24 and p. 30, n.7; Chamalières, p. 88 has red, blue, white and "dark"; Blesle, p. 124: Thiollier reports red, blue, green; Lavoûte, pp 134 and 136, has "polychromy" with white. Andalusia: LTB 1957, p. 544 and colour plate showing red and brown with blue, white and yellow; Segovia: al-And 1935, p. 428: yellow, red, blue, brown.

17. J. Bousquet, "Les origines de la sculpture romane, sont-elles lointaines ou proches? Un exemple: le motif de l'entrelacs en éventail", CSMC 1978, pp 51-72: the motif "'en bretzel' like the Alsatian biscuit" was transmitted from Ireland to Carolingian to Romanesque, and in stone carving died out shortly after 1100, sooner or later according to the area (or according to the archaeologist).

18. L. and J. Hill, Raymond IV de St-Gilles, Comte de Toulouse, Toulouse 1959. Raymond in 1086 "came to Saint-Gilles, where he received his sister-in-law, Emma, whom King Philip of France, tiring of his wife, had hoped to marry. Emma's father Roger of Sicily, probably because he

suspected Philip, sent his daughter to stay with his son-in-law while the negotiations were in progress. The Norman captain of the ship carrying Emma´s dowry, lacking confidence in the latter´s brother-in-law, left France without leaving the treasure in Raymond´s hands. Raymond, having little esteem for the king of France then married his sister-in-law to the young count of Auvergne, son of his old rival and enemy Robert, count of Auvergne...From his father´s side, Raymond sustained claims to part of eastern Velay, a region nominally shared between the counts of Auvergne and the bishops of Le Puy..Raymond was extending his influence over the lands and rights belonging to the patrimony of the House of Toulouse..[p. 17]. [By] 1095 he had assumed the titles of thirteen counties: Toulouse, Cahors, Albi, Lodève (all from his brother William) and Rouergue, Agde, Béziers, Nîmes, Uzès, the Gévaudan, Viviers, Venaissin, which constituted his earlier possessions. The count of Die was his vassal and the count of Foix recognized him as sovereign. His influence extended into the Velay and to Provence.." [pp 21 ff]; K. Werner, "Kingdom and Principality in Twelfth-century France": Chapter 8 of T. Reuter (ed.), The Mediaeval Nobility, Amsterdam/New York/Oxford 1979 (see Chapter V, n. 109) gives the greatest insight into the paramountcy and hereditary legitimacy of the princely families of France, of which Toulouse was one. On the whole, Raymond maintained good relations with his half-brothers, counts of Barcelona; the need to create a stable area for commercial traffic between the Rhône, Toulouse and Barcelona probably weighed with both sides. Raymond´s territory coincides neatly with that of plait capitals. The marriage of his son Bertrand to Helen of Burgundy, and his own marriage shortly beforehand to Elvira of León are signs of the more widespread alliances which brought new artistic stimuli to Languedoc. The links with northwestern Spain will have added to the existing ties with Catalunya to create further opportunities for the arrival of other Andalusian influences. The queen at the court of León in the last decade of the century at latest, was Zaïda, daughter of the emir of Seville.

19. There is doubt that the carved lower parts of the door are original (Doors, p. 139); they are of different wood and some of the planks appear to have been cut down in size (pls 77 and 79). They were certainly there before the early 17th century and the alterations to the valve were probably not made later than its installation in the south portal of the new Gothic church begun about 1460 (Doors, p. 132). That the carving tradition was still alive in the 13th century is shown for example by the carved window surround in Blesle illustrated by Cahn, fig. 84. The lower panels at Lavoûte-Chilhac are most likely taken from other Romanesque doors, however, rather than newly made.

20. Cahn, Doors, pp 136-7, reviews examples of flaring arms on crosses of pre-Romanesque date; a large proportion

have Spanish affiliations. Several, such as the two Visigothic crosses in the Camara Santa, Oviedo, are illustrated in HE II, figs 417 and 421-422, also one carved in relief over the portal of San Juan de Baños (fig. 272); the cross on the Agates casket, fig. 427, and the arms of Mozarabic ivory crosses with flaring arms (EK Elf, nos 48 and 49; AHIII, figs 35, 477, both attributed to a workshop at San Millán de la Cogolla, late 10th century), should also be added to his list. The Romanesque León crucifix (Lasko, Ars Sacra, pl. 152, figs 82-83) flares slightly on the upper vertical arm towards the wider bar at the top. Small flaring crosses are carved on the Taüll bench figs 100, 101.

21. E. Lévi-Provençal, Inscriptions.. no 57.

22. The church was dedicated in 1024 or 1025 by Bishop Etienne of Clermont. The inscription reads:

> HIC TIBI REX REGUM
> HOC CONDIDIT ODILO TEMPLUM
> AGMINIBUS SUPERIS
> QUEM MISCUIT ARBITER ORBIS

According to Bousquet (CSMC 1978 p. 65) the reference to Odilo is most likely composed by his successor as abbot of Cluny, St Hugh, when the cult of Odilo was at its height. In 1063 his body was raised by Peter Damian, legate of Gregory VII, at a time when it was already performing miracles. "It was his tomb at Souvigny that attracted the greatest crowds, but would not Lavoûte also have been eager to celebrate him? we do not feel compelled to accept a link with the donation from one of his "descendants"(!), another Odilo of Mercoeur, canon of Brioude around 1137" [as indicative of the date of the inscription]. "The church was clearly intended as a family mausoleum, Odilo associated with it his four brothers, already deceased, and his nephews, many of whom had been or were dignitaries of the church of Le Puy". Pierre, one of these nephews, was bishop of Le Puy from 1050 to 1072; he received the pallium in 1051 and was in León in 1063. Cahn, p. 132, is less convinced of the early date of the doors.

Odilo was responsible for the reform and attachment to Cluny of Moissac, which he visited in 1049, leaving in charge his young kinsman Durannus who was later also bishop of Toulouse. Durannus is commemorated in Moissac cloister with a relief, companion to those of the apostles. Le Puy, Moissac and Lavoûte-Chilhac are thus all directly linked to the Mercoeur.

23. Madinat az-Zahra´: Maldonado, Tudela, pl. XXXVII, the cording edges the corbel member itself along the straight oblique profile, outside the curls. Cording on vertical and oblique corbel face: LTB, AEAyA 1936, p. 45, in the patio of Abd ar-Rahman III. The carved mihrab panels in the

Mezquita are edged with cording, and so are the corbels on the inside of the mihrab.

24. L. Goldschmidt, Elf.I (1914), no 31; J. Hubert, J. Porcher, W. Volbach, Carolingian Art, London 1970, pl. 209. The border treatment of the Narbonne panel is similar to the edgings on al-Mughira´s casket, EK Elf., no 31; JBCC pls 14-17. Lasko, Ars Sacra, p. 271, n. 36, suggests a metalwork model for the beading round the cross. The guilloche border of the most elaborate Narbonne workshop altars, including the Toulouse altar by Gilduinus, and the Rodez altar, is identical with that on the Narbonne ivory, showing once again the shared stock of motifs in this area.

25. J. Bousquet, "Les origines.." CSMC 1978. There are no Andalusian examples. Bousquet quotes (pp 70-71) an ivory casket in the V&A Museum (Goldschmidt, IV, 1926 (re-ed., 1975, no 16, pl. VI 16 b and a), attributed to England (it is associated with a hint at foliated pseudo-Kufic, and is itself elaborated with veined leaves) and the olifant in the British Musuem on which snakes form the knot (EK Elf no 65). The Codex Rotense written at Nájera (late 10th century) shows it on a capital, and the León Antiphonary, in a horseshoe arch over the Matthew symbol. The diploma of 1054 for Nájera contains one in an initial (ARE 1934, p. 16 and pl. V).

26. Berry roman, pls 10 and 11.

27. Segovia: TB, al-And 1935, pl. 16; Tudela: Maldonado, Tudela, pl. XXVII; Catalunya: G. Gaillard, Premiers essais..1928, pl. II,5; with down-turned leaf, pl. II: 6,7. Hernandez, "Un aspecto..", 1930.

28. A composite rosette of this type is carved on corbel B-1 at Tudela, Maldonado, Tudela pl. XXXVIIa and fig. 19, with trefoils rather than half-palmettes, and fragments of eaves or hood moulding over doors from the mosque of Madinat az-Zahra´ are carved with such rosettes. A lattice enclosing palmette crosses , from Sa Coloma near Nájera, restored in 923 by King Ordono of León, is illustrated in L´Art Mozarabe, fig. 71, p. 252. This is a stone chancel plaque.

30. Doors, p. 145.

31. Cahn, ibid, p. 144, comments on the fact that "the distribution of the four sets of doors cuts across all lines of institutional affiliation". The abbess of Blesle held the lordship of the town, and the lords of Mercoeur were installed in the burg (p. 118). A Mercoeur presence is thus involved in three of the four places where these doors survive (Le Puy, Lavoûte-Chilhac and Blesle). Powerful families may have been the strongest institutions where patronage was concerned.

32. Doors, pp 84-116. "Two latticed grids constructed
with.. four vertical strips of wood which come to grip a
single horizontal board of equal width at equidistant
points by means of interlocking joints" (p. 89). He
observes that this type of construction is encountered in
both Islamic art and in the Latin West, but in examples
later than this one. It can be added that the shape of the
vertical strips resembles the arms of the crosses in many
"star and cross" tile ensembles of Islamic wall facings.
Confronted quadrupeds and tilting horsemen are standard
Islamic motifs.

33. An analogous elaboration is seen at Tudela; on corbel
B-6 the half-palmette in a circle scroll is not continuous
and the leaf is doubled, Tudela pl. XL.

34. Cahn, Doors, p. 126, gives Limousin illumination as a
parallel and illustrates (fig. 7) the stone carving over
the doorway of San Fede at Cavagnolo in Piedmont, late 12th
century, as a rare architectural example of this type of
interlace border with figures; it has a carved cornice to
mark the horizontal above the arch F12, and spandrel
figures F19. AHIII, fig. 295, shows a plaster frieze in the
Aljafería with a pair of bands that lace at intervals with
a cartouche containing a (non-figural) motif (fig 51). Wood
panels with carved figure motifs within a similarly laced
border from the Fatimids' Western Palace, now in the
Islamic Museum in Cairo (G. Wiet, Album du Musée Arabe, pl.
22; E. Kühnel, Islamic Art and Architecture, London 1966,
pl. 21) are a good example of the universality of
Mediterranean style in the 12th century.

35. Cf. the marble dado of the mihrab of al-Hakam II, and
the general Islamic tendency to concentrate decoration
upwards F5.

36. Fikry thought Gauzfredus introduced the style of
carving of the doors to Le Puy from Spain, and that it was
copied by local craftsmen who made the other doors; Marçais
postulated a model from Africa which inspired Gauzfredus;
Bréhier proposed a Mozarab: in each case an innovator.

37. Cahn, Doors, Chap. VIII. In considering iconography,
p. 28, he contemplates "a broadly shared system of formal
conventions adapted to particular materials and modes of
workmanship rather than intrinsically grounded in the
experience of a particular craft". Cf. also Hernandez,
1930, p. 41: "..what travelled was the craftsman".

38. De diversis artibus, ed. C.R. Dodwell, London/New York
1961; T. Lyman, CSMC 1978, p. 126.

39. Cahn, Doors, pp. 144 and 149.

40. Cahn, Doors draws attention to the similarity of the
polychromy on the Cordoba ceiling beams and the Le Puy

doors. Pyrenean crucif.xes were painted in the same range of colours, also with imitations of hispano-moresque silks: M. Durliat, Christs romans, Perpignan 1957, p. 24. In CA 133, 1976 Durliat quotes the statue of Our Lady of Le Puy, known from an engraving by Veyrenc in B. Faujas de Saint-Fond, Recherches sur les volcans éteints du Velay et du Vivarais, Grenoble/Paris 1778, fig. 5, opposite p. 14. The earliest reference to the statue is in a donation by Raymond de St Gilles in 1096. In the engraving the hem of the garment and its vertical braid have a row of four-petal florets each in a ring, and the robe of the Infant is similarly decorated. The wide sleeves of the Virgin are bordered with mock-Kufic.

41. Cahn, Doors, cites (fig. 84) a carved wooden window frame of the 13th century at Blesle. He also comments, pp 61 and 154 (notes 34 and 38) on the fame and quantity of wooden statues in the Auvergne, particularly images of the Virgin in Majesty and Christ on the Cross. His account of the lost statue of Our Lady of Le Puy (p.61) differs in detail from that given by Durliat (op.cit. note 40) and follows I.H. Forsyth, The Throne of Wisdom. Wood Sculptures of the Madonna in Romanesque France, Princeton 1972, pp 103 ff. Cahn lists the following crucifixes: Lavaudieu, Blesle, Lavoûte-Chilhac, Arlet, Auzon, Lavoûte-sur-Loire, Montsalvy, Valuéjols, Saint-Flour and Chanteuges; and the following bust-images of saints: St Chaffre at Le Monastier, St César at Maurs, St Baudime at Saint-Nectaire (Les Trésors des églises de France, Nos 417, 428, 447, pls 79-811), St Peter at Bredons. The St Baudime bust is dated in Trésors to "late 12th century". T. Lyman CSMC 1978, p. 125 gives strong reasons for dating it c.1100. Forsyth, op. cit. lists the Auvergnat Madonnas pp 135 ff.

42. A. and O. Grabar, "L´essor des arts inspirés par les cours princières à la fin du premier millénaire; princes musulmans and princes chrétiens", Occidente e l´Islam 1967, pp 845-892, on the priority and influence of secular court and noble patronage over religious art. A. Grabar has frequently stressed this influence in recent writing.

43. And even extended north as far as to Cologne. The network of long and medium-distance trade routes carrying slaves and cloth as their leading commodities would sustain the contacts of such a craft "freemasonry" by providing the facilities for people to travel and ideas to spread. Trade in timber also signifies here: cf M. Lombard, "Un problème cartographié. Le bois dans la Méditerranée musulmane VII-XIe siècles", Annales E.S.C. 1959/1, for the cumulative scarcity of timber as Andalusian civilization expanded, though most of recorded supplies came from Africa and further east. C. Verlinden, L´Esclavage dans l´Europe médiévale, I, Bruges 1955; id., "The Rise of Spanish Trade in the Middle Ages", EHR, 1940; W.G. East, An Historical Geography of Europe, London 1948 quotes the description of Langres by Idrisi "remarkable for its buildings, commerce,

"Remarques sur le commerce maritime en Afrique au XIe siècle", <u>Mélanges....Marçais</u> 1957, pp 51-59, describes the rôle of Jewish merchants in a network comprising Spain, Sicily and North Africa, linked with the Rhône; M. Durliat, <u>Histoire du Roussillon</u>, 1962 quotes G. Duby on a route through Roussillon from the Rhône to Andalusia . J.-M. Lacarra, <u>Un arancal de aduanas del siglo XI</u>, Zaragoza 1950 gives details of the passage of the Pyrenees from Béarn to Jaca, a town that grew up considerably during the century. The customs document shows expansion of trade with Andalusia into Gascony: many of the trading terms and names for clothings and fine leatherwork are Arabic. The links between Le Puy and Bigorre were perhaps made worth while because of these developments; for more on the development of Jaca, id., "Desarrollo urbano de Jaca en al Edad Media", <u>Est. Ed. Med. Corona de Aragon</u>,; 19, pp 139-155.

44. M. Durliat, <u>CSMC</u> 1976, p. 101. For Roda, p. 103; <u>Les Structures sociales de l'Aquitaine, du Languedoc et de l'Espagne au premier âge féodal</u>, Paris 1969 (Colloquy held at Toulouse, 1968), <u>passim</u>, especially P. Bonnassie "Conventions féodales.." p. 203 on the supremacy of the count of Barcelona, and p. 215, "Raimond Beranger..was probably the richest man in Europe"; J. Bolet y Siso, <u>Las Monedes Catalanes</u>, Barcelona 1908; L. Nicolau de Olwer, <u>La Catalogne à l'époque romane</u>, Paris 1932; L. de Valdeavellano, <u>Historia de Espana</u>, 5th ed., Madrid 1973, vol. I, part 2, Chap. X, with bibliography p. 219; J.M. Villas Vallicrosa, "Valoración de la cultura romanica en la epoca de Santa Maria de Ripoll", <u>Ests sobre Historia de la Ciencia espanola</u>, Barcelona 1949, pp 43-64; id., <u>Nuevas aportaciones para el estudio de la transmisión de la ciencia a Europa a traves de Espana</u>, Barcelona 1943. R. Beer, <u>Die Handschriften des Klosters Santa Maria de Ripoll</u>, Vienna 1907-1908, 2 vols; J. Puig y Cadafalch, <u>Le premier art roman</u>, Paris 1928; id.,A. de Folguera, J. Goday i Casals, <u>L'Architectura romanica a Catalunya</u>, 3. vols, Barcelona 1909-1918; C. Higounet, "La rivalité des maisons de Toulouse et de Barcelone pour la préponderance méridionale", <u>Mélanges...Halphen</u>, Paris 1959.

45. W.W.S. Cook and J. Gudiol Ricart, <u>AH VI</u>, 1950, illustrate many examples. "The painting is on a single plane which...makes no attempt at the third dimension" (p. 15). Ricart, p. 327, commenting on the group of sculptures of Erill, insists on an oriental (even Chinese !) element which he derives from Hispano-Arab culture. W.W.S. Cook, "Stucco Altar Frontals of Catalonia", <u>Art Studies</u>, ii, 1924, p. 41 ff; id., "Earliest painted panels of Catalonia", <u>AB</u>, vi, 1923; M. Durliat, <u>Christs romans</u> Perpignan 1957; id., <u>Vierges romanes</u>, Perpignan n.d.; id., <u>La sculpture romane en Cerdagne</u>, Perpignan 1957 gives p. 82 a list of fifteen crucifixes of wood and painted; M. Delcor, "Les vierges romanes en Cerdagne et en Conflent dans l'histoire et dans l'art", <u>CSMC</u> 1970, p. 45 ff.

46. F. Hernandez, "Un aspecto de la influencia del arte
califal en Cataluna (basas y capiteles del siglo XI)"
AEAyA, xvi/4, 1930, pp 21-49; G. Gaillard, Premiers essais
de sculpture monumentale en Catalogne aux Xe et XIe
siècles, Paris 1938; M. Durliat, "Les débuts de la
sculpture romane dans le Midi de la France et en Espagne",
CSMC 1978, pp 101-113.

47. Now generally agreed to have been completed for or
soon after the dedication of 1022: Durliat, art. cit., pp
103-105; J.-Cl. Fau, "Un décor original..." CSMC 1978, p.
131; J. Bousquet, "La dédicace ou consécration des églises
et leur rapport avec la construction", CSMC 1972, p. 66
contests this, arguing (from the letter written by Abbot
Peter to Pope Benedict VIII in 1023, complaining that when
Abbot Peter summoned various bishops "they refused even to
come to the consecration of the new church built in this
place.." because of harrassment by the laity) that the
occasion was not a success, and therefore that the abbot
did not mean that the building was finished!; that there
are no records of new donations or indulgences and we
should therefore deduce that the abbey was as destitute as
the abbot makes out. It may be countered to this argument
that when there is strife and complaint the stakes are
worth the conflict and no one is destitute. By this date
there had been some highly lucrative expeditions into
Andalusia (ELP II, pp 284 and 329) foreshadowing the paria
system that was to bring such wealth to the county of
Catalunya and its confederates. At all events, what Abbot
Peter says is that the new church has been built.

48. Details linking the Roda capitals with those of the
porch of Saint-Benoît include spiral columns among the
acanthus leaves, the solar-like flower on the console,
multiple strand stems, refined chip carving scrolls, a
profile animal head hidden in the corners. This last motif
is taken up at Moissac in the porch (figs 89, 301); Fikry
gives drawings of the Le Puy acanthus capitals. At Conques
and Rodez, as at Le Puy, it is the interlace and associated
foliage treatment that provides the link with Roda. Rodez
capitals: J.-Cl. Fau, "Un décor.." pp 129 ff, figs 4 and 6;
M. Schapiro, "A Relief in Rodez" Romanesque Art, London
1977, p. 286, fig. 6 (Studies in Western Art: Acts of the
XXth Int. Congr. on the History of Art, I, Princeton 1963,
pp 40-66). The capitals at Bessuéjouls, often similar to
examples at Conques, share motifs also with Saint-Benoît
(Val de Loire roman, figs 31 and 38, Rouergue roman, figs
70. 76,77). E. Vergnolle p. 78 distinguishes the northern
palmette capitals devoid of proper interlace from the
meridional, but barriers were not impervious.

49. P. Deschamps, "Tables d´autel de marbre éxécutées dans
le Midi de la France au Xe et au XIe siècle",
Mélanges...Lot, Paris 1925; M. Durliat, "Tables d´autel à
lobes de la province ecclésiastique de Narbonne (IXe-XIe
siècles)", Cah. Arch.XVI, 1966, pp 51-75. D. Jalabert, La
flore sculptée... illustrates, pls 14, 15, 16, such motifs

on the altars of Rodez, Gerona, and, pls 17-20, Saint-Sernin and Cluny, with examples from Syria, in an emphatic denial of any Islamic influence.

50. Also G. Marçais , AMO, fig. 108.

51. Cahn, Doors refers p. 18 to the "ornate and extravagant letter forms encountered in the Latin epigraphy of Auvergne, Spain and the south of France in Romanesque times" as "another and no less vital dimension of the impact of Kufic writing". cf also A. Grohman "The Origin and early Development of Floriated Kufic", Ars Orientalis 2, 1957, p. 194; G. Miles, "Classification of Islamic Elements in Byzantine Architectural Ornament in Greece" Actes du XII Congrès intern. d´Etudes byzantines III, Belgrade 1964, pp 281-290; id., "Byzantium and the Arabs: Relations in Crete and the Aegean Area", Dumbarton Oaks Papers 18, 1964, pp 3-32; R. Ettinghausen, "Kufesque in Byzantine Greece" in The Latin West and the Muslim World, A Colloquium in Memory of G.C. Miles, New York 1976, pp 28-47.

52. GG 1938, p. 20, in an analysis of capital decoration.

53. The scroll corresponds to Fau´s phase 2 of capital carving at Roda, exemplified on the capital below it: "characterized by the presence of palmettes or trilobed fleurons into which the three strands of the [interlaced] ribbon expand at the ends".J.-Cl. Fau, CSMC 1978, p. 130. cf AHIII fig. 71, a capital from Tudela with an identical treatment of the caulicoles, which have grooved stranded stems that expand at the ends into fleurons.

54. A. Grabar, "La décoration architecturale de l´église de la Vierge à Saint-Luc en Phocide et les débuts des influences islamiques sur l´art byzantin de la Grèce" CRAcIBL, Dec. 1971.

55. Maldonado, Tudela, figs 17 and 18.

56. J.-Cl. Fau, CSMC 1978, pp 130-131, "grooved ribbon branching into leaves".

57. CA 1976, p. 459 and passim. He discovered lobed arches in the original roof.

58. Maldonado, Tudela illustrates throughout the book examples from Madinat az-Zahra´ that furnish models for the motifs of carving in the mosque of Tudela. Theophilus, as Cahn argues, would take it for granted that his readers were able to carry out the techniques of woodwork (pp 148-9). T. Lyman, "Arts somptuaires et art monumental: bilan des influences auliques pré-romanes sur la sculpture romane dans le sud-ouest de la France et en Espagne" CSMC 1978, p. 176, makes a strong case for the decline of the sumptuary arts being the motive for Theophilus writing the book; this would explain why he does not devote attention to the

rising art of stone carving either: it threatens to overshadow them.

59. Languedoc roman, 1975 (with bibliography), pp 141-148; the doorway, fig. 37. "Though polychromy using local basalt may not be exceptional, its use on the tympanum, combined with a studied refinement in the encrusted designs, is admittedly surprising. When, furthermore, this decoration is associated with a rare example of a motif of Islamic inspiration, it is clear that Saint-Pierre-de-Rhèdes underwent northern [sic!] influences easily explicable by the priory´s situation on the route across the Cévennes from Le Puy. Above all, it is the twin columns that demonstrate the extent of Saint-Pierre´s debt to its position on the old Gallo-Roman route to the north. We have seen this type of column used in the Velay, Rouergue and Gévaudan. The fact that they are also met with at Loupian on the coastal plain leads us to the conclusion that Saint-Pierre marks a stage in the propagation of a feature". The route went north from further south than Loupian.

60. Basalt decoration is listed in CA 1950, p. 266: at Villeneuve-lès-Béziers, Cassac, Quarante, Puissalion. It is found as a surface rock along a line running from l´Escandorgue to Agde, Languedoc roman, p. 146.

61. R.S. Ventura, "Un grupo de iglesias del Alto Aragon" AEAyA 1933, pp 215-235; R. Crozet, "Petites églises..." CCM 1969/3, p. 187 ff.

62. Languedoc roman p. 19.

63. See L. Valdeavellano, Historia, I/2, p. 166, Bibliography to Chapter VIII; Ch. Verlinden, "The Rise of Spanish Trade in the Middle Ages" EHR 1939; C.E. Dubler, Über das Wirtschaftsleben auf der Iberischen Halbinsel vom XI zum XIII Jahrhundert (Beitrag zu den islamisch-christlichen Beziehungen) Geneva 1943. The long-term transhumance of shepherds described by Le Roy Ladurie, Montaillou, village occitan de 1294 à 1324, Paris 1982 is likely to have existed centuries before, if on a smaller scale.

64. Cahn, Doors p. 32, n. 25 lists the following: Shroud of St Chaffre and griffon silk of Le Monastier (Trésors des Eglises de France nos 426 and 427); fragments found inside the altar of Saint-Michel d´Aiguilhe (F. Enaud, BM 1964, pp 37-57); id., Mons hist. France 1961, pp 136-140); the chasuble of Saint-Rambert-sur-Loire (Mons hist. France 1966, pp 63-80). There are similar examples in Catalunya also, e.g. the Battló crucifix from Olot (J. Ainaud de Lasarte, Museo de Arte de Cataluna Romanico, 1980, p. 119).

65. F. Enaud, "Remise en état de la statue de la Vierge à l´enfant d´Orcival" Mons. hist. France 1961, pp 79-89, illustrates fragments of the cushion p. 84. On the side, beaded medallions alternately containing griffons and

quadrupeds are bordered by the inscribed bands, all in repoussé silver. The statue is of wood overlaid with silver and silver gilt. See note 40 on the Le Puy Virgin and Child, now lost.

66. Bull. Arch. 1896; BSNAF 1925; C. Urseau, Monuments Piot 1926. R. de Lasteyrie, Architecture religieuse à l'époque romane, 1929: it was opened in 1923 and found to contain i.a. "important Spanish cloths with Kufic inscription", a ring with an "inscription which seemed like a European transliteration of three Arab words", and a "covered box of turned wood like contemporary Spanish ones". The Bishop died in 1149.

67. Cahn, Doors, figs 85 and 82.

68. In the gallery of the little church of Durro, in the Val d'Aran near Taüll, stands a seat made up of various disparate panels. Two of these are clearly two halves of what was the side of a piece similar to the Taüll bench. It is curious that in Archivo Mas in Barcelona is a small photograph of a seat with two such half panels. A note on the back states that it is in Erill la Val, a church sited directly below Taüll (fig 102). One panel is apparently the same piece as that on the left in fig. 103 at Durro, but the other is different. Archivo Mas have no negative of this snapshot. So far efforts to find the third half-panel or any more such pieces have been unavailing.

69. In the absence of the abbey's archives, lost during the Revolution in 1793, only fragments of the history of Moissac's relations with Spanish affairs remain:
    a) Count Bernat II of Besalú, of the same family as Hunald, abbot of Moissac from 1072 to 1085, gave to Saint-Pierre in 1078 the foundations of Camprodon, Santa-Maria in Arles-sur-Tech and San Pau of Vallosa. The association was not a happy one, the Pyrenean monks resented and disputed the authority of Moissac (J.A. de Lasarte, "Moissac et les monastères catalans de la fin du Xe au début su XIIe siècle" AduM 1963.
    b) In 1102 Diego Gelmirez, Bishop of Santiago de Compostela, stopped at Moissac on his journey to Rome, where he was to receive the pallium (Defourneaux, p. 120 n).
    c) Bernard of Sédirac, monk of Moissac, born at La Sauvetat de Savères a few kilometers from Moissac, and Archbishop of Toledo since the capture of the city by Alfonso VI of León in 1085, found his efforts to go on crusade in the Holy Land thwarted by insurrections in his episcopal city as soon as his back was turned. He was absolved of his vow by Urban II in 1096 as he passed through Rome, and returned to Spain, on the way recruiting a number of monks from the monasteries of his native province, to staff his administration with men more loyal than the Spaniards, whose independence of spirit had balked him of his projected enterprise. From Moissac he enlisted Geraldus, whom he first appointed cantor of Toledo and then

archbishop of Braga; Geraldus was canonized after his
death. Others of the recruitment were

Pierre from Béziers, archdeacon of Toledo, then
bishop of Osma

Bernard from Agen, cantor at Toledo, then bishop
of Sagonte,

Pierre from Agen, bishop of Segovia,

Another Pierre, bishop of Palencia
(Valdeavellano, I,1, p. 537)

Raymond, who followed Pierre as bishop of Osma
and succeeded Bernard at Toledo in 1124; there he developed
the famous school of translators and was much concerned
with urban development and irrigation.

Jérome of Perigord served also in Toledo, became
bishop of Valencia when the Cid captured the city
(Defourneaux, pp 35-6) and thereafter bishop of Salamanca.

M. Schapiro, "The Romanesque Sculpture of Moissac" AB 1931
(repr. in id., Romanesque Art, London 1977, to which
reference is made hereafter) discusses the capitals from
the point of view of the figure style and iconography. He
enumerates the subjects of the cloister capitals on p. 135.
M. Vidal, Quercy roman, pp 131-1133 also gives a list with
the same numbering, which is adopted here. Figure capitals
are all illustrated in Schapiro, and in the standard work:
E. Rupin, L'Abbaye et les cloîtres de Moissac 1897, re-ed.
1981, often all four sides, and also the decorative
capitals.

70. At Saint-Sernin in Toulouse there is one capital in
the south transept triforium decorated totally in the style
of a Moissac cloister capital; it has thick acanthus
leaves, but is much less flaring in shape. The decoration
is an all-over coiling stem and sunk-centre leaves, and it
has the striated volute stem support: T. Lyman, AB 1965,
fig. 36. If Lyman's account is followed, this sculptor left
Toulouse in about 1083, when the Benedictines returned to
Moissac after their attempted takeover of Saint-Sernin, and
subsequently worked there, where his style of decoration,
identifiable in other details (op.cit. pp 33-34) and linked
with Santiago and León, was applied to the flaring shape
characteristic of the Moissac cloister capitals. The origin
of the volute stem motif is puzzling. Capitals in the
cloister museum (M. Vidal, Pierres romanes au Musée de
Moissac 1963, figs 1 and 2) show a possible stage of
evolution towards it, and an apse capital at Loarre
also. Vidal dates the Museum capitals to the late-11th
century, "pre-cloister", and attributes them to the
Romanesque chapter house. They have points of resemblance
with Mozarabic capitals, notably at Santiago de Penalba and
San Miguel de Escalada (L'Art Mozarabe, figs 32, 33, 38),
especially that at Peñalba with palmettes in hearts and
rigid veining of acanthus under the volutes. There is a
parallel effect in the Aljaferîa, AHIII, fig. 280, from the
fronded scrolls, but the Moissac device is distinctive.

71. Examination of the motifs on the ivory cross of Fernando and Sancha fig 111 and AH IV, fig.268, Palol & Hirmer, figs 68-70 and of other work of the craftsmen working for the court of León would yield many details showing that Moissac sculptors had close familiarity with their style and methods: the type of monster masks, often disguised (figs 73,74,112,3), asymmetry, dancing gait, folds rendered with double lines, for example (AH VI, figs 269-275, 277-281; Palol & Hirmer figs 66, 67, 74-76, 78-81).Figs 301 a-d) show capitals with treatment of foliage closely related to that of the cross, and the tendrils of Santiago and Moissac. However preponderant the German element in the ivory carving (Lasko, Ars Sacra, p. 148-9), its distinctive character is partly Andalusian, in spite of the quite different energy of many of its figures. Grooved stems, ring- and multiple-bindings, fleshy or hollow curled leaves D4 (e.g. Hispanic Society casket, EK Elf no 28, [JBCC pl. 12], once the obsessive drill holes and cut-off· edges are discounted), birds, back-to-back half-palmettes and stiff profiled flowers, are all Cordoban motifs. Fikry cited the "fleshy acanthus border" (Lasko, op.cit. p. 150) on the back of the León crucifix as debased Kufic (Fikry, p. 260, fig. 323), and this may be a valid example of convergence between an Ottonian acanthus border, exemplified on the panel of the Two Magi in the British Museum (Lasko, op. cit.p. 101) and the kind of inscribed border seen round the Fez mimbar panel fig.44 , the former being modified in the direction of mock-Kufic. The regular notches hollowing the small intermediary leaves of the border on the cross are repeated in the notches of the Moissac impost inscription, giving reason not to dismiss Fikry´s parallel of the León border motif with Kufic, even though taken in isolation the border motif of the cross might pass muster as a traditional debased acanthus. This approach is different from the mock-Kufic of the Oviedo Arca Santa fig.81 which emulates a true inscription. In León where these pieces were made, "Christian" and "Arabic" would not be mutually exclusive terms, considering the sizeable Mozarab population (C. Sanchez Albornoz, Estampas de la Vida en León, Madrid 1926; M. Gomez Moreno, Iglesias Mozarabes 1919.

72. Typical of Santiago de Compostela: GG 1938, LXXIX, figs 15, 18, 20; also at Frómista, Jaca, Toulouse, Saint-Sever-des-Landes (Gascogne romane, fig. 30) and La Sauve-Majeure (Guyenne romane, figs 79, 80, 82; 83) with chevron binders instead of the Andalusian twisted stem.

73. R. Argaud, "Sur les chapiteaux prétendus hispano-moresques et byzanto-arabes du cloître de Moissac", Bull. Arch. Midi..France iv, 1940, p. 17, interpreted it as a repetition of the name of Allah foward and reversed. His argument has not convinced other Arabists. (fig.229)·

74. G. Marçais , "Sur l´inscription arabe de la cathédrale du Puy" CRAcIBL 1938, repr. Mélanges...Marçais, Algiers 1957, p. 207, fig. 2.

75. The ambiguities of this motif, derived from the meeting of two acanthus leaves (GG 1938, p. xxi) and its relation with half-palmettes and in which the lam-aliph schema often seems implied, recur throughout Romanesque border decoration, from imposts at San Pere de Roda onwards.

76. Dr M. Bayani confirms in conversation she knows of none in any oriental manuscripts. I have found none in the following: J.D. Weill, Catalogue générale du Musée Arabe: Les bois à épigraphes jusqu´à l´époque Mamlouke, Cairo 1931. No 3361, 9th century, has a thin line up the centre of ascenders but no wedge hollow; G. Wiet, ditto, Stèles funeraires; B. Roy and P. Poinssot, Inscriptions arabes de Kairouan, Paris 1950; and of course E.Lévi-Provençal, Inscriptions arabes d´Espagne, Leyden and Paris 1931, except for the four quoted below in notes 79-82.

77. EK Elf, no 32, JBCC pl. 19, dated 969-970.

78. EK Elf, no 34, JBCC pl.26, 11th century

79. E.Lévi-Provençal, Inscriptions arabes d´Espagne, 57.

80. Ibid., 58.

81. Ibid., 65.

82. Ibid., 68.

83. Vita Beati Geraldi, qu. Defourneaux, p. 35; M. Schapiro, Romanesque Art, p. 50 ("From Mozarabic to Romanesque in Silos" AB 1939).

84. GG 1938, Frómista: LXX, 15-18, LXXI, 22; León: XVI, XXII, XXIII, 16, 20, also caulicoles: León, XXV, XXVII with a crossbowman, no bolts; Jaca: XL,8, also with caulicoles, XLI, 13 14 LI; Santiago: LXXVIII, 21, LXXX, LXXXI, LXXXIV, 1.2. etc. The characteristic treatment of caulicoles as nearly vertical and touching corkscrew volutes is found at Saint-Benoît in the porch capitals and is marked on the Mozarabic capitals of San Cebrian de Mazote (Ig.Moz., fig. 73) and Escalada; it reappears at Saint-Sever-des-Landes (Gascogne romane, fig. 32), and on this capital the horizontal leaf cylinder beneath the lowest of three pairs of caulicoles or volutes is a link with the Berry (Berry roman, figs 56, 93) where it is typical; the similar caulicoles at Saint-Benoît will also signify the Mozarab connexion through Gascony, the Berry being strongly under the influence of Saint-Benoît in its first phase (E. Vergnolle, "Les chapiteaux de La Berthenoux..", GBA 1972, and Saint-Benoît-sur-Loire.. 1985).

85. León: i,.a., GG 1938, XVI,7; XVII, 9-10; XXI, 7,8; XXV. It is frequent also in Saint-Sernin in Toulouse: south

transept triforium, (Lyman, <u>AB</u> 1967, figs 25, 38 on imposts; 31, 36 on capitals.

86. <u>Haut-Languedoc roman</u>, fig. 13, door capital; <u>GG 1938</u>, XVe, (transept); L. Grodecki, "La sculpture du XIe siècle en France, Etat des questions", <u>Inf. d´Hist. de l´Art</u>, 3, 1958, fig. p. 107: Saint-Bénigne in Dijon, "before 1017" (the necks of the monsters give an idea for the Moissac volute stem support); id., "Les débuts de la sculpture romane en Normandie, Bernay" <u>BM</u> 1950.

87. G. Marçais , <u>AMO</u>, p. 61.

88. In Fez: H. Terrasse, "Chapiteaux oméiyades d´Espagne à la mosquée d´al-Qarawiyyin de Fès", <u>al-Andalus</u> XXVIII/1. pl. 4; Madinat az-Zahra´: Maldonado, <u>Mem. Exc. Mezquita de Madinat al-Zahra´</u> 1966, pl. XXII; Seville: <u>al-Andalus</u> 1966, pl. 8, and figs 17, 75, 54 (drawings of decorative bands).

89. <u>Tudela</u>, corbels A4, fig. 104; A8, B3, B4, B5, B6, B7, B8, B9 (here the hollowing of the two straighter folioles is close to the carving technique of the Moissac inscription). Maldonado demonstrates their similarity to decoration at Madinat az-Zahra´.

90. <u>L´Art mozarabe</u>, fig. 71.

91. Ibid., figs 17, 28.

92. Ibid., figs 14, 16; especially the portico, but inside, fig. 16, the middle capital of the left-hand row and a few others; for volute stem, figs 32, 33; other similar shaped capitals in San Miguel de Terrasa, Barcelona (<u>Palol & Hirmer</u>, pl. 49).

93. <u>L´Art mozarabe</u>, fig. 23. Also 11th century Toledo: <u>AHIII</u>, fig. 270.

94. <u>GG 1938</u>, pls LIV and LXIX, 10; LXX, 14.

95. An early feature: at Escalada, <u>L´Art mozarabe</u> figs 19, 30, 31[?].

96. <u>GG 1938</u>, LXX, 14, and LXVIII, 4, 7, 11. The bird capital 14 has a plain fillet "heart-and-dart" impost, as also 16, 17, 21, 11, very much "woodwork" technique. 4, 7. 11 have coiled stems, not leaves, associated with "snail shells" axial grooved vertical volutes, "piton", and a pendant palmette under the console; the pendant palmette in a heart is less popular in Andalusia than erect, or pendant, leaf bud or pine cone. It perhaps came to Cordoba from Byzantium with the dome mosaicist (cf <u>Tudela</u>, fig. 9). Cordoban design has a marked upward turn, its motifs rarely droop; the corbel shell or down-turned leaf is the more remarkable. Pendant palmettes alternate with upright ones on a plinth of a pilaster at Madinat az-Zahra´ (<u>LTB 1957</u>, fig. 516) and pendant pine cones in a heart-shaped stem

scroll are quite usual (ibid., figs 521, 522, 523). These in the same scheme as the Tudela pendant palmette are a distinctive trait of the repertoire of San Pere de Roda and a Narbonne workshop active in the Rouergue (J.-Cl. Fau, "Un décor original.." p. 131 and fig. 2; id., "Le bassin roman de serpentine du cloître de Conques" Actes Congr. Etudes de Rodez 1975, fig. 3). At Santiago, GG 1938, LXXIX, 14.

97. A distinctive Spanish Romanesque feature, unexplained iconographically, appearing particularly at Santiago, Frómista, Jaca (West door master), the nave and north door of León, and on the "Spanish master capital" in Saint-Sernin in Toulouse. It must originate in heavy acanthus tips, but assumes its own identity. Cabanot Les débuts.. believes it may originate in Gascony; it is very marked at Hagetmau.

98. cf the fleur-de-lis on the church bench from Taüll.

99. Tudela, XVIIIe, conspicuous on ivories, e.g. EK Elf, nos 22, 23, 26, 27, 28, 35; (JBCC, pls 6, 10,7, 12, 23. The effect is attenuated on most Romanesque ivory carving but the capitals of the arches framing the apostles on the SS John and Pelayo reliquary of 1059 are so treated (Palol & Hirmer, figs 66, 67); San Pere de Roda: ibid., fig. 52.

100. e.g. Antioch, 5th century frieze, A. Grabar, Byzantium, London 1966, fig. 301.

101. Cahn, Doors, pl. 7 for Le Puy, the upper part of the vertical batten carrying the Latin inscription; pls 37, 39, 41, 42 for Chamalières; Cahn´s parallel with the Figeac Homiliary, pl. 44 (Paris, Bib. Nat. lat. 3783, fol. 52), can hardly bring the quest for a derivation to an end; the stems ending in a cleft palmette, i.e., two half-palmettes back-to-back, abound in Andalusian decoration: AHIII, figs 110, 113; Maldonado, Memoria.. passim.

102. Maillezais, Vendée romane, fig. 2, "first half of 11th century"; F. Garcia-Romo, "Un Taller Escultorico de Influjo Hispano-musulman en el Loire Medio (antes de 1030-1050)" al-Andalus, xxv, l, pl,. 7; Saint-Outrille-en-Graçay, Berry roman, pl. 16, "early 12th century"; Villesalem, D. Jalabert, La flore..., pl. 40d.

103. A tendency to bulbous volutes is evident at Santiago, on the chevet, on the capitals of the Platerias doorway and in the transepts (GG 1938, pls XCII, XCIII, LXXXII, LXXXIII and LXIV). In the transept the balls on the ends of acanthus leaves serve the same purpose. Capital 2 of pl. LXXXIV has two registers of volutes, corresponding to the "snail shell" of the "Spanish capital" at Toulouse set below the volutes on the angle. The same tendency exists at Jaca, but in Spain it is primarily at León that the feature is developed. It is marked at La Sauve-Majeure, Agen, Nogaro, Cénac (J. Secret, "Les chapiteaux de Cénac" AduM 1963, p. 601 n.), and Cuxa. It is also seen at Saint-Sever-

des-Landes on the earliest plain leaf capitals of the north chapel, Gascogne romane, fig. 29, and on the figure capitals of the south chapels (Cabanot's second phase of sculpture), figs 30-55. It is exaggerated in the León manner on some capitals at Hagetmau and Saint-Sever-de-Rustan, ibid., figs 38-44, 82, 85, and at Lescar (Pyrénées romanes, figs 94. 97, 98, 100, 101 [with the crossbowman motif used here to do duty for the usual prisoners], 103). At Lescar the peg-legged huntsman of the mosaic donated by Bishop Gui (1115-1141) portrays a Moor, and Spanish connexions are clear. Durliat does not allow the "snail shell" volute to be Spanish but thinks it is local (BM 1971, p. 118), possibly developed in the Agenais or at La Sauve; it is, however difficult to leave out of account the capitals of San Cebrian de Mazote, and some at Escalada. The appearance of this feature at Saint-Sever probably ante-dates it at León. It is curious that it appears at Santiago in the three figured capitals, two with versions of the history of St Faith and one with a similar composition but unidentified subject, in the chapel of St Faith and in the transept (GG 1938, LXXX and LXXXI: the numbering is muddled, the central photographs nos 23 and 24 being reversed). These have frequently been connected with a capital at Conques depicting the story of St Faith, since the subject and the composition with a row of figures are both similar, but S.M. Alvarez has rejected the idea of anything more than "una mediación gráfica" ("Artistas, patronos y publico en el arte del Camino de Santiago", Compostellanum XXX 3-4, 1985, p. 404). There are no volutes on the Conques capital.

104. see S.M. Alvarez, "Une sculpture du style de Bernard Gilduin à Jaca" BM 1973, p. 9 n.8; M. Durliat, "Les origines de la sculpture romane à Toulouse et à Moissac" CCM 1969, p. 355 ("enigmatic", but elsewhere agrees it is Spanish); T.W. Lyman, "Notes on the Porte Miègeville capitals.." AB 1967, p. 28. Alvarez calls it "Frómista-Jaca type". On one face the figure is holding out a folded cloth at both ends. On the iconography of this motif, Lyman, art.cit pp. 26-27.

105. AB 1967, fig. 26; Haut-Languedoc roman, fig. 35.

106. GG 1938, LXIII, 23, 15. There are more examples in the higher parts of the building, many badly worn. Aragon roman fig. 67 shows the Daniel capital clearly. He appears to hold bunched drapery or a book instead of wearing the folds on his chest.

107. Gascogne romane fig. 41.

108. The longest foliole extends alternately above and below the stem beyond it, but does not curl round it as at Moissac. The treatment of hems on the capital resembles that of the fragment set over the doorway at Loarre. The angels stand on lion heads, the saint on a plinth or possibly on stilts[?] (p.34).

109. San Miguel de Fluvia, the site consecrated 1045, church dedicated 1066: W.M. Whitehill 1941, p. 83. see Chapter IV, n. 41.

110. Daniel capital: GG 1938, LXIII, 13; cf. also LXII, 7.9; LXV, 25, a motif taken from the Cordoba leaf roll corbel D16; launched early at Santiago, GG 1938, LXXIX, 17, 18 but not much developed in Spain. Adopted at Moissac, fig.22, in Burgundy (Vézelay, Autun, Anzy, Charlieu), Conques, La Trinité in Caen.

111. Spiral columns on capitals: Madinat az-Zahra´, AHIII , figs 114, 116-119; Cordoba, fig. 11; Granada (Loja), LTB 1957, fig. 475; Ripoll and Cornelha; Aljafería; Saint-Benoît-sur-Loire; discussed by Garcia-Romo, AE 1954, p. 44, with illustrations for Saint-Benoît-sur-Loire, Saint-Hilaire, Méobecq.

112. GG 1938, XLI,9. These capitals at the south-west corner of the crossing are usually classed with the capitals of the central arcades as of a later campaign than the rest; they differ in style, but that is not necessarily a chronological difference.The triple bindings adduced as a late feature join scrolls on the cross of Fernando and Sancha dated 1063 and in the Aljafería, AHIII , figs 290b, c; 292d, 293, 299. Binding of scrolls at Moissac is triple, not chevron.

113. Tudela pls XL, XLI; the extended leaf, B6, B1, fig. 24; A6, figs 10a, b.

114. A. Duran Gudiol, El Castillo de Loarre, Zaragoza 1971, new ed. 1987; K. Watson, "The corbels in the dome of Loarre", JWCI 1978, pp 297-298, where I argue that the corbels may be earlier than those of Toulouse.

115. Huesca under Muslim rule was a lively cultural centre and the Mozarab community was large. cf. Pat. Lat., fol. 157, col. 528 ff: "Dialogi contra judeos" by the convert Pedro Alfonso, baptized in 1106. The Mozarabic Bishop Sancho of Huesca was a person to be reckoned with. A. Duran Gudiol (Arte Altoaragones..., Zaragoza, 1973, p. 49) surmises that his death or resignation was awaited before installing the new bishopric, planned first perhaps at Loarre, then in Jaca. The eldest son of King Sancho Ramirez of Aragon, the future Pedro I, like others of the king´s entourage, appears to have received an Andalusian education: he signed consistently in Arabic, cf. A. Duran Gudiol "La Iglesia de Aragon" Anthologica Annua, 1963, pp 163, 166, 169, 173, 174, 181, 193; R. Menendez Pidal, La Espana del Cid, p. 571. I am much indebted to Dom Antonio for his advice and help at Loarre.

116. The first campaign of building goes well beyond the height of the door, which is encroached on on the north by the aisle wall. I have checked this observation on site

(March 1982) after discussions with Christopher Bailey, to whom I am much indebted.

117. Tudela, corbel A9, fig. 14, a fragment from the Great Mosque of Tudela.

CHAPTER IV

ANDALUSIAN FEATURES IN ROMANESQUE DECORATION

II. THE LOBED ARCH (F21)(1)

Previously unknown in western architecture though portrayed in manuscript illumination (2), and of very limited and modest application in the East (3), the lobed arch appears in al-Hakam II´s extension to the Mezquita (961-965) as one of the most striking features of both structure and decoration. Here, at its first introduction as a major architectural element, it is already treated by the Cordoban architects as a theme capable of many variations. It inspired a long and inventive tradition in Andalusia and the Mahgreb. That some degree of debt is owed by Romanesque designers to this Cordoban invention is universally recognized, even though few close correspondences have been established. A summary review of the types, function and geometry of Andalusian lobed arches is the necessary context for an examination of French developments.

THE LOBED ARCH IN ANDALUSIA

Types of lobing in the Mezquita

Type 1. Lobing may be applied to the face of an arch as a series of segments of a small circle carved in relief. The earliest known example of this is the oft-quoted great arch that spanned the gateway at Ctesiphon (4). The arches between the squinches supporting the dome over the mihrab in the Great Mosque of Qairawan fig.137 are decorated on the same principle; the decoration is independent of the voussoir jointing. With this type the lobes are no more than an embellishment of an already existing arch form. The type is rare in Andalusia: it is simulated in plaster on a few doorway interiors (AHIII, fig.138), and on the axial arcades of the mihrab tract the decorative plaster lobed round the back of the voussoirs of the upper semicircular arches, giving the uncarved voussoirs a marked fish-tail extrados (AHIII fig.154), are perhaps an adaptation of the same principle. It is characteristic of one type of French arch, the earliest known architectural example of which is the triforium arches at Cluny (fig.138).

Type 2. Alternatively the soffit of an arch may be lobed by suitably shaped the ends of each voussoir. Again there are modest antecedents in Asia (5). The ancestry of this open form on the larger scale applied in the Mezquita in the 10th century has been explained as an adaptation of the Roman shell niche, whereby the half-dome behind the face of the niche is eliminated to leave the scallops of the opening profiled on the void. The fluted squinch niches in the mihrab dome at Qairawan illustrate this process. They make this monument once again the likely direct inspiration for Cordoban invention. The shell is still in evidence in the Mezquita as a decorative motif, though never immediately associated with lobing (AHIII figs 144, 157, 181).

Type 3. An intermediate type between these open and closed lobed arches arises when there are multiple archivolts, and one or several of these is constructed of voussoirs with ends appropriately shaped. The lobe is blind, but the relief is higher than when the voussoir face is simply carved as in type 1. This third type is first found at Cordoba, and the majority of blind lobes in the Mezquita are of this kind, with an independent arch form created by the lobed archivolt. An example is the second archivolt of the central entrance arch to al-Hakam II´s extension (AHIII fig. 139), on the north face of the Villaviciosa chapel, made more striking by the fact that the centre is raised in relation to the centre of the inner archivolt (F16). French architects also frequently lobed the outer archivolts of arches, keeping a plain soffit fo the opening profiles.

Applications of Lobing to Architecture in the Mezquita

Lobed arches in the Mezquita are put to both structural and purely decorative uses. Structural uses comprise:
i. The great arches spanning the three central naves at the entrance to the extension of al-Hakam II. While the soffit of the arch into the central nave is plain, and the outer archivolt lobed (type 3), on the side aisles the position was reversed, with a lobed inner soffit (type 2) and plain outer archivolt (AHIII figs 137, 140).
ii. The free-standing interlacing arches of the Villviciosa chapel, and of the mihrab tract screens, in combination with round-headed and horseshoe arches (type 2).
iii. The five-lobed squinch arches of the mihrab tract dome (type 2). These are set under a decorative mitre arch, and both again are under a horseshoe-shaped window; the base of the fluted squinches of the lateral domes (AHIII figs 143, 161) also forms a horizontal five-lobed arch.
iv. Arches in the transverse arcade of al-Hakam´s 11th bay, enclosing the maqsura, between columns C and D (fig.29, plan)(6), and G and H.
v. A surviving fragment of one of Almanzor´s arches piercing the previous east wall to give access to his extension (fig.27). In these last two examples iv and v, the lobes are convex. Decorative uses comprise:
vi. The simulated outer archivolt on the inside of the main west doorway (AHIII fig.138)(7)(type 1).
vii. Blind arcading, or arcades: a. trilobes along the top of the mihrab alfiz (fig.18). b. trilobes within the mihrab as separate arcades on each wall panel (fig.18). c. blind niches over the windows flanking one of the west doors (AHIII fig.198).
viii. Trilobes in plaster on the panels between the squinches in the mihrab chapel dome (fig.11).

Except for the trilobes of viii. which have all-over plant decoration, the lobes of all the above arches are, or are made to appear to be, built up from voussoirs (8). Without exception the extrados is apparent, and it follows the lines of the lobe in every case, though not concentric with the intrados. On the inner arches of the arcade over the mihrab (viia) space only allows the back of the top to be completed; the backs of the lower lobes obscure each other, but the extrados of the lower lobes of the two outermost arches are lobed.

Lobed round arches are rare in the Mezquita, the few examples being simulated in plaster. The inside of the main door of al-Hakam´s west façade (AHIII fig.138) has a simulated brick and stone archivolt of nine lobes, on a circle with its centre raised above that of the tympanum, so as to fit, according to an elaborately calculated mathematical module, a mitre arch above it within the alfiz (9). The uniform arch line is broken because the central lobe is given prominence with more and narrower voussoirs and is peaked, and its centre raised. Another door interior on this façade has simulated voussoirs in red and white plaster. The extrados has a raised centre and the head of each voussoir is painted in the contrasting colour with the point of a small series of lobes (10), giving the voussoirs a fish-tail shape. A door interior on Almanzor´s east façade is similarly painted with a band of small red lobes meeting in the centre of each white voussoir, to similar effect. Here the eccentric extrados is abandoned (11).

The majority of Cordoban lobed arches are open (type 2), and are based on a pointed arch form. The geometry required some manipulation to adjust the proportions betweem the height of the arch and the radii of the lobes, especially as a mathematical unit was frequently sought (12). The diagram sketched under the plaster in a passage at Madinat az-Zahra´ (LTB 1957 fig.281) is evidence of a preoccupation with this discrepancy and the principles of its solution. For varying numbers of lobes, and especially when intercrossing arches were involved, the design needed to be of some sophistication. There is great virtuosity also in the different systems of voussoir arrangement that were applied henceforth. C. Ewert has shown in a series of publications the growing mastery of the geometry of intersecting arches (13), from the irregularities resorted to in the Mezquita to more theoretically successful formulae, through the 11th century at Malaga and Zaragoza into the 12th at Almería and Soria. None of this development was taken advantage of by Romanesque designers.

The two lines of trilobe arcades within and above the mihrab can be seen each to use a different design. Over the mihrab the central lobes of the intrados are not circular at all; the centres of the extrados are almost at the top of the soffits. The two lower lobes of each arch are less than a semicircle and their decoration does not simulate voussoirs; they are thus seen more as the result of the fish-tail shape of the impost. This waisted shape is given some prominence as it recurs throughout the mihrab tract, at the spring of juxtaposed lobed and horseshoe arches (AHIII figs 154, 156, 159, 183 etc.). It possibly had some part in the waisted shape of the voussoirs forming the points of one type of Romanesque lobed arches, including arches at Santiago, Cahors and Meymac (figs 141, 145, 185). Inside the mihrab the soffits of the separate trilobe arches have a top lobe of about three-quarters of a circle, or a stilted semicircle, while the lower lobes are semicircles or less; all three lobes are of the same radius. The centre of the extrados of the top lobe is raised well above that of its soffit, like all the unlobed arches of the extension. The trilobe openings between the ribs of the dome of the entrance chapel (Villaviciosa), and the plasterwork trilobes contained in pentagons round the spring of the ribs of the dome over the mihrab tract, are similar in shape to these trilobes inside the mihrab, but the centre of the extrados is not raised so high.

Fikry's statement (14) that trilobes based on concentric semicircles "abound" in the Mezquita is thus incorrect. The top three lobes of intercrossing five- or eleven-lobed structural arches on the east wall of the Villaviciosa chapel (AHIII figs 148, 149) might be read as concentric trilobes, but this is accidental. Apart from this ambiguity, trilobes in the Mezquita are all built on equilateral or taller triangles, conforming more or less closely (though rarely quite rigorously) to the Madinat az-Zahra´ diagram drawing.

Andalusian Lobed Arches other than those in the Mezquita

Toledo: Cristo de la Luz. Many of the openings in the zone between the arcades and the domes in Cristo de la Luz (fig.35) are trilobed (15). The "rigorous geometry" invoked by Fikry as characteristic of Andalusian work is far to seek: they are all based on triangles taller than equilateral, but with no overriding ambition to rigour, evidently.

Zaragoza: Aljafería. Three new variants of lobing appear in the Aljafería. They appear in the following list as xiii, xiv and xv, after the different shapes evolved on non-architectural decoration.

Andalusian decorative carving provides examples of a wider variety of trilobe shapes, and some fragments show forms closer to concentric types.

ix. The arcade framing rosettes, carved on a marble plaque found in the Alcazaba of Malaga (AHIII fig.243c), is a very flattened trilobe built on a chord shorter than the diameter; the three lobes form only three-quarters of a semicircle.

x. The intrados of the arch on a fragment of stucco wall-facing from the baths of the Cordoba Alcazar (AHIII fig. 237 "painted in red, yellow and black") is close to the Madinat az-Zahra´ diagram scheme; the centre of the extrados is set on the circumference of the top lobe.

xi. Almanzor´s marble basin in Seville (AHIII fig.249) has trilobes considerably steeper than the equilateral. The trilobes on the façade of Saint-Etienne in Nevers are similar in shape (fig 155).

xii. In the 11th century the trend towards steeper arches increased; the Palencia casket has trilobes with vertical sides (AHIII fig.369).

xiii. The polylobed portico in the Aljafería (fig.139) foreshadows the narrow pointed arches of Almoravid architecture in North Africa and Spain (16) and the long points, lightened by notches in the depth of the relief, foreshadow the delicate lambrequins of Almohad lobes (17).

xiv. The arcading round the gallery of the oratory in the Aljafería (fig. 51) is an interlace with plain horseshoes of nine-lobed arches, with each lobe less than a half-circle (the cusps are elongated to disguise this); in the process the interlace creates five-lobed arches on an equilateral triangle. These are echoed on some capitals (fig.40).

xv. On the lower order the mixtilinear arches suggest at the notched angles the rather wide-angle double points of some Romanesque lobes (Journet ⌣⌣⌣); the spring has a convex curve which in Cairo on the Bab Zuweila (1087) fig.140 was to be even more pronounced, and above it a curl which anticipates the solutions arrived at in some Limousin examples such as Meymac, Collonges, Palisse or Tulle (figs 141-144).

Some capitals in the Aljafería are decorated with lobed arches with peaked tops harking back to caliphal fantasy (fig. 332). They look forward to Almoravid conceits in Marrakesh and Fez (second third of the 12th century)(AHIII figs 138, 249, 334-7).

LOBED ARCHES IN MOZARAB AND EARLY ROMANESQUE ARCHITECTURE IN NORTHERN SPAIN

Lobed arches are not known on any Mozarab buildings; occasionally they appear in Mozarab illuminations (18) but never with the consistency, with which horseshoe arches occur for example, to signify a special affinity. Nor do many lobed arches survive on early Romanesque buildings in Spain. The great exception is at Santiago de Compostela (19), where they must be among the earliest on any Christian buildings. The transept arches into the crossing of San Isidoro in León are also lobed; their date is unknown.

At Santiago concentric five-lobed arches in the axial chapel of San Salvador, one of the earliest parts of the buildings, are known from an old print (20) . Similar arches survive over the Platerias doorways (fig.145) and on the transept gables where a five-lobed concentric arch alternates with mitre arches. Round the apse are blind trilobe niches on colonnettes; they appear to be concentric. Corbels prevent the extrados showing clearly, but it appears from photographs to be lobed also (21). Here as with the Platerias five-lobed arches, the joints of each lobe converge on the centre of the lobe. This practice is unknown in Andalusia, though as was noted earlier the same fish-tail shape which is caused from such jointing is insistent in the maqsura arcades as an effect of the horseshoe arch forms, on the many imposts of the multiple arches.

The transept arches in the crossing at San Isidoro are (22) of six and two half-lobes; the half-lobes rest on a tall vertical impost, which corresponds to the stilted round-headed order of the nave arcades. The lobes are semicircular and tangent, constructed with finely cut narrow voussoirs whose joints converge on one centre only. In the west wall also a six-lobed doorway with a concentric horseshoe extrados was pierced to give access to the Panteón from the new church dedicated in 1149 (23).

The Arca Santa in Oviedo (fig 146) has a five-lobed arch scratched on one of the panels under the silver sheet, among other experimental lines drawn with compasses (24). The arch is two-centred, the top lobe has a considerably larger diameter than the rest, and the lobes are not exactly tangent at the points (25). It is on this great reliquary, donated to the cathedral by Alfonso VI and his sister Urraca in 1075, that the front and side panels with their embossed and gilded scenes are bordered with continuous Kufic inscriptions (mostly meaningless, fig. 81).

The "tomb of Mudarra" from San Pedro de Arlanza (26), removed from the cloister to that of the cathedral in Burgos, is inscribed with the date 1105 (era 1143). It is in the form of a doorway block with a round eleven-lobed arch framing twin lobed arches. The lobes are round horseshoes, each on a separate voussoir, and wide apart. The cornice crowning the structure is supported on roll corbels of the double roll type known from Gormaz and Silos (Chap.V), except for one of the two central ones which has a lion head and no rolls. In connection with this structure two later Spanish examples claim attention here: the wooden church bench from Taüll and a stone window.

Though the arches are not lobed but edged with Romanesque billet moulding, the 12th century wooden church bench from Sant Climent de Taüll in Barcelona Museum (figs 100,101) is sufficiently close in design to the Arlanza stone structure, and to the stone window of Rebolledo de la Torre fig.147 (probably of later date than Mudarra´s tomb) to suggest once again that woodwork shared largely in transmitting ideas of design and detailing throughout the Romanesque period. The details of this rare survival are common to Islamic and Romanesque decoration. The piece has horizontal lines of lobing above and below the triple arcade. Along the crest the lobes are notched to give an effect like the arches on the towers of La-Charité-sur-Loire. The largest lobes, along the foot, have a grooved border and are immediately reminiscent of the lobes on altar tables. There are traces of paint remaining. Polychrome, slender columns (F8), trefoil motifs between the arches, lattice work, horseshoe arches, oculus or rosette (D15), stars (D3) and stepped motif along the base (F18) are all typical of Islamic practice, but not exclusive to it: this is not a mudéjar but a Catalan Romanesque artifact, exhibiting the extent of a common tradition with Andalusian work.

THE LOBED ARCH IN FRANCE

Previous Studies and Classifications of the Lobed Arch in France (27)

Fikry divided Romanesque lobed arches into two groups on the criterion of fidelity to Euclidian principles, in the last resort on whether or not the arches and their lobes conform to perfect circles or semicircles. A first group "following the rigid geometry of the Arabs" he centred on Le Puy, whose monuments, including their lobed arches, he argued must have been designed by an architect familiar with Islamic practice. His second group was one he explained as influenced by manuscript illuminations or by designs on portable objects, and with no direct relation to Islamic architecture. He demonstrated how similarity to the first group waned as proximity to Le Puy grew less, and deduced from this fact that Le Puy was the source of the feature. This classification produced a reasonable contrast in distribution: concentric lobed arches tend to cluster round the Massif Central, the freer forms being mostly found further west.

Fikry lent great importance, as proof of Islamic origin, to strict geometry in the design of the lobes on the Le Puy monuments; however, in complete contrast to the variety and, in many cases, sophistication of Cordoban trilobes and five-lobed arches, those featured at Le Puy are constructed on the simplest possible geometry: they require no mathematical preparation and are based on a division of concentric semicircles into three, four or five segments, such as can be achieved with any pair of compasses and a straight edge. We find none of the subtleties in placing the centres of pointed arches, or in planning the voussoir jointing, that are the raison d´être of the lobed arch designs in Cordoba or Zaragoza. As noted in Chapter II the number of round-headed arches decorated

115

with lobes on Andalusian buildings is extremely small, and what examples there are offer elaborations unheeded by the Le Puy designers.

Héliot amplified Mâle's two categories of French lobed arches: those with lobed soffits and those with lobes carved only on the face. He introduced a new category by noting the undulating form of some lobes, consisting of less than a half circle, most frequent on doorways in the area round Limoges and asociated with "Limousin" torus moulding (see n.98). In geographical distribution this Limousin group lies half way between Fikry's "geometric" Le Puy group in the Massif Central, and much of his derived or non-Islamic group in the west. Héliot thus made a three-fold classification: first, following Fikry, a "group showing direct Muslim inspiration emanating from Le Puy in the late 11th century", mainly consisting of blind trilobes; second, the "Limousin" group whose beginnings he placed south of the Limousin, in Quercy, with the south door of Cahors in the second decade of the 12th century; third, a proliferation mainly in west France, and largely in the last quarter of the 12th century, by which time he considered lobed arches established as native practice, not essentially dependent on Muslim examples nor the influence of the pilgrimage route to Santiago, though with periodic approximations to Spanish or North African forms. This chronology will need some revision.

Since virtually all Romanesque lobed arches are included in an area west and south of the Rhône, Saône and Loire, Héliot concluded that it must be from Spain that the lobed arch first entered French architectural decoration in the late 11th century, and that its diffusion was due to the opportunities offered for contact with Spain by the pilgrimage to Compostela and the Cluniac involvement in the Spanish church; that starting with the geometry to be achieved with ruler and compasses, french builders soon elaborated their own, non-Islamic repertoire: the simple examples of Le Puy and Cluny were followed by the first independent design at Cahors, and the elaboration of lobe design in the centre of France, initiated at Cahors, was independent of any but local inspiration.

E. Vergnolle in her thesis of 1966 made a detailed study of lobed arches in the centre and west of France, supplementing and correcting Fikry's lists, and preceding her study by a review of Islamic examples. She followed Héliot in regarding the south door of Cahors cathedral as the earliest in France with a lobed inner profile, and as the prototype for the series of Limousin lobed dooways. These in their turn she saw as the decisive influence on arches of various uses in the Angoûmois and Saintonge. The Cahors doorway therefore asssumes particular importance in her analysis, since it "contains all the elements that were developed separately afterwards"; these elements were not Andalusian. She concluded that no more than the basic idea of the lobed arch had been taken from Muslim models;

116

Romanesque sculptors concentrated their interest and experiments on the decoration and form of the point between the lobes, while the tendency of Muslim arch design was towards an elaboration in series by interlacing and other repetitive linear devices.

Classification

The chronology of Fikry, Héliot and Vergnolle is brought into question by much work (not least their own) since 1970 (28). Building on their analyses of French lobed arches, their classifications can be amplified into a series of representative examples and areas whose locations show a typological progression moving roughly from east to west across France. Lobed arches in France will be examined here under the following rubrics:
I. Cluny: arches decorated with multiple blind lobes (Ctesiphon or altar table type).
II. Rhône and Velay: concentric arch geometry for trilobes and derivatives (Santiago type).
III. Quercy and Limousin: i. undulating Limousin moulding; ii. lobes with volute or elaborated points; parallels with 11th and 12th century Andalusia (Cahors type). Volute points later spread to the west.
IV. Convex lobes: a miscellany, Egyptian and North African parallels.
V. Saintonge, Angoûmois, Berry: edged lobes, a renewed reference to Andalusian models.
VI. Some lobed arches depicted in sculpture.

I.   Cluny: the transept arcades (fig. 138).

The arris of the shallow niches of the triforium in the transept of Cluny III is carved in low relief with a series of round horseshoe-shaped lobes. These are not tangent, but set more or less regularly at short intervals. The closest parallel for this embellishment is to be found on the semicircular arches between the squinches supporting the mihrab dome at Qairawan (fig.137)(29).

Santiago might historically be looked to as likely to have provided the direct model for Cluny, but the lobes of the surviving examples there, on the transept gables and over the Platerías doorway, and the trilobes round the apse exterior, are semicircles, are independently jointed and have tangent lobes; Qairawan with only approximate circle segments carved into the arch face, and the lobes not tangent, is in this respect a closer parallel. If the Cluny arches were a direct copy of some model, it has not survived.

Associated features in the Cluny transept.

Other features in the transept are consistent with a western Islamic inspiration for the lobed arches (30). These arches are separated by fluted pilasters crowned by acanthus capitals which, alternating with corbels, support

117

a cornice on which stand the rectangular plinths of the twin tapered columns (F6) of the clerestory.

i. The corbels have a rectangular vertical face and billet moulding on the scotia curve. The shape is more Cordoban than classical; the billet moulding on corbels is a frequent Romanesque development from the roll motif (31).

ii. At Qairawan tapered colonnettes, their bases resting also on projecting rectangular plinths, support the arcade framing the squinches and intermediary niches of the mihrab dome. At Cordoba similar colonnettes support the arcading over a. the mihrab (AHIII figs 168-169); b. the trilobe arcades inside the mihrab (AHIII fig.180); c. the arcade round the uppper level of the Villaviciosa chapel (AHIII fig. 148); and d. the similar arcades under and in the maqsura domes (154).

iii. The larger acanthus capitals on the columns supporting the entrance arch into the Cluny transept are genetically similar to capitals of the 9th and early 10th century at Cordoba (AHIII figs 51ff, 81; LTB 1957 figs 471-473), particularly the liking for a triangular hollow under the volute, and the plain wedge treatment of the acanthus stems (less marked, in fact, in the Mezquita than elsewhere on Andalusian capitals)(32) and the crossed stem motif (D1).

iv. The colonnettes under the ribs in the central maqsura dome at Cordoba are paired (F6), as are the columns between the windows of the clerestory above the lobed arches of the Cluny triforium.

v. Fluted pilasters are, of course, a classical feature; it is one much used in al-Hakam II´s extension of the Mezquita.

Altar Table Influence

On the other hand, neither Qairawan nor Cordoba has lobes continuing below the spring of an arch, nor has Santiago. The series of Syrian and Pyrenean altar tables bordered with lobes (33), some in the shape of a stilted arch, and with horseshoe-shaped lobes, provides a possible inspiration for this aspect of the Cluny transept arches: a particularly attractive hypothesis since a lobed altar table was at Cluny by 1095 (34). This very altar cannot be the exclusive inspiration however because the Cluny altar lobes are exactly semi-circular, not horseshoe-shaped, and they do not end at the edge of a plane; the similarity of the triforium arches to the Cluny altar is therefore less striking than to other lobed altars or mensae (figs 148, 149)(35).

The triforium lobes have no incised outline, unlike most altar table lobes; it may well be however that they were originally painted with an outline. Andalusian arches were painted (36), and the Taüll bench also has traces of paint. It is carved with both plain and outlined lobes, and is a reminder of the possibility of inspiration from wooden models. Altar tables also may have been painted. The lobing of the transept arches may be primarily an adoption from wooden furniture or the bases of statues. The fragment of the tomb of St Hugh in the Musée Ochier shows his effigy standing on a plinth with shallow lobes carved along the base, as on the Taüll bench and the lid of the shrine of Bishop Ulger (37).

Cluny Doorway (fig. 158)

The inner archivolt of the great doorway of Cluny III repeats the lobe motif of the triforium arches with angels enclosed in horseshoe lobes (38), suggesting a conscious connexion between doorway and interior (39). This feature on the portal hints even more strongly than the triforium arches at links with the marble atelier responsible for the series of 10th and 11th century lobed altar tables, not only because of the lobes, but through correspondences of the Cluny archivolt decoration both with the figures in medallions on the Toulouse altar (40), one of the masterpieces of the atelier, and with the heads in scrolls of the San Pere de Roda doorstep (fig.151). This doorstep, and even more emphatically the lintel and threshold fragments by the same workshop from Perpignan (41) with guilloche border, lion heads carved inside lobes (fig.150) and large rosettes at the corners (these also beloved of Burgundian sculptors) are other examples of the application of the "altar table" style of decoration to doorways, in these cases by the makers of the altar tables themselves.

Reference to the sanctuary made on the doorway was not new at Cluny, or even at Perpignan; it is not a classical nor an oriental practice however, but Cordoban. What can be regarded as the Islamic equivalent of the apse with its altar, the mihrab, is deliberately imitated on the doorways of the Mezquita; the Puerta San Esteban is the earliest of monumental doorways on a religious building west of the Euphrates; its reference to a mihrab is patent. In view of the familiarity of the marble sculptors of the east Pyrenean seaboard region with Cordoban traditions of design (42) it may be postulated that their associations with Cluny contributed to an Andalusian element at Cluny, and, included in this, to the decision to make the doorway an announcement of the sanctuary. The decision, however it was inspired, was a momentous one for mediaeval architecture. The dominance of classical influence on both the west door design at Cluny (triumphal arches) and the triforium (tapered colonnettes, fluted pilasters and acanthus capitals) is undeniable, but that does not exclude a contribution from an Andalusia equally indebted to the classical tradition. The doorway lobes, like the shape of the triforium corbels, are a persuasive indication that the Cordoban treatment of classical themes played a part in the handling of classical themes at Cluny. Even if subordinate, an Andalusian influence must be admitted to exist here (43).

To Summarize

The features distinguishing the triforium lobes (44) are five:

i. Their low relief, carved into an already-built arch face. Precedents are the great arch at Ctesiphon, dome arches at Qairawan, altar tables. Low relief is not confined to the Cluny group of lobed arches: it is also characteristic of many arches of "Le Puy type" to be treated in the next section. The lobed decoration at Cluny may well have promoted the adoption of the lobe motif down the Rhône and in the Velay, but the prevalence in those areas of the trilobe, and adherence in design to an arch constructed on concentric semi-circles within which tangent lobes are inscribed, justifies their classification as a separate group of which the earliest examples surviving are at Santiago, not Cluny.

ii. The horseshoe or stilted shape of the lobes. Precedents are again Qairawan and certain altar tables, though not the surviving altar at Cluny itself. The windows of Asturian churches, San Miguel de Liño in particular, are pierced with half or complete rosettes, some of which have horseshoe-shaped "petals" (fig.152).

iii. The absence of any carved outline, extrados or embellishment. The precedent is again to be found at Qairawan and on some altar tables.

iv. The arrangement along the edge they decorate: the lobes are not tangent and are thus separated by blunt points, detracting from the impression of geometric rigour. Blunt points, of course, follow necessarily from horseshoe-shaped lobes. Precedents are altar tables where lobes, whether half-circle or horseshoe, are spaced; Qairawan, where the width of the point is not dictated by the shape of the lobes; Ctesiphon, where also the lobes are not tangent; the Perpignan threshold and lintel.

v. Lobes running down the jambs. Earlier examples of lobed jambs are unknown. Precedents: some mensae rounded at one end and rectangular at the other (45), lobing of wooden objects, illuminated page borders, exterior of the dome of Sousse Great Mosque.

None of these five features is like the Andalusian treatment of lobes; the influence of Cluny, rather than Spain, must have disseminated them in France. Arches decorated with blind lobes carved on the arch face are found from the Rhône to the Atlantic; with our knowledge of the use of lobed arches at Cluny limited to the surviving triforium and the reconstruction of the west door, her influence can only be confirmed where

a. the lobe type is similar, in one or more of the five ways listed above, to the triforium or to the doorway lobes, or as on an altar table;

b. the application is similar. which is to say either when interior arcades or arches are lobed, or (which was Cluny's most inspired and fertile contribution to lobed decoration) when lobes are applied to doorway arches.

A selection of examples whose main dependence is on the traditions established at Cluny will now be proposed,

taking them first by lobe type in descending order of their
closeness to the Cluny model and then by similarity of
application. As they appear on each example the features i-
v summarized above will be noted in brackets.

Examples of the Influence of Cluny. a. Similar Lobe   Types

    (Saint-Lazare, Autun [i-v]; Tournus [i,ii,iv]; Les Aix
d´Angillon [i,ii,iv];Nevers, Saint Etienne and Saint-Cyr
(cathedral) [i-iv]; Viré [i-iv]; Dore l´Eglise [i,iii,iv];
Parassy [i,iii,v]; La Charité-sur-Loire [iii,iv]; Catus
[i,ii,iii,v]; Montbron   [i,ii,iv];   Trizay;   Plassac;
Agudelle; Vandré [i,ii,iv]; Ladignac [ii-iv]; Soye-en-
Septaine [i,iv]; Le Villars [i,iii,iv].

    The triorium   arches in the apse of Saint-Lazare at
Autun are exact copies of those at Cluny (46). Elsewhere
the distinctive features noted above are found isolated,
adapted in various ways or affected by other types. Often
lobes are semicircular; many do not end at an arris; in
some cases the points receive special attention and are
embellished; in others the relief is heightened or the
lobes form a separate archivolt as at Santiago.

    The high arches on the crossing tower at Tournus
follow next after Autun as near-relations of the Cluny
triorium   lobed arches (Bourgogne romane, figs 24,25).
Each arch has nine spaced round horseshoe lobes cut into
the surface of the arch face, disregarding the jointing.
They are separated by fluted pilasters. Modifications of
the Cluny example are that there is a clear line along the
(unlobed) extrados and the lobing is restricted to the
archivolt: it rests on colonnettes supporting capitals. On
the courses below these arches the horizontal line of
miniature lobing identical with that on the tower at Cluny
appropriately recalls a First Romanesque corbel table as a
link with the lower part of the tower and other earlier
parts of the building (cf also the Taüll bench). The
carved band of rosettes and circles framed in arcades,
again imitating the Cluny tower, evokes the bacini
incrustations which were a characteristic Italian response
to   Islamic   decoration.   Dramatically   enhanced
interpretations of this theme, with masks as well as plant
roundels or rosettes framed in trilobe arches are found
reused from the Romanesque church at Saint-Maurice in
Vienne (47). If Gaillard´s chronology be correct, the
latter stand at or near the head of the French trilobe
series to be discussed in the next section. The theme,
rosette in trilobe, is familiar from Andalusia (AHIII
fig.243)(48). On a group of doorways in the Brionnais
including Belleville, Salles, Semur, La Bénisson-Dieu, the
rosette has been attached as a splayed palmette to the
points themselves, in shallow decorative trilobes, widely
spaced to give full scope to the elaborated points so that
they occupy the whole space of tympanum (fig.153)(49).

The mid-12th century church of Soye-en-Septaine (Cher) has an intermediary archivolt of 15 horseshoe lobes in the doorway arch, set under a horizontal corbel table. The tympanum of the doorway of Le Villars (S&L) is bordered with little blunt-point lobes. The low relief lobe of Cluny triforium is reproduced exactly on impost blocks and archivolts in the small decorative arcades round the exterior of the apse of Les Aix d'Angillon (Cher) fig.154. Similar small tympana decorated with twin lobes, and in one case with a rosette (fig.184) are encrusted into the north wall of the cathedral of Nevers, clearly reused, and over the lobed doorway of Saint-Hilaire (Cher) fig.156.

A close imitation of the Cluny triforium type is the archivolt of the blocked north door at Viré, a few kilometres east of Cluny, where the arch is even flanked by fluted pilasters as at Cluny. At Dore l'Eglise (PdeD) similar but semicircular lobes decorate the outer archivolt of the doorway. On both these arches the lobes appear to have been carved after the arch was built, or at least laid out, with no correspondence between lobe and voussoir. At Parassy (Cher, close by Les Aix d'Angillon) the lobes only differ from those of Cluny in being semi-circles (fig.157): they are shallow, carved in the face of the arch, not outlined, not tangent, and they run all down the jambs.

The soffits of the arcading in and outside La Charité-sur-Loire (fig.37) are carved with small lobes built of independent voussoirs with shaped ends. They resemble Cluny in being spaced, not contiguous circles. The line joining the points of the lobes forms a semicircle while the beaded extrados is round on the interior arcading of the apse, but two-centred on the exterior arcades; it runs close to the backs of the lobes, avoiding any similarity to the Andalusian raised extrados (50). The enriched rectangular colonnettes supporting them however are reminiscent of al-Hakam II's central arcade. They are found again at Plaimpied in the Berry (figs 292, 38). Ladignac gives another rare example of a soffit cut with Cluny-type lobes.

On the windows of the chapter house at Catus (Lot, fig.159) lobes are carved on the face of the arches. They have an incised outline (51) but the relief and basic arrangement is modelled on Cluny; an engraved border and convex rosettes stress the debt to the marble atelier tradition, but more immediate is likely to be the example of the convex rosettes which bedizen the north door of Saint-Etienne, Cahors.

The lobed arch is not an early feature in the south-west and west of France (52), and by the time it was adopted there many models were available and original sources less in evidence, combined or revised. The Cluny precedent is still apparent however at Montbron in the Saintonge (fig.160), on the outer and the second archivolt. The lobes are stilted or horseshoe-shaped and carved in low relief into the arch face. Unlike the Cluny model the lobes

are themselves enriched, imitating metal or ivory work
rather than the products of the marble atelier, which as
far as is known never reached futher west than Limoges
(53). The type of lobing at La Charité appears to have been
a dominant influence on a number of buildings in the west;
for examples, on arcades at Trizay and Plassac (fig.161)
and a window at Agudelle, where there is added enrichment
of the intrados (154). On the façade at Vandré (CM) the
lower voussoirs are shaped into small spaced lobes; above,
the spaces are filled with triple points of evolved "Cahors
type", perhaps an illustration of the way the elaborated
point evolved.

Combination with Chevron: Overlappings Points (Parassy, Les
Aix d´Angillon, Nogent, Pezou, Arlempdes, Bains, Landos, Le
Puy porche du For, Perrecy les Forges, Nogaro).

The chevron ornament on the outer order of the Parassy
doorway suggests that a combination of Cluny lobing with
this northern motif (54) lies at the origin of a popular
12th century elaboration of lobed decoration on outer
archivolts: this consists of deepening the hollow at the
back of the lobes to suggest a scotia moulding behind, and
a torus in front, with the points of the lobes lapping
across the hollow to rest on the torus. Restoration at the
head of Parassy doorway has produced this developed form by
emphasizing what was originally no more than a slight
difference of relief; this can be seen at the unrestored
foot of the jamb.

At Les Aix d´Angillon (fig.162) the developed form is
used on alternate arches of the triforium. The nave arcades
are two-centre arches, reminiscent of the nave arcades of
Cluny and Autun. The small raised rosettes (F4) in the
spandrels of the arches below, imitated from Cluny, are
evocative of similar medallions in the side tracts of the
maqsura of Mezquita: a frequent motif in Islamic
architecture fig.11 (55).

At Nogent-le-Bernard (Sarthe) the chevron and lobes
are associated. Not far away, at Pezou (fig.163), up-river
from Vendôme, the chevron archivolt frames convex-lobed
cushion voussoirs more familiar further south, at Poitiers
and beyond (fig 209)(56).

In the Velay, at Arlempdes, Bains (fig.164) and Landos
the doorways each have lobes with overlapping points; in
the Porche du For on the east door into the south transept
of the cathedral at Le Puy, relief lobes overlap a facetted
intrados (fig.165)(57). As earlier at Perrecy-les-Forges
the points wrap right round the torus, implying a row of
circular holes in a casing, illustrated complete in an arch
of the canon tables of Theodulf´s Bible at Le Puy, and
carved on the outer archivolt of the doorway of Cluny III.
This threading of the torus is done again at Nogaro, (we

remember the affiliation of Bigorre to Le Puy in 1062) on the arches of the chapter house and it is repeated vertically on the pilasters (fig.166). There seems to be a return to Cluny here, this time to the doorway lobes and medallions.

In this form with overlapping points the Cluny type of lobe has had a wide dissemination (58). Its most imaginative exploitation was in the west of France, where it played a part in the development of beak-head ornament on the one hand, and the singular Aquitanian human- and horse-head voussoired doorways on the other, in a fertile combination with the animal head tradition, well-established in the local corbel sculpture. There a series of occasional details signifies a fresh current of Andalusian influence some decades later than Cluny (59).

Scalloped Profile (Moissac, Beaulieu, Souillac, La Souterraine with Le Dorat, Celles-sur-Belle and Thouars).

As well as the doorways already noted in connexion with Cluny-type lobes (Viré and Dore l´Eglise with an archivolt lobed like the triforium arches, Parassy with jambs thus lobed as well and associated with chevrons, and the Velay group where the chevron is combined with the Cluny lobe), another group of doorways drew on the Cluny example, for the practice of lobing right down the jambs. Leaving aside the direct copy at Autun, in the two cases where this practice has been so far mentioned, at Parassy and on the interior arcades at Les Aix d´Angillon, there is an association or a combination with chevron. This predilection for sharp points occurs again among a Limousin group of lobed arches in whose beginnings the Moissac porch master was involved. The type of lobing in this group is very different from Cluny, with open, large-scale shallow scallops executed in Limousin moulding. Arches are not necessarily included in the lobing, it is carried at Moissac down the length of the jambs and trumeau, at Beaulieu and Souillac down the trumeaux, combined with sculpture. At La Souterraine (Creuse) the doorway has no sculpture, and both archivolts and jambs are thus lobed (fig.169). Three further doorways with similarly treated archivolts at Le Dorat, Celles-sur-Belle and Thouars (fig.170) are to be included in the group (60).

The Influence of Cluny. b. Similarity of Application.

1. Lobed Interior Arcades. (Autun , La Charité. Les Aix d´Angillon, Clermont, Issoire, Champagne, L´Hôpital Saint-Blaise).

Lobing of interior arcades, of the transept as at Cluny, or the sanctuary and apse (which may well have been the case at Cluny since identical arches are found at Autun) was adopted at La Charité and Les Aix d´Angillon. At Autun and Les Aix we have seen the Cluny example closely followed, with the lobing carried to the bottom of the jamb. There are three further cases where lobing was carried out not on solely decorative triforium arcades like these but on structural tribune arches. These are at Notre-Dame-du-Port in Clermont Ferrand, at Issoire and at Champagne (fig.171). In each case the openings are trilobes, equilateral triangles or taller at the two former, and concentric at Champagne in conformity with other examples of lobed arches in the Rhône valley (61). This application of lobing is an extension of the Cluny decorative innovation in the triforium, La Charité with its arcades suggestive of a structural feature providing an intermediary stage. The scale of the tribune lobes at Champagne, combined with their relation to people, who stand framed in them to look down into the church, is unprecedented in surviving Islamic examples, which are all high above any floor. The form of these arches, and similar arches in l´Hôpital Saint-Blaise (Landes), in each case derives from an inspiration other than Cluny.

2. Lobed Doorways

It is consistent with the importance of Cluny in church politics that the Third Church doorways should have a wide influence on doorway design. It seems likely that the west doorway of Cluny was the earliest with a lobed archivolt and if this is so its impact was extensive, and found many forms of response as it was received into different contexts and building practices.

It cannot be known whether in this instance at Cluny the lobed archivolt was a case of 1. incidental convergence with Andalusian building philosophy and practice (the intention being solely to refer to an altar table or to the triforium in the sanctuary) 2. direct emulation of some Andalusian doorway treatment, easily seen in Toledo or another newly-occupied Andalusian town, or 3. based on a model transcribed already into Christian terms somewhere in the frontier region (as suggested by the doorway of San Juan de Buso with its engraved lobes filled with at least a reference to mock-Kufic (fig. 172) in a sort of relief (62), or the Perpignan fragments (fig. 150), but however inspired, many of the ideas it generated will be seen to have accepted the Andalusian associations by adopting further Andalusian features.

II. The Velay and Rhône Valley: Concentric Trilobes and Polylobes and Other Trilobes

A distinctive type of lobed arch, constructed on the most elementary geometry, is characteristic of the Rhône valley and the Velay. Le Puy has been assumed to be the centre of its dissemination. The design consists of the centres of the lobe circles being set round the circumference of a semicircle, or of the half-hexagon, dekagon etc., inscribed within it, and the lobes inscribed within an outer semicircle concentric with the first (figs 164, 165, 175, 176). In the case of a trilobe the diameter

of each lobe is equal to the radius of the inner
semicircle. Whatever the number of lobes, they are tangent
and the points between them plain and sharp (fig. 173).

Trilobes are the most common type of concentric lobed
arches in the region, other than on doorways. At Le Puy the
chapel of Saint-Clair has one five-lobed window arch,
caarved in the Cluny fashion on the face of the voussoirs
without taking account of the joints between their
alternating colours. On the cathedral in the Porche du For
is the eight-lobed doorway with overlapping points; all
other lobed arches on the monuments of Le Puy are trilobes
(68). Apart from the great decorated doorway of Saint-
Michel d´Aiguilhe all these trilobes are small arcades over
windows or niches, andy many are carved into the face of an
archivolt, thus ending at an arris.

Though there is a concentration of concentric lobed
arches in the Velay it is no longer possible, in the light
of the chronologies established at the Congrès
Archéologique of 1975 (69), to continue asserting that the
monuments of Le Puy were the centre from which lobed arches
were disseminated throughout France. At this congress
Santiago was more than once cited as the precedent for
lobed arches. E. Vergnolle explained those on the Saint-
Clair chapel (70) in this way; since she dates the chapel
to 1180 it hardly seems necessary to turn to Santiago for a
model, but Le Monastier (fig 177) offers perhaps one of the
earliest French examples of a trilobed arch on colonnettes,
and J. Bousquet (71) refers to Santiago as the inspiration
for this.

The church of Le Monastier was begun about 1076,
starting with the west end, and was completed before 1136.
Shallow niches with finely jointed voussoirs forming
trilobes run in a triple arcade along the exterior south
wall of what corresponds to the west bay of the nave
interior, thus belonging to an early part of the building
campaign. This arcade is now hidden by the roof. The arches
rest on short half-columns, all originally on attic bases,
with capitals of plain smooth leaves with thick ends (F3)
turned out and down in two registers, and heavy volute
stems above them. They are less exuberant but similar in
type to the capitals on the apse exterior at Santiago or
the earliest capitals at Saint-Sever-des-Landes. The
moulding of the impost blocks is more delicately cut than
at Santiago (72). This arcade may be presumed to have been
in place before the lower storeys of the bell tower at Le
Puy (figs 176, 177).

It would be satisfactory to establish an influence
from Cluny in the adoption of the lobed arches at Le
Monastier, for the abbots of Cluny were closely involved in
the building of the church there and Abbot Guillaume was a
close friend of St Hugh (73); but Cluny offers no suviving
model for these trilobes.

Le Puy

The bell tower of Le Puy has on its third floor the only examples in the city of lobed arches that can be dated in the first half of the 12th century. These are a separate archivolt of blind trilobes with a round arch extrados, surmounting round arches, on colonnettes over twin openings (F6,11); in the centre the colonnettes are double.

The gable and the structural organization of the bell tower, says Durliat, are imitated from Limoges, where both the tower of Saint-Martial and that of Limoges cathedral followed the same design (74). It is not known whether the towers of Limoges had lobed arches to provide a model for these at Le Puy also; voussoired trilobes similar in shape to those on the Le Puy bell tower and façade occur in exterior arcades at Solignac in the Limousin, but there are none on the surviving members of the group of Limousin belfries ·(Saint-Léonard, Saint-Junien, Collonges, Brantôme); the doorway of Collonges has concentric trilobes but in a different tradition with elaborated points (fig.142). The tower of Saint-Apollinaire at Valence however which has the same structure as those of Le Puy and Limoges, is shown in a lithograph before the 19th century restorations with blind trilobes exactly like Le Puy, also on the third floor, and with a 9-lobed arch on the 5th floor. Bousquet notes the similarity of the trilobes on the south façade of Saint-Apollinaire to those of Le Monastier (75). Saint-Apollinaire was consecrated in 1095 by Urban II, and it may be assumed that building was at least contemplated at this date.

On the fifth storey of the Le Puy bell tower, dated by Durliat to about 1180, are plain trilobe openings without colonnettes or multiple archivolts. Similar arches at Chamalières (HL, not the earlier church at Clermont Ferrand) and Chanteuges, over windows or niches, are likely to be copies of these openings on the bell tower. They all have jambs closer together than the width of the arch (not the Andalusian style (76)).The trilobes on colonnettes, at Saint-Vidal, Saint-Etienne Lardayrol and Roffiac all date, like the two previous examples, to about 1180 (77).

The lobed doorways of Landos, Saint-Vincent, Bains (fig.164) and Arlempdes (78) are again based on the concentric geometry characteristic of the Velay, while the overlapping points connect them also with the Cluny group.

Rhône Valley

The bell tower at Saint-Apollinaire, Valence, which originally had a 9-lobed arch on the fifth storey and blind trilobed arches on the third also has blind concentric trilobe arcades on colonnettes on the nave exterior, alternating with round-headed windows under round-headed single billet moulding. Twin concentric trilobe arcades open from the tribunes onto the nave at Champagne, and small similar arches but with wide rounded points pierce the diaphragm arches between the domes. They all rest on a short colonnette between each pair, like the Andalusian ajimez (F11)(79). The same arrangement of support is used for the little twin bay in the façade of Saint-Jean-de-Muzols nearby (fig.1). An oculus (D15) on the west façade at Cruas is framed in a concentric 6-lobed arch on columns under a round-headed moulding, probably similar to the original aspect of the 5-lobes over the Platerías doorway, before the eccentric achivolts on columns were added and the wall thickened there. There is an example down-river at Saignon in the Vaucluse with a run of four sets of paired trilobes sharing a colonnette (F11), separated by pilasters and flanked by a pair of round-headed arches at each end.

At Saint-Pierre in Vienne the bell tower has trilobes without colonnettes framing a round-headed opening supported on colonnettes; in the porch extension capitals support a trilobe arcade with no extrados (fig.179), similar to the interior arcade in Saint-Pierre in Lyon, where blind shallow trilobes are held on fluted pilasters. Not all trilobes are so modest however. In Lyon cathedral itself there also survives a Romanesque doorway in the nave, with an archivolt of nine lobes containing grotesque figures (80). In the same vein are fragments of arcaded cornice remaining in Saint-Maurice in Vienne (47). Blind round-headed shallow niches are inscribed with trilobes framing large medallions carved with relief masks, rosettes or plant interlace, described by Vallery-Radot (81) as "like Muslim ceramics". The great rosettes (D15) are in keeping with the penchant for such decoration at Cluny and its imitators (82), the lintel at Moissac an early manifestation of this taste. The motif was also in vogue across the Pyrenees in the Romanesque as it had been in the caliphal period (AHIII fig.243c); in Barcelona is an illustration of the model emulated: on the 11th century tower built over the Roman wall (83) are reused pieces of a late Roman frieze with mask and floral garland, and gorgon head corbels. Medallions, oculi and pierced circular windows are characteristic of Spanish decoration from Ramiran buildings onwards. "More and more eyes are turned to Sicily and the south Italian ports" in looking for precedents for Le Puy, declares Durliat. The medallion rosettes in trilobes of the Rhône valley churches make thoughts run also to the Spanish ports (84).

The domes of Le Puy are modelled on those of Saint-Martin d´Ainay in Lyon (85); there also are found the human heads with animal ears and prancing cat dancers of Le Puy cloister, and of the impost block of the lobed arch capital 17 in Moissac cloister (fig.180)(86). The early capitals in the church of Le Puy belong to the group which includes Tournus, Figeac, Saint-Pierre-Toirac and San Pere de Roda (87). Lyon, Valence, Montélimar, Vienne, Tournus all have polychrome decoration: at Valence and Vienne coloured cement or terra cotta is incrusted in the stone, a method employed at Madinat az-Zahra´. It is thus logical to see the trilobes of Le Puy as members of a group formed in the great thoroughfare from the Mediterranean northward provided by the Rhône valley.

Trilobes in the Limousin and Further West

The simple concentric form of trilobe occurs only sporadically west of the Massif Central. The trilobes on the north nave exterior of Solignac (HV) are associated with a reminiscence of First Romanesque arcading on a lower register. Roll corbels (F1) support the cornice above. Connexions of the Limousin with the Auvergne (Aurillac and La Chaise-Dieu) are mentioned by Maury (88) and they might account for the lobes and corbels of Solignac; the latter have a nearer possible source at Fleury if restorations of the exterior of the church are faithful, but the only extant lobes in Saint-Benoît-sur-Loire are on the north door tympanum framing the seated Christ and evidently derived from a manuscript; ther are no trilobes or roll corbels at Aurillac. On the towers of Saint-Yrieix and Le Dorat runs an arcading of trilobes with split points and fish-tail voussoirs, resting alternately on slender columns (F8) and, at Le Dorat, on the angle pilasters of the octogon, at Saint-Yrieix on these or on more robust engaged half-columns: an alternation of supports (F7) with perhaps an attenuated reference to the _ajimez_ scheme of twin windows (F11). Trilobes under a half-round moulding also decorate the tower of Saint-Estèphe (Char.).

A small window in the apse under a miniature arcade in Berry fashion at Nourray (_fig_.181), not far from Saint-Benoît-sur-Loire, has an outer archivolt resting on colonnettes under a round-headed moulding which has four lobes; the points at the sides occur at joints of the voussoirs; the point at the top is cut in the central voussoir and is sharp. The cornice below the window is carved with scallops above and below: a device familiar in the Saintonge. The arcade rests on twin colonnettes (F6).

Trilobes in the Rouergue: Saint-Pierre-Toirac, Bessuéjouls

Niches in the north and south walls of the choir at Saint-Pierre-Toirac (Lot)(_fig_.15) are crowned with concentric trilobe arches supported on colonnettes with interlace capitals and backed by a torus moulding. The form of trilobe approximates to the Velay/Rhône type more than to its neighbour, the Cahors south door, the only other trilobe associated with such moulding. Some of the capitals at Saint-Pierre are recognizable as of the same type as the plait capitals of Tournus or Figeac (_fig_.182). Those supporting the trilobe arcades under the rectangular section ribs of the vault (F22), for example, belong to this group, and suggest a date for the niches at the turn of the century at latest (89). The trilobes are by that token earlier than any at Le Puy, or than the south door at Cahors, and they may even be earlier than those of Le Monastier. The question of the torus moulding will be discussed in connexion with Limousin lobes in the following section.

Bessuéjouls has a bell tower approximately contemporary with Toirac, or a little earlier (fig.183)(90). Here a single trilobe is the central arch of a run of five. It is taller than concentric, and higher than the round arches flanking it; the joints coincide with the points, and find a common centre within the arch. The extrados is slightly lobed (F15). This trilobe echoes, or is echoed by, the central panel of the splendid carved Romanesque altar (D1,D2,D6) now in the chapel within the tower (Rouergue roman fig.74); the panel is surmounted by a trilobe with almost vertical sides. Grooved moulding is carved to represent a lobed extrados. The trilobe panel shares capitals and pilasters, originally furnished with half-columns, with flanking round-headed panels. Carved in the style of the marble atelier of Narbonne, this altar is dated by Fàu to directly after 1065, following the closure of the first Conques workshop (91). The trilobe motif is found again flanked by round arches on a piscina from Lassouts, contained within a horseshoe under a mitre-shaped gable (ibid.fig.116), nearer the concentric form than the Bessuéjouls examples.

Nivernais and Auvergne

The half-quatrefoil shape of trilobe of the Bessuéjouls tower and altar appears further north on the triple arcade framing the high windows in the gable on the west façade of Saint-Etienne in Nevers (fig.155). These trilobes compete with Bessuéjouls for the claim to be the earliest lobed arches on a French façade (92). They surmount the single billet moulding over plain round-headed windows, as a round-headed archivolt, with an extrados of single billet moulding and a lobed intrados. The jointing converges on a single centre within the arch. The single billet moulding, making the arcade remotely reminiscent of the arcade over the mihrab with its semicircular extrados (F17) is, as Gomez-Moreno observed, a close link with Santiago: a link strengthened by the association of round and mitre arches on the transept façades, and the existence of roll corbels (albeit of elaborated form) in quantity round the eaves (93).

There are Islamic analogies for the billet moulding and mitre as well as the lobed arches. The late 10th-early 11th century mosque of Sidi ´Ali ´Amman at Sousse (94) has alternate mitre and round-headed niches on the façade (and vertical lobing of the angles of the exterior (F21) of the dome drum, which is insistently evocative of the jamb lobing of Moissac); the minaret of the Great Mosque of Sfax of the same period uses a striking giant version of billet moulding to frame round-headed bays, some of which enclose lobed niches (95). The blind arcades on the upper register of the minaret of the 11th century Qala´a of the Beni Hammad (96) frame shell niches faced with a festoon of decorative intercrossing mitre and round arches, adopted from Andalusia.

The trilobes of Bessuéjouls and Nevers are very different in shape from the concentric forms of Santiago, and even more remote from Andalusian architectural forms than the lobed arches of Santiago. They are nearer the shape of the arches on the Palencia casket (AHIII fig.369, mid-11th century) and the lobed arch flanked by round ones on the lid of the shrine of Santo Domingo de Silos c.1170. The single trilobe in the north gable at Issoire (97) is in the same vein as Saint-Etienne but both its shape, and its position between two round-headed arches, make it resemble that at Bessuéjouls more closely. The extrados is slightly lobed. The points are formed on fish-tail voussoirs however, and the lobes are thus independently jointed.

The tribune arcades at Issoire and in Notre-Dame-du-Port, Clermont Ferrand have already been noted as stemming from Cluny as to their application. They are trilobes built on taller triangles than the façade arches of Santiago, Bessuéjouls or Issoire, closer to Cordoban forms. Whether the design came to Notre-Dame from the earlier cathedral of Clermont cannot be confirmed, but it is likely since Notre-Dame was so closely modelled on that building (98). These tribune arches, together with the concentric trilobes of Champagne, are the nearest Romanesque approximation to Cordoban structural use of lobed arches. Painted decoration at Issoire now stresses the similarity with Cordoban arches by providing them with an extrados; this may have been the original intention with many such arches that now are bare stone and have no extrados.

III. Quercy and Central France. Cahors South Door

The south door of the cathedral of Saint-Etienne, Cahors (fig.185) originally led into the cloister. It has two trilobed archivolts of very different types, neither of which can be classed with the groups previously described. The peculiarity of the soffit archivolt is the elaboration of the trilobe points; that of the second archivolt the finishing of the voussoirs with a Limousin moulding (99). The shape of the Cahors trilobe is also quite unlike any other trilobes, Andalusian or Romanesque, though it resembles Andalusian architectural examples in being contained within a larger segment than a semicircle (figs 186,187). Unlike Andalusian arches however the jambs are set within the width of the arch diameter.

The dominating feature of the soffit is the treatment of the points between the lobes; they split into volutes. To accomodate this elaboration the centre of the top lobe is depressed by the width of the moulding framing it, and the radius increased by that measurement, resulting in a reduction of the width of the voussoirs carrying the point, which threatened to look very clumsy if the radius of the top lobe conformed to the basic equilateral triangle scheme; this change would also give more light (fig. 178).

Elaborated points, split, voluted or carved with little motifs, are characteristic of a relatively large group of lobed arches in central and western France, but no other attempt at this shape of trilobe exists among them, and most examples have more than three lobes. The point may be carved on a single voussoir, often shaped in the same manner as the Cahors soffit, or the point may occur at the junction of two voussoirs. This difference is primarily a function of the stone employed rather than of design.

The lobing of Limousin moulding is a less frequent feature than the elaboration of the points, and is confined to central France. The combination of the two features is rare; it occurs only at Vigeois, La Souterraine, Saint-Paixent and Tulle, beside Cahors. Most arches with a lobed soffit of the Cahors type (i.e. with elaborated points) are framed with several orders of unlobed Limousin moulding.

The two features exhibited at Cahors need separate examination, since it is no longer possible to assume the south door of Cahors stands at the head of both series: the consecration of two altars in 1119 by Calixtus II (100) has until recently been accepted as dating the completion of the whole cathedral apart from the sculpture of the north doorway, and 1119 was therefore taken as a terminus ante quem for the south door. The detailed study of Saint-Etienne by E. Bratke (28) argues a new and later chronology, rejecting the consecration of two altars as signifying the completion of the whole monument. Comparisons of the sculpture of the north door with the Moissac doorway and Saint-Pierre in Angoulême fix the north door after both these, and the south door is shown to coincide with the north in time. Though her dating of completion of the tower porch of Moissac at 1131 and of Angoulême cathedral in 1136 is not fully substantiated and perhaps too late by a decade, possibly more, there is no doubt that she is correct in asserting that the porch and doorway at Moissac antedate the east end of Cahors (where capitals copy those in Moissac porch), and that the west end of Cahors, which includes the lobed south door, is later than the east end.

IIIa. Arches with Lobes with Volute or Elaborated Points. Waisted Voussoirs.

The Volute

The curl motif which adorns the points of the Cahors south door soffit trilobe is much in evidence in Andalusian decoration, from the beginning as applied to the lobes of roll corbels. It was not applied to the points of lobes. An example that may antedate Romanesque ones is a basin set in the floor of the court of the Mosque of Sidi ´Oqba (the Great Mosque) in Qairawan. It is carved in white marble with three descending levels of lobed borders, and the points of the lobes are divided into volutes (102). On ground level the basin is surrounded by strips of black and white marble.

The Jointing

The jointing of the lobes of the Cahors south door arch is dictated by two waisted voussoirs. They separate the lobes whose joints radiate from the centre of each lobe. The arrangement is unknown in Andalusian architecture; the jointing of Cordoban arches never takes account of the lobes and always converges either towards the impost, or onto a descending vertical beneath it. But lobed arches at Santiago, both the trilobes of the apse exterior and the five-lobed arches on the transept over the Platerias doorway are jointed independently for each lobe; the voussoir forming the point tapers at either end. This seems to be the case also at Saint-Pierre-Toirac, but not at Le Monastier, Bessuéjouls or Nevers, where the whole arch is jointed as one: perhaps this closer adherence to Andalusian practice indicates a position at the head of the French series of lobed arches.

Lobes are jointed as separated arches at a number of other French sites, including Meymac, Saint-Amand-de-Coly, Vigeois, Lubersac, Les Rosiers d'Egleton and Saint-Yrieix. At Meymac (fig.141) the jointing of the tympanum above the voussoirs is rough and uneven, but the voussoirs nonetheless adhere to the scheme on all five lobes, as they do at Saint-Amand, Vigeois and Lubersac; and on the blind 7-lobed arch on the apse exterior at Les Rosiers (fig.189). Flattened trilobes on the tower of Saint-Yrieix are the most westerly example of this type of jointing. At Palisse (fig.143) the waist of the point voussoir, so marked on all these latter doorway and window arches, is hardly retained and the effect of jointed lobes almost lost. At Tulle (fig.144), in the Creuse group like Bénévent l'Abbaye (fig.190) with joints at the points, and in the west of France, the joints converge on the centre of the whole arch, not on the lobe centre.

Three Restorations Reconsidered

Three examples of trilobes, generally dismissed as 19th century fantasies, need to be considered: at Moissac, Saint-Antonin and Collonges. At Moissac the entrance into the church from the porch is now made through two trilobed doorways, as restored between 1910 and 1914 (fig.191)(103). They were an original feature. Judging by analogies they are more accurate restorations than is usually allowed: there are two cases of similar trilobed arches, both restored, it is true: at Saint-Antonin in the twin windows of the tower restored by Viollet le Duc (fig.49)(104) and at Collonges under the tympanum (fig.142), restored in 1923 (105). The latter includes pieces of the original soffit and at Saint-Antonin a fragment of the original central impost was recently discovered (fig.192) while other pieces of voussoir are included in the restoration. At Saint-Antonin the façade was originally incrusted with Fatimid bowls, fragments of which survive (fig.48). Here the lobes were certainly not independently jointed, as the re-used fragments show; At Collonges the small fragment of lobe voussoir suggests the voussoirs should be waisted. The shape of the restored point is not authenticated; the joint may well have been sloped more towards the point as at Cahors to avoid the thickness resulting now in the central scallop.

At Moissac there is yet another example of lobed arches: the reliefs on the side walls of the porch are framed in trilobes. These are not to be dismissed as merely rendering a device of manuscript illumination for framing figures: far from following the line of a figure´s head and shoulders or a hierarchical composition of three figures to surround them with an arch that thereby becomes three-lobed, as is patently the way manuscript trilobes arise, these arches (and their imitations on the tympanum at Cahors) disconcertingly bring the points of the lobes exactly above the heads of the figures (fig.193)(106). They must be intended to represent real architecture. Colour perhaps added a desired illusion of depth to suggest that the figures were acting in or outside real buildings, rather than standing in cramped poses under arcades. Thus, though Moissac has no authentic surviving examples of a true lobed arch it has four separate references to lobed arches: the representation on capital 17 in the cloister (fig.194), the porch relief, the lobed jambs of the portal and the restored inner dooway inside the narthex. A further element confirming Moissac´s connexions with the "Cahors" group of lobed arches is that Limousin moulding is used in three orders on the great Moissac doorway. The representation of a "Limousin" belfry with gabled angles on the east relief of the porch is another point of contact.

The Spanish Elements at Moissac (see Chapter III, note 69)

Unlike Conques, Saint-Pons-de-Thomières or La Sauve-Majeure, all of which were favoured by the kings of Aragon (107), Moissac is not recorded as benefitting from gifts in the recaptured Muslim cities such as would bring its artists into contact with Andalusian monuments and works of art. The troublesome connexion with Camprodon, barely beyond the Pyrenees, is one of the monastery´s few material links with the peninsula. Yet the Spanish contacts are pervasive: Abbot Hunaldus (1072-1085) who succeeded the Auvergnat Durandus de Mercoeur was half-brother to the count of Béarn, a region where trade from Zaragoza through Jaca into south-west France was vital to the economy (108). The close personal ties represented by the fact that Bernard Archbishop of Toledo came of a noble family of the Agenais, bordering the Moissac area, and that he recruited Giraldus from Moissac, who became cantor in Toledo and archbishop of Braga, are manifest in the Toledan imprint on the cloister capitals discussed in Chapter III. The Catalan connexion must be responsible for the unusual treatment of a corner animal head on a narthex capital, the foliage convention of which is imitated at Cahors and Collonges: the rare corner head among Roda capitals is at its source, perhaps transmitted through Saint-Benoît-sur-Loire (figs 301, 89; see Chap.III, n.48).

The influence of Mozarabic illuminations on the iconography of the tympanum postulated by Mâle is now discounted (109) in favour of northern influences from Carolingian apse paintings, but there has been no consideration given to the origin of the declamatory function of the doorway, and the idea of transferring thither the features of the sanctuary. The conception is Andalusian, transmitted through Cluny. Another Spanish element at Moissac is the unusual theme of the Martyrdom of the Three Spanish Saints, illustrated on capital 37 of the cloister (St Fructuosus, bishop of Tarragona in the 3rd century and his deacons Augurus and Eulogius) whose relics the abbey must presumably have possessed.

It is universally recognized that Moissac is the source for the sculpture of Cahors: capitals in the east end of Cahors are imitations of the capitals in the narthex of Moissac and the north doorway of Cahors derives its conception and many details from the great Moissac doorway, as do the doorways of Beaulieu, Souillac, Collonges and ultimately in some measure Vézelay (110). It is therefore reasonable to seek the inspiration for the south door of Cahors at Moissac also, where both volute cusps and Limousin moulding were to be found.

No firm dates can be assigned to any lobed doorway at present; those of Meymac and Vigeois cannot be later than the end of the third decade of the 12th century, which is certainly contemporary if not earlier than Cahors. The façade of Meymac is placed by Héliot (111) at the end of the 11th century, though he ignored the implication for the dating of lobed arches: that it is earlier than Cahors, which he placed in 1119 at the beginning of the series. Vigeois he thought "largely completed" by 1124 (112). By this time there were lobed arches to be seen at Cluny, Santiago, Nevers, Bessuéjouls, Le Monastier, Vienne and Saint-Pierre-Toirac. Thus jointing to the lobed centre (Santiago and Meymac), Limousin moulding (Meymac, Vigeois and Moissac), and trilobe (Saint-Pierre-Toirac, Le Monastier, Bessuéjouls and Moissac) were already to hand by the end of the third decade of the 12th century, and the originality of Cahors south door lies in its felicitous combination of the results of previous experiments and not in a new invention from Andalusian precedents. Meymac, Cahors and Vigeois represent three experiments with the form of lobed arches and their points.

Meymac

135

At Meymac the line of the soffit is based on a round arch, and the impost is its diameter: the lobing is formed within concentric circumferences. The voussures framing it are pointed arches, with their centres at the two bottom cusp points of the soffit. The whole space between the round lobed soffit and the pointed archivolts is too high to be spanned by single voussoirs (F16)(fig.141). An analogy for the way the Meymac soffit springs from the capitals, with the point extending beyond the impost, is to be found in the oratory of the Aljafería (AHIII figs 284-285), where the mixtilinear arches end in a circular lobe, and the inner profile of the base of this lobe is divided into an upcurled soffit and a round lower part that is shaped as a convex lobe resting on the impost (113); the width between the jambs is thus greater than the width of the soffit. This curl occurs on a number of later lobed Limousin arches, for example at Tulle (fig.144).

Vigeois (fig. 188)

At Vigeois the arch design is unusual (114). The outer orders are pointed, and centred on the cusp points at the spring of the soffit, as at Meymac (115), but the soffit and the framing archivolt are constructed on a circle whose diameter is well above the impost; it is thus a deliberate horseshoe arch; Andalusian models would seem likely, though the impost is less than the standard Andalusian one-third of the radius below the centre (116). The nearest arch shape, apart from Déols cloister door (fig.195) is on buildings in the Near East and North Africa: arcades on the minaret at Aleppo, finished in 1090, are of similar profile; they enclose lobed rosette medallions. An arch in a niche on the façade of the minaret of the Great Mosque of Sfax is similar. It became popular in Spanish Romanesque later (117). The consoles or pseudo-capitals under the impost (the right-hand one, with Peter and Paul in mandorlas, is in the Moissac style) carry the profile of the opening back to jambs as wide apart as the widest opening of the arch, which again gives the entrance a more Andalusian aspect than most French lobed openings, but the points carved with animals, remote from Andalusian practice, prevent the doorway being classed as totally under Andalusian influence in design. Cahors and Meymac both have jambs set within the width of the arch, unlike Andalusian.

The Volute Cusp

The origin of the voluted point is uncertain. There are no examples in earlier church or Islamic architecture apart from the basin at Qairawan already quoted; it must be sought in the decorative use of a curl motif in other contexts. Lombard carvings, Christian manuscripts wall-paintings and ivories (118), scroll patterns in Andalusian architecture as well as corbel (119) and arch decoration all provide convergent models. French corbels, like Andalusian, have curls carved on the sides; Toulouse and

Conques both can offer numerous examples; but paradoxically roll corbels are markedly rare in the area of distribution of this doorway type with volute-point lobes (Maps III,IV).

The lobe points of Meymac doorway are carved in granite and the twin volutes are little more than a double point. At Vigeois in contrast, the volutes of the two upper cusps are carved with animals and the lower two cusps also have a motif carved on them. These place the arch stylistically in a more evolved category than Cahors, though the relative dates remain uncertain, and Vigeois is probably earlier. Lubersac, like Vigeois, has figure motifs and there are further examples at Saint-Hilaire in the Berry, Montmoreau (Char. fig.196) and Petit-Palais (Gir. fig.197), all of the second half of the 12th century. Les Rosiers, Saint-Amand-de-Coly and Palisse have volutes like Cahors.

The division of the point at the junction between two voussoirs is rather a matter of the material employed than a distinction in intent. It is not surprising that greater elaborations occur with limestone than with granite: Vigeois and Lubersac, though the building is of granite, have limestone voussoirs. Most of the churches in the Creuse with lobed arches are of granite and the point is divided between two voussoirs, often without much attempt to develop a volute: La Souterraine and Bénévent-l´Abbaye for example both have split rather than volute points.

Often in the west of France (for example at Puisseguin (Gir), Châtres (Saintonge romane figs 196-7), Aubeterre (Char), Echebrune (op.cit.fig.175) the two halves of the point, or the two volutes, are set as at Collonges on either side of a central rib to make a triple point. This development culminates in the convex points of Tayac and Neuillac (fig.199). The jambs and arches framing windows in the western area, as at Rioux and Vandré (op.cit.figs 185,207), show another popular variant in late Romanesque decoration, where the volutes occupy as much space as the lobe openings, or more. This type of point also became widespread in later 12th century decoration in Spain (120). The form of the points at Journet (Vienne) is no more than a simplified version of this type. Alternatively, it may be classed, like Le Waast (fig.200), as under a direct influence from Egypt or as a derivation from the angled profile of the mixtilinear arches of Zaragoza; it may be the result of a convergence of such stimuli.

Journet lobes.

Junction with the Jambs

At what part of the lobe circumference the spring of the arch should begin was evidently a problem with which designers of lobed arches were always experimenting. At

Cordoba the spring begins at different places on the circumference of the bottom lobe, but never at more than the half-circle, whereas in France it even sometimes begins at the point.

At Cahors the line of the junction resembles many in the Mezquita, for example the dome decorative trilobes, and entrance arcades to the maqsura, but since the jamb is vertical, without the Andalusian scotia impost dictated by the horseshoe arch, it avoids the characteristic Andalusian profile with the jambs wider apart than the spring (121). Approximately the same line is followed at Saint-Amand-de-Coly, Montbron and Les Rosiers.

At Meymac, Collonges, Tulle and Palisse lobed round arches spring from the point itself, and at Vigeois the impost block is used as the lower half of the final point; the bottom voussoir joint is horizontal, not convergent on the centre ·of the lobe circle, making the jointing less subtle than at Cahors. A single up-turned curl is usual with multilobe arches with fvolute points: the arcading on the tower of Saint-Yrieix even manages to achieve it with trilobes. Many arches further west use this solution, as Montmoreau (fig.196), Châtres, Condéon (fig.202) and Aubeterre in the Charente, Echebrune, Genouillé, Neuillac (CM), Puisseguin and Petit-Palais (Gir).

Less than half a lobe takes the spring to the crown of a lobe at Lubersac (fig 201), Saint-Ybars (Ariège), Saint-Antoine (Gers) and a coherent little group of late doorways in the Berry including Colombiers fig 204, Malicorne (with a five-lobed oculus above), Saint-Hilaire. An economical method of construction, with each voussoir forming half a lobe and point, at La Saunière, Saint-Maurice and Saint-Sulpice in the Creuse, gives a half point at the spring. This is a late return to the primitive jointing of Le Monastier.

IIIb. Torus (Limousin) Moulding with Lobes

Cahors, Vigeois, Tulle, Déols and Saint-Bonnet all have examples of one lobed archivolt of Limousin moulding. In the first three cases it frames a lobed soffit with volute or elaborated points, and is itself enclosed in an unlobed archivolt of Limousin moulding (three at Tulle). At La Souterraine the lobed soffit is framed by three achivolts of lobed Limousin moulding and this is carried down the jambs as well.

The lobed jambs of La Souterraine make plain the close relation of the above series of arches to the lobed jambs of the Moissac doorway, thus adding three more sites to this "Limousin moulding" group: Moissac, Souillac and Beaulieu, all by the same atelier if not the same sculptor (Quercy roman figs 120, 146).

The cloister door at Déols (fig.195), now ruined and blocked, presumably originally had lobes open on the void, like the Moissac jambs, and if this was so it is the only example of an open archivolt of Limousin moulding (122). The lobes appear to be bracket-shaped, a sharp joint alternating with a rounded. The arch is a horseshoe and the columns are in line with the wider part of the arch, and are relatively short, giving the arch an Andalusian "top-heavy" aspect.

The jambs of Moissac doorway have a lobed torus against the void, and the moulding imitates the form of a lobed column engaged in a lobed jamb. The face of this jamb is bevelled at the edge and enriched with the same ribbon motif that surrounds the tympanum. This simulated engaged column appears again, lobed but without the corresponding ribbon enrichment of the flanking wall, on the trumeau down the centre of the sides; it has a downturned-leaf capital (D16) and emerges below the figures of Jeremiah on the east, Saint Paul on the west (123). A comparison of the face of these jambs with the triple moulding of jambs, lintel consoles and lintels of the Platerías doorways at Santiago suggests, if not direct connexion, a common inspiration. Although the lobes of the moulding at Santiago behind the consoles are not against the void and the relief is shallower than that of the Moissac moulding the same contrast of planes is created. The parallel is more precise in the similarity of the Santiago moulding to the trumeau of Beaulieu where the torus comes at the angles. The plaster mouldings in the Aljafería, sparse remnants of the kind of work that was everywhere to be seen in the cities of Andalusia during the 11th century, suggest a source of inspiration for this kind of treatment of the edges of architectural members.

The five-lobed arch with a plaster extrados in the tower of San Lorenzo in Toledo (AHIII fig.266) is an example of Spanish 11th century plaster work, and of the kind of model available for such Limousin doorways with five lobes as Meymac and Vigeois. At the latter the archivolts framing the five-lobed soffit keep comparatively closely to the lines of the soffit, but Meymac has the same wide space between the top lobe and the crown of the next archivolt as there is at San Lorenzo; this may be explained as an influence from the caliphal practice of raising the centre of the extrados, perpetuated at San Lorenzo (F16).

The trilobe niches of Saint-Pierre-Toirac can be connected with this group of arches with Limousin moulding, by reason of their moulding. In this case it is a hood framing the arch, not a roll moulding in an angle. The only comparable hood treatment of a lobed profile is also on a member of the Limousin group: it is used at Souillac over the very flat trilobe of the Theophilus relief (Quercy roman fig.115). The little volutes between these lobes connect the panel with the form of volute point seen at Cahors. Little upturned volutes at the crest of one of the

139

incrusted Samson reliefs at Saint-Pierre-Toirac provide a link between Souillac and Saint-Pierre, already suggested by the use of lobed hood moulding in both, and confirm the association of both churches with the "Cahors" group of lobed arches that combine volute points and Limousin moulding (124).

While Saint-Pierre-Toirac has a claim to head the Limousin series by reason of a date before the end of the 11th century (125), Le Dorat (Limousin roman fig.3), Thouars (fig 170) and Celles-sur-Belle, which all repeat the multiple lobed archivolts of La Souterraine, stand at the end of the series. They have capitals at the impost line, unlike La Souterraine, and the corresponding columns below are not lobed, nor are the jambs. Thouars introduces a less austere Poitevin note to the composition, with a round-headed floral hood moulding over the door and carved capitals and imposts. Le Dorat, in the tradition of Meymac, has a wide space (F16) between the twin door arches and the next archivolt. A console in the central spandrel (F19) shows that a figure was intended to occupy it. The way the moulding turns at the bottom of the final lobes into a vertical, before reaching the impost, points the affinity of this group with the trumeaux of Beaulieu and Souillac.

Whereas at La Souterraine the top central lobe is widened and flattened on the outer archivolts to make almost a round arch, in these three later examples it is heightened and narrowed, creating a more Andalusian aspect, enhanced by the strongly stressed radial jointing (F14) of the voussoirs. The affinities of Gothic taste with Andalusian begin to make themselves felt. In spite of their irregular lobes and the strong recession of orders, both of which features are quite un-Andalusian, this group of arches has a closer parallel than any other French lobed arch with one Andalusian example : the arch on the south wall of the Villaviciosa chapel which also has several orders, like La Souterraine, and multiple lobes (AHIII fig.146).

The lobed arcades on the upper storey of the façade of Petit-Palais in the Gironde (fig 197) perhaps owe something to Celles-sur-Belle for their multiple deeply undercut moulded archivolts and elaborated points. The arch shape is however different and the moulding is not fitted in an angle in the Limousin manner. Petit-Palais, late in the 12th century, can point to very few precedents for this original combination of existing elements. The façade design as a whole inherits the Andalusian scheme already integrated into French design. The interior arcades of Blanzac in the Angoûmois offer a late example of a lobed torus decoration (fig.205). The edging of the voussoir of the outer order with horseshoe, or rounded rectangular lobes in shallow relief reflects the example of Montbron (fig.160); it is reminiscent also of the rounded rectangular scroll stems on the wooden door at Lavoûte-Chilhac (fig.77).

IV. Arches with Convex Lobes

The monuments assembled under this rubric do not form a coherent geographical group, and different influences including the Islamic can be seen as inspiring them. The two best known French doorways with convex lobes are at Le Waast far north of the usual distribution of lobed arches (fig 200) in the Pas de Calais, and Ganagobie (BA)(fig 206), again outside the normal lobed arch area. The lobing of the doorway of Le Waast is compared by Enlart and Héliot (126) to the decoration on the late 11th century Cairene gateways, Bab el Nasr and Bab el Futuh (127), and the similarity is close. Enlart regarded it as the result of Godefroy de Bouillon´s participation in the First Crusade (128). Le Waast is one of the few cases where a direct contact with the eastern Mediterranean best explains a form.

Héliot quoted a correspondence (129) with Spain carried on by Ide de Lorraine, countess of Boulogne, mother of Godefroy of Bouillon and patroness of the church, as an argument for looking for a Spanish source for the Le Waast arch, but no close parallels can be found for the form in Spain, and oriental parallels are many.

Arches with convex lobes are not uncommon on buildings in Egypt of the late 11th and early 12th century. Creswell illustrates examples at Aswan, on three Cairene gateways, on the Mosque of al-Aqmar (1125) and at Qasr al-Hallabat (130). Almanzor´s arch into his extension of the Mezquita is a century earlier than any of these (fig 27), and arches like magnified roll corbels, even carrying the reference to a central band of decoration imitating the fillet between rolls, were built in the Aljafería and in Granada (131). The development of cushion voussoirs (from which such rolls are carved) in North Africa and Egypt, where they often occur, may have been inspired from Andalusia in the first place.

The Spanish source suggested by Héliot for the late 12th century doorway at Ganagobie is more plausible than one for Le Waast: Zamora and Salamanca (132) have doorways with enlarged volute-type points, but even so closer parallels for the shape of Ganagobie´s voussoirs exist in Cairo (133).

The confident use in later Spanish Romanesque decoration of convex lobes and cushion voussoirs and the play with the motif as a reminiscence of the acanthus leaf tips of Mozarabic tradition as at Puente la Reina (134) suggest that in Spain it was a native development stemming from the Andalusian tradition, and France received it from Spain. The ribbed convex lobes at Les Eyzies-de-Tayac and at Neuillac (fig 199) are similar if less exuberant developments of volute points. These two doorways fit in other respects into their local context (Limousin moulding at Tayac; a typical Saintonge façade at Neuillac), and do not suggest any exotic inspiration.

A series of arches with cushion voussoirs shaped into multiple cylinders can be traced from Saint-Hilaire in Poitiers (fig 207). The tall arcade over the doorway on the north face of the tower has an inner archivolt of triple cylinders. The doorway at Pezou (L&Ch)(fig 163) has one of double cylinders and outside it the archivolt of chevrons. The small church of Saint-Amans (fig 208) near Agen has an outer archivolt with voussoirs carved as cylinders at the point, framing an arch with chevrons overlapping a torus, repeating the association of motifs noted at Pezou. Nearby, at Saint-Robert (fig 209) an outer archivolt of triple cylinder voussoirs is highly decorated. The inner and outer rows of "cylinder ends" are carved with crosses, circles, spirals or palmettes in circles, giving the effect of impressed plaster, and these motifs are repeated on a hood moulding, on the imposts of the capitals, and on two of the corbels holding the cornice immediately above the arch. Similar discs are carved on the voussoirs of the doorway of Porqueras (Gerona)(AHV fig 66) and in the Saintonge the rosette disc (D15) was also popular. At Saint-Robert the arch, recessed in the wall, is enclosed in a frame formed by a corbel table and simulated colonnettes carved up the wall from the imposts to the outermost corbel. This resembles an alfiz and thus gives an effect more Spanish (like Porqueras or Cubells) than local, or than the Berry arches with rosettes in spandrels to be treated below.

Examples in the Saintonge

There is something similar to the above voussoir treatment in the use of discs on the doorway of Saint-Quantin-de-Rançannes in the Saintonge (135). Some of the rosettes are not circular but ellipses, and they do not form the soffit but are only on an outer archivolt. A line of horsehead corbels, above the arch and its flanking carvings, connects the doorway with the group with cushion voussoirs.

The series of churches in the Saintonge with horsehead arches has taken the convex voussoirs of the windows of Saint-Eutrope in Saintes a stage further. The axial window of the chevet of Matha-Marestay (136) has two archivolts of cylindrical voussoirs. Each consequent circular "point" of the soffit is carved with a rosette in relief, and above this with a human head in the majority of cases, with some birds, monsters or animals. The outer archivolt is carved with uniform scrolls curling round the nail head of the cylinder end. The same effect is obtained by the cylindrical voussoirs of the arches flanking the horsehead doorway at Saint-Fort (137). The voussoirs of the flanking niche are like unfinished horseheads, and illustrate the tendency prevalent in the Saintonge though not confined to that region (cf Bellegarde du Loiret, or Pezou fig 163) to treat voussoirs in the Andalusian manner as radiating units clearly marked off one from another. This feature is already seen on the chevet at Saint-Eutrope in the 11th century and on many later arches, often doorways with an adumbration of an alfiz (138). Other notable examples of this tendency are in the cloister of Saint-Aubin in Angers (fig 330) and on a window arch in the apse of Saint-Pierre, Chauvigny (139). Cylindrical masonry is used round the apse of Jarnac-Champagne (140) and at Saint-Estèphe (Char) a band of it separates storeys on the tower (141). A precedent for this is in the series of churches in the High Aragon east of Biescas, where the exteriors of the apses are decorated with lines of vertical cylindrical blocks (142). These Aragonese churches also have openings framed in rectangular recesses (F12) and twin columns (F6). Asturian precedents for rectangular frames round openings lead some scholars now to question any Islamic element in these buildings (143) but at San Juan de Buso the door archivolt hints unmistakeably at a Kufic-inspired scroll (fig 172)(F2).

On the lobed outer archivolt of a window at Agudelle (CM) and on the upper arcade at Plassac (fig 161) the joint of the voussoirs comes at the point of the lobes, which is therefore thickened to make almost a convex lobe. This is remote from the treatment of convex points like roll corbels in the Andalusian manner (144). At Rioux the "Cahors" volute point is so much developed as to become flat if not convex, and this form is common in later 12th century decoration in the Saintonge. At Puisseguin it is associated with down-turned leaf capitals (D16). An unemphatic reference to convex lobes is perhaps intended in the frequent scallop border of Saintonge decoration, exemplified at Rioux inside the apse, and at Blanzay (fig 212) where it forms an archivolt outside a split lozenge-shaped leaf, which may well imply a lam-aliph.

V. Lobed Arches with Edged Lobes

A characteristic of all Andalusian decoration, from as early as the San Esteban door (145) to the Alhambra (fig 210), whether in carved stone or moulded plaster, is the insistence on outlining and differentiating basic elements of structure. Not only are openings framed, but voussoirs, archivolts, cornices or panels are picked out with moulding or fillets. The curve of the lobes of arches is stressed by bordering a real or simulated extrados with a line of decoration or moulding, often both. At Zaragoza in the 11th century amid all the complexities of combined curves and straight lines that form the arches of the great screens and the arcades of the oratory the principle is retained, and two centuries later at Granada care was taken even to mark the structure of the cells of the muqarnas (stalactite ceiling) with fillets, carving or paint (146), and an arch with a smooth soffit may be given a plaster moulding simulating long voussoirs with a lobed extrados (fig 210).

Outside Spain Islamic examples are less consistent.
The arch of the Bab Zuweila in Cairo (fig 140) for example
has grooves marking the intrados line and an independent
extrados that ignores the series of lobes in the upper part
of the arch. The Almoravid mosque of Tlemcen of c.1135
leaves the lobes of some of its arcades without an extrados
(AHIII fig 338)(147).

In France where most lobed arches have a recession of
orders the outer archivolts are not generally lobed, so the
line of the soffit is only a negative shape. In the Cahors
group which constitutes the majority of open arches the
design concentrates on the soffit, primarily on the point
dividing it from the next lobe (148). There are some cases
in France however where some concern to emphasize the
extrados and embellish it in a more Andalusian manner is
apparent. Multiple-lobed orders of course automatically
create the effect of a lobed extrados. The lobe, framed by
the succeeding archivolts, acquires some breadth and
becomes a band of positive shape, though the outermost
lobed may be unbacked (149).

To consider the early examples of lobed arches already
discussed: the extrados of the trilobes on the gable at
Nevers (fig 155) are backed by a round arch of billet
moulding (F15); this corresponds to the five inner arches
of the arcade over the mihrab in the Mezquita, but at
Cordoba the extrados of the two outer arches, where there
is room, are lobed. At Nevers the lobe is not repeated on
the extrados.

At Bessuéjouls both the gable and altar arches have a
lobed extrados (F15). On the altar the trilobe is
emphasized by a projecting grooved archivolt; on the façade
the ends of the voussoirs are merely shaped into a lobe but
the extrados is not stressed by any decoration or moulding.
The case is the same with the façade trilobe at Issoire
whereas the painting on the tribune openings of the
interior makes them look more Andalusian than any other
lobed arches in France, with broad bands of decoration
marking a simulated (but not lobed) extrados.

A number of French arches have the inner edge of the
their lobes emphasized by a bevel or incised line (Saint-
Antonin, Montmoreau, Malicorne) that gives a modicum of
breadth beyond the negative shape of the lobe. The arch on
capital 17 in Moissac cloister (fig 180) is the ealiest
example of this feature on any surviving in France. The
five lobes of the relief on the tympanum of the north door
of Saint-Benoît-sur-Loire are given a plain fillet edge
within the cloud border.

The majority of examples of edged lobes is to be found
among the group of later lobed arches in the west of
France: for example, all with split or volute points,
Condéon (fig 202), Puisseguin, Aubeterre, Echebrune,
Châtres, Esnandes, Agudelle, Plassac (fig 161). The blind

lobes at Catus (fig 159) and a little group with examples of the late retention of the Romanesque lobed arch on Gothic buildings in the Berry, such as Saint-Amand, Ivoy-le-Pré (with oculus) or Saint-Hippolyte also show this finish on the inner edge.

A more lively group in the Berry combines this edging with a spandrel rosette, which links them with the rosettes associated with arches in the Saintonge already discussed, and with arches in Lérida and Balaguer. To this group belong Colombier and Malicorne (fig 204) and the splendid oculus over the door at Villefranche d´Allier. Malicorne has a more modest oculus over the door. Saint-Hilaire nearby has no rosettes but instead virtually circular little faces on the points themselves.

In western France elaborations on the bevel of the lobe and on incised borders give a more Andalusian look to the lobes than is possessed by lobes elsewhere in France except the Issoire tribunes. At Montbron (fig 160) the unlobed archivolts (third and fourth) of Limousin moulding frame a lobed soffit with split points; the second and fifth archivolts are carved on the face with hollowed lobes outlined with incised motifs; on the outer archivolt the lobes are embellished with drilling and little scallops. Similar decoration is used on the arch over the funerral monument of Robert of Montbron (+1209). The lobed intrados of the main portal at Condéon (fig 202) has a wider simple moulding tooled with foliage, and there is similar decoration but double moulding at Saint-Hippolyte-de-Biard on the miniature lobes of its outer voussure. The interlace or drilled edging of the medallions on the 11th century ivory casket from Pamplona, offers an example among others of a kind capable of inspiring such decoration (AHIII figs 363-4.

The fine long points of the lobed archivolt on the west front at Aunay, fancifully created out of a plant motif, come close to the profile of Zaragoza arcades but the lobes are not backed, whereas at Zaragoza there was originally certainly some plain or carved lobed moulding in plaster along a simulated extrados.

The inner archivolt at Montmoreau (fig 196) is unusually delicately carved: the two volutes on the points are held together with a binding, the lobes are bordered with a fillet separating them from the three-petalled undercut florets in the spandrels and the ground of cross and lozenge between them. The Gothic doorway of Saint-Martin in Brive is flanked by lions framed in small three-lobed niches. The lobes have beaded edges and an incised extrados.

The Outlined Extrados

In summary, the extrados so firmly stressed in Andalusian lobes is given some scant recognition in some of the earliest surviving French examples of lobed arches (Moissac capital 17, Saint-Pierre-Toirac, Nevers, Bessuéjouls) but mainly restricted to the shaping of the voussoirs themselves.

A torus moulding backs the trilobe at Toirac, but in the case of lobed "Limousin" arches with multiple archivolts, as at Cahors or Le Dorat, the torus is associated with the line of the archivolt outside it, and the outermost voussure therefore has no lobed extrados; it follows that no special attempt was made to observe the Andalusian principle. In this "Limousin" group in cases where volute and elaborated points occupy the attention, the extrados lost importance (for example at La Souterraine), but in other cases the moulding stresses the line of the lobe (Thouars, Celles-sur-Belle). With trilobes of Le Puy type the extrados is always of minimal importance, thus belying a strong directly Andalusian element.

In western France towards the middle of the 12th century and later an extrados or an inner border to make a positive shape assumed greater importance in the design of the lobes. This is expessed either in a plain fillet or grooving, or in tooling or beading similar to borders executed in ivory carving or metal work (for example Condéon, Saint-Hippolyte-de-Biard, Montbron). At Aunay the lobes are entirely subservient to the floral carving.

French lobed arches thus seem to reflect the influence of Andalusia more directly towards the end of the Romanesque developments, judging by the composition at Thouars, Celles, Condéon; the edged arcades in Saintonge like Plassac, Agudelle and Trizay (fig 211); the doors and oculi of the Berry (Malicorne, Colombiers, Saint-Amand, Villefranche).

The group of doorways and arcades of the Angoûmois and Saintonge with their simple lobed round arches detached from the surrounding decorated archivolts constitute an interpretation of the Cordoban lobed arch which takes little account of its later developments as they appear in Zaragoza or Balaguer in the 11th century (150). In the decoration of these 11th century Andalusian palaces the plaster work disguising the brick arcading is elaborately carved and moulded to create ambiguous structural effects so that soffit and extrados almost lose their meaning, though each lobe is always firmly outlined (eg AHIII fig.297).

In two respects however some parallels can be drawn between these emiral palaces and the near-contemporary Romanesque buildings at the beginning of the series. First, the strong composite mouldings (AHIII figs 294-297)(151) of the Andalusian plaster work provide antecedents for the lobed mouldings on the lintel corbels at Santiago, on the lobed jambs at Moissac, on the trilobe surround at Saint-

Pierre-Toirac. It can be seen as a formative influence on the whole development of Limousin moulding. Second, we can take from Balaguer two from many examples of decorative motifs used equally on buildings, ivory and metal which were transmitted to Romanesque (152): a painted border has a version of the naturalistic scroll D9 fused with the circular palmette scroll D5 in the same way as on Mozarabic metalwork (AHIII fig 480). Again the lobes of a circular window (hitherto unpublished) in the remaining wall of a ruined Romanesque chapel on the castle site (fig 47) are edged (D12) like medallions on a caliphal ivory; the composite moulding and spandrel rosettes (D15; AHIII figs 385, 398a) recur on Romanesque windows in the Berry (Colombiers fig 204, Villefranche, Gassicourt, Fleuriel). The example of applying ivory, metal and textile motifs to architectural sculpture was followed at least as early as the last decade of the 11th century at Saintes (the choir dedicated 1096.Saintonge romane figs 512-517) and made their own .by sculptors who a few decades later decorated first Angoulême (copied exactly at La Couronne fig 39 and Genouillé (Saintonge romane fig 206) then Aunay, Corme-Ecluse, Marignac (Saintonge romane figs 206, 167, 155-160, p.172) and many other churches in the Saintonge (153). The unusually uncompromising decoration and lobes of Genouillé doorway show how the Andalusian style became ultimately dessicated in transmission.

VI Lobes Portrayed in Sculpture

A few capital and relief sculptures give evidence that lobed arches had an interest for builders quite early in the Romanesque period. An apse capital at Saint-Révérien (Nièvre) illustrating the Israelites in the Fiery Furnace shows them under a round-headed arch with a soffit indented with ten horseshoe-shaped lobes. These are spaced as on the lobed arches of La Charité and Ladignac (fig 213). One of the columns supporting the arch has spiral decoration like columns at Santiago; the other is rectangular, like the La Charité arcading. Above the central arch the central tower and one of those flanking it are portrayed with their conical roofs supported on a corbel table.

At Gargilesse (Indre, fig 214)(63) ribbon issuing from a corner mask along the top of a capital with a figure scene, forms a canopy or cloud which runs as lobes with an axial grooving. At Cahors similar horizontal lines of lobing end in the corner volutes over acanthus on the exterior window capitals (fig 215).

On the façade at Souvigny (64) a lobed canopy surmounts a figure scene. The tympanum over the north door of Saint-Benoît-sur-Loire is carved with a seated Christ and the four Evangelists, each contained in the lobe of a five-lobed arch. Manuscript illumination is the obvious inspiration but the carving of the lobes aims at giving the arch an architectural quality. On the façade at Foussais (Vendée) a niche relief shows a triple horizontal arch held on spiral columns with a deep soffit, the edge of which is notched to match the chevron-over-scotia archivolt of the niche containing the sculpture (fig 215).

Capital 17 portraying the imprisonmnent of St Peter in the cloister at Moissac shows the soldiers sleeping under an arch carved in relief with lobes along the arris of the archivolt. The arch is surmounted by a hipped pointed gable, reminiscent of the interior of the central door in the west façade of the Mezquita or the squinch arches of the dome, particularly as the top lobe is larger than the others (F16), with a longer radius of the central lobe. The final lobe at the spring rises vertically: the arch rests on a tower with keyhole shaped blind windows and a (?) pointed door with a square framing cornice above. This shape of lobe is not met in Cordoban architecture, though the arcades on the Palencia casket (AHIII fig. 369)(65) have trilobes on a vertical spring. The consoles on this capital are of the same form as the corbels over the lobed triforium arcade at Cluny (66). There is an ambiguity about the lobes on the capital 17 arch. The sculptor has apparently aimed at cutting away the spandrels, except at the top, to make the lobes stand proud as a series of arches. This treatment resembles that of the lobes on the Cabestany and San Martí de Empurias altars (67). They might even be read as the niches of a First Romanesque gable rather than a lobed arch, except that the "tower" at the side has no indication of the pilaster strips indispensable to that architecture.

None of these capitals betrays any special debt for the lobe motif to manuscript illumination, the inspiration being directly architectural.

Summary

Andalusian lobed arches have been reviewed and previous classifications revised to group French lobed arches into five broad types; these, though mutually interacting, fall in their origins into a series of geographical areas centred respectively east to west, on Cluny, the Rhône valley with the Velay, Quercy and Limousin, Angoûmois and Saintonge. I. Cluny III generated several different developments based either on the characteristics of the lobes (shallow relief cut from the arch face, horseshoe shape) or the applications of lobing a. to triforium or tribune arcades b. to doorways. The lobing of Cluny West Door represents an Andalusian component at the inception of the evolution of the Romanesque façade and this strengthens the thesis that the Romanesque monumental doorway owes its ultimate inspiration to the Puerta San Esteban, the earliest example west of India of the entrance to a religious building that "copies" the sanctuary within. The combination of lobed arches and the rosette motif popular in Andalusia as all round the Mediterranean has novel interpretation on doorways in the Brionnais. II. In the Rhône valley and Velay, trilobes and a few polylobed arches constructed on concentric semicircles demonstrate some influence from Santiago where arches were lobed in this way before the end of the 11th century, but not a strong enough influence to promote the independent voussoiring of lobes. At Champagne, and in the Auvergne at Clermont and Issoire, functional tribune arches are built as trilobes. III. Westward again, the trilobed south door at Cahors exhibits the combination of two departures from the two former types a. an open-lobed soffit with lobes separately voussoired and volute points and b. multiple-lobed orders with Limousin moulding; Moissac is proposed as standing near the inception of these; Saint-Pierre-Toirac with moulding, and Meymac with the "Santiago" independent lobes, may be earlier. The waisted-point voussoir may owe its shape to shapes noted in the Mezquita. The origin of the volute point is uncertain. The moulding has antecedents in the slender columns and mouldings of Andalusian palace architecture, adopted at Santiago. IV. Convex lobes in most cases result from elaborating the voluted points of the "Cahors" soffit; they occur mostly in the central and western areas. Le Waast and Ganagobie are special cases outside the usual distribution area of lobed arches, and have parallels in Egypt. V. An emphasis on the extrados, always present in Andalusia, which was not sought after in the previous groups of Romanesque lobed arches, coincides with the dissemination of sculpture in western France that draws on Andalusian themes and ivory carving style and betokens a renewal of conscious reference to Andalusia. The artistic links observed in the earliest Romanesque capital sculpture in the Berry with the Saintonge, Gascony and North Spain are seen persisting with a group of mid- or late-12th century doorway arches with analogous edged or backed lobes. VI. Some representations of lobed arches in sculpture are examined and the preoccupation of Moissac with this feature is noticed.

.

1.   The terms "lobed", "polylobed", "trilobed" have become established to describe what should more properly be termed "cusped" or even better "scalloped" arches (OED: lobe "a roundish projecting part, usually one or two or more separated by a fissure"; cusp "a point, pointed end, peak. Each of the projecting points between the small arcs in Gothic tracery, arches etc."; scalloped "having the border, edge or outline cut into a series of segments of circles.."), since it is space that is in most cases the "roundish projecting part", not the solid part of the arch. I follow nevertheless the practice originating in French writing and now generalized in using lobe for the concave shaping of the profile and point for the cusp between these. The bibliography is more extensive than for any other Islamic feature thought to have influenced Romanesque art. See n.27.

2.   Lobed arches portrayed in Christian manuscript illumination for canon tables, for framing figures and occasionally portraying architecture have no doubt affected Romanesque arch design. Realization of these in stone however begins in the West in Andalusia. This is one of many examples of how Cordoban art is one of the fullest expessions of Carolingian ideas: cf J. Hubert, J. Porcher and W. Volbach, Carolingian Art, London 1970, pl. 73: B.N.lat. 8850 (Gospel Book of Saint-Médard of Soissons: beginning of St Luke): the seven-lobed arch is like a maquette for a Cordoban, with moulding, and voussoirs alternating both in colour and in carved decoration with plain. The concave lobing of the extrados is similar to the shaping of the exterior angles of the dome drum of the Great Mosque of Sousse, and to the shallow lobes of the Romanesque series of arches, and sometimes jambs, with Limousin moulding (section IIIb of this chapter).

3.   The series of pre-Andalusian Islamic examples of all types of lobed arch is listed in many of the works cited in Chapter II n.1 (Qusair al-Hallabat, Raqqa, Ukhaidir, Samarra, al-Aqsa Mosque in Jerusalem, Egypt, Qairawan) and especially LTB al-And 1956; LTB 1957 pp 490-495; Héliot, BM 1946.

4.   EMA I p. 282, fig. 326.

5.   AMO p. 45-46; in stone, only Qusair al-Hallabat, LTB 1957 p.492, see also p. 491.

6.   The authenticity of this arch for the original building is questioned by M.-L. Arscott (Chapter II, n.6), but Brisch and Ewert maintain it is genuine. Among other remains, a plaster fragment from Granada (AHIII fig. 317) shows the same arch decoration in use in Andalusia, but not until the 11th century.

7.   The masonry is plastered over and painted.

8.   Many arches in the Mezquita are bonded into the wall
for about half their height and are only voussoired across
the top (eg AHIII p. 56, fig. 67).

9.   E. Camps Cazorla, Módulo, Proporciones y Composición
en la Arquitectura Califal Cordobesa, pp 99ff, figs 66 and
67. This   work is liable to criticism   for being
insufficiently based on survey measurements and too much on
photographs. The   principles   deduced are nonetheless
consistent and convincing.

10. Ibid., figs 43 and 44, p. 84.

11. Ibid., figs 45 and 46, p. 85.

12. Ibid.; passim.

13. C. Ewert, "Spanisch-islamische Systeme sich kreuzender
Bogen" I (Cordoba), M.F. 2. 1968; II (Malaga), M.M. 7,
1966;III (Zaragoza) M.F. 12, 1978; IV (Soria), M.M. 8,
1967; "Islamische Funde in Balaguer.." M.F. 7, 1971; "Der
Mihrab der Hauptmoschee von Almería" M.M.13, 1972; "Die
Moschee von Mértola (Portugal)" M.M. 14, 1973; "Die Moschee
am Bab al-Mardum in Toledo.." M.M. 18, 1977. The centres of
the lobes of both intrados and extrados are set on the line
of pointed arches. They are regular and concentric at
Malaga and Zaragoza. At Cordoba they are neither concentric
nor do the radii maintain uniformity.

14. A. Fikry, L´Art roman du Puy et les influences
islamiques, Paris 1934, pp 190-196 etc. Fikry´s
documentation only consists of about one hundred examples,
and these include arches of very different architectural
importance, consisting not only of major elements such as
doorways, series of tribune arches and exterior decorative
arcades, but minor isolated windows, niches, niche outlines
within sculptural compositions and decorative motifs on
capitals or impost blocks. His distribution maps can in
fact prove no more than that, even assuming Le Puy had the
earliest lobed arches, Le Puy was an important focus of
inspiration in its own vicinity, and not the direct source
of the use of lobe decoration elsewhere.

15. C. Ewert, "Die Moschee am Bab al-Mardum in Toledo"-
eine ´Kopie´ der Moschee von Córdoba", Madr.Mitt.18, 1977,
figs 5-9.

16. eg Tlemcen AHIII figs 343, 347 and Aljafería portico
294; 12th century, Ewert, "Der Mihrab der Hauptmoschee von
Almería" figs 12 and 13; AHIV fig. 13, p. 18. The tendency
increased in Almohad and later building.

17. AMO, pp 239, 247.

18. A lobed arch in the Tabara Beatus (AD 970): the painting of the Church of Sardis, though the lobed arch is possibly only the upper half of a wheel window. Madrid, Arch.Hist.Nac.Cod. 1097B.

19. K. Conant, The Early History of Santiago de Compostela, fig 21.

20. AHV, p. 212.

21. GG 1938, fig. LXXXVII.

22. AHV, fig 314, p. 188.

23. ARE, fig LXXXIII; J. Williams, Art Bull. 1973, p. 184 gives the reasons for regarding with scepticism this date as signifying that of the completion of the "new" basilica. There is at present no means of establishing the date when the first opening, between the Panteón and Fernando´s church was walled up and this doorway inserted one bay to the south. It must be within "late 11th to mid-12th century".

24. ARE, pp 28-30; Camps Cazorla, op.cit. figs 62-65, pp 96-98; Lasko, Ars Sacra, figs 152,153, p. 157; de Palol & Hirmer pls 74-76; and M. Gomez-Moreno, "El Arca Santa de Oviedo Documentada", AEA XVII, 1945, Pl. III)

25. Ewert, "Malaga",(MM7, 1967), quotes the sketch on the Arca Santa core (fig. 146) to argue that by the 11th century geometric schemata were worked out ahead of building, rather than resorting to mathematical modules.

26. ARE p. 96, pl. CXVIII.

27. G. Gaborit, "Les arcs polylobés dans la Saintonge et l´Angoûmois", Bull.Soc.Archéol.de Saintonge et Aunis V, 1928; R. Crozet, L´Art roman du Berry 1932 lists "Islamic" lobed arches in the province; A. Fikry, Le Puy 1934 Chapter IX p. 185 ff, "Les arcs polylobés"; R. Crozet, "Les arcs polylobés en Berry" and F. Laborderie, "Les arcs polylobés..Limousin" Bull.Fed.Soc.Sav. Centre de la France 1936; Ch. Daras, "L´orientalisme dans l´art roman en Angoûmois" Bull.et Mém.Soc.archéol.et hist. de la Charente 1936: lobed arches are suggested as a means of plotting a network of pilgrimage routes across the Angoûmois; J. Colle and G. Foucaud, "Les arcs polylobés dans les églises d´ Angoûmois-Saintonge" Le Pays d´Ouest 1946, with better photographs than heretofore; P. Héliot, "Les portails polylobés de l´Aquitaine et des régions limitrophes" BM 1946; P. Héliot and M. Menores, "Sur quelques arcs polylobés..."GBA 1950; J. Colle, "Essai sur les influences mozarabes dans l´art roman du Sud-Ouest" Rev.de la Saintonge et d´Aunis 1956 (Lobed arches, quatrefoil columns, concentration of decoration around openings, octagonal towers); E. Vergnolle, Les influences islamiques, l´arc polylobé. Thèse 3e cycle, Paris 1966 (unpub.); id.,

"Les arcs polylobés dans le Centre-Ouest de la France"
Inf.d´Hist.de l´Art V 1969. Héliot (1946), Daras (1936) and
Vergnolle (1966) all give a summary of Boissonnade´s data
concerning the presence of the French in Spain in the later
11th century. L. Torres Balbás, "Nichos y arcos lobulados"
al-And XXI, 1956 pp. 147-172; 1957 pp. 488-495.

28. i.a. E. Bratke, Das Nordportal der Kathedral Saint-
Etienne in Cahors 1977; E. Vergnolle, "Les chapiteaux de La
Berthenoux" GBA 1972; CA 1976 (Velay), passim.

29. Qairawan: dated 836-875. AMO p. 9. By the end of the
9th century the mosque was in essentials more or less as it
was described by al-Bakri two centuries later, and as we
see it now. A. Fikry, La Grande Mosquée de Kairouan, Paris
1934.

30. Conant,CRA p. 118, speaks of the pilasters and paired
columns in the transept elevation at Cluny "inching the
wall outward..". The wall is similarly "inched out" in the
arcades of the Mezquita by means of the pilasters bearing
the upper order of arches; in the maqsura tract, by
colonnettes, cf AHIII figs 129, 135, 154, 156,etc.

31. Early examples at Nevers, Conques south door, Saint-
Hilaire in Poitiers.

32. H. Terrasse, "Chapiteaux oméiyades d´Espagne à la
Mosquée d´al-Qarawiyyin de Fès", al-And.28, 1963; Cluny:
Conant, CRA pl 67b on wall return; see Dl.

33. Lobed altars: P. Deschamps, "Tables d´autel de marbre
exécutées dans le Midi de la France au Xe et au XIe siècle"
Mélanges F. Lot 1925, pp 137-138; M. Durliat, "Tables
d´autel à lobes de la province ecclésiastique de Narbonne
(IXe-XIe ss)" Cah.Arch. XVI 1966, pp 51-75; A.A. Barb,
"Mensa Sacra: The Round Table and the Holy Grail" JWCI xix,
1956.

34. In 1095 Pope Urban II dedicated the main altar:
Durliat, art.cit. p. 163, n.l.

35. Durliat, loc.cit., n.33: Suréda, Gerona, Cornella,
etc.

36. Ewert, Malaga, p. 250 gives evidence that the lobed
arches of the maqsura chapel that have no carved decoration
were painted, and the tradition was maintained in the 11th
century at Malaga and Zaragoza. Id., Cordoba 1978 p. 76:
all stucco facings with red, blue, gold, black outlines;
capitals gold.

37. St Hugh: photograph "Reserves in the attic" of Musée
Ochier in Cluny, in Courtauld Institute Conway Library;
Ulger: Cahn, Doors, fig. 85.

38.   Reconstruction of the west door, K. Conant, Cluny, Les Eglises et la Maison du Chef d´Ordre, Mâcon 1968, fig 185. F. Henry and G. Zarnecki, "Romanesque arches decorated with human and animal heads" JBAA 1958, (repr. G. Zarnecki, Studies in Romanesque Sculpture London 1979) point the connexion with the Catalan area: the doorstep of San Pere de Roda and the Perpignan doorway fragments, figs 150,151.

39.   Durliat, CSMC 1977 p. 20 quotes A. Grabar on the need to investigate how painted apse cycles were used as "models" to "transpose" onto monumental doorways, and this correspondence is accepted or assumed by most writers on the development of the mediaeval Christian doorway, i.a. Y. Christe, Les grands portails romans, Geneva 1969; G. Bandmann, "Zur Bedeutung der romanischen Apsis" Wallraf Richartz Jhb 15, 1953; T.W. Lyman "L´Intégration du portail dans la façade méridionale", CSMC 1977 who concentrates specially on the development of the meaning of arcading in apses and on façades; R. Hamann McLean, "Les origines des portails et façades sculptés gothiques" Gesta XV 1976; D.J. Gardelles, "Façades à étages d´arcatures des églises mediévales", BM 1978. Durliat places the Roussillon "lintels" at the head of Romanesque sculptured doorways. It is not wholly certain that they are in their original position and were not carved as altar frontals or antependia, cf. Lyman, art.cit. p. 60 quoting P. Ponsich, but this uncertainty does not affect the apse/doorway correspondence theory which is supported by other works by those same sculptors: Arles-sur-Tech façade, Perpignan door etc. The existence of lobing exactly like that of the Cluny transept on arcading in the apse of Autun confirms Conant´s conclusion that the lobes were repeated in part of the sanctuary at Cluny too (cf CRA pl. 66; he also gives the nave arcades a torus with overlapping-point lobes). It may be taken that the lobes of the doorway in fact refer to the sanctuary.

40.   Languedoc roman figs 20-25.

41.   P. Ponsich, "Saint-Jean-le-Vieux de Perpignan" CA 112, 1954; id., Etudes romanes III, 1953; M. Durliat, La sculpture romane en Roussillon III, p. 59. P. Ponsich CSMC 11, 1980 for convincing reassertion of dating to 1025.

42.   The connexions of the sculptors of Narbonne and Roussillon with Andalusian sculpture have most recently been pointed by Durliat, CSMC 1978, p. 102; 1979, p. 161; for Ripoll and other associated capitals, F. Hernandez, "Un Aspecto..." AEAA 1930, and G. Gaillard, Premiers essais..., Chapter 1.

43. Andalusian ideas are likely to have impinged on Cluny not only from Spain but from Montecassino whence came a powerful inspiration for Cluny III. North Africa is as likely as Spain to have exerted influence there CRA p. 223.

44. The only certainty about the doorway lobes that can be deduced from surviving drawings and reconstructions appears to be that they were shallow, horseshoe-shaped and framed carvings of angels; their spacing is not clear.

45. eg Corvey, Kunst und Kultur am Weserraum 800-1600 pls 160, 166; A. Barb, JWCI 1956, pl 6. a. Mensa from Ephesos, c. Mensa from Mettlach. Pharaoh's dining table (fig 149) in a miniature in the Vienna Genesis has volute points.

46. Autun lobes: A. Grivot and G. Zarnecki, Gislebertus, Sculptor of Autun 1961, A8 and p. 63.

47. The arcade is illustrated, CA 1923, pl 117: "balustrade re-used on the exterior" and BM 1952, p. 297: "high arcade under cornice on north", apparently indoors. Saint-Maurice in Vienne was begun by Archbishop Léger (1030-1070) and left unfinished at his death. On stylistic grounds it had been assumed since M. Deshoulières (CA 1923) that there was an undocumented "complete rebuilding" of Léger's unfinished church in the mid-12th century (cf J. Vallery-Radot, BM 1936 and 1952), until Gaillard disputed this in 1950 and subsequently ("La date des travées romanes de l'ancienne cathédrale de Saint-Maurice de Vienne", Bull.Soc.Hist.Art Fr., 1950, repr. in Etudes d'Art Roman, Paris 1972; also "Essai de classement des sculptures delphino-rhodaniennes au début de l'époque romane" and "Le tympan de Saint-Alban-du-Rhône" in the same volume). He argues the improbability that Guy de Bourgogne, later Calixtus II, should allow the cathedral church of his see (which he occupied from 1088 to 1119) to remain unfinished throughout his tenancy. There is no evidence that it was not ready for the consecration of the high altar and cemetery in 1107 by Pope Pascal II; Guy was solemnly inducted there as Pope in 1119. To meet the now obligatory proviso that a papal consecration be not taken as the basis for dating the completion of a building, Gaillard proposes completion "shortly after 1107". F. Salet, "Valence" CA 1974, totally rejects this argument and holds to a mid-12th century rebuilding, without producing any new evidence.

48. Two arcades with a horseshoe arch of seven lobes which frames a niche containing a large six-lobed rosette on the minaret of the Great Mosque of Aleppo, finished in 1090: Creswell, MAE, p. 215, fig. 117.

49. BM 1936, pp 288-291; J. Evans, Cluniac Art of the Romanesque Period, Cambridge 1950, pl. 66a.

50. In contrast to Meymac (fig.141) and Vigeois (fig.188) where the next archivolt, like the shallow porch at Dore l'Eglise, gives a definite effect of a raised centre, in the Andalusian manner (F17).

51. The grooving recalls the lobes on the Moissac cloister capital 17 (fig. 194) to be discussed in section VI.

52. Much of the Saintonge was virtually unpopulated until some years into the 12th century. C. Higounet, "Les hommes, la vigne et les églises romanes du Bordelais et du Bazadais", Rev. hist. Bordeaux, 1952 I/2: The Benedictines' need for wine for the host led to large schemes of land reclamation beginning in the 11th century and continuing until the end of the 13th. R.C. Watson, The Early History of the Counts of Angoulême, doct.thesis, Univ. of East Anglia 1978 (unpub.) also stresses the scarcity of population, especially in the Saintonge and even in parts of the Angoûmois until the 12th century.

53. In the time of Abbot Odolric (1025-1040) a white marble altar was brought to Limoges from Narbonne for the abbey of Saint-Martial. A wall had to be breached at Capdenac to get it through, reported by Geoffrey of Vigeois, (qu. M. Durliat, Cah.Arch. 1966).

54. A. Borg, "The Development of Chevron Ornament" JBAA XXX, 1967, pp. 122-140.

55. Also AMO, figs 22 (Qairawan), 39 (Sousse), 55 (Qala´a of the Beni Hammad).

56.See also Section IV: at Saint-Robert they are again associated with chevron.

57. Porche du For, dated late 12th century by Durliat, CA 1976. This arch is built over an earlier opening.

58. It was particularly popular in England, eg. the choir exterior at Canterbury, and thence to a number of churches in Kent.

59. F. Henry and G. Zarnecki, art.cit.: the authors note the animal head framed in a V-shaped leaf motif transposed from Cordoban basins. Andalusian also are the emphasized extrados of lobed arches and the outlined voussoirs very marked at Angers and Aunay (fig 330); the human head with animal ears referred by these authors to Roman models also occurs on Cordoban marble basins and on Islamic and Mozarabic ivories. Heads are already associated with lobes on the outer archivolt of Cluny doorway.

60. The jambs of Souillac have not survived; another example of this type of doorway is vouched for by fragments in the museum at Brive.

61. Rhône valley, see below. Champagne has superposed columns (F9) supporting the ribs of the nave vaults.

62. R. Crozet, "Petites églises de la vallée du Gallego (Espagne)", CCM 1969/3. The series of churches all has twin columns on the interior walls to support the vault ribs (F6).

63. A. Heimann, "The Master of Gargilesse, a French Sculptor of the First Half of the Twelfth Century", JWCI 1979.

64. J. Evans, Cluniac Art..pl. 129b; at Souvigny the abacus is lobed, 3b.

65. Palencia casket: J. Beckwith, CC pl. 32; AHIII fig.369; EK Elf, No 43.

66. The impost block now surmounting capital 17 is carved with masked bacchanalean figures of Roman (ultimately oriental, cf. O.M. Dalton, The Treasure of the Oxus, London 1964, No 18, fig. 43, p. 8) inspiration. They raise the possibility of closer connexions between Moissac and Le Puy than previously established, (cf. the cloister frieze at Le Puy, and fragments of cornice carvings in the museum there) which need further investigation. These prancing figures are at Anzy-le-Duc and also at Lyon in Saint-Martin d´Ainay, strengthening the evidence for contacts between Moissac and the Rhône/Velay - on the route to Cluny of course. Moissac´s link through Durannus with the Auvergne has already been stressed in Chapter III.

67. Durliat, Cah.Arch. 1966.

68. Possibly five lobes at the arches of the west façade. Although Viollet-le-Duc declared that Mallay had reserved the "grandiose and original aspect" of the west façade, there is some doubt about the upper part with small five-lobed arches.

69. CA 1976. The bell tower: the first two or three storeys [?]1130 or later; the rest not finished until 1180 or later. It was rebuilt to the old design in 1887; Saint-Michel d´Aiguilhe: façade, 1180; Saint-Clair chapel, c. 1180; west end and façade of cathedral, 1180.

70. ibid., p. 324.

71. ibid., p. 453. I am much indebted to Prof. Bousquet for photographs of the trilobes (fig 177) and for his helpful comments.

72. But the jointing of the arches is more primitive; ibid., p. 455, fig. 10; GG 1938, pls LXXXII-LXXXIII.

73. J. Bousquet, "Le Monastier", CA 1976, pp. 444-445.

74. ibid., p. 153; J. Vallery-Radot, "De Limoges à Brantôme, au Puy et à Valence" GBA 1929, pp. 265-284, countered the accepted view that Brantôme was the earliest of the "Limousin" belfries and regarded it as a simplified imitation of the towers of Sainte-Marie and the cathedral at Limoges, which also radiated their influence to Le Puy and Valence. The type of belfry was possibly in the Quercy by the early 12th century since it is portrayed on the

porch relief of the Flight into Egypt at Moissac. The crossing tower at Collonges, another of the same type, is variously dated to early 12th century (J. Maury, <u>Limousin roman</u>) and 1140 or after (M.-M. Macary, <u>Collonges</u> 1972). At both Moissac and Collonges there were trilobe arches, but not of Le Puy design (Section IIIa).

75. <u>CA</u> 1976, p. 480. The south façade trilobe appears to be monolithic.

76. P. Ponsich, "Architecture préromane de Saint-Michel de Cuxa et sa véritable signification", <u>CSMC</u> 1971, pp. 17-27: Andalusian horseshoe arches have jambs as wide apart as the widest part of the arch above; Persian, Roman and Visigothic arches have jambs as close as the imposts.

77. <u>CA</u> 1976, p. 593.

78. <u>ibid</u>., Saint-Vidal, p. 647, second half of 12th century; Lardayrol, p. 593, same date; Bains, p. 633: given to Conques by Pons de Polignac in 1105, but the door is again after 1150. Chamalières, p. 471, the same, etc.

79. The soffits of the tribune arches are grooved to make a longitudinal decoration like arches in the Mezquita (<u>AHIII</u> fig. 214) and the Aljaferìa (<u>ibid</u>., fig.293). The latter are of plaster and are pointed arches with many lobes.

80. illustrated in <u>BM</u> 1936, p. 306; the door, <u>CA</u> 1935, p. 144. Saint-Pierre in Vienne, not finished at the death of Abbot Goulard in 1107. The porch and tower are dated 1161 by Deshoulières.

81. <u>BM</u> 1936, p. 297; illustrated <u>BM 1952</u>, p. 356; <u>CA</u> 1974, p. 546.

82. For example the altar frontal of white marble carved with rows of different sized and shaped rosettes, K.J. Conant, <u>Cluny</u> 1968, fig. 184; rosettes on the towers of Cluny, <u>ibid</u>., fig. 188 and Tournus. A cornice soffit from Ile Barbe (<u>BM 1936</u>, p. 302) shows Andalusian scrolls round a rosette more elaborate than the standard Auvergnat soffit type.

83. A. Duran i Sanpere, "La Torre Poligonal (num. 6) de la Muralla Romana", <u>Cuadernos de Arqueol. y Hist.de la Ciudad</u>, Barcelona 1969, no 13, p. 51, figs 7, 11-13.

84. M. Durliat, <u>CA</u> 1976, pp. 19 ff., refers to the trade route north to the Champagne, the many contacts of Le Puy and Le Monastier with the Empire and with Piedmont, and the route linking Lyon and Toulouse via Le Puy, with an emphasis more on trade than on pilgrimages.

85. The squinch domes of Saint-Martin-d´Ainay in Lyon can be dated 1107 and resemble those of Tournus also. Vallery-

Radot, "La limite méridionale.." BM 1936 accepted that Le Puy received its dome form from the Rhône but believed the trilobes of the area derive from Le Puy. To do so now is to insist on an unreasonably late dating of building activity in the Rhône valley, since Le Puy is put so late.

86. CA 1935, p. 108. On p. 111 are masks similar to those of the vertical marble plaque of Moissac doorway (fig. 74).

87. Durliat, CA 1976, discusses in his Introduction the group of capitals at Le Puy of the second half of the 11th century in the Roda tradition with fleurons and interlace, "The most lively type until the figured and historiated sculpture of Saint-Sernin and Moissac". He quotes Aurillac, Conques, Nant, Saint-Guillaume-le-désert, various Languedoc churches. The type goes as far north as Issoudun. He does not include the Berry or Cluny, where figured sculpture is likely to be earlier than that of Saint-Sernin and Moisssac; Vergnolle, GBA 1972.

88. Limousin roman, pp. 100-101. A consecration in 1143 is accepted by him as a likely date ante quem for Solignac.

89. cf. J.-Cl. Fau, "Un décor original.." CSMC 1978.

90. The church is reported in Rouergue roman as given to Saint-Victor, Marseilles, probably at the same time as Bozouls nearby in 1082. Bousquet, Chapiteaux.. p. 183 agreed with Gaillard in dating Saint-Pierre shortly after this donation, but in "Le Monastier" CA 1976 he corrects this account and states that it was a priory given to Pébrac en Velay in 1085. "Its stylistic links with that region should be underlined".

91. The pine cone motif on the panels flanking the altar trilobe is a link with the Andalusian sources of the latter workshop, through San Pere de Roda: J.-Cl. Fau, op.cit., p. 131 and id., "L'apparition de la figure humaine dans la sculpture du Rouergue au XIe siècle", Actes XXVIIe Congr.Soc.Sav., Montauban 1972. Similarity with a jamb fragment of the great west door, Conant, Cluny 1968, which has pine cone and crossed stem in something of the same style as the Bessuéjouls altar, might suggest this dating of the altar is too early. The interlace medallions however are in its favour.

92. Saint-Etienne in Nevers, begun about 1083 under the stimulus of large gifts, and it is reported as complete with its towers at the time of its dedication (15th December, 1097): CRE p. 115.

93. ARE pp. 120-124; AHV p. 123. The idea would thus be bandied to and fro. From Nevers perhaps to Santiago, where it was re-shaped by Andalusian models. From Santiago back to the Auvergne. Meanwhile the roll corbel travels in the opposite direction, having been long in the Auvergne in the form in which it reached Santiago ?.

94. <u>AMO</u> p. 76, fig. 39.

95. <u>ibid</u>., plate, p. 95.

96. <u>ibid</u>., fig. 50. Marçais, p. 127, dwells on the commercial importance of the coastal cities of Ifriqiya after the Hilalian invasion of the mid-11th century devastated the cities of the interior. They needed vast supplies of wood (M. Lombard, "Un problème cartographique; le bois dans la Méditerranée musulmane, VIIe-XIe siècle", <u>Annales E.S.C.</u>, 1959/1) and travelled far to find it. The Rhône might well bring down timber as well as slaves, furs, etc.

97. Dated by Conant <u>CRE</u> c.1130.

98. M. Vieillard-Trouerikoff, "L'ancienne cathédrale de Clermont..", <u>Cah.Arch</u>. 1960, pp. 199-247.

99. "Limousin moulding" is a narrow torus set in the angle between successive archivolts, usually carved on the inside edge of a voussoir; it is often but not always continued down the corresponding jamb as a thin nook shaft or colonnette of the same diameter, with or without a small capital at the impost line. In the Limousin the capital is frequently undecorated. This moulding is found mainly on doors and windows in the Limousin (Hte Vienne, Corrèze) but with outliers in Quercy and Poitou, Périgord and Angoûmois, throughout the 12th century.

100. R. Rey, <u>La cathédrale de Cahors</u> 1937; Devic & Vaissette, <u>Hist. de Languedoc</u>, II, p. 385.

101. The dating of Moissac porch sculpture is still fluid, based on extrapolations from the only written authority, the Chronicle of the abbey written by Aymery de Peyrac, abbot from 1377 to 1406. Abbot Ansquitil (+1115) is credited with the "portale pulcherrimum..". His successor Roger's statue crowns it. For Angoulême, P.M. Tonnelier, "La date de consécration de la cathédrale d'Angoulême" in <u>Mél. Crozet</u>, p. 507; P. Dubourg-Noves, <u>Iconographie de la Cathédrale d'Angoulême..</u>, 1973.

102. H. Saladin, <u>La mosquée de Sidi Okba à Kairouan</u>, Paris 1899, pl. XIV. Points decorated with flowers, perhaps contemporary, at Tlemcen: W. Marçais, <u>Les monuments arabes de Tlemcen</u> Paris 1899, p. 147, fig. 15.

103. M. Vidal, <u>Quercy roman</u>, p. 96. In conversation she confirmed that there are surviving fragments that justify the trilobed twin doorways "in principle".

104. M. Méras, <u>Saint-Antonin-Noble-Val</u>, Rodez 1969, p. 27.

105. M.-M. Macary, <u>Collonges</u>, 1972, p. 1

106 <u>Quercy roman</u>, figs 22-25.

107. Conques, <u>Defourneaux</u>, p.14 (possessions in Navarre), p. 151 (mosque in Barbastro); Saint-Pons: <u>ibid</u>., p. 150 (mosque in Huesca); La Sauve: <u>ibid</u>., p. 154 (rights in Ejéa).

108. M. Schapiro, <u>Romanesque Art</u> p. 50; J.-M. Lacarra, <u>Un arancál de aduanas del siglo XI</u>, Zaragoza 1950; A. Meillon, <u>Les possessions de l´Abbaye de Saint-Savin de Lavedan à Saragosse au XIIe siècle</u>, Tarbes 1923.

109. E. Mâle, <u>L´Art religieux du XIIe siècle</u>, 1923; L. Grodecki, "Le problème des sources iconographiques du tympan de Moissac", <u>Moissac et l´Occident au XIe siècle</u>, Toulouse 1964; N. Mezoughi, "Le tympan de Moissac, études d´iconographie" <u>CSMC</u> 9, 1978, pp. 171-200.

110. Many typically Limousin features are found early at Moissac: Limousin moulding; the lobed profile adopted at La Souterraine and Le Dorat; the gabled belfry pictured on the relief of the Flight into Egypt (<u>Quercy roman</u>, fig. 23, also pictured at Beaulieu, fig. 144); Macary, <u>Collonges</u> 1972 quotes MM. and S. Gauthier, <u>Visages du Limousin et de la Marche</u> 1950 as suggesting that the tower of Saint-Martial in Limoges initiated the gabled belfry. Vidal opines that the relief illustrates a local monument "in the area by about 1110".

111. P. Héliot, "Observations sur les façades à arcades aveugles..dans les églises romanes", <u>Bull.Soc.Ant.Ouest</u> 4, 1958, pp. 364-458: Meymac was given in 1085 to Uzerche, and building began then.

112. Vigeois: <u>Limousin roman</u>, p. 24. The church was built between 1082 and 1124. A. de Laborderie, <u>Bull. Soc. Arch. Corrèze</u> iv, 1932.

113. This is an early version of the "serpentiform impost" from which Almohad art "drew a more elegant and richer form" (<u>AMO</u>, p. 233). Marçais traces its beginning from stelae in Qairawan of the early 11th century, through a basin in the Qala´a of the Beni Hammad and the Aljafería (mid-11th century) to Tlemcen and Rabat in the 12th. "It might be considered as a memory of Vitruvius´ "prothyrid console" but the Hispano-maghrebi decorators endow it with plant apparel formed of long palm leaves which accommodate it to the general spirit of the style". The up-turned curl at Zaragoza is peculiar to this site.

114. No measured drawings are available. The following observations apart from references to Cahors south door are deductions from photographs, as are all the calculations of Cazorla in <u>Modulo...</u> I am very grateful to George Michell for his measured drawings at Cahors, Le Puy and Bains.

115. Pointed arches are common in the Limousin from an early date. cf. Limousin roman, p. 49: "le tracé brisé, indiscutablement préféré en Limousin dès la fin du 11e siècle" (indisputably the preferred form in the Limousin from the late 11th century).

116. The same form of intrados is used on the façade of Petit-Palais, Gironde, for the arcades flanking the semicircular lobed doorway; the arches above are round horseshoes (fig 197).

117. Aleppo: MAE fig. 117, p. 215; Sfax, AMO, pp. 95, 102; Spain: Maldonado, Toledo, fig. 8.

118. Anglo-Saxon pen case in British Museum, J. Beckwith, Ivory Carvings in Early Mediaeval England", London 1972, No 46.

119. Corbel from Reading, Victoria & Albert Museum; Cordoban corbels.

120. cf. AHV, Zamora Cathedral, fig. 411; La Magdalena, Zamora, fig. 430; Oseiro, fig. 504; Orense, fig. 512; Cirauqui, fig. 302; Puente la Reina, fig. 303; Estella, not illustrated.

121 See n. 76

122 The lobed doorway of Déols has hood moulding with foliage carving while the Moissac jambs have a ribbon edging. Most Limousin lobed arches are strictly undecorated.

123. Quercy roman, difa 29, 30.

124. The niche arches of Saint-Pierre-Toirac are on colonnettes and capitals, and the trilobe is concentric. Nonetheless, the moulding of its intrados, its proximity to Cahors and its early date all argue for its inclusion at the beginning of the Limousin series, before the norms became established. It may provide a link between the trilobe arches of Le Monastier, also of this shape and on columns and capitals, and the Cahors series.

125. The plait capitals are of a type similar to those of Aurillac and Figeac, J.-Cl. Fau, CSMC 1978; they have the "galons perlés" of the end of the series; J. Bousquet, Les Chapiteaux de Conques 1956. The rectangular thick ribs on the crossing F22 are an early feature.

126. C. Enlart, "L'église du Waast en Boulonnais", GBA 1927. P. Héliot, CA 1936.

127. cf. K. Creswell, MAE.

128. This does not preclude the possibility of an influence from Egypt two decades later, which would be more

appropriate for this doorway. Recorded journeys of individuals can only be regarded as indications representing many more unrecorded connexions.

129. A letter from Osmond, bishop of Astorga, to Ide concerning relics; it is countersigned by Alfonso VI (Chalandon, Histoire de la première croisade, Paris 1925, pp. 196, 264); Héliot, BM 1946.

130. K. Creswell, MAE.

131. AHIII fig. 293, and cf. a "large roll-corbel with leaves carved on the soffit...of stucco" from a house in Elvira, ibid., p. 173 and fig. 231.

132. AHV, Zamora cathedral fig. 411; Sa Maria la Mayor de Toro, figs 423, 424; Salamanca San Martin, fig. 433; San Juan del Mercado, fig. 434.

133. A similar kind of point is on the trilobes of the diaphragm wall ajimez at Champagne.

134. AHV, fig. 283; Mozarabic capitals: Ig.Moz., figs 435, 452 for example. Later Islamic arches, on the contrary, tend to break up the line of lobes into finer and finer points, cf. AHIV, figs 2,3,13, in an evolution towards the creation of stalactite ceilings.

135. Saintonge romane, fig. 147.

136. ibid., figs 1, 98; Avy, fig. 166, has vertical cylinders on a fluted cornice.

137. F. Henry and G. Zarnecki, "Arches decorated..", pl.VII,4; Saintonge romane, fig. 139.

138. Saintonge romane: Saint-Eutrope, Saintes, fig.1; Corme Royale, fig. 71; Saint-Quentin de Rançanne, fig. 147; Vandré, fig. 207; Nuaillé, fig. 208; Abbaye aux Dames, Saintes, fig. 22, the lower window.

139. J. Evans, Art in Mediaeval France, Oxford 1948, pl. 16, "c.1100".

140. Saintonge romane , fig. 192.

141. Saintonge romane , fig. 185. Bellegarde (Loiret) and Pezou (LetCher) fig 163, are examples of its use away from this area where it is commonest.

142. R. Sanchez Ventura, "Un grupo de iglesias del Alto Aragon", AEAA 1933, pp. 215-235; Aragon roman, pl. 16 and pp. 123-4.

143. See Aragon roman p. 123, and I have heard similar comments in the faculty at Zaragoza.

144. However, the niches on Bab Zuweila in Cairo share this feature (fig 140).

145.A fragment now used in the setting of the grille flanking the door to the south, carved with foliage, has a curved border suggesting that a lobed arch was represented in the carved plant decoration a century or more before structural lobed arches were built in the Mezquita. It may on the other hand only be part of a curved scroll stem (AHIII fig. 38).

146. AHIV, figs 100-103.

147. H. Terrasse, Art hispano-mauresque, fig. LXV.

148. As stressed by E. Vergnolle in her thesis 1966.

149. Multiple lobed arches all belong to the group with Limousin moulding: Cahors, Vigeois, La Souterraine etc. Petit-Palais with its series undercut in depth only has moulding on some lobes, and is perhaps to be regarded as the exception.

150. C. Ewert, Balaguer 1971, pls 12-15, 44.

151. ibid., pls 12, 13, 34, 35.

152. ibid., pls 13, 31 and 34b show motifs apopropriate to ivory or textiles. The town was important for trade as well as defence. The castle changed hands often in the last years of the century, or was held under tribute, and finally taken by Urgel in 1105.

153. Andalusian and Mozarabic ivory carvings, as all authorities agree, are an important element in the style of the capitals at Saintes (Saintonge romane , figs 13, 14), and these in their turn are a patent source for later sculpture in the Saintonge.

154. L. Anfrey, L´Architecture religieuse en Nivernais au moyen-âge, Paris 1951, refers to many towers with polylobed arches influenced by La Charité, eg. Rouy, Garduzy, Saint-Eusèbe in Auxerre, Saint-Laurent l´Abbaye, Semelay, Varzy. Tournus probably represents what was imitated by La Charité from Cluny.

CHAPTER V

ANDALUSIAN FEATURES IN ROMANESQUE DECORATION

III. THE ROLL CORBEL

Stone corbels carved with lobes down the profile, and with this motif carried across the front to simulate a series of horizontal rods, constitute a distinctive group among the many forms of Romanesque corbel. They will be discussed in this chapter under the term "roll corbel" (1).

Since the publication in 1923 of the second of Mâle´s articles on Islamic elements in Romanesque architecture (2) the ultimate Andalusian origin of the feature has been universally accepted. In 1936 Torres-Balbás reviewed the whole history of the form from its origins in Roman corbels, but French examples have received little systematic study (3).

The division by Torres-Balbás of Romanesque roll corbels into three broad classes is a useful descriptive classification:
i. Plain "rod corbels" (modillones con baquetones)
ii. "Wood-shaving corbels" (modillons à copeaux, henceforth "fillet roll corbels"): the rods are interrupted, or tied, across the face by a vertical fillet of varying width which generally projects beyond the rods and is either plain, or carved with incised decoration
iii. Roll corbels on which the central fillet is replaced by a plant, mask or figure motif in high relief. Animal and human heads form a large proportion of this class.

All these types have antecedents in Andalusian corbels, and before discussing their associations in France it is helpful to look at the context and development of different types in Andalusia and in Christian Spain (4).

The method of roofing whereby eaves are carried on a stone corbel table is one of the most frequent and distinctive characteristics of Romanesque architecture throughout France. The only example of its use before the Romanesque period however is not in France but in Spain, first in Andalusia, and from the 10th century on Mozarabic buildings in the north as well. In both cases the corbels are exclusively of roll form. In the Mezquita roll corbels appear in the second third of the 9th if not in the 8th century. With one exception they are the only form used. The multiplicity of levels at which the influence of a single element of one culture can operate on another is vividly illustrated by the history of this feature, in which the adoption into Romanesque of the Cordoban roll form with many adaptations (including elimination of the roll) accompanies the wholesale acceptance of both the corbel table itself as a structural device and the decorative use of corbels in general.

Roll corbels in Andalusia: shape

The most elementary form of roll corbel, and probably the earliest (5) is seen on the interior arcades of the first mosque (fig.2). These examples are not independent members of a corbel table, but parts of the cruciform stone imposts supporting pilasters that rise to carry the upper wider rows of arches, while the other two arms are the springers of the horseshoe arches of the arcades. These arms are carved in a concave profile, corresponding to the spring of the horseshoe arches, and the face is carved to simulate three or more rods laid horizontally one above the other between a flat vertical face above and a fillet below. Variations in the height of the columns, all of which were reused, could be adjusted by the height of this impost, and the number of rods thus varies between three and four-and-a half.

This basic form is subsequently found on elements other than corbels in Andalusian building into the 11th century and later, particularly door pivots, gargoyles and arches (fig.29), and the profile of machicoulis in mediaeval fortifications both Muslim and Christian can be seen to derive from it. Mozarabic corbels also mostly consist of an extension of this form.

Rod corbels in the Mezquita: decoration

Some corbels on the arcades of the earliest part of the Mezquita are carved on the sides of the lobes with circles in low relief, to imitate the ends of the rods. Many more are carved with foliage in very low relief all over the side; often in this case curling tendrils correspond to the rod ends; alternatively heavy curls spring from among the leaves. This latter decoration, distinguishing the architectural and plant motifs, is foreshadowed in an unusual merlon from Palmyra, of the 1st or 2nd century AD, decorated with a series of volutes among acanthus (6).

The rare surviving traces of colour observed by F. Hernandez Jimenez (7) in the shallow hollows on the carved sides of corbels in the Mezquita suggest that originally all the corbels of the arcades were painted with plant scrolls even when they were not carved.

Fillet Roll Corbels: the Corbels of the San Esteban Door Cornice

The nine uniform corbels supporting the cornice over the San Esteban door are each carved with six rolls (AHIII fig.68)(8). The face is divided by a central narrow fillet which runs vertically from the vertical face at the top to the level of the underside of the first roll; this roll is set back from the plane of the face. The fillet then turns sharply to follow the concave curve of the profile and still projects beyond the plane of the lobes at each side.

These corbels are too inaccessible and too weathered to show much original decoration, but it can be seen that some had curls carved on the sides, and others had circles marking the roll ends, with a hollowed dot at the centre.

Fillet Roll Corbels: the Corbels of the North Façade of the Mezquita

Fillet corbels similar to those over the San Esteban door were used in 958 on the Mezquita to support the eaves of Abd ar-Rahman III´s reinforcement of the north façade of the sanctuary giving onto the patio. Here the edges of the sides are decorated with interlaced lines to represent the rod ends, or curls, and the front vertical face and shallow central fillet, wider than the fillets over the San Esteban door, are carved with simple chip-carved geometric or stylized plant motifs such as linked palmette scrolls. They all have seven rolls (AHIII fig. 96; LTB 1957, figs 269-273).

The eaves overhang the wall to a considerable extent, and the corbels therefore are elongated horizontally more than those previously described. On Mozarab buildings of this century the eaves tend to be even wider and corbels correspondingly more horizontal in shape relative to the vertical.

Fillet Roll Corbels: Interior Arcades of the Second Extension

al-Hakam II´s extension (961-965) being provided with newly-made columns, the imposts were all of a height; the corbels nearly all have a uniform five-and-a half rolls. Their surface decoration uses a great variety of motifs however, though these are always very restrained; they include inscriptions, grooves, cording, strapwork interlace, or simple geometric patterns (LTB 1957 figs 278 and 363-365). Another innovative variation was to eliminate the vertical face at the top and give the profile a smooth S-curve; the central fillet barely projects, or is sometimes even cut away and left as a hollow; it still follows the same profile as the rod ends. Some corbels of this type in the central aisle are double, with two fillets or grooves. The sides may be left as plain lobes [for painting?] or carved with circles, curls etc. Usually in France the vertical face is pronounced, but on the Porte Miègeville corbels of Saint-Sernin (fig 220) and on some others in south-west France it is much reduced in height.

Fillet Roll Corbels: Almanzor´s Extension

The third extension of 987 contains many fillet corbels, both on the interior arcades and on the patio façade (LTB 1957 figs 379-381). Some are carved on the sides with curls, and there remain occasional traces of the red paint that emphasized the hollows. Often the curls on one side, or just a bottom curl, or all but the top one,

are turned upward instead of down. This detail, especially
applied to the bottom curl, recurs on roll corbels at
Santiago, and in an early context in France, at Tournus,
and at Conques over the north transept door; this is the
classic "Auvergnat" corbel with many examples in the
vicinity of Clermont which closely resemble those of this
type in Almanzor´s extension, as many authorities have
observed (fig 222).

Though Almanzor´s columns are uniform in height the
number of rolls, and hence their size, is much less uniform
in this building campaign than in the previous one. The
rolls vary in number from five to seven; corbels with the
greater number of smaller rolls are on the easternmost
arcades, and on the sides of these the lobes are left
without emphasis or carving.

Twin windows (F11) under arches flank Almanzor´s
series of doorways on the east façade exterior. They are
supported in the centre by a colonnette on a console. This
console is a fillet roll corbel, with the fillet so
extended as to produce a rectangular profile (AHIII fig
219) (9).

 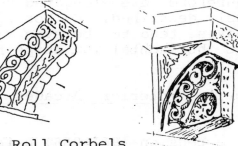 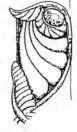

Decorative Fillet Roll Corbels

The roll corbel was evidently de rigueur in 10th
century Andalusia; some craftsmen more concerned with
decoration than form, while making no attempt to shape
their corbels into lobes, still made the form implicit in
the decoration. This created another variant of the fillet
corbel consisting in a smooth unlobed profile that might be
concave or square, with the different planes of rolls and
fillet eliminated altogether, but with the concave profile,
or imitation concave profile on the square, carved with a
border of circles or curls. In the most numerous cases
these were expressed as the tendrils of a plant scroll
covering the whole side, with a stem sprouting curling
tendrils or leaves to trace the concave profile line.

This motif appears as a simulated corbel carved at the
top outer corners of the marble wall-facings of the mihrab,
on a rectangular projection that is made to look as though
it supports the arch and alfiz. The concave profile
outlined by the curled tendrils is followed by the stem of
a leaf, and the leaf itself curls round to fill the rest of
the rectangle: the "down-turned leaf" motif (fig.19)(D16).

From the mid-10th century this scroll-carved corbel,
with a concave, oblique or rectangular profile, was used

frequently in Andalusian buildings, for example on the doorways of al-Hakam II´s halls in Madinat az-Zahra´ (<u>fig.</u> 230, <u>AHIII</u> fig.209), and the doorways of his and then of Almanzor´s extensions to the Mezquita (<u>AHIII</u> figs 192,193).

Stone and plaster corbels with similar decoration are preserved in the museums of Malaga, Granada, Almería and Toledo (<u>AHIII</u> figs 322, 264, 231). At Tudela the fillet roll corbels of the mosque, probably of the late 10th century (<u>fig</u> 45) are of two types, both based on models at Madinat az-Zahra´. One has a classic concave profile, the other a straight oblique profile (10); in both cases there is plant decoration on the sides and the curls are interpeted as half-palmettes of different types. The marble basin from Seville in the National Museum in Madrid, made for Almanzor´s palace of al-Zahira, is carved on one long side with a relief of trilobe arcades resting on such corbels (<u>AHIII</u> fig.249).

Plaster Corbels

The decorated or elaborated fillet, like the motifs in higher relief of the corbels on the arcades of the second and third extensions to the Mezquita and on Almanzor´s north façade are added in plaster (11). Splendid plaster corbels with decorated fillet and scroll carving on the sides have been found in excavations at the Great Mosque of Almería, dating probably from the first half of the 12th century (12). Much use was also made of plaster in the Aljafería, including the supports of the ribbed vault, remains of which are now shared between the museums of Zaragoza and Madrid. The striking feature of these members is an advanced development of the down-turned leaf motif; it introduces a distinct type of Andalusian corbel, precursor of the most characteristic and inventive types of Romanesque corbel (<u>fig.</u> 52).

The Down-turned Leaf Motif.

This motif which we have aleady met on the simulated corbels of the mihrab panels of the Mezquita was employed two decades earlier at Madinat az-Zahra´, on corbels along the eaves on the terrace of the Salon Rico (AD 946)(13). They are carved with rolls on either side of a strongly dominant central convex leaf (<u>fig.</u>20): one is reminded of the convex shape of the arcade corbels of Abd ar-Rahman II´s extension (<u>AHIII</u> fig.48). Torres-Balbás describes the form, to be perpetuated for some centuries in wood in Spain and the Maghreb, as "prow-shaped". Rougher limestone versions among the fragments recovered in excavations (14) show that doorway arches in Madinat az-Zahra´ were supported on consoles of similar design. The motif is interpreted too as a simple shell, done in plaster, on some impost corbels in the arcades of the last two extensions of the Mezquita, including some in the central nave of al-Hakam II (15).

In the 11th century the leaf or "prow" motif developed independently. It was especially popular for wooden beam ends; examples survive from the Aljafería, Malaga, Granada (AHIII figs 290, 317, 316). The culmination is in Segovia, where it alternates with roll corbels in the supports for the wooden roof of the nave of the church of San Millán (16) already described in Chapter II (fig.46).

On the complex carved plaster support of the dome of the oratory in the Aljafería (fig.52, AHIII fig.287) a tall vertical leaf bracket with bracts overlapping its point ("prow") is recessed by cube-shaped corbels projecting above and below it. These latter are basically of square profile, with the outer corner finished as a thin dowel. Analogies for this shape are found in North Africa (17) and (fig.223) in Le Mans, where they may be equally early (18). The Aljafería corbels are all decorated with carved scrolls, and on some of these the scrolls form a concave line of circles or curls, as on the mihrab panel corbels of the Mezquitá, but this line is no longer treated as an essential part of the design: on many the "rod end" curls have been abandoned and the surface decoration pays scant regard to architectural function, conforming to the general disregard of structure in the decoration of this building. The vertical leaf of the brackets is a direct copy of the caliphal down-turned leaf. The small corbels above and below them, having softened into a flattened S-curve their rectangular profile which originally had contained the leaf motif, show how relief motifs other than a leaf or shell, such as were exploited in Romanesque corbel art, might evolve.

This down-turned leaf or shell is entirely at variance with the classical norms of upward growth; it origin is certainly Andalusian and not Roman. It is only an occasional motif on Romanesque corbels, where its place is occupied by animate motifs in full relief, or a more classical "tongue" leaf with an upward lift (19); but what has previously been overlooked entirely is its adoption in Romanesque decoration to an important function in the design of certain types of capital, as a replacement of the volute. The leaf volutes on the capitals of the late 10th and early 11th century at Ripoll (fig.21), Cornelha, Vich and Bages in Catalunya, whose Andalusian inspiration has been analysed by Hernandez and Gaillard (20), have a direct sequel at Santiago, Loarre, Conques and Moissac (figs 21-25) and after them throughout France in the 12th century; a rustic example is Mourens in the Agenais (fig.26). They may well have contributed also to the "leaf canopy" concept at Saint-Benoît-sur-Loire which had a sequel in the Berry with renewed reference to roll corbels (Berry roman figs 56, 93).

Mozarabic Roll Corbels

The roll form of corbel is one of the several Andalusian architectural features brought to northern Spain in the 10th century by Mozarab émigrés (22). One of their earliest surviving buildings, San Miguel de Escalada, founded in AD 913, has examples round the apse of shapes that are close to the Cordoban model (23). In general however Mozarabic corbels have three distinctive characteristics which put them outside the sequence from Andalusian to Romanesque.

a) The topmost roll is larger in diameter than the rest, thus reverting closer to the usual Visigothic shape, with a single heavy cylinder-shaped roll, that long survived in the Asturias (24).

b) They support for the most part very wide eaves, and are thus elongated horizontally (sometimes vertically as well, to balance) in comparison with the Cordoban, while keeping about the same thickness. Exceptions to this generalization are the many roof corbels at San Millán de Suso (Cogolla) (fig.227)(25), which originally retained the square profile of the Cordoban rectangular type, and the classical Cordoban consoles supporting the horseshoe arches of the pseudo-dome of San Miguel de Celanova (AHIII fig.449). In contrast outside, under the eaves, run typical elongated Mozarab corbels.(26).

c) The concave profile is usually abandoned in favour of a straight oblique line, as already assumed by some corbels at Madinat az-Zahra´ (fig.230). An exception is Hornija, where the roof corbels retain a strong concave profile (27).

Mozarabic eaves corbels are decorated on the sides with the traditional sub-Roman and Visigothic chip-carved rosettes and helices appropriate to wood carving. The pierced flange of some corbels at San Millán de Suso also suggests a woodworking rather than a stone-carving tradition. While there is clearly a debt to corbels like those on Almanzor´s east façade doorways, the handling of the decoration shows strong influence from carpentry practices.

Wooden Corbels

Wooden corbels survive in Christian architecture in Spain (none is reported from France) from the Asturian church of Valdedíos (AD 893), the Mozarabic church of San Miguel de Escalada (AD 913) and the ceiling of the church of San Millán in Segovia (28). Two wooden corbels survive from the series that ran along the whole length of the nave roof at Escalada. They are identical in form with the stone corbels that support the gables at either end of the eaves (29).

In trying to trace from surviving examples how the corbel form was transmitted to Romanesque architecture, the rare presence among them of corbels of plaster and wood is a reminder that the perishable nature of these materials makes it impossible for us to be acquainted with more than the vestiges of a building practice that included at least as much activity on the part of plasterer and carpenter as

of the worker in stone. The history of the introduction of
the roll corbel, or indeed of any kind of corbel, to
Romanesque architecture will thus always be fragmentary,
and furthermore the rôle of secular building practices in
this history is entirely without Romanesque illustration.
Fig.309 is an illustration of a modern secular reference to
this ancient tradition. Where wood and plaster corbels
survive in Andalusia and Christian Spain however they are
exactly like their stone counterparts, and this fact must
compensate in some measure for the fact that the major,
perishable part of the evidence needed to complete the
history has not survived (30).

Ceramic Corbels

A few pre-Romanesque ceramic corbels survive in
France, at Pommiers (Loire), Germigny-des-Prés and Saint-
Benoît-sur-Loire (31). They are all very thin and only made
to hold a shallow decorative cornice. They do not therefore
enter into consideration of the origins of the Romanesque
corbel, which was primarily a structural member.

It must be emphasized that apart from these ceramic
examples no corbels of any kind exist in French
architecture that might be considered as antecedents of the
Romanesque corbel.

Corbels in North Spain

The presence of roll corbels on Romanesque buildings
in Spain is no cause for surprise. They follow logically as
the next group to be discussed, though the earliest
Romanesque corbels to survive are probably in France, at La
Trinité in Vendôme, Poitiers, Jumièges and Conques.

Plain rod corbels of stone have recently been
uncovered in place in the Aljafería, intended as housings
for the pivots of doors (32). Such pieces are prototypes of
the most common type in 12th century Spanish Romanesque:
carved into plain horizontal rods on a concave curve,
usually with no indication of curls or other decoration on
the side. These were the standard support for eaves and
weather roofs over doorways right through the 12th century
on numerous rural churches (fig.231).

Double and Composite Rolls

Undecorated roll corbels with a double series of rods,
created by lobing a wide central fillet, now crown a rubble
wall, probably of the 14th century, near the gateway of the
castle of Gormaz. The castle was built by the semi-
independent rulers of Zaragoza, the Beni Hud, in the late
10th century. The corbels are thought to have been
originally set over the gateway when the castle was built
(33). The castle changed hands several times in the
fighting between Navarre and Zaragoza during the 11th
century. These corbels at Gormaz are the earliest examples

172

of a type that gained some popularity among Romanesque corbel sculptors: similar corbels with double and even treble rows of rolls or curls have been found not far from Gormaz, during excavations of the 11th century chuch at Silos. They are now in the cloister museum (fig.232). They came to light amid the debris filling the stairs between the cloister and the transept of the earlier church, and perhaps were part of the Puerta de las Virgenes (34).

Smaller corbels of the same form are used to hold the cornice of the "tomb of Mudarra", inscribed era 1143 (AD 1105); this monument was formerly in San Pedro de Arlanza and is now preserved in Burgos cathedal. Some of the re-used corbels on the gable of Santa Susanna in Compostela are of this type also (35). It is found in France among the vast variety of forms of roll corbel at Saint-Etienne in Nevers and at Anzy-le-Duc, at Blesle also (figs 233-236) and it is quite common in the Berry (eg Châteaumeillant, Vic l´Exemplet, Avord, St Jeanvrin).

Problems of the Transmission of the Roll Corbel Form from Andalusia to Romanesque: The Fillet Corbel and its Rarity in Spain.

The square fillet profile of the consoles on the mihrab panel and in Almanzor´s doorways is found further elaborated in north Spain, exemplified already both on the 10th century Mozarabic corbels at San Millán de Suso and on 11th century corbels in the Aljaferia, but the classic fillet corbel from which it derived is rare in Spanish Romanesque, whereas it is common in France, particularly in the Auvergne. The only cases of its occurrence in Spain are in León (one fragment, see below) and at Santiago de Compostela. Here fillet roll corbels are not uncommon, on the chevet of the cathedral, in the patio of the church of San Clemente, on Santa Maria del Sar and (re-used) on the gable of the church of Santa Susanna. For this reason the hypothesis has been widely entertained (36) that along with other features thought to originate in France, this type of "Auvergnat" corbel was introduced to Compostela from France, where they had been adopted direct from Andalusia at some earlier date. Gomez-Moreno suggested Saint-Etienne in Nevers (1068-1097) as the focus of French influence on Santiago and the source of the transmission of the fillet corbel thither (37) but most other scholars have looked to the Auvergne. The exuberance of the Nevers corbels is not repeated at Santiago. The double roll form of the Gormaz corbels described above needs taking into account in this context. As it is only an elaborated version of the fillet corbel, Gormaz can be included in the list of pre- or early Romanesque fillet corbels in north Spain, representing a model for those in the museum at Silos, those on the Mudarra tomb from Arlanza and those at Santiago.

Mozarabic Corbels as transmittors

A Mozarabic origin is often postulated for French roll corbels, a Christian source being seen as the most likely means of transmission from Andalusian architecture. It is true that the principle of eaves brought out over a stone corbel table is a characteristic of Mozarabic buildings a century and more before its widespread adoption in France, yet the Romanesque corbels of France and Spain (38) rarely adopt Mozarabic shape or decoration. Where the roll form is used on Romanesque buildings it is much closer to Cordoban forms than to Mozarabic, and its developments rarely appear to be dependent on Mozarabic examples. A few exceptions, particularly in similarities of decoration, might be used to argue that the Mozarabic type played some limited part in the transmission; there are corbels with Mozarabic features at Saint-Hilaire in Poitiers (fig.237, no 9) and Saint-Etienne in Nevers in the 11th century, and from Saint-Sauveur in Nevers (fig.240) in the 12th. In the area of Mozarabic building itself in north-west Spain, Romanesque corbels show little sign of Mozarabic influence.

Early Corbels in León

There are however two examples of roll corbels firmly dated to the early 11th century that provide evidence for a transitional stage beetween Mozarabic and Romanesque types of corbel within Spain. Gomez-Moreno (39) illustrates a stone corbel that was found in the filling of the city wall of León, demolished by Almanzor in AD 988 (40) and rebuilt by Alfonso V (999-1028). The corbel has the characteristic elongated shape, and chip-carved rosettes on the sides, but the top roll is the same size as the rest, thus deviating from normal Mozarabic practice. The concave curve is filled by a grotesque carving, a nude figure with open mouth and hands held between its legs, that would look quite at home in 12th century France, in the Berry or the South-West.

Associated with this corbel in so far as it was in the same filling was a fragment of another roll corbel, plain with a central fillet, again of the elongated horizontal Mozarabic shape but without the large top roll. This find is of importance in any attempts to assess the "French" origin of the fillet roll corbel at Santiago, for these archaeologically attested pieces bear witness to early developments in north Spain beyond the typical Mozarabic, and tending towards Romanesque types. They are scant evidence from which to argue that the Romanesque corbel originated entirely in Spain, but they demonstrate that both the fillet and the high relief forms of the later 11th century at Santiago, Frómista and elsewhere need not be due exclusively to an influence from France.

An awareness of the form, even in the absence of any signs of the structural use of corbels, is reflected occasionally in details of capital carving: one example of this is in Catalunya at San Miguel de Fluviá (fig.241).

174

San Miguel de Fluviá

The exterior of this church (begun cl045, consecrated 1066)(41) is in First Romanesque style and it has no corbel table round the eaves, but the characteristic little arches. These are carved at their consoles with little bearded heads in a tradition that continued unchanged in Spain into the 12th century (for example at Javierrelattre near Jaca), as well as developing into the highly popular Romanesque head corbel. The consoles are carved at Fluviá by the same hand as the capitals of the interior and among them one capital has corners strongly suggesting a roll corbel. This detail brings San Miguel into the discussion, and a short examination of other Andalusian elements in the building is appropriate since it shares a number of motifs with Saint-Hilaire in Poitiers and Saint-Benoît-sur-Loire, which as will be seen were in their different ways key monuments in the developments and dissemination of the roll corbel in France. The connexions of the sculpture in the tower-porch of Saint-Benoît with San Pere de Roda have been noted in Chapter III, and San Miguel also can be seen to have derived much inspiration from the latter.

An example of Fluviá´s connexions with Poitiers and beyond is a wave-scroll with the shortest foliole at the centre and a long one parallel to each side of its zig-zag stem. It is used on an interior cornice and on imposts at San Miguel; it also decorates soffits 8-9 and 9-10 on the cornice of the tower of Saint-Hilaire (fig.237) and is taken up at Saint-Outrille in the Berry (Berry roman,fig.12). One such impost crowns one of the capitals at Fluviá which has the "Coptic" frontal figure, emerging here from a zone of heavy acanthus leaves (F3) with spiral stems. The volutes are encased in a downward sweeping leaf (D16) (fig.134).

The use of the frontal figure (42) on a capital in this way and the partiality for human heads at Fluviá appear as innovations in this region (Roda had animal heads almost hidden at corners of capitals); much of the rest of the repertoire is explicable as derived, though in a very crude rendering, from earlier work in the neighbourhood, (Ripoll and Roda), and contemporary work at Zaragoza and Balaguer: interlace, beaded and corded astragals (figs 242-3), flat plane plant carving all characterize the Roda style; there too the Cordoban pendant pines (D2), the vertical triangular hollow under the volute and twisted columns were already to be found. At Zaragoza, in about the same decade, twisted columns are combined with heavy acanthus tips (F3) as they are at Fluviá (AHIII fig.280b). The heart-shaped leaf with drill holes of figs 241 and 243 is a motif from further west: it is characteristic of the group of western Mozarabic marble capitals from Hornija, Sahagún and Escalada that marks the height of Mozarabic capital carving (AHIII fig.435-436). These illustrate early stages in the process of dividing the acanthus into the juncture of converging folioles to create the fleuron typical of Romanesque foliage capitals (43).

Downturned leaves sweeping from below volutes, as on the frontal-figure capitals like fig.134 are also nearer the shape of western Mozarabic capital foliage (see AHIII fig.452 where the rising acanthus is perversely represented as a falling palm) than the shape of the corner leaves that at Ripoll replace, and at Zaragoza decorate, the volutes. But the influence of the downturned leaf of Ripoll too is operative at Fluviá (fig.242), as it is at Elne (44).

It is the capital of the north crossing arch (fig.241) where the roll corbel theme is quoted. It is given corners composed of a leaf canopy with a triangular hollow beneath. In this there is a convergence of a patent reference to a roll corbel on the one hand, and a leaf volute on the other. Vergnolle follows the expression of this conceit, with a stronger emphasis on the downturned leaf motif, from the Saint-Benoît leaf canopy to the group of Berry capitals with roll- corbel-like volute stems enclosing a corner head. Fig.136 shows one of the many elongated heads at Fluviá, here an animal, that links with elongated faces at Saint-Benoît-sur-Loire (45). The impost and the capital´s middle zone are treated in the same hollowed refined chip carving as the scroll resembling that at Poitiers. The leaves call to mind the triangular hollows of the Toledan Kufic inscriptions; a technique scantily used at Saint-Hilaire and with limited application in the Saint-Benoît porch, but conspicuous in the inscription of capital 50 at Moissac.

Corbels at Frómista, Jaca and Santiago

Among the fully Romanesque buildings in Spain the corbels which are most relevant to the study of roll corbels in France are those of San Martín in Frómista, San Pedro in Jaca and Santiago in Compostela, together with the few that survive at Loarre (46). The first three form a group with carving styles and motifs in common, though the variety of types at the two former is more restricted than at Santiago, and only Santiago has fillet corbels. Typical of the group are animal heads with long necks, and crouching figures of beasts or human beings. Both roll and other motifs are often set against a plain label marked off from the block by grooves or a change of plane.

Frómista

There are many plain rod corbels at Frómista. Curls or lobing of the sides accompany some of the figure corbels, and some figures are set against rods. There is a predilection for placing little crouching figures low down within the concave profile, against the plain label. Some capitals have volute stems sprouting curls on one face (fig.122) and one has curls on one volute and leaves on the other (47).

176

Jaca

Jaca has many plain rod corbels, with either three thick rods or many small ones. There are also many like those on the upper parts of the chevet at Santiago with a plain tongue-like leaf, its tip sometimes curling over a large knob; this motif corresponds to the typically Spanish and south-west French ball capitals, as on the south door at Conques. There are some corbels with a lobed profile edging the label which is set behind high relief figures of animals; these generally fill the whole concave space and the vertical face is much reduced (fig.244). The link with Saint-Sernin in Toulouse is manifest in the corbel by Gilduinus reused on the Gothic apse (48). The side is edged with three layers of lobes or waves, resembling more the moulding behind the consoles of the Platerías or Pamplona cathedral doorways (figs 245-248)(49) than any treatment of corbels seen elsewhere. The metopes of the south apsidiole at Jaca have low relief animal carvings (probably by the master of the west tympanum) and one rosette (slightly dished). The soffits have a variety of large rosettes; they resemble those on the chevet at Moirax (fig.249).

Santiago: the chevet

The roll corbel is much in evidence on the cathedral, but nowhere in uniform series. Much of the chevet is masked, but Gaillard illustrates the corbels and describes those of the different parts (50). These include fillet corbels of "Auvergnat" (better "Almanzor") style on St Peter's chapel and on higher levels. Though curls are given great prominence on the sides they have no horizontal stems attached; the scotia curve of the profile is paramount, and even where curls are duplicated or reduced to shallow lobing the curve is clearly marked. The figures on the corbels of the St Faith chapel are so similar to those over the Platerías doorway and to the full relief figures on the roofs of the St John and St Faith chapels that they must be by the same hand. In some cases these corbels are edged with little lobes, as at Fromista and often at Jaca, in one or more rows. This kind of shallow edging became popular in the 12th century in the Saintonge (51). In other cases rolls are deeply carved into curls at the sides and run as rods across the face behind the figures. None of the corbel tables of the eaves shows any sign of rosettes on soffits or metopes, which are undecorated.

On one exterior facet of the clerestory of the polygonal apse, the Cordoban type of fillet corbel, with roll stems starting on a concave line, is associated with the series of trilobed blind arcades resting on capitals which must originally have stood on colonnettes. The cornice has a corded moulding. Corbels with motifs other than rolls, such as large tongue-like leaves, heads or crouching figures, retain lobing down the profile edge.

Gaillard follows Torres-Balbás (52) in regarding this fillet roll corbel as re-imported to Spain from the Auvergne, since it is widespread round Clermont and scarcely met in north Spain outside Santiago. Gaillard adds two items to the argument: first the "Auvergnat style of the capitals near the entrance to the Saviour´s chapel, showing the king and bishop with angels holding inscribed banderoles, and a capital with linked sirens; second, the five-sided lintel over the little door between the chapels"(53). These in fact are found at Conques and Bessuéjouls also, at least as early as in the Auvergne, and chronological priorities remain debatable. The pentagonal lintel has antecedents in the Mezquita (AHIII figs 138, 186,189,190).

The Platerías Doorway: Rosettes and Corbels

Over the Platerías doorway (fig.250), where only some of the corbels have rolls, much is made of the rosettes (D15) between them, both on soffits and metopes. The rosette itself is richly varied, in considerable relief, and surrounded by a broad decorated border. On the metopes a little boss is carved in each corner (F19). The general effect is of medallions (F4), in the style of the 8th century façades of the Mosque of Ibn Tulun in Cairo, or more contemporary Sedráta: an oriental taste already indulged in 9th century Ramiran architecture at Naranco and Lillo (54).

The corbels over the Platerías doorway are mostly animate, with crouching humans, animals and monsters, full figures or protomes in lively postures, some with rolls or lobes at the sides. The composition of these corbels suggests that the tongue form of leaf that appears frequently, often combined with rolls, on the upper parts of the chevet (55) was a labour-saving adaptation of the crouching beast that is so frequent among the corbels over the doorways.

The lion-head consoles (figs 245-8) supporting the lintels are part of the original scheme for the doorway, and not part of the restorations after the fire of 1117, and they must be earlier than 1100 for they are imitated at San Esteban de Corullón where an inscription gives the years of its construction as 1093-1100 (56). Furthermore the feroces leones (57) over the trumeau and under the chrism are, as Gaillard pointed out, by the same hand as the monsters on the roofs of the St John and St Faith chapels (60) which were dedicated in 1105, and the doorway consoles belong with these works. They must thus antedate the similar consoles of the lintels of the Saint-Sernin Porte Miègeville (fig.251) and the south transept portal of San Isidoro in León by a decade or more.

Carved on these lintel consoles at Santiago are enormous heads with holes pierced for ears (or horns?) that have vanished. They fill the curve of highly elaborated roll corbels with a simulated trilobed extrados (F21). Each is different, but the lobed moulding of the extrados keeps the same sinuous line on all four corners, rising vertically above the console to make a stepped lintel profile: an outline reminiscent of the Puerta San Esteban niches and the simulated consoles on the marble relief plaques flanking al-Hakam II's mihrab; and here in the animal heads furthermore is the downturned leaf (D16) of these mihrab panels (61) pursuing its Romanesque development as a full relief sculpture. In south-west France it wil culminate on the consoles of doorway lintels in full-figure scenes, as at Nogaro, Tasque, on the Porte Miègeville in Toulouse and at Saint-Sardos near Agen (fig.252).

The westernmost console of the Platerías doorways retains the horizontal bars of a roll corbel right across the face behind the outward-twisted lion head, with two large curls bending down from the top. This twisted head recurs at León without rolls, on the south transept door; at Toulouse it is still backed by vestigial rolls. Even at Santiago the ends of the rolls on this console are not carved into curls, whereas the other three consoles have asymmetrical curls carved on the sides in quite high relief.

The multiple moulding of the consoles runs all round the doorway openings; it recalls the plaster mouldings framing the decoration in the Aljafería, and suggests itself as an inspiration for the moulding on the lobed south doorways of Moissac and Cahors.

Against the hypothesis of an Auvergnat provenance for the fillet corbel at Santiago is the fact that this form is closely integrated with the figure sculpture of corbels and doorways at Santiago (62), and this sculpture is not in the style of the Auvergne, or even of Conques, but in the highly characteristic "fleshy" style shared with Toulouse, Frómista and Jaca, but at its most extreme at Santiago, at the Spanish end of the spectrum, as for example the Woman with a Skull on the eastern tympanum. It is also associated with trilobed arches; these have no wide distribution in Mozarab or Romanesque buildings in north Spain, and Santiago comes nearer to French than local practice in lobing semi-circular arches. Conversely the example of Santiago was certainly the inspiration for many corbels and lobed arches in France.

Corbels at Iguácel

The corbel table on the west front of this little church has not previously attracted much comment. The church lies in a Pyrenean valley north of Jaca and is mainly noted because of the early date of the inscription (AD 1072) over the doorway (62).

The themes of the capitals and corbels (figs 253-260)
are closely allied to themes in the great churches of the
Santiago pilgrimage road, in Jaca, Frómista, Santiago, and
in Loarre; the scrollwork resembles that in the Panteón.
The inscription stating that the church of St Mary was
completed in 1072 (Era 1110) is set in a series of slabs on
the west front and is protected by a horizontal weather
roof of stone slabs supported on corbels (63). The soffits
are carved with rosettes (D15) and edged with billet
moulding. Between the inner archivolt of the west door and
the archivolt with a double torus (fig.253) is a line of
narrower voussoirs set longitudinally in First Romanesque
fashion (see St Juan de Buso fig.172 and the early chapel
at Loarre, Aragon roman fig.70). They are carved with
interlacing heart palmettes like the majority of imposts of
the apse and windows (D11). Like the volute stems of
capitals and corbels, the looping frame of these palmettes
has an axial double grooving.

At the east end the eaves of the small apse rest on
slabs similar to those of the west door, edged with billet
moulding and carved on the underside with rosettes. They
are held on corbels carved with interlace, rosettes or
knobs on a straight oblique profile (fig.255). None of the
corbels on this church includes any of overtly roll form,
but some on the west front, and perhaps some on the apse
also (they are too badly weathered to see clearly) bear
hints of the roll motif.

The corbels over the doorway are much more elaboate
than those round the apse, and though they are clearly
carved by the same hand as the capitals of the windows and
interior apse arcade the result is much more finished in
effect: the artist is presumably the "master" who signs his
name along with the epigrapher on the inscription:
"Magister harum picturarum nomine Calindo Garces". We must
take it that he consideed his carving merely as support for
his more important work as a painter (64). The corbels are
decorated on the sides to simulate in the upper wider
portion a half capital, with a volute which in some cases
enfolds a down-turned leaf (D16). The faces of the corbels
are carved, some with heads of men or animals, some with
whole figures or even scenes, and some merely with
palmettes or interlace in relief or engraved. Two of the
eleven corbels have an archaic barrel-shaped bottom, the
rest a straight oblique profile. In general the style of
capitals at Iguácel is a crude version of sculpture at
Jaca, Santa Cruz de los Seros, Loarre or Frómista, (65),
but both the design and composition of the Iguácel doorway
corbels are quite individual (66).

The volute and vertical bar that occupy the upper
section of the sides of each corbel create a system
peculiar to this series. It echoes the volute on the
capitals, and also a curious vertical bar that often rises
between these volutes to replace the console. At Jaca in
the nave (67), at Santiago (68) and in the Panteón this

same system is applied, but with greater refinement, to capitals. The treatment of the stems of the capital volutes themselves at Iguácel is distinctive. It occurs on 11th century capitals, at Tournus and at Frómista, and less frequently at Santiago and León (69). The volute stem is wide and rectangular in section, with parallel axial grooving, and rises vertically before flaring from about half way up the capital. Two capitals in the museum of Jaca cathedral, said to come from rural churches nearby, have volutes similar to those on the Iguácel capitals and corbels.

North to south the eleven corbels show a great variety of motifs. The face of No 1 has a fir-tree motif like corbels in the patio of the Mezquita. Nos 2 and 3 have the barrel-shaped bottom of Visigothic tradition: on this lower section of the sides, a palmette framed in a heart. The "barrel" is surmounted on No 3 by a human head with turban-like hair, even more cap-like than that of St Peter over the Porte Miègeville doorway (fig.261), or the St Isidore over the Puerta del Cordero in León, and similar to the projecting heads on capitals in the Berry (Berry roman, fig.56), whose ancestry is at Saint-Benoît-sur-Loire (70). The lower strand of this hair is crossed by the strand above at the side, and a slender-bodied bird's neck has slipped through the gap. Two discs below the volute here give a suggestion of roll ends at the sides.

No 4 is more elaborate: a bearded human head (in lower relief than the head of No 3) emerges above a now damaged ox head, while the figure's left hand grasps either a horn or a raised knife. The hair is even taller and more cap-like than on No 3, with rows of curls in the Jaca style noted by Alvarez (71). Another grinning head pokes out below the volute at the side (72). Like volute stems on capitals at Jaca, Santiago and Frómista, the vertical bars on the sides of corbels 2 and 3 are carved with scales. No 5 again has vestigial rolls in the form of discs at the sides. A human leg is all that remains of what must have been a projecting figure, perhaps an angel, since the lower section of the side is grooved and may portray wing feathers.

No 6 is a bold ox head; it has deteriorated badly in the last ten years. Either a now damaged human head surmounted it, or the mane above the frontal ridge is treated as a series of plaits. The vertical bar of the sides is again scaled. No 7 shows traces of a human figure with raised arms and a scabbard or horn hanging diagonally from the waist. The volute ends in a downturned leaf palmette and springs from some obscure motif involved in the main design. No 8 has simple three-strand interlace. No 9 has another human head with cap-like plaited hair of Jaca style like No 4, projecting above grotesque legs, perhaps originally an animal dompter with the animal's head, like the man's arms, broken off.

No 10 is a man with elongated head under a devouring monster. This is a theme familiar from the earliest French Romanesque sculpture, in the crypt of Saint-Bénigne in Dijon, at Bernay and at Saint-Benoît where the elongated head is specially marked. The motif is repeated several times on the earliest capitals of Saint-Sernin in Toulouse, on the Porte des Comtes and in the interior transept. The head on the Iguácel corbel is reminiscent of the Lazarus capital in the Panteón, but it is even closer, because of the hair-line, to the St Martin capital and other porch capitals at Saint-Benoît-sur-Loire (Val-de-Loire roman figs 20-25). No 11 at the corner is a simple undulating scroll enclosing deeply hollowed five- and six-petalled rosettes, with a heart palmette and volute on the sides (73).

This is an early Romanesque example of a corbel table placed over a doorway and the inspiration is Andalusian. The same influence is marked in the bases of the colonnettes framing the windows and those in the interior (fig.253). They are close in shape to the Cordoban bases analysed by Hernandez (74) in connexion with an Andalusian influence on Ripoll. The bases favour the argument for accepting that the early date given in the inscription applies to the sculpture of the church.

On the south front a narrow fillet traces the line of a stepped alfiz (F12,18)(75)

Corbels at Loarre

The roll corbels in the dome of Loarre and the four now set with the "frieze" over the south doorway (figs 263-268)(76) stand apart from the group formed by Frómista, Jaca and Santiago. There are resemblances with corbels at Toulouse. Head 1 is similar to heads carved by Gilduinus or his follower (fig 269) and the composition, at least, of the dome corbels is of the same type as that of the re-used cornice fragment in the fourth bay of the northern nave gallery at Toulouse (77) and the corbels over the Porte des Comtes (fig.270). The corbel of Head 1 is the most Toulousan, with a plain rectangular vertical front; beneath it is a strongly moulded torus which curves into a label behind the head, while the curl which ends the torus is set back, in line with the rest of the curls. This corbel is set into the wall beyond the sculptor's intention: two curls are all but lost and there is a trace of drapery round the neck disappearing into the wall.

Head 2 (fig.265) must also have been intended to project further; the profile curve only begins at the wall about half way up the corbel, and the beard touches the wall without any sign of a neck. The torus here is simply articulated by two grooves and there is no label between head and curls. The top curl is considerably larger than the following ones which diminish in size, Mozarabic fashion. The curl stems on this corbel do not swell towards the profile as they do on the other dome corbels and on those over the doorway.

Both these heads are set so that they look down almost vertically, and this is even more marked with Head 3 (fig.266), behind which the series of curls sprouts from the horizontal. The relative size and shape of the rolls is the same as with Head 2, and there is again no label. This placing of the heads is not the most usual on corbels, and curls rarely spring from the horizontal, though crouching figures sometimes look down vertically, as for example at Poitiers (corbels Nos 3, 8, 11, figs 237-8), Saint Sever or Aubiac (fig.271). The fourth dome corbel is unreadable, it was probably a quadruped with head turned backwards.

The upper parts of the doorway corbels also are worn away. Three are ox heads, one is the body of a quadruped facing the wall, of a type with head turned back 180 degrees, familiar at Jaca including a console in the dome and a corbel on the south chapel (fig.244) and at Santiago over the Platerías doorway. There is no label between curls and head and the horns rise over a hollow and continue across the vertical front. The curl stems swell like those of Heads 1 and 3, but without the graceful curve of Head 1.

An ox head corbel of very similar character to those at Loarre, associated with a palmette scroll, is among those surmounting the Bab al-Futuh in Cairo, dated 1087 (78). There is a kinship among examples of ox heads on Romanesque roll corbels, at Conques (North door), Toulouse, Lescure (fig.273) and Anzy-le-Duc. At Conques and Anzy the relief is flat. Capitals at Varen (Aveyron) have ox and ram heads in low relief spitting chip-carved half-palmette scrolls and interlace; the eyes and nostrils are carved in similar fashion to the Loarre corbels (Languedoc roman fig.131). In addition to the Andalusian roll form F1, the downturned leaf D16, pendant pine D2, splayed eagle D17 and harpies are other Andalusian motifs that recur on capitals at Loarre.

The historical arguments propounded by Duran Gudiol for dating the main building of Loarre and its decoration before the disgrace early in the 1080s of Garcia, bishop of Jaca and brother of Sancho Ramirez (79) cannot be set aside, and similarities of sculpture at Iguácel with capitals at Loarre might validate this dating. On the other hand the variety of styles of carving and of themes at Loarre gives an impression of eclecticism and argues against regarding it as a centre from which influences radiated. A full classification and study of the many capitals in the building is needed. Motifs fully integrated into the corpus of sculpture at Jaca predominate, but there are also analogies, clear even without prolonged study, with Frómista, León, Santiago, Conques, Toulouse and Moissac at the least; the scroll work is of many types, on imposts and capitals alike, and the treatment of drapery is also diverse. The frontal figure of Nogál and Fluviá appears several times; the Moissac scroll version 2 only once (80). There are a number of versions of the superposed animal composition of Jaca, in a clearer rendering than at Iguácel: lions are ridden by men or monsters so that the heads appear one above the other at the angle under the volute; they are attacked by birds whose wings or tails are held in a lion or monster maw at the console. Saxon and Limousin illuminations are among the sources of this theme, but the superposition of animals on caliphal basins and the registers of animal attack or animals in scrolls on ivories, for example the Silos casket (AHIII figs 367-8) have shared in its formulation; the griffins of the Silos casket are reproduced on a high window at Loarre (81).

Unlike the capitals, the corbels at Loarre have little to do with the pilgrimage churches of more western Spain, but belong with the Portes des Comtes series of roll corbels and are associated in style with the Gilduinus atelier. They perhaps come from a cornice over the original doorway: the positioning of the dome corbels is higher than any other such, and raises doubts as to their original position. Angel and other figures in domes in other cases, as at Frómista, Jaca, Conques or Parthenay le Vieux, are all much more visible. The corbels over the west door at Lescure are similar in structure (fig.273); they clearly derive from Toulouse, but the curls at Lescure are smaller and lighter. The model had little repercussion elsewhere.

Despite the similarity with Toulousan corbels, the shape of the curl stems of Head 1 and the ox-head corbels is distinctive; the nearest comparison is with a less graceful curve in the stem of the same conception, in the decoration of the vertical band of the impost over capital 17 with the imprisonment of St Peter, in Moissac cloister (fig.272)(83).

The unusual refinement and peculiar style of the Loarre corbels dissociates them from the capitals of the church; the resemblance of Head 1 to heads by Gilduinus, on his altar and in the figure of the evangelist Matthew (fig. 269) on the marble plaque of the Majesty now in the ambulatory in Saint-Sernin, allows the hypothesis that the Loarre corbels are an early work of Gilduinus. The place of Loarre in the Spanish connexions of Conques, as well as of Toulouse, remains to be investigated.

The two badly worn corbels: the quadruped body over the doorway and the south dome corbel which is possibly the same motif, are evidence that other motifs than heads were used on corbels at Loarre. Many more corbels must lie buried.

THE ROLL CORBEL IN FRANCE AND COMPOSTELA

The extensive use of corbels, and the wide variety of roll corbel types displayed at Santiago mark it as a centre of development of Romanesque corbel types. The geographical position of Galicia, bordering Andalusian territory, and the cathedral´s outstanding attraction as a focus of pilgrimage make it a natural source of influence in the wide diffusion of the feature throughout France and Spain; yet while its influence in the later 11th and 12th centuries is patent, as will become clear in the following review of the French material, it cannot be invoked as the source of all French developments of the motif, since roll corbels were used in France well before the present cathedral of Santiago was begun.

The series of French roll corbels begins as early as the fourth decade of the 11th century at Vendôme with the fillet type, and there are enough examples for which a probability of a date in the next few decades is very high (Poitiers, Lyon, Tournus, Jumièges, Conques, Méobecq, Ennezat for example), to show that even if the date of one or other of these monuments is disputed, the feature was established in the repertoire of builders in a number of areas by the third quarter of the century at latest. Apart from Poitiers, all the above are fillet corbels, and at Poitiers they too are in a majority among other forms based on them.

It can no longer be maintained that the corbels of Chamalières and of Saint-Bénigne in Dijon are earlier than the 12th century (85), but with Vendôme the fillet form is still the earliest among surviving Romanesque corbels in France. Because it had little dissemination in the rest of northern Spain the hypothesis remains attractive that this Andalusian feature arrived in Santiago with the indubitably French structural features (the "pilgrimage formula") as the contribution of the builder Rotbertus. He is named in the Codex Calixtinus beside the <u>mirabilis magister</u> Bernardus as responsible for the building started by Bishop Diego Pelaez (86). The names are more French than Spanish. That a French builder should find a receptive, and creative, interest at Compostela in such a motif is the more probable since the roll corbel will not have been unfamiliar in Galicia, even if its classic Cordoban form was not then in the current local repertoire of stone-work.

French roll corbels will now be discussed in geographical groups, taking first Vendôme and its neighbourhood Maine and the Loire area, then Poitou in which Saint-Hilaire (before 1049) provides the earliest example; Normandy (Jumièges, 1040-1067); the Rhône-Saône valley and Brionnais (Tournus[?]); Auvergne (Ennezat begun before 1078); Nivernais (Saint-Etienne begun by 1083), and Berry-Bourbonnais, where the plain fillet corbel has at once lost its predominance; Conques (corbels probably by c. 1070; Toulouse (Saint-Sernin begun before 1080); the South-West.

La Trinité, Vendôme

The earliest datable examples of French roll corbels are at La Trinité (87). On the exterior, the eaves of the very high south transept rest on corbels, most of them badly weathered and very difficult to see. We rely on the reports of Abbé Plat: during restorations he was able to ascertain that several fillet corbels were among them, and he implies that this was the form they all take (88). There is no record of any metope or soffit decoration. Only one example is illustrated, in a drawing by E. Chauliat published by Plat, who states: "billet moulded cordons and wood-shaving corbels of the classic type were used in 1032 on the transept of La-Trinité-de-Vendôme and a little later at Rivière..". The corbel illustrated has four rolls and a projecting central fillet in two planes. The interlace on the vertical face and the scroll down the concave face of the fillet are entirely in the style of the corbels of ´Abd ar-Rahman III´s façade in the Mezquita. The profile appears to be more curved than that of the fillet corbels on the tower of the church with which La Trinité was closely associated: Saint-Hilaire in Poitiers.

Roll Corbels in the Neighbourhood of Vendôme

Roll corbels are known from Angers, Rivière, Sainte-Radegonde, Preuilly, Montoire, Langeais and Le Mans. Saint-Benoît-sur-Loire can be included in this group: though Fleury is not very near Vendôme the river forms a connecting link, and it has no nearer neighbours.

A single corbel, with curls engraved on the sides and an eagle carved in high relief, is illustrated from Le Ronceray d´Angers (89). At Saint-Julien in Tours (90) Ch. Lelong found a plain fillet corbel in the Gothic chevet which he concluded is reused from the abbey church begun about 1084 by Abbot Gerbert. It can therefore be associated with other vestiges of that building. These include capitals with a linked scroll motif (D5) "with no analogues in Touraine" and downturned leaf volutes (D16). Other corbels are carved with lions devouring men, crouching figures and other motifs which like the capitals do not belie the suggestion that Saint-Julien was in contact with the sculptors of north Spain and south-west France.

Roll Corbels at Saint-Benoît-sur-Loire

The roll corbels of the chevet and transept façade of Saint-Benoît-sur-Loire were restored in the 19th century, but old prints show them likely to be faithful copies (91). In type they are close to the examples at Tours and Montoire, with subdued variations on fillet and plain roll forms (fig.276). The choir and transepts were not begun until about 1067. The little sub-arcades in the tympana of the transept cornice are also in Nevers and the Berry (figs 154, 155).

Le Mans

The surviving Romanesque chapels of Notre-Dame-du-Pré and La Couture in Le Mans present an extraordinary selection of corbels. They are all uncompromisingly a rectangular block, but the concave profile line is marked in some way down the sides, and several, without seeking the elegance of the classic fillet form, pay full tribute to the Andalusian model; at La Couture with curls or circles on that line (figs 223,224).

Poitiers, Saint-Hilaire

The earliest roll corbels at Saint-Hilaire are more decorative than structural; they support only a narrow cornice, marking the second storey of the bell tower, part of the building mentioned in the Chronicle of Saint-Maixent as dedicated in 1049 (figs 237-239). The cornice was masked by the transept in the alterations that involved enveloping the tower within the church, carried out before the end of the 11th century (92). It is the non-figural corbels which of course are most reminiscent of Andalusian precedents, and close parallels in 10th century Andalusia can be found for the scrolls, rosettes and geometric patterns on the vertical faces of the majority (corbels 1, 3-7, 9)(93). Carving on the vertical face is' a trait found on some of the North door and chevet corbels at Conques (figs 125,128,277).

The key fret or castellation down the fillet of corbel 9 calls to mind the edging on some corbels at San Millán de Suso, and is among the rare parallels occurring between Romanesque and Mozarabic corbels. Apart from corbel 10, the only one of the eleven without rolls, and which has a rounded vertical face unlike the rest, all the corbels have curls with the stems running back to the wall and thus filling the whole side. On most of them the stem is horizontal, but on corbel 3 the stem of the bottom roll of the three rises almost vertically. The same is true of corbel 7, but there is a fourth roll curled upward at the bottom, as there is on corbel 9 where the stems are thin and deeply cut like one on the north door of Conques, and like many in the Auvergne. On corbels 3 and 7 the stems widen at the base like the two with figures over the south door at Conques (figs 278-9). The horizontal stems are not infrequent in the Berry and Bourbonnais, probably influenced from Poitiers, and they occur sporadically in the Auvergne (fig.226, Saignes). It is not Andalusian practice to fill the side with these stems, and stems are never horizontal on Andalusia corbels. Curls used in other contexts, for example in Hibernian illumination or Anglo-Saxon ivory carving (94) will have played their part in this deviation from the Cordoban norm.

Cornice Slabs, Saint-Hilaire.

The classical inspiration is evident, but the roll corbels and their decoration do more than hint that it is mediated through Andalusia. The face of each slab meets the next with a simulated triglyph. Above runs double cording Dl2); cording is a frequent border in the decoration of the Mezquita (AHIII fig.178, round each corbel)(95). It is also characteristic of Spanish Ramiran carved stone decoration and a typical Mozarabic manner of decorating an astragal (AHIII figs 415, 435-6, 452, 454).

Soffits 1-2, 2-3 and the oblique edge of 9-10 have close analogies with Cordoban decoration .1-2 is a "heart and dart" Dll with horizontal link, (fig.19, mihrab panel and LTB 1957 fig.262, a painted dado at Madinat az-Zahra'). This is the only example on the Saint-Hilaire cornice with any reference to the classical rosette soffit. 2-3 is an angular meander D7 (cf LTB 1957 figs 513-4, fine chip carved motifs on bases at Madinat az-Zahra'). The edging on 9-10 is a derived Roman ovulo moulding (cf LTB 1957 fig.526). The wave scrolls of soffits 8-9 and 9-10 however resemble scrolls at San Miguel de Fluviá (fig 134); they reappear at Saint-Outrille.

Some metopes are carved with animals, as from a bestiary, in shallow two-plane relief: a dromedary and a saggitarius were thought by Crozet to be reused, the latter being cut down to fit between the corbels. There is a relief with confronted lions on soffit 7-8 in the same naive style, which as part of the cornice slab is unlikely to be a reused piece. It reinforces the arguments against the once prevalent notion that all such "primitive" carvings are survivals of an earlier period (96).

Fillet Roll Corbels in Poitou

Plain or elaborated fillet corbels account for nearly half of the eleven corbels accessible for study on the east wall of the tower of Saint-Hilaire (nos 1,2,5,6 and 9). Elsewhere in Poitou they are scarce. There are a few among the different types at Parthenay-le-Vieux and a small number again at Montierneuf and in museums in Poitiers (97); in the great majority of cases if corbels have the roll form at all they are combined with an animal or human head in high relief.

Less infrequent are corbels with rolls on a convex profile (98). These have a typological affinity with the "prow" corbels evolved from the downturned leaf in Andalusia. It is found in Romanesque Spain at Compostela (Santa Susanna), and on the tomb of Mudarra from Arlanza. It is a form exploited in the Berry, on parts of Saint-Etienne in Nevers and at Anzy-le-Duc.

188

Political Affiliations

Since roll corbels are comparatively rare round Poitiers, the political affiliations of the patrons of the buildings may explain their distribution. Three buildings with early examples of roll corbels are directly associated with the name of the countess Agnes: La Trinité in Vendôme, Saint-Hilaire in Poitiers and also Tournus, where she and Geoffroi of Anjou were generous patrons of Saint-Philibert (99). In 1049 at the time of the dedication, her son Gui Geoffroi, later Duke William VIII of Aquitaine, was lay abbot of Saint-Hilaire; again in the close comital entourage the Treasurer was Josselin, second son of the lord of Parthenay. Both Saint-Jean-de-Montierneuf in Poitiers, begun by the Duke about 1069 (100) and Parthenay-le-Vieux have roll corbels. Those of Montierneuf were probably in place by 1074-1075.

The associations are not overwhelming however. Saint-Nicolas in Poitiers (c.1050) and the Abbaye-aux-Dames in Saintes (dedicated in 1047) were both founded by Agnes and there is no sign of roll corbels in either. In the case of Parthenay the eaves are unlikely to date earlier than after 1092 when it became a priory of La Chaise-Dieu (101). Auvergnat influence is evident in the quarter-barrel vaults of the aisles, and the few fillet corbels may well reflect the growth of popularity of the form in the Auvergne.

Maillard (102) attributed the alternation of piers (F7) at Saint-Hilaire to the Norman origin of Emma's architect Walter Coorland. The alternation of supports at Jumièges was a novelty in Normandy however, and an origin has been sought for them in Burgundy at Saint-Bénigne in Dijon. The fillet roll corbels at Jumièges were also a novelty, unless the primitive-looking corbels of La Couture in Le Mans can be attributed to the early 11th century buildings of Abbot Gauzbert, cousin of Emma (103). Something of their cubic shape is characteristic of Norman corbels, at Jumièges and Boscherville, but the latter are much more "classical Cordoban" (figs 225, 281).

Relations of Poitou with Spain

Apart from the opportunities for Andalusian features to come to Poitou from Normandy and Burgundy, there is no lack of evidence that Spain itself played an important rôle in the political thinking of the counts, as it did with the rulers of Normandy and Burgundy. The pilgrimages of William the Great to Santiago, and his frequent exchanges of gifts with the kings of Navarre and León are a measure of the importance he attached to his relations with Spain (104). William's son Gui Geoffroi (Duke William VIII) is the most likely leader to have been designated by Ibn Hayyan as "commander of the cavalry of the Roumi" who took Barbastro in 1063 and held it for a year. At all events, Gui Geoffroi brought many ornaments and slaves back from the campaign, and renewed his father's friendships with the Spanish monarchs which had subsided during the troubled years of his mother´s regency and remarriage (105).

The concern to assure control of Gascony, culminating in Gui Geoffroi´s assumption of that ducal title (by forced sale) in 1052, is attributed by Martindale (106) in large measure to the importance for Aquitaine of the route to Spain. Dynastic marriages bear this out. William the Great had married a daughter of the Duke of Gascony; the first wife of Alfonso VI of León/Castile was Agnes of Poitiers (107) a daughter (or sister?) of Gui Geoffroi; another (or, a?) daughter of the latter also named Agnes was married as a child to the son of Sancho Ramirez of Aragon, Pedro (later Pedro II), in 1086 in Jaca. The latter´s half-brother Ramiro, acceding to the throne of Aragon in 1134 married Gui Geoffroi´s granddaughter, again named Agnes. In this way firm links were established with the most influential monarchs in Spain.

The close association of the Duke´s vassals, the counts of Bigorre and the viscounts of Béarn, with the court of Aragon in the early decades of the 12th century reflects the continuing importance of Spanish affairs in the power struggles of the great feudal houses (108). All these activities created opportunities for craftsmen and ideas to travel.

Other types of roll corbel in Poitou

Later building campaigns at Saint-Hilaire, but still in the 11th century, continued to use the roll form, but not the fillet type. There is one plain rod corbel on the north transept interior, and under the eaves of the northern radiating chapels metopes carved with paired heraldic beasts are set between roll corbels with animal heads (109). On the north façade of the transept there is a cornice similar to that on the tower but simpler, with a plainer moulding. The metopes are undecorated, and the soffits are carved in very shallow relief with animals in "primitive" style. They rest on corbels, the great majority of them with rolls; three have a bull head, the muzzle pointing down vertically and the neck differing little from the profile of a fillet, but less carved away from the cubic block. The difference in style of these corbels from those on the tower makes plain the difference in date.

Several roll corbels with heads or a plant motif survive on Monthierneuf and in museums in Poitiers. Other examples of roll corbels with heads are at Chauvigny (both Saint-Pierre and Notre-Dame), Saint-Savin, Bonneuil-Matours and La Chapelle-Morthemer; it is notable that all these lie to the east towards the Berry where the roll form is virtually standard. A plain concave rod corbel is among a very few other roll-derived forms on the apse of Saint-Jouin de Marnes.

The popularity of the roll motif clearly declined in
Poitou in comparison with regions further east, in Berry-
Bourbonnais, Nivernais or Auvergne. It was discarded in
favour of head corbels. The roll form is sparsely used at
Notre-Dame-la-Grande, and on the turrets a few animal heads
still have manes described by little curls.

The widespread adoption of heads on corbels in Poitou,
first as an addition to or elaboration of the fillet on
rolls corbels, later by themselves, as on the chevet of
Saint-Pierre at Chauvigny or at Notre-Dame-la-Grande, goes
in parallel with the dense distribution in Poitou of arches
decorated with heads (110).

Though the roll form was superceded, the practice of
supporting cornices and eaves on decorative corbels became
firmly established. There is hardly a Romanesque church,
early or late, throughout all the dominions of Aquitaine,
without a corbel table under the eaves. The characteristic
façades of Poitou, and the bordering tributary provinces of
Vendée, Limousin, Périgord, Angoûmois, Saintonge, Guyenne
and Gascony all make constant use of cornices on corbels,
most of these carved with heads.

That the ultimate Roman origin of the corbel table, as
seen on the architraves of Roman triumphal arches or
gateways still standing, for example at Saintes, was still
present in the minds of the Romanesque designers is evident
in the classical aspect of many details, but the fact that
the earliest corbels to survive are roll corbels shows that
the Andalusian mode of treating the classical tradition had
been operative in disseminating its adoption.

The cornice on the tower of Saint-Hilaire is the
earliest surviving example of a corbel table in the Duchy.
The fact that corbel tables were widely adapted to the
function of eave supports, at Vendôme and subsequently at
Saint-Hilaire, and not only used in the Roman manner on
cornices, again shows that Andalusian influence prevails.
While animal-head corbels already support a cornice above a
doorway in Diocletian's palace in Split (111) and suggest a
Roman ancestry for the highly popular head corbel, the use
of the roll motif as the support for the animal heads at
Saint-Hilaire, first on the cornice of the tower then under
eaves, must be due to the influence of the Andalusian
tradition already manifest at Vendôme supporting the eaves,
in the surviving corbels on the south transept.

Roll Corbels and other Andalusian features in Normandy

Jumièges

The plain fillet corbel made an early appearance in
Normandy at Jumièges (begun 1040, consecrated 1067)(fig
225). All the roll corbels surviving on this building are
of this type. They can be seen in situ: on the western

191

façade supporting a cornice with triple billet moulding among others with single rolls or similar variations, uniform under the eaves of the north tower, and under the eaves of the crossing tower. On the south tower the fillet is used without the flanking rolls, and a cornice on the east face of the lantern tower has concave corbels with a square stud, among others with rolls. The roll corbels tend to a stocky cubic shape characteristic of all Norman roll corbels. The central fillet projects strongly. There are signs of grooving on the underside and down the fillet, and on the sides the ends of rolls are defined as circles along the concave profile. No other decoration is to be seen.

Twin columns (F6) flank the otherwise very plain entrance to the abbey church, in the same alignment as the columns supporting the mihrab arch in the Mezquita, for the doorway is not splayed. That this feature, also seen on the west towers, is as much Andalusian here as Italian (112) is made more likely by the presence of roll corbels which are unknown in Italy. A window in the west wall of the south transept has an extrados with horizontal slabs, as in High Aragon, and there were twin windows (F11) in the crossing tower. The insertion of columns on the outer angles of towers and transept piers is a Muslim feature which does not survive in Andalusia (113). The alternation of supports (F7) in the nave is not found over-frequently in Romanesque architecture, and roll corbels often occur on the buildings with this feature (114).

The plain fillet-type corbel of Jumièges is the only roll form to be met in Normandy, and it was not widely adopted. The tower of Saint-Pierre in Aizier has them (115). The 12th century churches of La Trinité in Fécamp (on the radiating chapels), Saint-Nicolas in Caen and Saint-Georges in Saint-Martin-de-Boscherville are among the few with a full series of corbels similar to those at Jumièges.

La Trinité in Caen

There are no roll corbels at La Trinité, but a deliberate reference is made to them on certain capitals with two registers of plain leaves, the upper leaves forming volutes (fig.282). These capitals, placed at tribune level under the cross ribs of the second and third double bay, and on the west front where the console comes against the jamb return, have consoles shaped as plain rod corbels, with no fillet; in the tribune examples the "rod" is rather angular than rounded, but still recognizably a roll corbel with a scotia profile. This transposition of a corbel to a capital differs from the reference evolved in the Berry from a leaf canopy, but it is curious that it was done at La Trinité where several themes on capitals (cat-masks, monsters, foliage types including a suggestion of the inverted Berrichon leaf zone, corner heads under a leaf canopy) are often reminiscent of themes prevalent in the

Berry where they derive from the porch of Saint-Benoît-sur-Loire.

A much larger number of Norman churches has plain, not roll, corbels round the eaves, many with heads. La Trinité in Caen, Domfront, Thaon, Lessay, Sèqueville and Abbetot are among early examples. Corbels are not much used under cornices on façades. Imitations of Mozarabic capitals have been noted (116), but the sculptors of Normandy also used Islamic models. The eared mask of the capital signed Britus at Bernay and similar motifs in Caen (fig.325) bear a close resemblance to the mask on an oliphant in the Hermitage museum in Leningrad. This motif may have been transmitted by a Mozarabic intermediary, such as the masks on the ivory crosses (117). Reference was made in Chapter II to the capitals of La Trinité with ram heads that render the rams´ horns with the same fronds that frame the ram and lion heads on Cordoban basins.

Twin columns (F6) also are not uncommon in Normandy: at Manéglise, Quilleboeuf, Montivilliers, Fécamp for example. Quilleboeuf has indented if not lobed soffits on the tower, and voussoirs alternating (F13) in plane on the outer archivolt of the west door. At Montivilliers the south transept arch (fig 330)(118) has voussoirs alternating in a manner strongly suggestive of Cordoban inspiration. Voussoirs carved on a horseshoe arch at Evrecy in the 9th century may well already betoken an Andalusian stimulus (119) renewed at Montivilliers in the 12th. Corbels on the tower of the latter church are concave with an intermediate ridge: a not so distant reference to the roll form. The intercrossing arches (F20) of the transept façades at Graville Saint-Honorine have a moulding running round both jamb and intrados so that the jambs appear to have slender corner columns (F8). The jointing of the arcading with the filling of lozenges gives prominence to the radiation of the voussoirs (F14). The roof is held on head corbels. All these parallels are evidence that those responsible for designing details of decoration for Norman buildings were conversant with the Andalusian decorative repertoire.

Relations of Normandy with Spain

The Normans from early times were no strangers to either Andalusia or Christian Spain (120). In the 11th century, apart from the frequent participation in military activities throughout the century (121) connected with the names of de Toeni, Montreuil, de Roucy or Burdet (122) and the growing control of South Italy and Sicily which brought their ships to and fro into the Mediterranean, there are Norman names among the merchants and traders who settled the new towns along the route to Santiago (123). In the 12th century Rotrou du Perche, related to the de Roucy, and the cousin and a close associate of Alfonso I of Aragon, not only liberated cities but was given the lordship of a part of Zaragoza and probably of Tudela also.

In Galicia the bishop of Santiago first concerned with the new cathedral, Diego Pelaez, was accused by Alfonso VI of involvement in the plot of the disgraced Rodrigo Ovequiz, exiled to Zaragoza, to hand over Galicia to William the Conqueror (124). Whether justified or no, the accusation assumes quite intense communications between Normandy and Spain.

Roll Corbels in the Rhône/Saône Valley, Tournus, Ile-Barbe and Saint-Martin d´Ainay

Tournus and Lyon mark the easternmost limit of the area containing roll corbels. There are plain fillet corbels on the radiating chapels of Saint-Philibert. It is unlikely that they are First Romanesque work, from which elsewhere they are consistently absent. The masonry of the chapels must require an earlier date than the abbacy of Pierre (+1105), and Gaillard (125) shows the capitals belong with those of the cloister. The sainted Abbot Ardain was buried in 1056 in "his" cloister. There is no reason to dispute such a dating for the corbels, though the chapels may have been re-roofed with corbel eaves during the work culminating in the consecration by Calixtus II in 1120; if so, it is strange they had no sequel nearby, and a mid-11th century date is more likely. The domes of Tournus and Saint-Martin d´Ainay in Lyon are similar; that of Saint-Martin was part of the building begun in 1102, but roll corbels are not on the main church; they are on the Ste Blandine chapel which was already standing. That the chapel antedates the new building is to be deduced from the fact that there are no roll corbels on the latter.

On the chapel the soffits are carved with hollow rosettes of Auvergnat type, but a soffit slab from Ile-Barbe nearby (126) is decorated with scrolls of a type that abounds in the decoration of ´Abd ar-Rahman III´s Salón in Madinat az-Zahra´, in particular in the fragments of the terrace eaves with their bracket-shaped medallions (fig.20). The Ile-Barbe soffit has a hollow four-celled rosette more like the wooden soffits at San Millán in Segovia (fig.46). This slab contributes to the evidence for the primary rôle of the Rhône valley in disseminating Andalusian influence in France, already conjectured in discussing lobed arches in the previous chapter. The simple hollow rosette of Auvergnat soffits may well have evolved from such intermediaries in wood and stone as this fragment from a cornice at Ile-Barbe.

Auvergne

Ennezat, founded between 1061 and 1078 (127) is in all likelihood the earliest surviving representative of the Auvergnat church type established by the vanished cathedral of Clermont (128). Round the eaves is a corbel table on fillet roll corbels, all identical; the soffits have a hollowed four-petal rosette in the centre, exactly like the

194

drawings of Viollet-le-Duc from Notre-Dame-du-Port and Ebreuil. The fillet roll form thus begins the series of corbels in the Auvergne; it was destined to predominate right through the Romanesque period in a wide radius round Clermont. The churches of Auvergne are "impressed with a powerful uniformity of style" (129) in which its corbel tables form one element. The cathedral of Clermont, now superceded byi the present one, and the vanished abbey church of La Chaise-Dieu (130) founded in 1043 must also have played a dominant rôle in establishing the eaves system typical of the Clermont region.

The most immediately striking decorative feature on the larger churches is the exterior wall patterning of coloured stone mosaic (fig.287); an equally characteristic feature on both large and small buildings is the treatment of eaves, which are supported on fillet roll corbels close to the Cordoban type of Almanzor´s extension, even to the device of turning the bottom curl up to meet its neighbour. The soffits · are frequently carved with miniature hollow rosettes. Round the apses of the major churches: Saint-Nectaire, Saint-Saturnin, Notre-Dame-du-Port, Issoire, Brioude, stone mosaic forms large rosettes corresponding to the more Roman-like carved metopes of the Santiago or Toulouse doorways. On the gable of the south façade of Saint-Genès at Thiers the stone mosaic rosettes substitute for encrusted bacini, and similarly over a window at Le Monastier (fig.36).

The scarcity of easily worked stone for sculpture in the volcanic Puy-de-Dôme can explain why few sculptors were employed for architectural detail compared with areas where soft stone is plentiful (131). Coloured stone mosaic patterns and uniform corbels and soffits for exterior decoration could be carried out by less skilled or inventive masons and leave the sculptor free to concentrate on capitals. On the exteriors an almost mechanical perfection of execution seems the aim, rather than originality of invention. Subtle embellishments distinguish some finer work, as on the earlier cathedral of Clermont (132).

Pont-du-Château is a minor church and the corbels are rather more peremptory, for instance the curls are only excavated to a very shallow depth and the design has become quite rigid (fig.285). The concave profile of the fillet is reduced to a small bite out of the rectangle, leaving an angular "tête de bélier". The curls spring from a curve but the profile of the lobed plane is almost straight. There are no carved soffits.

The complete Auvergnat system is found further north in the Bourbonnais not far from Clermont, on the 11th century parts (nave, transept and north aisle) of Saint-Léger at Ebreuil. Whether the roofing is as early as the walls is not certain (fig.284). To the north and west of Ebreuil in the Bourbonnais and Berry begins the area where hollowed rosettes cease and the fillet corbel is only one among a very large repertoire, though the roll form is much in evidence. A more mixed treatment of corbels becomes more common as the distance from Clermont in any direction increases. For example Craplet (133) illustrates two corbels from Glaine-Montaigut, one with a crouching figure, the other a roll corbel with foliage in comparatively deep relief down the face: an unusual treatmnt of a corbel, its closest parallel corbel 1 of Saint-Hilaire in Poitiers. The vertical face is narrow, the curl stems fill the side and the bottom curl turns up to join the one above in a heart framing a fleur-de-lis.

On the southern border of the Auvergnat corbel area, at Blesle, a small apse, which Walter Cahn (134) dates to the early years of the 12th century, has a corbel table under the eaves which includes two corbels with rolls on a concave profile. Both have animal heads, one designed on the same scheme as corbel 7 of Saint-Hilaire; next to this is one with a motif similar to the bat of corbel 9 at Saint-Hilaire, but without rolls. Another chapel has an example of a double roll on a convex profile (fig.235) and one, without rolls, has a grimacing mask in the Berry style, like the recut corbels at Les Aix d'Angillon (fig.286). The cornice has a row of discs along the vertical face, but no carved soffits. A later campaign at Blesle was responsible for the choir, and here are eaves with uniform Auvergnat corbels, with deep-cut curls and horizontal stems (135). Inside the church at the crossing the lintel of the squinch is supported on a corbel carved with an elaborated form of rolls, resulting in a kind of gigantic billet moulding.

On the late Romanesque east end of Saint-Julien in Brioude (fig.287)(136) the chapels present a great variety of corbels, human and animal heads, complete figures, heavy plain rolls, quadruple and double rolls and the metopes are carved with varied rosettes D15; the apse, transept and nave eaves on the other hand have uniform fillet corbels; on the apse the rosettes are mosaic on the metopes and hollow on the soffits.

These two churches mark the southernmost limit of the Auvergnat type of corbel table. Southward from here Conques stands alone, midway between the Auvergne and Toulouse, where a distinct form, intimately connected with northern Spain, is centred on Saint-Sernin. On the east, north and west borders of the Auvergne the classic form is modified in other ways.

Roll Corbels in the Brionnais: Anzy-le-Duc, Saint-Laurent, Charlieu

The chevet before restoration at Anzy-le-Duc is reported to have had roll corbels with hollow rosette soffits. Several corbels on the north wall of the nave and on the south transept are variants on double and fillet roll forms (fig.236), but there is no attempt at any consistency of style. The corbels with double rows of rolls are not excavated deeply into curls (unlike those of Clermont, which in this resemble those of Silos and Gormaz) but are similar to the variants appearing on Saint-Etienne in Nevers. On the south transept are two corbels with animal heads carved in low relief on the vertical face, very like the ox-head corbel over the north door at Conques (fig.221).

Some capitals at Anzy-le-Duc share themes with capitals in the Berry and are in the same rigid style; its monster masks evoke also more distant contact, with La Trinité in Caen. The corbels have more of the vitality of invention seen in those at Nevers, and a number of shapes and ornaments are shared with Saint-Etienne.

The eaves corbels of Charlieu and Saint-Laurent-en-Brionnais also include some of roll or derived roll form.

Roll Corbels in the Nivernais

Saint-Etienne in Nevers was given to Cluny in 1067-68. The church, begun before 1083 and finished by 1097, has numerous corbels, and almost all of them are elaborated and diversified versions of the roll corbel treated with considerable virtuosity and exuberance (figs 233,234). The curved profile is emphasized, often multiplied into several planes so that the fillet is slender. The fillet is rarely shaped to the profile but is given a variety of strange forms. This tendency to keep the rectangular block as a base, and the many geometric and curving patterns on the sides, bring this series close to the type of corbel of San Millán de Suso. The same style persisted in the city into the 12th century with the corbels of Saint-Sauveur, one of which, now in the museum, has three Mozarabic features: stems carved to suggest roll ends along the curved profile, castellation along the top border, and a whorl carved in the side (fig.240). The nearest parallel is with the riotous shapes of the corbels on the east and north transept chapels of Notre-Dame-du-Pré in Le Mans.

The few head corbels at Saint-Etienne are without rolls. More classic fillet corbels have very narrow fillets projecting strongly so that the profile of the fillet is nearly rectangular, with a very curved indentation. The curve of the line on the plane of the rolls starts in all cases vey near the top, a detail which these corbels share with those of Santiago, Frómista and Jaca, and with some on the eastern parts of Saint-Sernin (i.e. the face is nearly eliminated, like some in al-Hakam II´s extension, LTB 1957 fig.363). The corbels of Saint-Etienne provide a model for some of the less unadventurous essays in corbel sculpture in the Berry.

Roll Corbels in the Berry-Bourbonnais

In this area, lying between Poitou, the Nivernais and the Auvergne, the corbels show characteristics acquired from each of its neighbours. The roll motif is very frequent on both early and late buildings, and the traditions of the strongly characterized surrounding areas previously described can be seen to mingle, but with differences: on the one hand, it is patent that corbels were often not given to an expert sculptor, but were left to a journeyman or mason not specialized in carving, who made much of simple variations on the roll theme, cutting rolls into billets, enlarging one roll, carving rolls in the fillet as at Gormáz, Arlanza, Nevers or Anzy-le-Duc, or following a few well-established models: heads with a minimum of relief carving, other simple motifs, or the classic fillet type. On the other hand, uniform series of fillet roll corbels in the Auvergnat manner, or of any other type of corbel, are infrequent (138).

At a time when Viollet-le-Duc's theory still held sway, namely that the origin of the roll corbel lay in a carpenter's caprice, and entirely within the Fench architectural tradition, Enlart (139) suggested the Berry region as the cradle of the motif. Since 1923 when Mâle established the origin of the form in Andalusia these corbels have received little attention; the view has prevailed that sculpture in general in the Berry was a passive receiver of influences from its artistically stronger neighbours: the Middle Loire, Poitou, Nivernais, Burgundy, Limousin and Auvergne (140).

Méobecq, if the original chevet can be accepted as belonging to the church dedicated in 1048, as appears most likely (141), is much the earliest site in the province with roll corbels, and among the earliest in France. The corbels on the eaves are part of the 19th century restorations of the east end, but some original pieces which they replace remain stored in a (very dark) corner inside the church. They consist of roll corbels, some with a plain or billet fillet and others with animal heads of similar type to the Saint-Hilaire corbels; they differ in that the stems of the curls spring from the curve of the profile and do not run back horizontally.

Given the disappearance of all the great buildings of the early Romanesque period in the province, such as in Déols, Issoudun or Bourges where about a dozen churches stood in the 12th century (142), Saint-Benoît-sur-Loire appears to exercise the strongest influence on early capital sculpture. Vergnolle shows in detail the close links between capitals in both the tower porch and choir of Saint-Benoît and the earliest capitals in the Berry at Méobecq, Saint-Genou (1066-1070), Neuvy-Saint-Sépulcre (in cult by 1077), La Berthenoux, Plaimpied (1080-1092) and La Celle-Bruère. Saint-Benoît has no corbels on the tower porch however, and those on the east end (fig.276) are not sculpturally inspired; corbels in the Berry may therefore owe more to a different source from that of the capitals.

Corbel Types

The plain fillet roll corbel occurs everywhere in the Berry among other types, in versions similar to those at Poitiers (corbels 4,5,6 and 9 on the tower: Châteaumeillant, Vic l'Exemplet, Avord: figs 291,292). Often, as at Déols or La Champenoise, Bengy (fig.290) or Neuilly-en-Dun, the curl stems are horizontal as at Poitiers. Many others keep to the profile line on the sides, and describe the roll ends as circles or spirals, as at Nevers. Plaimpied has both kinds (fig.288). Variants with knobs, billets, barrels or bars, the stock-in-trade of masons, recur frequently.

Heads are comparatively rare, particularly combined with rolls. At Saint-Genès in Châteaumeillant and at Plaimpied they look out horizontally, as at Nevers; the downward facing of 3,7,8,10 and 11 on the Saint-Hilaire cornice, as at Split and marked also at Loarre, was not taken up in the Berry. Often heads are treated in peremptory rather than classical fashion (Saint-Jeanvrin fig. 289, Bengy, Malicorne). Figures are even rarer than heads (atlantes at Châteaumeillant, where the corbels are among the most finished and varied in the region).

The tendency towards rigidity of style, exemplified on the capital carving in the treatment and exaggeration of themes initiated at Saint-Benoît: feline masks, the "col berrichon" (turned-down stylized leaf frieze round the lowest register of the bell) or the vertical cylinder of horizontal leaf fronds, is expressed on the corbels by a preference for impersonal geometric devices and mouldings as against animate motifs. On the whole there is little in these corbels either of the animation of Poitiers with its animals or the opulence of Nevers with experiments in shape.

Only in rare instances, and on none of the churches thought to be earlier than the 12th century, are there uniform series of roll corbels. Such series occur at Déols on one level of the tower (144), on the apse at Selles-sur-Cher, and at Neuvy Pailloux; even at La Champenoise though they look alike there are slight variations. There is no sign of the decoration of soffits or metopes with rosettes, so the influence from the Auvergne is not overwhelming even where there are regular series of fillet corbels. La Berthenoux, Avord and Déols share a variant of a rod corbel with a rosette in relief in the centre.

At Châteaumeillant and at Saint-Jeanvrin (145) adoption of the convex profile creates a motif very near the Cordoban leaf-shell (figs 289, 292), and there are some with double rolls. At Avord floret and half-palmette motifs are reminders of connexions with woodwork. Among the series of crude human and animal heads at Saint-Jeanvrin is a horse-head corbel like those at Saint-Sever (Landes); the framing curls are not so deep or finely cut (fig.289, next to the convex corbel). A common Poitevin source is possible, yet a number of surprising details of capital sculpture suggests that the artistic links of the Berry with the South-west and Spain were also very close (146): they share for example an affection for fairground scenes; for a mask replacing the central consoles; eyes drilled for inlay. The characteristic Berry horizontal leaf cylinder is found equally in Gascony and the Berry (147), and relates to the Andalusian incurled leaf motif D4.

Volute Stems with Curls

Another shared detail is the reference to roll corbels on volute stems. The roll corbel was so prevalent in the Berry that it affected the design of capitals. At a number of churches, among them Neuvy Saint-Sépulcre, La Celle-Bruère and Plaimpied (148), a projecting corner human head under a veil is framed by stems sprouting curls which meet above it to provide a diminished volute. Vergnolle traces the motif back to a leaf canopy on capitals at Saint-Benoît: one in the porch with a figure bending at the corner under an oppressive volute (149) for example, and in the choir a corner head projecting likewise under a leaf canopy. At Plaimpied and Neuilly-en-Dun the head framed by rolls in this manner is transferred back to a corbel (fig.288)(154); whether the conversion from leaf canopy to a volute stem with curls took place at Saint-Benoît on corbels now lost, or the leaf only became a curl in the hands of the Berry sculptor with his urge to formalize, and whether Spanish examples contributed to the development, remains to be decided: a parallel process took place on capital volute stems in Spain.

Volute Stems with Curls: Spain

The bent figure on the corner of the capital in the porch of Saint-Benoît, designated as the source of the Berry motif, is similar to figures on capitals in the Panteón in León (151) and under a similar heavy canopy. Both on these capitals and at Saint-Benoît the eyes are inlaid with lead (as they are on León ivories as well). Capital 22 in the nave at Jaca and capital 15 at Loarre (152) follow the same scheme, the bent figure at Jaca under a double leaf, plain on top and foliated below, at Loarre under the traditional devouring monster, as on the Porte des Comtes at Saint-Sernin, which descends from the work of the master of the crypt capitals at Saint-Bénigne in Dijon (153). At Loarre the curve of the figure is less marked and the volute has no curls or sprouts, but the capitals warrant inclusion because the head of the attendant, like the rider's head on a capital of similar composition (154) is veiled and very like the Berry heads under discussion.

At Santiago the chevet capitals 13 and 16 (155), on which again the eyes are pierced for inlay, both have figures whose heads occupy the angles, and the stem of the volutes is carved with a line of little curls. At Jaca the foliage capital No 10 in the nave, with a strong Mozarab-type leaf, has curls on the stem, and the volute sweeps into a downturned leaf (D16). The west door capital 4 with men and snakes (D17)(156) has the volute stems and one caulicole stem carved with curls. At Frómista there are curls on the volute stem of the bird capital in the nave (Gaillard's no 14), and on one volute stem each of the Adoration capital no 12 and the superb dompter capital no 1 (157); the other volute in each case is carved with scaley leaves connecting the notions of curl and tendril (the scaley leaves that decorate the vertical bars on the corbels at Iguácel). Many capitals in the Panteón have volute stems branching into scrolls or bearing flowers. No 19 is close to a capital at Saint-Sever de Rustan where an alignment of curl scrolls makes the volute stem (158). A comparative study of other details of motifs in the two areas should lead to more precise correlations than can be advanced at present.

The associations of these volute stems at Frómista reflect Andalusia influence in addition to their own reference to Andalusian corbel and arch forms. The bird capital has Moissac's linked scroll motif (D5), generally recognized as deriving from Andalusian decorative carving (159). Some of its many variants at Frómista (160) have close parallels at Saint-Benoît, for example the scroll lining the mandorla behind Saint Martin (161). The console on the face of the bird capital takes the form of a pine cone (D2). The console of capital no 1 is almost eliminated, and a lion mask (D17f-see introductory notes to Appendix I part 2) occupies the centre of the capital face. Though lions have widespread associations and can hardly be used as a diagnostic of Andalusia influence, the many uses to which the motif was put in Andalusian decoration: spitting foliage, framed in a V of foliage, approximating to a human face in an eared cap (cf Berry roman fig.83) cannot be left out of account in considering the affiliations implied by its appearance here.

Roll Corbels in Sainte-Foy in Conques

Roll corbels are in the majority among the many corbels at Conques (figs 293-295)(162). They are all of limestone. Those of the north and south transept doorways may date from the last stages of the fist building campaign, ending a few years after the death of Odolric in 1065 (163). A systematic classification of the many forms in relation to their placing would allow more far-reaching conclusions than can be attempted here, and would contribute usefully to deciding the chronology of the building. This is still not agreed upon by the scholars most concerned, but earlier datings are gaining ground.

M. Aubert distinguished five building campaigns up to
1119 and dated the west portal to 1130. For G. Gaillard
(164) the present church, begun under Abbot Odolric (+1065)
between 1041 and 1050 was finished soon after the accession
of Bégon III in 1087. He observed that the structure is all
of a piece and that references to Bégon's work are confined
to his building of the cloister. More recently J.-Cl. Fau
(165) had dated the corbels of the transept doors to after
1080 and probably early 12th century, and most of the
capital sculpture, after the sandstone plait capitals of
Odolric's campaign, before 1110; in agreement with the
orthodox French view he places the tympanum some quarter
century later (166). In his view the last years of the
first building campaign saw the beginnings of historiated
capitals and the abandonment of the interlace tradition.

J. Bousquet (167) however puts the climax of
sculptural activity, including the great tympanum of the
Last Judgment on the west doorway to "a period of
exceptional creative activity" around 1100, and L. Grodecki
adopted the "new thesis" of Z. Swieckowsky (168) for the
anteriority of Conques over any Auvergnat sculpture, which
he suggested begins at Mozac c.1095.

The case is strong for the earlier datings of the
sculpture, including the tympanum, since the capitals at
Conques which are copied at Santiago are close in style to
the Conques tympanum sculpture, and the copies at Santiago
date before 1105 when the chapel of St Faith was dedicated
by the bishop of Pamplona (169). The fact that the north
and south doorways at Conques leading into the transept
arms are overlaid by the nave walls which impinge on both
the arches and the cornices above them can only mean they
belong to an early stage in the building (fig.278)(170).
This being so, the "ball" capitals of the south door and
the incurled leaf (D5) scroll are an established type some
time before their introduction at Moissac and Toulouse, and
Spanish-type corbels with crouching figures (fig.279) begin
their career here or at Frómista.

The progress of work at Conques is generally agreed:
the building was begun round the whole periphery entirely
in red sandstone (172) and continued and finished in yellow
limestone, supplemented with schist. Sandstone is used for
the whole series of plaitwork capitals that appear in and
outside the chevet and on the north transept door. The
cornices of both doors and all corbels on the building are
of limestone, and so are the capitals of the south door.
The use of both materials together in the transept masonry
precludes any suggestion that there was an interruption in
the work to coincide with a difference in materials. The
correctness of this is borne out by the decoration of the
corbels on the chapels, which reflects the decoration of
the plaitwork capitals beside them (fig.128), so there was
no immediate change of workshop. The south door illustrates
the moment of rejection of the old plaitwok tradition and

the introduction of variation in corbel forms along with a new type of capital.

Corbels at Conques fall into three stylistic groups. The first group is fillet roll corbels, corresponding to both the earliest part of the building (chevet and north transept) and round the eaves of the chapels, and the latest: uniform fillet corbels support the eaves of nave, aisles and towers.

The second group consists of modifications of this classic corbel. The curls are smaller, sometimes only remaining as lobes on the sides, often multiplied to make a fine edging for the increased number of planes down the profile or along the fillet; in some cases the roll has entirely disappeared. Alternatively, the fillet is broadened to a panel containing some geometric or abstract relief decoration (knobs, bars, grooving or rods). This type is on the ambulatory and apse.

The third type is full relief carving of figures or heads. Only a few of these are combined with rolls, and there are many without. These are on the ambulatory and apse and they predominate on the transepts. Both second and third groups are represented on the south transept door.

Type 1

These are far from stereotyped on the east end. On the radiating chapels many corbels have motifs on the vertical face, linking them closely with the capitals between which they are placed. There are six similar corbels over the north door; the deeply excavated curls vary in number from four to seven. The stems are very thin and fill the side, springing from the top inner corner and branching lower down. The fillets are grooved and the vertical faces have various simple groove patterns, no 3 from the left with an ox head in shallow relief (172). On this corbel the four lower "wood-shavings" curl towards each other in pairs.

The Annunciation panel now in the north transept is framed in arches with a cornice above. The shape of the corbels holding this cornice is like this type of corbel but only a top curl is indicated (Rouergue roman, fig. 20). The cornice of the north doorway is a plain torus moulding; there are no carved metopes or soffits.

Type 2.South Transept Door

On this door the six corbels are less uniform than over the north door. Corbel 1, on the north is half-hidden in the nave wall. The six rolls are carved with zig-zags on the sides, creating a link with the Platerías consoles and the Jaca "Gilduinus" corbel which has a shallower chevron pattern on the sides. Corbel 2 is damaged; it was probably similar to corbel 3, which is carved with a crouching figure. They have curl stems with thickening sides, no 3 with curls upturned. These corbels are evidently recut or imitations; if they present the original design and not a shallower imitation of the sides of the north door corbels, they are of the same type as the corbels of Loarre and Toulouse but, as on the Poitiers cornice, the concave line is abandoned. No 4 has a large facetted knob on a plain concave panel and curl stems again running to the back, no 5 has instead three smaller knobs with star or spiral grooving. No 6 is a grooved fillet roll corbel. The shallow stems that fill the sides of the corbels, and much more strongly the edging of the cornice itself, recall the tower cornice of Saint-Hilaire: in fact the only comparison for the soffits is at Saint-Hilaire and their repetitions at Melle (Saint Savinien) and Airvault, apart from the single slab from Ile-Barbe with a scroll containing a hollowed rosette that probably comes from a similar cornice. The only original soffits on this south door cornice are 1-2 and 2-3. 1-2 has three slightly hollowed rosettes in linked circles formed of split stems, separated by a sheaf of three narrow leaves. The edge of the cornice is a single-billet moulding pierced with a foliage motif. The soffit 1-2 and cornice edge at Saint Hilaire are closely similar. This is the only approximation at Conques to the soffit rosette which is so marked, at Santiago and Toulouse in large and classical guise, and sparse and hollow in Auvergne, but it is markedly different from either the hollow soffit coupolettes or mosaic metope rosettes of Auvergnat cornices. 2-3 has a more elaborate scroll based on half-palmettes and linked circles, very like the carving on the Bessuéjouls altar panels (Rouergue roman fig.74); in both cases Andalusian analogies are close.

Type 3. Ambulatory, Apse and Transepts

Here the abstract variants of classic roll corbels are numerous. There are occasional plain rod corbels. Mostly the face of the fillet is narrowed, not widened as on the south door, and the number of planes on the sides increased, each edged by some kind of small or large curl or scallop, and provided with knobs or billets. There are figure and head corbels among them, but then mostly devoid of any suggestion of rolls.

The corbels on the south door with figures represent a stage before the abandonment of the roll motif by the figure sculptor. There is a cornice on the interior of the south transept façade (fig.295) and, as here and there on the ambulatory also, the quadruple billet cornice is punctuated with little figures: confronted animals or, the majority, angel busts (173). An atlas angel is in a pose frequent on Spanish corbels; the frontal eagle is familiar at Loarre and Iguácel on capitals, and on capitals and a corbel at Santiago (174).

The Spread of Influence from Conques

Conques is doubtless responsible for roll corbels at Lunac and Aubrac nearby. Corbels at Bessuéjouls on the tower's north and south façades, like capitals, ae closely allied to those at Conques. There is one angel atlas, and an eagle, a rider and a sphinx, which also connect with Santiago, but there are no rolls. Similarly at Perse rolls were rejected.

Apart from this local influence we may well see in Conques the pioneer roll corbels in stone that inspired the wholesale programme of Saint-Sernin.

Further Andalusian Elements at Conques

There are superposed columns F9 as buttresses on the exterior of the radiating chapels, and twin columns F11 in the tribune arcades and in the two upper orders of arcades in the apse.

The supports of the nave vault alternate F7 with engaged half-columns and pilasters to tribune level.

A slight impression of horseshoe arches is created throughout since arches are stilted and the voussoirs shorter than the blocks of the jambs, the edges thus created being cut away.

The serpentine basin in the cloister (175) has capitals with down-turned leaf volutes D16 and a frieze of animal heads and busts. There were also famous basins in the cloisters at Moissac and at Santiago: ablution basins were from early on an essential part of the fitting out of a mosque. The basins of Andalusian palaces with animal heads were described in Chapter II.

Several capitals have a downturned leaf D16 at the corners, some from the tribune and cloister and some in serpentine that may be from Bégon's tomb structure (figs 24, 297). Pine cones D2 are frequent in Conques sculpture and the basin has a capital with pendant pine.

The Conques atelier played an important part in developing the vermiculé technique on metalwork (fig.298) which owes much to Muslim design (176).

The portable altar in the Treasury, given by Bishop Pons of Barbastro (previously a monk at Conques) to Bégon, has oculi in the spandrels (F19) between the arcades framing the saints (177): a reflection of Andalusian spandrel rosettes. Some of the saints' haloes are lobed.

The close association between the interlace capitals of the chevet and the roll corbels between them makes it likely that an Andalusian influence contributed the facetted colonettes of the Rodez altar which has similar capitals. Facetted columns are rare in French Romanesque. Fau notes them twice more in south-west France, each time with interlace capitals: at Saint-André-de-Sorède and Saint-Pierre-Toirac (F21). The facetted colonettes in al-Hakam II´s nave provide a model which is associated both with roll corbels and with lobed arches (178).

The Relations of Conques with Spain, and Wider Affiliations

Already in the 9th century the relics of St Vincent of Zaragoza were coveted by monks of Conques and two monks despatched to find them (179). In the 10th century the Miracula reports the death of Raymond count of Rouergue, on the way to Compostela. In the 11th century is the story of quidam Arnaldus, contained in Book III of the Miracula, which assumes without comment the background of trading relations with Muslim Spain (180). Roger de Toeni in 1020 called at Conques on his return from a campaign against Andalusians, and went back to Normandy to found Conches as a priory in honour of St Faith (181). The outstanding rôle of Pierre d´Andouque in Aragon has aready been mentioned, and the many possessions in Navarre and Aragon that he secured for Conques in the last decades of the 11th century.

In the last third of the century the title to the county of Rouergue was assumed by Raymond de St Gilles, whose ascendency in Toulouse increased as the activity of his brother William declined. William IV left for the Holy Land early in the last decade of the century. Raymond´s third wife was Elvira, daughter of Alfonso VI of León. His niece Philippa, daughter of William IV, who later married William IX of Poitiers was the wife of Sancho Ramirez of Aragon (182).

Conques joined in the upsurge of prosperity of the 11th century. The administrative and commerical connexions of the monastery werre widespread (183) and corresponded to the economic perspectives of the counts of Rouergue, who aimed at making their province a zone of passage between the Massif Central and the Mediterranean. This situation is reflected in the dissemination of the style of the Narbonne marble sculptors round Rodez and Conques, bringing their interlace-and-palmette capitals to the north door and chevet; but this was only part of a network stretching from Andalusia to Champagne. The expansion of cities like Barcelona and Toulouse stimulated a flow of movement and exchange of ideas (184). There are enough details of iconography and style at Conques to show contact with Saint-Benoît, the Velay, Aragon and Moissac, apart from the most obvious links with Santiago, Toulouse and the Auvergne (185).

Roll corbels at Saint-Sernin in Toulouse

The corbels of Saint-Sernin have been much supplemented in the 19th century restorations (186).

Lithographs done before the restorations of du Mège and Viollet-le-Duc show there were corbels on the chapels and over the Porte des Comtes, but not under ambulatory, apse or transept eaves. Those that can be taken as original on the building are all roll corbels, but the corbels on a fragment of cornice fom Saint-Sernin preserved in a private collection in Paris (187) are without rolls.

Corbels on the building can be divided into three distinct groups: abstract variants of roll forms; human and animal heads; and more dramatic figures or busts. The first two types are found on the chevet, the second over the Porte des Comtes, the third over the Porte Miègeville. The first two resemble Conques corbels in having deeply excavated curls, but the concave profile line is more strictly adhered to.

The Eaves Corbels

The line of the profile is strongly marked and the stems of deeply excavated curls expand towards it. There are no classic fillet corbels; the variants of it are more emancipated from the rigid central line than the variants at Conques, with a broad-lobed central panel, a double, notched fillet, double rows of curls and a tongue-like leaf resembling the opulent elaborations at Santiago. A few animal heads were also part of the original scheme (188) and as at Conques there are occasional rod corbels, similar to those at Jaca.

The Porte des Comtes and the Fragment now in the North Nave Tribune (189)

There are two types of human head, one bearded and one unbearded, and ox, bear (or feline) and canine (baring its teeth)(fig.300). The top roll runs across the whole width below a vertical face, cut, or overlaid (on the fragment) by horns where an ox head is involved, but generally moulded as on a classical Roman corbel, as at Loarre. The heads are set low and detached from the plain panel that generally divides them from the curls. These, deeply excavated at the sides, have narrow stems sprouting from the curved line parallel to the profile. They look out almost horizontally (Haut Languedoc roman, fig.16).

The Porte Miègeville

The rolls are reduced on the sides to lobes (fig.220). There are contorted beasts, and a lion dompter, in the style of the Magus and rider panels on the doorway, paralleled at Santiago. The vertical face is very short and the concentration of the design is much higher D5 than on the Porte des Comtes corbels. Two busts and a plant motif are unconvincing restorations.

While the soffit rosettes on the Porte des Comtes are square, the soffits and metopes here have round rosettes like those of the tribune and Paris cornice fragments.

The two lintel consoles of the door (fig.251) are strongly reminiscent of the Platerías doorway consoles, but with differences implying a later date: they are more ambitious and less robust: the left one alone has vestigial rolls in the form of a lobed profile.

The Paris Cornice Fragment

Eagle and Gilduinus-type head consoles suggest a date near the Porte des Comtes corbels, but they appear to be devoid of rolls. The metope and soffit rosettes are contained in circles, like the tribune fragment. A line of floret D3 nail heads, and a line of little crosses along the borders recall the woodworking associations of corbel tables.

Further Andalusian Elements at Saint-Sernin

The earliest type of floral decoration in Saint Sernin, on a capital in the ambulatory (Haut-Languedoc roman fig.11), has on the impost a version of the heart-and-dart motif D11 combined with a floret D3 (compare AHIII fig.113). Impost decorations on the Porte des Comtes capitals (ibid.figs 12, 14) are also close to Cordoban border motifs.

Linked scrolls D7, balls and pine cones D2 are frequent in capital decoration. The chapels are buttressed with superposed columns F9 (fig.13). The figures in the spandrels F19 over the Porte des Comtes were framed in arches on which were carved inscriptions in relief F2 (fig.7). The only parallel for such relief inscriptions is over figures at Marcilhac (fig.6).

The central figure of Saint-Saturninus (now destroyed) is flanked by lions D17h. The placing of the three niches with figures is an elaboration of the Andalusian practice of decorating arch spandrels with a motif F19, usually a rosette. On the Porte Miègeville, as at León, this principle produces figures similarly placed standing out in deep relief.

Roll Corbels in the Lower Garonne Valley and Gascony

Two distinct types of roll corbel are found in the area comprising the Bordelais, the Agenais and Gascony. One is a heavy plain rod corbel without fillet (Saint-Macaire, Engayrac, Sérignac), the other a distinctive version of head or figure corbel. A Spanish influence is discernible (190) not only in the figure motifs and treatment of the roll, which are closely allied to Frómista, Jaca and Santiago, but in the presence of the plain rod form so rarely encountered elsewhere in France. The two types do not occur together. At Aubiac where there are plain rods the figure corbels have no rolls.

A characteristic of the figure corbels of this area is the diminution in relief, size and importance, and the multiplication in number, of the rolls, compared with other regions (191). A comparable development can be seen on the left-hand consoles of the Platerías doorways at Santiago (figs 245-8). The concave profile line is strictly adhered to.

Saint-Sever-des-Landes and La Sauve Majeure were the most dominant artistic centres (192). Both of these have examples of the figure type of roll corbel; those of La Sauve are preserved in the Cloisters Museum, New York. At Saint-Sever they support the eaves of the only north chapel to survive intact, and of the north and east walls of the straight parts behind it. These correspond to the earliest parts of the building (193).

The First Type of Roll Corbel in the South-West: La Sauve Majeure, Saint-Sever, Saint-Pierrre-du-Mont, Roquefort, Lagrange, Cadillac (L&G), Saint-Sardos, Moirax

La Sauve-Majeure

The group of twelve corbels in the Cloisters (194) includes three roll corbels and one on which the scroll, held in the mouth of a lion, forms with the curling tendrils a similar line of curls (fig.219). The treatment of the lion's mane, the little scroll on its forehead and the hair and beard of a man on other corbels show that the same sculptor carved both roll and non-roll corbels. He carved capitals and imposts besides. On one corbel the rods are carried behind the two men seated in an embrace. The composition is paralleled at Saint-Sardos (L&G) on the doorway consoles (fig.252). On those corbels from La Sauve that have curls they continue to sprout horizontally across the front face at the top, treating the curls like a border motif rather than rod ends (195). On one corbel, one curl from each side is brought to meet at the centre.

Saint-Sever-des-Landes

At Saint-Sever (figs 302, 303) the chapels next to the apse on either side have corbels supporting the eaves, and there are also corbel tables along the east and north walls of the straight parts behind them. On the north these are roll corbels with animal heads or busts, seated quadrupeds or monkey figures. The poses resemble corbels of Jaca and Santiago, but the rolls are treated in a distinctive way and the animal heads have a characteristic liveliness. The heads are set on thick solid necks, unlike the long slender necks of many Spanish corbels, but their placing in relation to the corbel block is the same, with the aim of projecting the creature beyond the limits of the block.

The full-figure corbels on the north of the chevet are topped by a curl projecting inwards from either side, corresponding to the row of curls across the top of La Sauve corbels. This suggests a different hand from that of the animal busts, which places the heads under a horizontal rod or curled shaving. Though uniformity of the curls is apparently the aim, the stems on the head corbels are all thick, and swell towards the profile with a counter-curve, like the curl stems of the Loarre corbels, while the curls of the animal figures have no such subtlety. Neither type at Saint-Sever can be attributd to the same hand as the La Sauve corbels though they are all closely akin.

The north chapels of Saint-Sever were built earlier than the south, and there are no animate themes on the interior capitals. The capitals of the southern chapels were decorated by a workshop, active in many parts of the region, whose work is the earliest with animate themes at Saint-Sever (196); to them must be attributed the corbels on the exterior of the northern chapels (197).

The lion theme is among the most popular in the South West; it is shared by Andalusian and Romanesque iconography and has many possible sources; on its own it could not testify to an Andalusian connexion, but it can contribute to confirming links where others are suggested. Cabanot has perhaps too lightly dismissed the Cordoban inspiration for the cruciform impost and smooth acanthus leaves of some of the earliest capitals in Saint-Sever (198). Without denying the inventiveness of the Saint-Sever sculptor, the Andalusian precedent exists (AHIII fig.215, 142, 143). The base carved with lions and atlantes under one of these presents more Islamic parallels: excavations at the 11th century Fanal castle in the Qala´a of the Beni Hammad in Algeria revealed that doorway arches were supported on black marble lions (199); atlantes figure on the corbels of the Játiva basin.

Two Doorways with Consoles. Cadillac and Saint-Sardos

In the descendence of La Sauve and Saint-Sever corbels are the consoles on doorways at Saint-Sardos (fig.252) and Cadillac (near Miramont) (fig.304) in the Agenais. Lintel consoles in this Santiago or Toulousan tradition are not uncommon in the South West, but generally the rolls are dispensed with. A stepped arch profile F18 arises from consoles.

On the south door of the little church of St Martin at Cadillac two consoles with curls quite deeply cut in the sides but separated from the edge by a fillet are carved with a jawless lion head on the west and an eagle on the east. A bull head on the corner of the west capital impost might lead us to expect that the door capitals complete the series of evangelist symbols, but in fact the east capital also has a bull head. There is no lintel, the tympanum with the Lamb in a thick torus frame flanked by crouched reverted birds creates a stepped opening which in this case is exceedingly narrow. The capitals have snail volutes.

At Saint-Sardos the sculpture is less rustic than at Cadillac; a lintel is supported on consoles, and carved with the fine curls of La Sauve corbels. The figures are paired, like corbel 115 from La Sauve. On the east are two hunched, seated human figures, hands on knees; on the west, two lions with thir backs facing outwards; all the heads are lost. Across the front the curls are separated, like billet moulding, to allow the sides of the curls to be carved.

The lintel has an unusual motif, imitating drawn thread work, but interlaced and confused with branching plant stems that at one place have an animal head at the node. The central vertical panel of the five forming the tympanum has a heavier version of the Saint-Sever linked tendril scroll.

These two doorways belong to the same type as those of Nogaro, Tasque and Sévignac in Gascony. A lost prototype at Saint-Sever is to be postulated as the intermediary from the Platerías doorways at Santiago. Only Tasque of these three Gascon doorways preserves any reminiscence of the roll motif (200), in a beading that edges the concave profile.

Roll Corbels at Moirax

The church of Sainte-Marie was much restored in the 19th century, but the reports show that the decoration was reproduced with great fidelity (201).The chevet has many types of roll corbel (fig.249). Masks, lobed fillets and fanciful abstract shapes are all flanked by curls springing from a concave profile. These are sometimes developed to reproduce the "snail shell" volute popular on capitals in the South West and in north Spain.

The metopes all have large circular medallions of geometric interlace (D13), in relief without any hollowing. Nevertheless the closest analogy is with the dished circular rosettes on the soffits at Jaca. No metopes survive from Romanesque buildings in Bordeaux, from La Sauve or from Saint-Caprais in Agen (202); Moirax thus appears more isolated in this respect than it probably was. It represents the link in a sequence from Jaca and Saint-Sever to the densely-decorated metopes and friezes of the following decades in the Médoc (203), Angoûmois and Saintonge.

The links of the South West with the Berry are emphasized once again at Moirax. The corbel of fig.249 with a lion head framed in curls is the same composition as the volute-framed heads of the Berry; hence the similarity of the interlace knots of the Moirax metopes and the medallions at Saint-Outrille and Châteaumeillant (Berry

211

<u>roman</u> figs 10, 61, 62) are unlikely to be fortuitous. The twin column of the latter´s façade and the interlace medallion on the impost suggests that some elements of this shared decorative tradition may be Andalusian: the transmission by a wood-carving tradition is patent.

The Second Type of Roll Corbel in the South West, Plain, and Plain Fillet: Saint-Macaire, Aubiac, Layrac, Engayrac, Peujard

The plain type of corbel is found in the vicinity of the Garonne. Only at Saint-Macaire is it used exclusively (<u>Guyenne romane</u> fig.67). At Layrac there are a number of discreet variations derived from the roll corbel (<u>fig</u>.305).

Aubiac

The eaves cornice is restored (<u>fig</u>.306), but the corbels are only cleaned for the most part. There are crouching figures, animal heads with ringed necks, their curve strongly marking the concave profile, whereas on the roll corbels the line is almost straight. On some there is a central fillet flush with the rolls, and the rolls are treated on the sides simply as rod ends. The closest analogies are with the Berry or Bourbonnais (cf <u>fig</u>.288); neither Saint-Sever nor Saint-Sernin offer any close parallels.

Other Examples in the Agenais

There is a single rod-corbel on the west façade of Sérignac, a few kilometres west of Agen, on the north end of the cornice holding the weather roof over the doorway. The whole doorway massif appears to be added to the early 11th century nave about a century later. Unfortunately the chevet has lost its corbels.

Engayrac is a small church north of Moissac, of which it was a priory. There is a single rod-corbel (<u>fig</u>.308) on the axis of the scale-roofed apse; the rest of the corbels are plain concave. The metopes are perforated, as they are on a group of small churches in the Agenais and Bordelais mostly dateable just before 1100 (204): the capitals of the interior include one with felines like those of Saint-Sever, Moirax and Saint-Mont, which once more would date the church in the first decade of the 12th century.

Gascony. Saint-Macaire

This church has a trefoil plan chevet like Aubiac. Round the eaves of the chapels is a uniform series of heavy rod corbels. These are part of a heightening of the roofs undertaken during the 12th century. The corbel table is supported on twin colonnettes (F6) set on bases at the top of tall pilaster buttresses with engaged half-columns. This corbel table is unique in France; the corbels resemble those of rural Spanish churches like Villarmún near León (fig.231), and represent a late phase in the Romanesque adoption of Andalusian themes, corresponding to Andalusian references in the churches of Saint-Blaise and Oloron nearer the Spanish border.

L´Hôpital-Saint-Blaise

The church is in many respects a patent imitation of Andalusian architecture, as the vaulting F22 makes clear (fig.12). It also has lobed arches F21, pierced window grilles and summary roll corbels F1 (Pyrénées romanes figs 136-142).

Sainte-Marie, Oloron

The vault resembles closely that of Saint-Blaise, but with shell squinches and four-lobed oculi. The doorway is surmounted by arcades F17, has spandrel figures F19, encrusted reliefs which may be the vestiges of a kind of alfiz F12 and clearly separated voussoir motifs F14. The outer archivolt has a crossed stem running scroll D1 in flat two-plane relief. The trumeau is supported on symmetrically-composed pair of atlantes with turban caps. No corbels survive from this campaign (205).

Peujard

North of Saint-Macaire at Peujard a typically Saintongeais façade of the second half of the 12th century (fig.307) has an arcade of chevron-decorated arches F17 on double colonnettes F6 over the wide doorway; above it is a corbel table with various moulded corbels including one of plain horizontal rods and others with series of knobs, or knobs flanking a fillet.

Other Areas.The Limousin

Roll corbels are rare throughout the Limousin. At Solignac there are fillet corbels on the north wall of the nave (on which the arcading is trilobed) and a few on the chevet. The abbey church was consecrated in 1143. It had rich possessions not only in Limousin but in the diocese of Périgueux, and fraternity of prayer both with Saint-Benoît and La Chaise-Dieu: these contacts may explain the presence of the corbel form. The chapels are buttressed by superposed columns F9, found also at Saint-Léonard.

Close to the Auvergne border, Beaulieu in the south of the province has a few roll corbels, among a variety of types with heads and mason´s motifs, mostly straight or convex profiled, and Chambon on the northern border with the Bourbonnais has them or head corbels on the chapels of the chevet (206).

Dordogne

The occurrence of fillet roll corbels at Saint-Jean-de-Côle and La Chancelade is likely to be a reflexion of the influence of Périgueux where their presence is probably due to connexions with the Auvergne (see 105). This influence did not apparently extend much further. Roll corbels are uncommon in the Angoûmois and only present in the Saintonge in remotely derived forms.

Summary

The corbel table characteristic of Romanesque building has no antecedents outside Spain. The roll form of the earliest French corbels is a distinctive and novel feature of the Mezquita, where it appears on the interior arcade supports, under eaves and as lintel consoles. It developed in stone and wood in Andalusia in two basic ways: first, to the "classic" corbel with a slightly-projecting unlobed central fillet that follows the concave line of the lobed profile; and second, to the "prow-shaped" corbel on which the fillet is enlarged into a wide convex motif filling the concave space.

The earliest example of corbels in France is at Vendôme; it is of the classic type and has typical Andalusian surface decoration. Without such decoration the type is found also at Jumièges, Tournus and Méobecq before 1070, soon after at Conques and subsequently in the Auvergne, where it became widespread, and with many variations and simplifications in the Loire valley, Berry and Bourbonnais, where it also combined with heads and figures. It also appeared early (before 1050) at Poitiers, with Andalusian-type decoration, and together with examples where a head or figure replaces the prow of the second Andalusian type. Heads or figures were soon preferred without rolls in the west of France. In the South West and in north Spain, including Toulouse, the roll was combined with heads and figures with varying consistency. In Romanesque Spain the primitive rod type without a fillet had some currency and there are examples of these in Gascony and the Agenais.

Mozarabic versions had little influence, but the exaggerated fillet at San Millán de Suso suggests a tradition, perhaps mainly expressed in woodwork, that may explain the exuberant contorted shapes at Nevers and Le Mans. There is good reason to suppose that the frequent communications with Spain resulting from religious, political and commercial intercourse produced a shared building repertoire. The extent to which the roll corbel, let alone the general principle of a corbel table, retained an Andalusian association in the craftsmens´ minds apparently varied in different regions. The influence of the richly-carved Andalusian corbel tables in stone, wood and plaster is manifest in the setting of some of the earliest roll corbels at Poitiers and Conques, and in the soffits with single hollow rosettes of the Auvergne. An intermediary stage towards these, represented at Ile-Barbe near Lyon, underlines the rôle of the Rhône as a transmitter of Andalusian ideas, though after the early examples of Tournus and Lyon the roll corbel is absent in the great valley.

The distribution of roll corbels, which virtually excludes the Velay, Limousin, Angoûmois and Saintonge, and Poitou after about 1080, shows a quite independent pattern from the distribution of lobed arches.

CHAPTER V. NOTES

1.   In French they are called "modillons à copeaux"
("wood-shaving corbels"), following Viollet le Duc
(Dictionnaire raisonné de l´architecture française du XIe
au XVIe siècle, 1875, vol. IV, pp 307-318 ("corbeaux") and
p. 319 ("corniche"). His contention that they derived from
unfinished woodworking is not now accepted. The chisel is
not easily used in such a manner as to produce the effect
he illustrates.   In 1911 E. Mâle, "La Mosquée de
Cordoue...", Revue de l´art ancien et moderne, repr. in Art
et Artistes du Moyen Age 1968 (cf p. 33) pointed out that
the explanation, though plausible for eaves corbels which
simulated wooden beam ends, is invalid when applied to the
earliest known examples of the form, which are in the
Mezquita, carved in stone, and which support a pilaster in
an arcade. In Spanish the term is "modillon de lobulos". K.
Conant translates the French literally (CRA) as "chisel-
curl eaves-brackets" (p. 175 i.a.). As this description
really only applies to the variant with a central fillet
the term "roll corbel" has been adopted here as more
appropriate to all types.

2.   E. Mâle, "L´Espagne arabe et l´art roman" Revue des
Deux Mondes, 15th Nov., 1923, repr. Art et Artistes (see
n.1), Ch. III, p. 40.

3.   L. Torres-Balbás, "Los Modillones de Lobulos" I, AEAA
1936, Jan.-Apr., pp 1-62; II, ibid., May-Aug., pp 113/64-
149/90 (henceforth LTB 1936) is the only monograph on the
feature.   It is concerned primarily with proving the
contention of G. Marçais ("Sur trois formes décoratives de
la Mosquée de Cordoue", Actes du XIXe Congrès international
des orientalistes, Algiers 1905, Part II, Section 7, Paris
1907, pp 3-4) that the Cordoban form was derived from a
Byzantine adaptation of the common Roman S-shaped corbel
with a curved acanthus leaf motif, subsequently disfigured
in the sculpture of the period of "artistic barbarism"
after the fall of the Empire. Torres-Balbás´s study follows
the post-Cordoban development of this type of corbel in
Italy and Spain, down to a re-instatement of the original
classical acanthus corbel in the Renaissance. He gives a
brief summary of what published material he could find in
1936 on the feature in France, and makes a tentative
conclusion (pp 97-95): that the three classes of corbel
type that developed in Andalusia appeared in France mainly
in the reverse order in which they originally evolved
(which was from plain rod, to fillet, to figures), and that
influences emanating from Andalusia therefore came to
France from different places and monuments at different
times; that the sources were likely to be not only Cordoban
or Mozarab, and that carpentry should be remembered as a
possible mode of transmission.

French roll corbels were also considered by F.
Deshoulières, "Les corniches romanes", BM 1920, pp 55ff; R.

Crozet, L´Art roman en Berry, Paris 1932, pp 223-227; id.,
"La corniche du clocher de Saint-Hilaire de Poitiers" BM
1934, pp 341-345. F. Garcia-Romo, "Influencias hispano-
musulmanes...", Arte Espanol 20, 1954, pp 39-40, comments
on the coincidence of roll corbels and the type of
Corinthian capital he argues is Mozarabic, carved in the
mid-11th century at La Trinité in Vendôme, Méobecq, Saint-
Jean-de-Montierneuf in Poitiers, Le Ronceray d´Angers, and
Parthenay-le-Vieux. H. Saladin La Mosquée de Sidi Okba à
Kairouan, Paris 1899, before Mâle in 1911 and even before
Marçais in 1905 and 1907, had noted the similarity of
French roll corbels to western Islamic examples, but it was
not until after Mâle´s articles that Viollet-le-Duc´s over-
ingenious theory of their indigenous derivation from
planing or chiselling the ends of roof beams, was rejected.

4. The following account summarizes briefly the published
work in Spanish, in books and articles by Gomez-Moreno,
Torres-Balbás, Pavon Maldonado etc.

5. By the mid-9th century at latest this roll corbel form
was part of the Cordoban repertoire; it was by then
certainly in the Mezquita on the interior arcades and in
the decoration of the blind niches flanking the San Esteban
door. In fact it was probably already in use in the first
campaign of 786; there is a paradox affecting the dating
however (LTB 1957, p. 354 n.37; full references on p. 389.
See my Chapter II n.9).

6. cf Chapter II. M. Lyttleton, Baroque Architecture in
Classsical Antiquity, pl. 105.

7. Quoted in LTB 1957, p. 355 and fig. 157, and LTB 1936,
p. 45 and n. 71.

8. According to Gomez-Moreno (AHIII), part of the
reparations carried out by Muhammad I in 855.

9. A drawing in Ig.Moz., fig. 177, reproduced in Tudela,
fig. 294d.

10. B. Pavon Maldonado, Tudela, Madrid 1978, pls XXIV-XXVI
and pl. XLII. There is a full description and illustration
of the corbels.

11. LTB 1936, p. 51.

12. ibid, pl. XVIII. Some doubt remains as to whether they
belong to the 11th or 12th century.

13. B. Pavon Maldonado, "Quicialeras califales..."al-
And.44, 1967, Cron. Arq., p. 42. They support soffits
carved with elaborate medallions prefiguring the Auvergnat
association of roll corbels with (simpler) rosettes. The
metopes have an entwined stem motif, inherited from the
capitals flanking the mihrab of Abd ar-Rahman II (fig.4) of
830, which was transmitted to the "Cordoban" series of

capitals at Ripoll and into Catalunya. F. Hernandez, "Un aspecto...", AEAAyA, XVI-4, 1930, pp 21-49.

14. al-And 1935, Cron.Arq.III, p. 419/29.

15. LTB 1936, p. 48 (illustration) and p. 49.

16. LTB "Restos de un Techumbre de Carpinteria Musulmana..." al-And.1935, Cron.Arq.III, p. 426/36 and pl. 15. He quotes examples of the "prow" motif, "in its origin simply a curled leaf" in Malaga, in the National Archaeological Museum in Madrid (12th and 13th centuries), plaster ones in Almería, Tlemcen etc., and even in Cairo. It was still current in the 14th century when it is found in the Alhambra and elsewhere in Granada.

17. AMO, fig. 62, a corbel at Bougie repr. LTB 1936, p.43.

18. CA 119, 1961. At Notre-Dame-du Pré on the east chapel are some corbels akin to the 11th century corbels of Qairawan and Bougie; on the north transept chapel (fig.223) they have curls framing the motif, an Andalusian element absent from Ifriqiya. Rougher versions at La Couture (fig. 224) stress the roll. The drawing by Viollet-le-Duc (Dict. "corniches") brings out the resemblance to the more elegant Zaragoza model. Greatest prosperity at La Couture was during the abbacy of Asselin (d. 1072): contemporary with or shortly after the building of the Aljafería. The arches of alternating brick and stone in Le Mans (F. Lesueur, "Saint-Martin d´Angers, La Couture du Mans, Saint-Philibert de Grandlieu et autres églises à éléments de briques dans la région de la Loire", BM 1961) may show another stimulus from Andalusia. Some initiative is implied in flouting the long tradition that requires either a concave profile on a corbel or if the hollow is filled, only a narrow fillet. Even where this tradition may have allowed broad heads, for example in Poitiers on the transept at Saint-Hilaire and at Montierneuf, the profile is observed in the curved necks. Jumièges (fig. 225, right hand corbel) and Ebreuil in part, and later rustic work in the Berry and Auvergne (fig. 226) adopted the labour-saving retention of the rectangular block, but the traditional form was the stronger.

19. This tongue shape is common at Santiago, GG 1938 pl. LXXXVII.

20. F. Hernandez, op.cit.; G. Gaillard, Premiers Essais...

21. The "inverted volute" and "Berrichon leaf" (Berry roman, pls 22, 46. 47. 51) launched at Saint-Benoît (Vergnolle, GBA 1972) may be ramifications of this motif, made possible once the principle of upward thrust is abandoned. The Berrichon leaf also appears already at La Trinité in Vendôme.

22. Examples in the following: illustrations where not otherwise noted refer to M. Gomez-Moreno, Iglesias

Mozarabes 1919: San Miguel de Escalada, AD 913 (figs 62-63); San Cebrián de Mazote, (AD 916 (LTB 1936 p. 125/75 and pl. XXIV); Santiago de Penalba, AD 931-937 (fig. 115); Sa Maria de Lebena, AD 930 (figs 140-147); San Miguel de Celanova, AD 940 (pl. XCIII); Sa Maria de Vilanova (p. 251 and fig. 124); San Roman de Moroso (figs 161-162); San Pedro de Berlangas (Burgos), qu. LTB 1936 n. 104; San Millán de la Cogolla, AD 984 (fig.225); San Román de Hornija (p. 188, fig. 82, a more classic Cordoban shape); etc. In Catalunya the Puerta Ferrada of San Filiù de Guixols (late 10th century) (LTB 1936, pl. XXVI) has small derived roll corbels like billet moulding. They support an arcading of First Romanesque type. The gateway also has capitals with a curl profile, similar to a roll corbel, that might have some part in the ancestry of the shape of soffits with lobes like those on the south door at Cahors, with curls on the points (fig 185).

23. Ig.Moz. fig. 62.

24. Torres-Balbás finds no example of the roll form before Cordoba, but he quotes as antecedents the horizontal corbel at the entrance of San Pablo del Camps in Barcelona (6th century)(LTB 1936, p. 38) and "perhaps" would include the heavy stone Visigothic beam supports with one large roll or horizontal cylinder carved at the upper or the lower angle of a rectangular block (pp 36-37). This has its ancestry in the "crude simplification of classical acanthus corbels in 6th century North Africa". The Visigothic corbel persisted in Asturias in Islamic times, eg., San Pedro de Louroso (P. 123/73), Valdedios, Oviedo, Priesca.

25. The Suso (Cogolla) shape is close to corbels of Almanzor´s extension, see Ig.Moz. p. 307.

26. Though more classically Cordoban, the corbels retain the characteristic larger top roll.

27. Ig.Moz. p. 188, fig. 82.

28. There are many more from later in the the 12th century onwards, continuing the same tradition of design, in both Nasrid and Christian buildings.

29. Ig.Moz. fig. 64.

30. F. Henry and G. Zarnecki, "Decorated Romanesque Arches..." Studies in Romanesque Sculpture, p. 31, n.2; A. Borg, Architectural Sculpture in Romanesque Provence 1972, pp 117-118, quotes fragmentary survival, notably of capitals, in stucco, at Germigny, Cividale, Malles, Saint-Laurent in Grenoble, Saint-Rémy in Rheims, adding "the sum total remains extremely small, and it is impossible to build up any coherent picture of the nature of stucco developments". The loss of nearly all painting, on stone, wood and plaster, on sculpture or walls, probably constitutes an equally large gap.

31. CA 1931, p. 564; Bull.Arch.Com.Travx.Hist. 1934, p. 119. G. Plat, Art de bâtir..., Paris 1939, pp. 151, 162, 165-166, adds Auxerre and Sonesmes.

32. The door pivots cannot be illustrated. Photography was not allowed; Professor Iniguez had not yet published his own photographs or drawings of them, and his promised print of his photograph never arrived.

33. LTB 1936, p. 56 and pl. XVII.

34. ARE, p. 100. Gomez-Moreno dates the cloister well into the 12th century, and later than the door. Whitehill, 1941, pp. 155-193, Chapter III, "Santo Domingo de Silos", revised his previous early dating ("The Destroyed Church of Santo Domingo de Silos", AB 1932), though putting the door later than the lower cloister. There is still no certainty over whether the epitaph on an impost referring to St Domingo´s death in 1073 can be dated before 1076 when his relics were moved into the new church. Torres-Balbás LTB 1936, caption to pl. XXVIIa, concluded that the corbels were over the Virgenes door and dated them 1100. John Williams (22nd Int. Congr. for Med. Studies, Kalamazoo, May 1987) rejects such early dates.

35. LTB 1936, pls XXVII and XXVIII.

36. For example, LTB 1936, 135/85; GG 1938, p. 183.

37. ARE pp 123-124 cites other parallels between Saint-Etienne and Santiago: types of vaulting and masonry, the single billet moulding, exterior arcades, lobed and mitre arches.

38. LTB 1936 reviews the Spanish Romanesque examples (pp 133-137): León (San Isidoro, Sa Maria del Mercado and fragments in the city wall); Silos; Arlanza; Santiago de Compostela (Cathedral, Santa Susanna [modern with re-used corbels on the west gable], San Clemente, Sa Maria del Sar); Corullón (1093-1100); Frómista; Valdetuejar; Jaca; Sepúlveda (c.1100); Sa Cruz de la Serós; Sa Maria la Nueva, Zamora; Sant Andrés, Avila; Sa Marta de Tera; San Millán, Segovia; Lérida cathedral; Torres del Rio; Lorca; San Martín, Segovia and many later churches in Aragon and Sória. Loarre should be added to this list (K. Watson, JWCI 1978).

39. Ig.Moz. fig. 126, p. 257.

40. E. Lévi-Provençal II, p. 240.

41. Gaillard, Premiers essais... pp 85-93. He describes the capitals of San Miguel as "preparatory experiments for Romanesque decoration" based on a Cordoban scheme of capital structure. The extent of the Cordoban element in his observations was restricted to the elongated form and

Corinthian zoning; he traced the sculptor´s departure from his models in his reduction of volutes, caulicoles and the indented abacus, his introduction of an astragal, head and figure motifs and his manipulation of plant forms; W.M. Whitehill, <u>1941</u> p. 83-84. pl. 26; Puig y Cadafalch, <u>L´Arquitectura Romanica a Catalunya</u>, ii, pp 209-212. At first Cadafalch suggested that a First Romanesque church had been refurbished in the 12th century, with the addition then of the sculpture, but later revised his view. One of the pilaster strips on the exterior of the chevet stops below a window, and this has been thought to indicate a revision. The ground for the church was dedicated by Oliba, Bishop of Vic, and his nephew Guifre, Archbishop of Narbonne, in 1045. This was Oliba´s last recorded public ceremony before his death at Cuxa in 1046. The count of Fenollares disputed the title to the land, and there is no record of a consecration until twenty years later. Whitehill judging from the similarity of ground plan to those of Sa Maria de Roses and San Quirce de Culera, believes in a change of plan before 1066, with engaged columns with sculptured capitals being substituted for the pilasters originally intended, and shafted windows inserted in the apse. "Corbels sculptured with tiny bearded heads were inserted" to support the little arches, built of slabs set with the wide face down in the 11th century manner, and these are by the same hand as the many heads on the capitals inside. This preoccupation with heads is a further link with Poitou where the head corbel was widely used in the second half of the 11th and in the 12th century.

42. Cf Chapter III for this figure in Romanesque contexts connected with the circular half-palmette running scroll associated at Moissac with the Kufic inscription. In so far as it is not a self-evident motif or inspired by various manuscript paintings its prototype seems to be Coptic, eg., British Museum, 1533, Apa Pachom plaque, 6th-7th century, and 1523, Apa Dorothius plaque, 7th-8th century. The former has the looped drapery, the latter the triangular.

43. <u>GG 1938</u> p. xx, traces the fleuron development from Andalusia. Gomez-Moreno <u>Ig.Moz.</u> p. 205 defines the "classical" Mozarabic marble capital group. M.L. Schmitt, "Traveling Carvers in the Romanesque", <u>AB</u> 1981,1, p. 7, lists the triangular hollow under volutes with "a flat wedge to render the center of the [acanthus] leaves" and "palmettes, often strongly pronounced, framed by the outer edges of the colleret leaves with which they alternate" as three characteristics constituting <u>carving habits</u> of a defined <u>atelier</u> working at the porch of Saint-Benoît-sur-Loire, at Selles-sur-Cher and elsewhere in the Berry. She dates it in the last decade of the 11th century and after. Without discussing this chronology, invalidated by Vergnolle, or her argument which relies on the combination of these three elements, it can be noted that it is possible to trace from Andalusia a typological series for these features culminating at Saint-Benoît. The expanding hollow under the volutes is a striking element on the

capitals on the Carpio tower in Cordoba, included by Torres-Balbás among the sculpture of ´Abd ar-Rahman II (LTB 1957, figs 193-194), of a capital in the Instituto de Valencia de Don Juan in Madrid, and of another with wedge-shaped acanthus stems in Cordoba Museum (ibid. figs 191-192). It is a feature of several capitals in San Pere de Roda (capital no 12, fig.88). A Madinat az-Zahra´ capital (LTB 1957 fig.501) offers a model for the Mozarabic marble series (Ig.Moz. pl. lxxv; AHIII, figs 435-436 (Escalada), of which those from Mazote and Escalada illustrate the wedge stems and incipient fleurons very clearly. Ig.Moz. figs 86 and 83 show the triangular hollow at Hornija and furthermore the start of the exaggeration of the corner leaf that reaches threatening proportions in the "leaf canopy" of Saint-Benoît, in the Panteón and at Jaca (GG 1938 pls. XIII and XLIII). Vergnolle regards the Saint-Benoît canopy as the ancestor of the roll corbel frame for heads on the numerous capitals in the Berry (Vergnolle, "Les chapiteaux de La Berthenoux" GBA 1972, figs 13, 15).

44. Gaillard, Premiers essais..., figs 45, 48, 53.

45. Poitou roman pl. 12 has a similar head on a corbel of the chevet.

46. Gaillard (GG 1938), writing before the dating of San Pedro in Jaca to 1063 had been invalidated, and dismissing the documentation of Frómista for 1066, regarded the corbels of Jaca as providing models for Santiago, and then Frómista. Now that S. Moralejo Alvarez ("Sobre la formación del estilo escultorico de Frómista y Jaca" Actas del XXIII Congr. Int. de Hist. del Arte, Granada 1973: I, Granada 1976, pp 427-433) has demonstrated that it was a sculptor at Frómista who launched the "ephebos" motif on capitals throughout northern Spain and thence to Toulouse, it can be argued that Frómista is the earliest of the group. However, chronological priorities between the stone corbels of these three monuments are not vital here. Some Frómista corbels are illustrated in GG 1938, pls LXIII-LXV.

47. GG 1938, pl. LXVII; de Palol & Hirmer, pl. 98.

48. S. Moralejo Alvarez, "Une sculpture du style de Bernard Gilduin à Jaca", BM 1973.

49. GG 1938 pl. CXXV.

50. GG 1938 pp 182ff, pls LXXXV-LXXXVIII. He describes them as follows: "The corbels of St John´s chapel, one of the earliest, are decorated with strongly undercut little figurines in high relief but with slight modelling and rather inexpressive: a cat, an owl, another bird, a human figure. More elaborate motifs appear on the Saviour´s chapel: contorted monsters, a maw with two thin legs dangling from it (a motif which will be found exactly similar under the cornice of the Porte Miègeville at Saint-Sernin, Toulouse)...and above all there are roll corbels:

one has double rolls of the type of Santo Domingo de Silos and Burgos; one corbel with a tongue-like leaf has little scallops on the sides which are vestiges of the roll motif.

"On St Peter´s chapel there are several roll corbels next to the capital of the column buttress (which is decorated in bizarre fashion with large very undercut leaves). One of them is especially notable for its shape, which comprises a central projecting fillet; on each side the curls are deeply carved, the bottom one turning up and closing on the one above to create a sort of heart".

There is a similar corbel in the cathedral museum, recently on display for the Portico de la Gloria Symposium, 1988. The description fits exactly the corbels of Glaine Montaigut in the Auvergne, for example, cf. Auvergne romane, p. 24.

Gaillard continues: "The cornice of the chapel of St Faith, which dates from the second building period, seems more careful·ly executed than that of the three earlier chapels. The curls on the corbels persist in the form of little lobes, which, sometimes in two rows, border the figurines. These figures are carved in high relief and sensuously modelled: we see a monster, a charming female head, a whole figure of a wild-haired woman, crouching and exhibiting her obscene nudity..". [The crouching female, apparently being devoured by a monster though Gaillard does not note this, is the same as the corbel at the east end of the south façade at Bessuéjouls near Conques]. "..Roll corbels are found at every level of the chevet...every variety is represented at Compostela, but the most frequent type is one with a projecting central fillet..".

51. eg. Cadenac, Saintonge romane fig. 85; Geay, ibid., fig. 181.

52. GG 1938, p. 232; LTB 1936, p. 134/84.

53. GG 1938, pl. LXXXVI. But some argue for dating Santiago chevet capitals to Alfonso VII and Gelmirez, after 1109.

54. M. van Berchem, "Sedrata...", Ars Orientalis II; Naranco and Lillo: AHII, figs 363, 379.

55. GG 1938, pl. LXXXVIIa, b.

56. Gomez-Moreno, ARE, p. 133; Whitehill 1941, p. 282, n.7. Gaillard disputes this dating, p. 234.

57. J. Vielliard, Le Guide du Pèlerin, 1960, p. 102; GG 1938 pl. CXV.

58. Whitehill 1941, p. 282 n.: "one of the sculptors of the Puerta de las Platerías must have been at Santiago almost from the beginning...".

59. Torres-Balbás, "Intercambios artisticos..." al-And. 1935, pp. 416-424.

60. GG 1938, pl. LXXXVI.

61. GG 1938, pl. XXVII, nave capital 31. Gaillard speaks, p. 186, of "the strongly Spanish accent of these full volumes".

62. A.K. Porter, "Iguacel...", Burlington Magazine LII, 1928, p. 111-127; id., Spanish Romanesque Sculpture 1928, p. 63, and pp. 128-131; Gomez-Moreno, ARE, p. 77; GG 1938, pp. 128=131; Whitehill, 1941, p. 242; Aragon roman, pp. 185-189; J. Caro Baroga, "Sa Maria de Iguácel, su construcción y la inscripción commemorativa de esta", PdeV, 33, 1972,2, pp. 128-129; E. Zudaire, "La inscripción de Sa Maria de Iguácel", ibid.35, 1974, p. 136-7, 405-407; S. Moralejo Alvarez, "Sobre las recentes revisiones de la inscripción de Sa Maria de Iguácel", ibid.37, 1976, pp. 142-3, 129-130.

63. Many specialists who have made the arduous visit to the church remark on signs of disturbance in the masonry, particularly on the south front, and use this as evidence of an intervention which could invalidate the dating of the monument as it stands by the inscription over the west door. This reads: HEC EST PORTA DOMINI UNDE INGREDIUNTUR FIDELES IN DOMUM DOMINI QUE EST EGLESIA IN HONORE SANCTE MARIE FUNDATHA IUSSU SANZIONI COMITIS EST FABRICATA UNA CUM SUA CONIUGE NOMINE URRACA IN ERA T CENTESIMA XA EST EXPLICITA REGNANTE REGE SANCIO RADIMIRIZ IN ARAGONE QUI POSUIT PRO SUA ANIMA IN HONORE SANCTE MARIE VILLARROSSA NME ?? UT DET? DNS REQETE???UM AMEN (very unclear, readings vary)

On the return to the south: SCRITOR HARUM LITTERARUM NOMINE AZENAR MAGISTER HARUM PICTURARUM NOMINE CALINDO GARCES. Era 1110 is AD 1072. The crude capitals of the west door archivolts are adduced as what belongs to that date rather than the Frómista/Jaca theme capitals of the windows and interior. A. San Vicente (Aragon roman p. 187) (see n.75) attributes the greater part of the south front to an earlier Mozarabic church restored and improved with sculptures in 1072, and applies the inscription to the door, rather than the whole church. The stepped alfiz formed by the cornice on the south façade runs on to join the imposts of the windows. These have a different moulding, decorated with palmettes which are not taken into account at the joins. The corbels on the apse are in a different style from those of the doorway; these latter certainly belong with the capital sculpture.

64. A. San Vicente suggests that the "pictures" refer to painted outlines and embellishments of the inscription; there are remains of polychromy on the engraved inscription of the Jaca tympanum too, but who can say of what date?

65. A. Duran Gudiól, El Castillo de Loarre, 1971 p. 31, believes Galindo Garcez came to work on the capitals of Loarre after finishing Iguácel.

66 There are coincidences with motifs at Santiago to be investigated also.

67. GG 1938, XL,7; XLI,12; XLII,20; XLIV, 24 bis; XLV, 25.

68. ibid, LXXIX, 15, 16; 17 and 18 without volutes.

69. ibid, Frómista: LXV, 1.2; LXVIII, 3,5,8; LXIX, 10, 11; LXX, 14; LXXIII; LXXXI, 21, 32; Santiago: LXXIX, 15; León: XIX, 19.

70. Cf. also Frómista, ibid, LXXV,3, or Saint-Benoît porch, upper storey, Val de Loire roman, fig. 30, on the rider.

71. BM 1973, p. 12, as distinct from the rendering of hair at Toulouse. It occurs on the Carizo ivory (fig. 262) as S.Moralejo Alvarez observes. He has not noted it here at Iguácel.

72. Cf. Saint-Benoît tower porch, Val de Loire roman, figs 24, 25, 31, the devil's hair-cap; or Toulouse, Haut Languedoc roman, figs 26, 29, the angels' hair. This corbel is possibly a Sacrifice of Isaac, with the ram enlarged at the expense of Isaac. The little head at the side on the other hand, similar to the head over the door among the "balls" at Sa Cruz de la Serós (Aragon roman fig. 74) is perhaps an early recension of a motif of heads which is seen for example on the Virgin's throne on a later capital from St Pons de Thomières in the Musée des Augustins at Toulouse (P. Mesplé, Sculptures romanes, Toulouse 1961, No 264, Inv. 846A), but the iconographic sequence is not clear.

73. Corbels at Notre-Dame-du-Pré in Le Mans have a comparable motif; see n. 20. The combination of these features on this and the preceding corbel calls to mind the treatment of corbel sides on the North African stone corbel of the 11th century in the museum at Bougie, LTB 1936, p. 43.

74. F. Hernandez, "Basas y capiteles del siglo XI", AEAA, XIV/4, 1930, pp. 31-35.

75. Aragon roman, Col.pl. facing p. 184. The dating of the Iguácel sculpture remains a problem involving closely that of Jaca and Loarre. San Vicente quotes (unspecified) documents as confirming that the church was reconstructed, and describes it as a 10th century Mozarabic church to which the count and countess added apse, portal, columns and capitals, and a barrel vault that later collapsed. The masonry is rougher on the south elevation and the rectangular stepped frame formed by a cordon, a glorified

alfiz, is broken by the imposts of the windows and continued by a line of cornice carved with palmettes. "The renovation of 1072 respected the greater part of this old Mozarabic façade, adding Romanesque details round its two windows...". Whitehill (1941, p. 242) on the other hand, refers to Salarrullana y de Dios, _Documentos correspondientes al reinado de Sancio Ramirez (1063-94)_, i, pp. 7-8, to state that Sancho Ramirez granted the site to Sancho Galindez in February 1068, and to a quotation by A.K. Porter from R. Léauté y Garcia to the effect that Sancho Galindez in turn gave it, together with the church he had built (my italics) to San Juan de la Peña in 1082; Whitehill regards the whole church as 11th century, with alterations to the façade made soon after 1082. J. Cabanot has proposed tentatively (in conversation) that, taking into account the signs of disturbance in the masonry, the sculpture and windows were added some time after the inscription. The crude (?unfinished) capitals of the west door would on this reading be contemporary with the inscription and antedate the rest of the capitals and the west front corbels. A. Canella Lopez (_Aragon roman_, p. 165) gives yet another version: in the estates of Sancho Galindez, tutor to Sancho Ramirez, stood "an ancient sanctuary dedicated to the Virgin Mary, situated at Iuozar, now transformed to Iguácel"; this was a centre of pilgrimage for the faithful of the region of Garcipollera, and the count decided to restore it in cooperation with his wife, the widow of Galindo Atones. On completion, in 1072, it was endowed by various devotees, among them the king, who donated the property of Larrossa nearby. (San Vicente interprets the inscription as reading that the king erected a town called Rosa for the salvation of his soul and in honour of the Blessed Mary).

76. K. Watson, "The Corbels in the Dome at Loarre", _JWCI_ 1978, pp. 297-301.

77. T. Lyman, _AB_ March 1967, fig. 20.

78. This gateway has arches at the sides with cushion or cylindrical voussoirs (_MAE_, pl. 64 [the gate], pl. 66.6 [the corbel] analogous to the cylindrical apse decoration of the group of 11th century curches in High Aragon (fig. 275). At Diyarbakr (_MAE_, fig. 100 and p. 219) the riwaq of the Great Mosque has similar ox heads on impost blocks, two on the west and four on the east, probably reused in 1124 and 1163, as Creswell thinks the Cairene version the earlier.

79. A. Duran Gudiol, "La Iglesia de Aragon", _Anthologica Annua_, ix, 1961; id., _El Castillo de Loarre_, Saragossa 1971, pp. 7-19; 2nd ed. 1987, pp. 7-27; id., _Arte Altoaragonés de los siglos X y XI_, Sabinanego 1973.

80. It combines the scrolls of Moissac capitals 55 and the more Toulousan 41 and 68; at Saint-Gaudens they are separate, the former less delicate on an impost of a

tribune capital, the latter on a choir capital (G. Rivière, Saint Gaudens Zodiaque 1979, figs 19, 12.

81. GG 1938, XLIV, 23. This composition with birds´ wing-tips touching a lion´s or monster´s jaw is also met in a variety of manuscript illumination versions from pre-Romanesque times on: there is scope for a full comparative study. The 10th-century First Bible of Limoges (Limousin roman col.pl. p.12) has columns of the piled animal attack motif.

82. K. Watson, "The Corbels..", fig. 40d.

83. The masked demons with their strange rites depicted on this impost have a remote ancestry: they border a bowl in the Oxus treasure: British Museum, O.T.123919 (Cat. No. 18). They surround a lobed rosette on the ceiling of the Samakṣiplavitana Trinetreśvara temple in Than (J.M. Nanavati and M.A. Dhaky, "The Ceilings of the Temples of Gujarat", Bull. of Baroda Museum, XVI-XVII, 1963, fig. 30).

84. GG 1938 XCV, top right. It appears again at Sa Cruz de la Serós and at Anzy le Duc.

85. That the roll corbel was introduced into France early in the 11th century was formerly deduced from the occurrence of fillet roll corbels at Notre-Dame in Chamalières on the outskirts of Clermont, and at Saint-Bénigne in Dijon. If the narthex of Chamalières was of the 10th century, and the corbel table on the rotunda of Saint-Bénigne of the early 11th, then the Cordoban form in stone with central fillet and deep curls carved on the sides could be seen as established in France as part of a contemporary tradition: Almanzor´s extension of the Mezquita only began in 987 (the doors brought from the sack of Santiago by Almanzor in 997 were, according to Ibn Khaldun, used in the construction of the ceilings of this extension (ELP II, p. 250). These dates can no longer be accepted: there is little doubt that the roof of the Chamalières narthex was rebuilt in the 12th century, using the classic Romanesque Auvergnat system of fillet roll corbels supporting soffits with hollow rosettes (M. Vieillard-Troiekouroff, "La cathédrale de Clermont du Ve au XIIIe siècle", Cah.Arch 1960, p. 219). W. Schlink, Saint-Bénigne in Dijon, Berlin 1978, p. 53, shows the same is true for the vanished rotunda of Saint-Bénigne, which also had both fillet corbels and hollow rosettes (as seen in his pl. 25, figs 49-51, in the drawings of Dom Plancher of 1739 and P.V. Antoine of 1790. [The drawings of Antoine ae reproduced in J. Moreau, Dijon à la fin du XVIIIe siècle d´après les gouaches de P.V. Antoine, Dijon 1893, accessible in the Bibliothèque Doucet, 3 rue Michelet, Paris Ve]). Schlink shows that the wall was raised and the corbel table and dwarf gallery combination added later than the original part dedicated in 1018. He lists a series of "isolated examples" of roll corbel tables outside the Auvergne: Ebreuil, Anzy-le-Duc, Saint-Pierre-de-Montmartre

(Paris), Saint-Hilaire in Poitiers, "all in the 12th century". He therefore proposes a date for the Saint-Bénigne corbels after the great fire of 1137. This may be correct for Saint-Bénigne but is not acceptable for the initiation of roll corbels in France.

86. "Didascali lapicide qui prius beati Iacobi basilicam edificaverunt nominabantur domnus Bernardus senex, mirabilis magister, et Rotbertus, cum ceteris lapicidibus circiter quinquaginta qui ibi sedule operabantur...", Cod.Cal. iv, 9, fol. 182r, qu. Whitehill 1941, p. 271. The name Robert, if not purely descriptive, is less usual for a Spaniard than a Frenchman. The name was current in Normandy, the Ile de France and Burgundy, and vey much in the Auvergne, which had four counts Robert by the end of the 12th century (R. Rigodon, Histoire de l´Auvergne, Paris 1963, pp. 41-43); furthermore, Robert of Turlande founded La Chaise-Dieu in 1046, no doubt adding to the popularity of the name in following decades; a Rotbartus signed a capital in Notre-Dame-du-Port, Clermont.

87. The south transept with its south crossing piers is the only part taken unaltered into the present Gothic building from the church dedicated in 1040. The church was built by Agnes of Burgundy, widow of William V the Great (Duke of Aquitaine and count of Poitou). In 1032 she married Geoffroi Martel, count of Anjou (R. Crozet, "Eglises à déambulatoire entre Loire et Garonne", BM 1942. As Agnes also patronized the completion of Saint-Hilaire in Poitiers, begun by Emma of Normandy, cousin of William V, it is notable that on the crossing piers of La Trinité are capitals described as "brothers" of the acanthus capitals in the nave of Saint-Hilaie (Poitou roman, p. 54). This strengthens the case for dating the Saint-Hilaire corbel table in the mid-11th century. see also n. 92. "Berrichon leaf" here makes early appearance.

88. Abbé Plat, "La Trinité de Vendôme", BM 1906, p. 19; "L´église primitive de Vendôme", Bull.arch.Com.Trav.hist. 1922, p. 31. The drawing is published in BM 1913, p. 371. It is reproduced by F. Deshoulières, in his important article "Les corniches romanes..", BM 1920, p. 54, and again by LTB 1936, pp. 141-191. The sides are not shown.

89. LTB 1936, pp. 90-140.

90. Ch. Lelong, "Le clocher-porche de Saint-Julien de Tours...", CCM 1974,4. T.J. Jackson, Byzantine and Romanesque Architecture, Cambridge 1920 reports roll corbels at Sainte-Radegonde on the outskirts of Tours and at "the ancient baptistery of Saint-Léonard near Limoges".

91. E. Vergnolle, Saint-Benoît-sur-Loire.., Paris 1985; Val de Loire roman p. 72 and fig. 1; G. Chenesseau, L´abbaye de Fleury à Saint-Benoît, Paris 1931; Etudes ligériennes 1976; M. Aubert, Cah.Arch. 1930. P. Verdier, in Etudes ligériennes, p. 333, quotes the description in the

Vita Gauzlini, Chapter 31, of gifts to the abbot by the count of Gascony, including Arab bronze scales, a Spanish bronze lectern with lion cubs round its base, silks and carpets. He observes that the Four Horsemen on the capital of the tower porch use Arab stirrups. Gauzlin had close relations with Oliba of Vich, and with the count of Cerdagne. It is not permitted to examine the exterior of the abbey church at close quarters, fig. 276 is taken from the village road some distance away. The transept façade also has a cornice along the base of the gable resting on roll corbels. Gauzlin, son of Hugues Capet, was also bishop of Bourges; the choir and transept, begun about 1067, apparently so influential on Berry sculpture (Vergnolle, GBA 1972) must represent what went on in Bourges as well in the 11th century.

92. The roofing was entirely changed later in the 11th century when vaults were inserted in the nave. R. Crozet, "La corniche romane du clocher de Saint-Hilaire de Poitiers", BM 1934; M. Aubert, CA 109, 1951; Lefèvre-Pontalis, CA 1951; M.T. Camus, "La reconstruction de Saint-Hilaire-le-Grand de Poitiers à l´époque romane. La marche des travaux", CCM 1982.

The Chronicle of Saint-Maixent (qu. Y. Labande-Mailfert, Poitou roman, p. 58) states "Istud monasterium magna ex parte construxerat regina Anglorum per manus Gauterii Coorlandi, Agnes comitissa, que eum jussit dedicare, plurimam partem construxit", thus giving equal due to Emma and Agnes. Emma left Poitou in 1044. The dedication in 1049 was attended by thirteen archbishops and bishops, Agnes and her son William Aigret. This original church had a wooden-roofed nave and transept, with alternating piers in the nave, and the bell tower stood separate in the north-west angle of the crossing. At .a later date in the 11th century vaults were raised and aisles introduced and the tower was enclosed in the church. Y. Labande-Mailfert postulates three or four campaigns after 1049, while Crozet expessed uncertainty as to when the tower was finished and was "inclined to put the cornice a decade or so later" than 1049. Aubert and Lefèvre-Pontalis date it before 1049, which seems reasonable on purely logical grounds, since the cornice would be unnecessary if the tower was to be obscured by the vaults and connected to the transept, as it now is. Crozet states that the upper part of the tower was pulled down in the 16th century and, assuming the cornice ran all round, the exposed parts were then removed. Evidently the east wall section was also disturbed. The cornice slabs are inconsistent and an extra piece of cornice is used in the rough filling above corbels 7 and 8. The cording varies in width and on 1-2, 8-9 and 10-11 runs in the opposite direction from the rest. Slabs 1-4, 7-8 and 10-11 all have an identical quarter-round edge with palmettes in relief; on 6-7 the whole soffit is oblique, the remaining slabs have an oblique edge, not uniformly decorated.

The similarity of capitals in the tower and nave, in the tower porch at Saint-Benoît and la Trinité in Vendôme argues for accepting 1049 for saint-Hilaire.

93. LTB 1957, figs 271,272, 363. Corbel 9 has an exact model in his fig. 363 (al-Hakam II), corbel 5 in fig. 271 (the patio); corbels 4 and 3, like the corbel at Vendôme, could certainly be matched in the patio were illustration available. Corbel 4 is matched by a capital in a twin window of the Mosque of Tudela (AHIII , figs 78-79) and a parallel for corbel 3 is to be found in many border motifs.

94. This detail (eg. at Saignes, Ygrande, Déols, Neuilly-en-Dun, Saint-Jeanvrin, Vic-l´Exemplet, Châteaumeillant [Saint-Genest], and also at Blesle on the choir) converges with a device used for depicting a mane or hair, formalizing conventional curls, in insular manuscipt illumination (eg. Book of Kells), or in ivory carving (the Anglo-Saxon "pen-case" of walrus ivory in the British Museum (J. ·Beckwith, Ivory Carvings in Early Mediaeval England, London 1972, no 46), and in stone (a corbel from Reading Abbey, formerly in the Victoria & Albert Museum, P. Williamson, Catalogue of Romanesque Sculpture, 1983, no 40, now in Reading) as the hair of a gaping mask. That this convergence is not fortuitous but results from contact between England and Spain is suggested by the similarity of the bird behind the head of the monster on the pen case with birds on Andalusian ivories: V&A 217-1865; V&A 368-1880 (JBCC pl. 7 and pl. 21-22) or Mozarabic (the arm of the cross in MAN Madrid [J. Fontaine, L´Art Mozarabe, fig. 138]). Affinities between insular and Spanish ivory carvings are such that the V&A Adoration plaque (142-1866, J. Beckwith, Ivory Carvings..no 63) can still be claimed as English in spite of the twin windows, guardian eagle and incurled leaves of Andalusia. Foliage is even more closely similar to the Andalusian manner in the frame of the Anglo-Saxon Deposition plaque (op.cit. no 88, dated c.1150). The composition, large hands and feet and facial features, angular angels, rigid draperies, all have similarities with Spanish Romanesque ivories. Curls also appear in wall and manuscript painting to portray land or water. fig. 280 shows an example at Vicq in the Berry.

95. Mihrab panels (LTB 1957, fig. 328), mihrab cornice corbels AHIII , fig. 178) marble fragments from Alamiriya (AHIII , fig. 236); decoration at Madinat az-Zahra´ (LTB 1957, figs 255, 236, 512-513, 510); for edging arches or medallions (op.cit, fig. 531); a panel from Toledo (LTB 1957, fig. 556); on ivories (JBCC, pls 2, 6, 8, 10, 13, 23, 25, 28, 19d) or metalwork (LTB 1957, figs 612, 624).

96. Crozet says of the soffit carving: "they are foxes or wolves, not dogs as Lefèvre-Pontalis said" and comparable to the lions of the capitals of the ground floor. Opinion is growing that this type of carved slab, often a metope, is Romanesque. Cf. M. Schmitt, "Random Reliefs and ´Primitive´ Friezes...", summarized in id., "Traveling

Carvers..." <u>AB</u> LXIII, 1981, and E. Vergnolle and others at the West Front Symposium in Lincoln, 1988).

97. In the Musée des Antiquaires de l´Ouest, and in the Faculté des Lettres. R. Crozet, <u>Art roman du Poitou</u> 1948, p. 232, describes the form as "oriental".

98. Crozet, <u>op.cit.</u>, quotes them at Saint-Pierre in Chauvigny, Pouillé, Morthemer, La Chapelle-Morthemer, Civaux, Lussac-les-Châteaux, Villesalem, Pamproux, Fenioux, Argenton-Château, Prahecq, Fontaines and Aunay; this list must span most of the 12th century.

99. R. Crozet, "Eglises à déambulatoires...", <u>BM</u> 1942, investigates the relationships and activities of the comital family. Agnes was also responsible for the vanished abbey of Saint-Jean d´Angély (choir consecrated 1050).

100. M.-T. Camus, "Un chevet à déambulatoire et chapelles rayonnantes · à Poitiers vers 1075: Saint-Jean-de-Montierneuf", <u>CCM</u> 1978,4, pp. 357 ff., fig. 1. Montierneuf was dedicated in 1096. Among the corbels, either animal heads, or a single sphere below the vertical face, largely predominate, and as far as possible the motif is as wide as the block.

101. P.-R. Gaussin, <u>L´Abbaye de La Chaise-Dieu</u>, Paris 1962. The Romanesque church was founded in 1043; it has not survived. In 1092 it received the gift of a church and sufficient land to form a priory at Parthenay from the joint lords Gueldin and Elbon. Here at Parthenay-le-Vieux quarter-circle vaults and squinches in the crossing dome (supported on animal-head corbels) are Auvergnat features unusual in Poitou, suggesting the church was built, or completed, after this donation rather than before. The corbels are mostly of various shapes approximating to rolls on a convex profile, knobs, etc., and heads without rolls on the west façade. The few fillet corbels look suspiciously new, recut or possibly even an invention of the very evident restorations. The rest of the repertoire is consistent with the observed development in Poitou by the end of the century (see Montierneuf, n. 104 above). The influence of the Auvergne as a factor in the introduction of roll corbels would explain another anomaly of distribution: they are a rarity in Périgord but appear at Saint-Front in Périgueux, and doubtless in its wake at La Chancelade and Saint-Jean-de-Côle: in 1077 the goldsmith and enameller Guinamundus went to Périgueux from La Chaise-Dieu to make a shrine for the tomb of Saint-Front (P. Labbé, <u>Nov. Bibl. MSS II</u>, "Frag. de Petragoriensibus Praesulum").

102. E. Maillard, "Le problème de la reconstruction de Saint-Hilaire-le-Grand au XIe siècle", <u>Bull.Soc.Ant.Ouest</u> 1934.

103.However, F. Lesueur, "La Couture", <u>CA</u> 119, 1961, considers the abbacy of Asselin, who died in 1072, as the most likely time of building. Gauzbert, abbot of Saint-Julien in Tours, was involved in founding or restoring many other abbeys including Saint-Pierre in Bourgueil and Saint-Pierre in Maillezais (with countess Emma and count William) in the early years of the 11th century. There are vestiges of early 11th century work at Notre-Dame-du-Pré in Le Mans: small masonry and polychrome vo ssoirs (F14), and the corbels are of the same type as La Couture but more elaborately decorated.

104. Adhémar de Chabannes, <u>Chronique</u> (ed. Chavanon, 1897), p. 263; <u>Defourneaux</u>, p. 129, comments on the Duke´s purely pacific relations, whereas the involvement of Burgundy included military interventions from quite early in the century. Glabar´s <u>Historia</u>, which finishes before 1036 (<u>Pat.Lat.</u> 640-641, 642) mentions Cluny´s connexions with campaigns in Spain. Constance of Burgundy married Alfonso VI in 1080 after the death of (the first) Agnes of Poitou. In 1087 she sent gifts to Tournus through her nephew Duke Eudes, who visited her in León after an abortive military adventure (<u>Esp.del Cid</u>, p. 341, n.2; J. Saroihandy, p. 261; Defourneaux, p. 22). Two of Alfonso´s daughters married Burgundians, who made their careers in Spain.

105. A. Dozy, <u>Recherches</u> II, pp. 357-399, gives the whole text of Ibn Hayyan; <u>R.H.G.F.</u> XII, p. 162: "His temporibus, Dux Aquitaniae Guillelmus et quidam alii optimates Gauliarum... copiosum in Hispaniam conduxerunt exer-citum...multamque et variam superlectilem secum afferunt multaque mancipia adducerunt". The pattern is often repeated: on assuming a title, each member of one of the great houses has first to assert his authority at home; once this is secure he must accrue wealth to reward and maintain the loyalty of his following. For the Spanish kings, this was done by extorting greater <u>paria</u> payments from client <u>taifa</u> rulers; for the French princes Spain had the same attraction, but they had to make accommodations with the Spanish kings. K.F. Werner, "Königtum und Fürstentum des französischen 12. Jahrhunderts" in <u>Probleme des 12 Jahrhunderts</u> (Vorträge u. Forschungen, <u>Konstanzer Arbeitskreis f. mittelalterliche Geschichte</u>, V, bd. 12), Sigmaringen, 1968. Translation in T. Reuter, <u>The Mediaeval Nobility</u>, Amsterdam, N.Y., Oxford, 1979.

106. J. Martindale, <u>The Origins of the Duchy of Aquitaine and the Government of the Counts of Poitou (902-1127), Oxford, D.Phil.Thesis</u> 1964. The importance of revenues from the <u>paria</u> system of clientship is clarified in J.M. Lacarra, "Aspectos Economicos de la sumisión de los Reinos de Taifas", <u>Hom. J. Vicens Vives</u> I, Barcelona 1965. The route from Gascony: id., <u>Un arancal de aduanas del siglo XI</u>, Saragossa 1950 (a customs document from Jaca).

107. J. Verdon, "Une source de la Reconquête en Espagne: le Chronique de Saint-Maixent", <u>Mélanges..R. Crozet</u> 1963. He

assumes Gui-Geoffroi had two daughters Agnès, as does Defourneaux. A sister of Gui-Geoffroi would be more of an age for Alfonso, and she disappears before Alfonso married Constance in 1079-1080. The sources are not clear and as every ruling count was called William, so every lady seems to be named Agnès. Later historians forgivably confound these problems by confusing the lines of León, Navarre and Aragon, all issue of Sancho III the Great of Navarre (1000-1035) and hence all bearing the same selection of names: Ramiro, Sancho, Garcia, Alfonso, Fernando for sons; Elvira, Teresa, Urraca, Sancha for daughters. Thus the wife of Raymond de St Gilles is variously described as from León or Aragon. She was the daughter of Alfonso VI of León.

108. For example, William IX of Aquitaine, son of Gui-Geoffroi, married Philippa, daughter of Count William IV of Toulouse and his Norman wife Emma of Mortain, and disputed the county of Toulouse against Alphonse-Jourdain, the son of Raymond de St-Gilles and Elvira of León. In the first decades of the 12th century, support for Alfonso I of Aragon (El Batallador) or his rival Alfonso VII of León, son of Raymond of Burgundy, in their contest for the control of León/Castile fluctuated according to the wider rivalries of Poitou, Toulouse, Burgundy and Barcelona, Defourneaux pp. 160-172; P. Tucou-Chala, La vicomté de Béarn et le problème de sa souveraineté des origines à 1620, Bordeaux 1961. J. Martindale notes how the agreement between Centulle de Bigorre and Alfonso I reserves the fealty that Centulle owes to Gui-Geoffroi and his son from his obligations to Alfonso. Nonetheless, Centulle, like his brother Gaston of Béarn, held great honours from Aragon, while the Duke's suspicion of Aragon's designs on Gascony drove him to support Alfonso VII against Aragon. Indeed Alfonso of Aragon in 1131 for a time seized Bayonne with the support of the archbishop of Auch and other Gascons. Alphonse Jourdain, now count of Toulouse, like the Duke of Aquitaine rallied against the pretensions of Aragon (C. Higounet, "La rivalité des maisons de Toulouse et de Barcelone pour la prépondérance méridionale" Mélanges..Halphen, pp. 313-318). Alliances shifted at the death of Alfonso of Aragon in 1134; his brother Raymondo el Monje found a wife in Agnès, sister of the next Duke William of Aquitaine. For the wide ramifications of the family of de Roucy, see B. Guénée, "La mémoire capétienne", Annales E.S.C.33, 1978, p. 450: Félicia de Roucy was wife of Sancho Ramirez of Aragon, her sister Beatrice married Geoffroi II du Perche, and their son Rotrou made his career in the entourage of the Aragonese court. The descendants of Hilduin de Roucy, (father of Ebles who went to Spain in 1077 to make himself a kingdom with a letter of support from Gregory VII; the new Pope had not yet taken account of the importance of the existing Spanish monarchs as he was rapidly forced to do [Defourneaux, p. 138]) were leading potentates in Hainauld, Vermandois, Lorraine, Champagne, Burgundy, Luxembourg, Flanders, Picardy, Ile de France, Jerusalem and Perche, which is virtually in Normandy. There was also a connexion with the royal family of England, and

though Ebles was foiled in his Spanish ambitions, his county of Roucy gave him great riches, power and status; he was married to Sybilla, daughter of Robert Guiscard of Sicily.

109. Poitou roman, fig. 12.

110. see n. 30: Henry and Zarnecki, "Romanesque Arches.." Acquaintance with Andalusian motifs, such as those in their fig. 6, would rather illustrate the pervasive awareness of Andalusian art in this area than a strongly concentrated current of specific influence.

111. LTB 1936, p. 17. Lion-head corbels at Split are surprisingly like the two west jamb lion-heads on the Platerías consoles at Santiago. The difference is in the addition of rolls at Santiago.

112. L. Grodecki (BM 1950) suggests twin columns came from Cluny II to ·Bernay and thence to Jumièges.

113. Angle columns are frequent in Egypt: cf Creswell (short), figs 69, 71 (Mosque of Ibn Tulun).

114. E. Lambert, "L'ancienne église du prieuré de Lay-Saint-Christophe et l'alternance des supports dans les églises de plan basilical", BM 1942, pp 225 ff.: The idea is Byzantine in origin; it is found at Hildesheim; in Italy; in Spain at Jaca, León, San Pedro de Duenas, Sahagun, Santiago, Ripoll. In France at Saint-Nazaire in Carcassonne (like Jaca), Bozouls, Carennac, Conques in Languedoc; Clermont, Issoire, Orcival, Saint-Saturnin (all rectangular with three and four engaged columns) in the Auvergne; Saint-Menoux in Berry; Ruffec in Bourbonnais; Jumièges, Saint-Etienne in Caen, Graville Saint-Honorine, Bernières. Ouistreham in Normandy; Poitiers (Saint-Hilaire), Vertheuil, Le Mans (Notre-Dame-du-Pré), Avesnières (round and composite). The buildings italicized have roll corbels.

115. Normandie romane II, p. 23; last quarter of the 11th century: "a low pyramid of stone whose cornice is held on large corbels of excellent workmanship [several display chisel curls]".

116. G. Zarnecki,"1066 and Architectural Sculpture" Proc.Brit.Acad. 1966, pl. XII and p. 95.

117. EK Elf, nos 48 (Louvre cross), 49 (Madrid cross) and 64 (Hermitage oliphant). The turban hair-cap of the mahout (appropriate in this context) resembles the Spanish/Toulousan hair-style.

118. G. Zarnecki, op.cit. pl. VIII.

119. Art de Basse Normandie 3, 1956; M. Baylé, La Trinité de Caen, Paris 1979, figs 137-139.

120. E. Lévi-Provençal I, pp. 218-225, 310--312: in the 9th century a group stayed behind from a raid on Seville, was converted to Islam and settled on islands in the river; they supplied the city with dairy produce and the fame of their cheeses spread far and wide.

121. Defourneaux, pp. 129-133, 157, etc.

122. Defourneaux, p. 40.

123. J.-M. Lacarra, "Para el estudio del Mucicipio Navarro medieval", Prin.de Viana III, 1941; id., Documentos para el Estudio de la Reconquista y Repoblación del Valle del Ebro, Saragossa 1946.

124. For Rotrou, Defourneaux, pp. 158-159, with references; for Diego Pelaez, Esp.del Cid, pp 346-347.

125. G. Gaillard, "Sur la chronologie de Tournus", Rev.archéol.1957. J. Virey, Saint-Philibert de Tournus, Paris 1932 categorically states the corbels are 12th century. J. Vallery-Radot, Saint-Philibert de Tournus, Paris 1955 declares "crypt, transept, ambulatory and chapels form a whole, built by Abbot Pierre who died in 1105 and was buried in the transept arm".

126. Illustrated BM 1936, p. 302. For Saint-Martin, CA 1935, pp 122 ff; A. Chagny, La basilique Saint-Martin d´Ainay, Lyon 1935, p. 215. Saint-Martin was consecrated by Pascal II in 1107, having been begun in 1102 by Jaucerand. The Sainte-Blandine chapel clearly antedates the whole church by some decades.

127. Lefèvre-Pontalis, BM 1921, p. 77. Conant (CRA, p. 176) lists the following chronological sequence; the finishing of roofs cannot be attached to these dates with any certainty, but there is no reason to find them impossible: Ennezat, founded between 1061 and 1078 (thought by Lefèvre-Pontalis to be the oldest church in the Auvergne); Saint-Nectaire, 1080; Saint-Saturnin; Orcival, 1100 (rebuilt 1180s); Notre-Dame-du-Port, first half of 12th century, reconstruction work 1185; Issoire, 1130-1150; Riom, Mozac (or Mozat), finally Brioude. Mozac however, attached to Cluny under duress in 1095, was thought by L. Bréhier to have been built at once following this, while Z. Swieckowsky considers its sculpture the earliest of any in the Auvergne, with influences from Conques and the south arriving up the Rhône. For A. Gybal, L´Auvergne, berceau de l´art roman, Clermont-Ferrand 1957, not all southern influences stem from Conques but include some coming directly from Cordoba; among these he cites the stone marquetry, from the minaret, and from the Mezquita itself the corbels, and soffit rosettes, trilobes applied to tribunes, and exterior arcades. He quotes the mihrab of Qairawan and the minarets of Fez to add to the description of the Cordoban minaret. He adds that Auvergnat music (the

bourrée) is Moorish and notes that Toledan blades were made at Thiers "tempered in the miraculous waters of the Curolle".

128. M. Vieillard-Trouerikoff, "La cathédrale de Clermont...." Cah.Arch. 1960.

129. L. Bréhier, "Les origines de l´architecture romane en Auvergne", Rev.Mabillon, Jan. 1923.

130. P.-R. Gaussin, L´Abbaye de La Chaise-Dieu, Paris 1972. It was a favorite abbey of Raymond de St Gilles, who was married first to the daughter of Roger of Sicily, then to Elvira, daughter of Alfonso VI of León. the latter´s wife Constance of Burgundy, a niece of St Hugh of Cluny, sent for St Adelelme (Aléaume) from La Chaise-Dieu at the time of the troubles over the change of rite from the Mozarab to Latin, shortly after her arrival in Spain. Aléaume was given a chapel and a hospital at the gates of Burgos, and at his death in 1097 Abbot Pons of La Chaise-Dieu sent the former troubadour Raoul Passereau to Burgos to compose Aléaume´s Vita. Aléaume is also said to have arrived at the taking of Toledo in 1085 and led toops over the Tagus into the city (DHGE II, col. 77). Gaussin suspects rivalries with Cluny.

131. Z. Swieckowsky, La sculpture romane en Auvergne, p. 12, lists the local sources of coloured volcanic stone. The richer churches imported limestone for their capitals from considerable distances.

132. The sides are decorated with gracefully curved lozenges. The curls on this example have no stems but are outlined, like the patio corbels of the Mezquita, ns rhw bottom curl turns up. The fillet projects strongly right through to the bottom of the corbel and its upper vertical face continues well below the level of the first roll. This is the tendency of many Auvergnat corbels. The corbels of Chamalières show how faithfully such precedents were followed into the 12th century.

133. Auvergne romane, p. 24.

134. W. Cahn, Romanesque Wooden Doors.. p. 119.

135. Horizontal stems are characteristic of the corbels of the tower cornice of Saint-Hilaire in Poitiers; some corbels on the south door of Conques have them and a number in the Berry, including Plaimpied, Neuilly-en-Dun, Avord, Ygrande, Déols. Further investigation might produce some correlations connected with this detail. Rural Auvergnat churches, like Saignes (fig. 226) and Tauves adopt the feature.

136. M. Thibout, Auvergne et vennes, 1961, p. 55. Construction began early in the 12th century with the

narthex and worked eastward. The east end was completed before the beginning of the 13th century.

137. F. Salet, CA 127, 1967, pp. 162 ff.

138. R. Crozet, Art roman en Berry, p. 241.

139. C. Enlart, Manuel de l´architecture française.

140. Berry roman, pp 11-12.

141. Saint-Benoît-sur-Loire..p. 165 and fig. 160. The abbey church was dedicated in 1048. J. Favière (Berry roman) thinks the chevet no earlier than the last years of the 11th century, but Vergnolle has no difficulty in associating them with the capitals derived from Unbertus, as part of the first campaign connected with the 1048 dedication. F. García-Romo (AE 1954, p. 39 and 53) includes the capitals of the choir in the group he attributes to an Andalusian-influenced workshop active in the mid-11th century, and quotes the existence of rolls corbels as supportive evidence, along with vaults with square ribs, for a Spanish influence at many of the other sites he discusses as well: these are Saint-Sever; Saint-Hilaire and Montierneuf in Poitiers; La Trinité in Vendôme; Le Ronceray d´Angers; Parthenay-le-Vieux and Saint-Savin (no roll corbels at these last two). Sainte-Radegonde in Poitiers, Maillezais, Cormery also have the vaults and capitals only. Saint-Benoît should also be added to his list of roll corbels. He discusses the same group in "Un taller..." Prin.de Viana 1962.

142. Berry roman p. 12. Déols is mostly ruinous, apart from the tower. A few fragments of sculpture survive in the museum at Issoudun.

143. E. Vergnolle, "Les chapiteaux de La Berthenoux...", GBA 1972, pp 259 ff and Saint-Benoît-sur-Loire.. Chapter 8.

144. The classic roll corbels at Déols on the tower have some points of resemblance with those of Jumièges, particularly in the blocky cubic shape of the corbel. The chevron window archivolts are also a northen feature (A. Borg, "The Development of Chevron Ornament", J.Brit.Arch. Ass. 1967), and the stepped double niches under the fragment of sculpture (Berry roman, fig. 103) also have a Norman flavour. Crozet speculated on the extent of Norman influence on façade design in the Berry, quoting the presence of Eudes of Déols, who inspired the new church at Neuvy-Saint-Sépulcre, at the dedication of La Trinité in Vendôme in 1040. The analogy of the corbels with those of Jumièges is not complete: the sides of the Déols corbels have horizontal stems like the Poitiers tower corbels, unlike those of Jumièges. The tower of Déols was not built until after 1107 (Berry roman: the choir was consecrated in 1107 and towers, nave, transept and narthex were built soon

after that). By then the roll corbel was widespread in many forms.

145. Saint-Jeanvrin is first mentioned in 1115, being confirmed by Pascal II as a possession of Déols. Its capitals resemble those of St Genès, Châteaumeillant (CA 1931). Themes on the capitals include birds with entwined necks and affronted lions (D17a,h). The corbels are so varied that E. Lambert gave the church particular attention as the probable pioneer of roll corbels in France. This cannot stand.

146. It was Crozet's contention that the Berry received the roll corbel from Poitou, and he insisted on the importance of other influences from further south-west. Déols had many possessions in Poitiers, Saintes and Agen; Dèvres had a church in Agen and two villas in the Saintonge, while several churches in the Berry have relics of Agen's Saint Caprais. Crozet ARB lists the following as examples of roll corbels to compare with those in the Berry: Saint-Jean-de-Côle and La Chancelade (Dordogne), and Courpiac, Clairac (L&G) and La Sauve (Gironde), where animal heads and other motifs are combined with rolls. The decoration of chevet exteriors with arcading is, as he observes, similar in the Berry and in the south-west and Saintonge; at Nevers and La Charité the resemblances are equally convincing.

147. Gascogne romane, fig. 32; Berry roman, fig. 93.

148. Volute stem rolls, Saint-Sever de Rustan (Gascogne romane, fig. 86), Frómista, Bayeux (fig.124). The corner head motif also at Preuilly-sur-Claise, Saint-Genou, Ardentes, etc.

149. Vergnolle, GBA 1972, pp 249 ff.

150. These differ from ordinary roll corbels with heads, in that the rolls continue to the top of the corbel instead of leaving a plain impost until the concave profile begins. The head is framed in the rolls. The position of the head, too, echoes the capital motif.

151. GG 1938, pl. XIII, 29-30 (the garments are drawn with curl volutes!). The following references in the text are to Gaillard's capital numbers at each site.

152. ibid., Jaca, pl. XLIII; Loarre, pl. LXIII.

153. L. Grodecki, "La sculpture du XIe siècle en France. Etat des questions", L'Inf.Hist.Art 1958, fig. p. 107.

154. GG 1938, pl. LXIII,15.

155. ibid., pls LXXVIII,13; LXXIX,16.

156. ibid., Pls XLI,10; XLVIII,4.

157. <u>ibid</u>., ₁ˌs LXX,14 and 12; LXVII,1.

158. <u>Gascogne romane</u>, fig. 86.

159. <u>Quercy roman</u>, pp. 132 ff. Capitals 21, 41, 50, 55, 63, 68. The derivation is from the circular scroll, D5 of my list of motifs in Appendix I.

160. <u>GG 1938</u>, Pls LXIX,9, 10; LXVII,7.

161. <u>Val de Loire roman</u>, pl. 23

162. The documentation is summarized in M. Aubert, <u>L´église de Conques</u>, Paris 1954, p. 69; <u>Cartulaire de l´abbaye de Conques</u>, ed. G. Desjardins, 1879; <u>Chronicon monasterii Conchensis</u> in Martène and Durand, <u>Thesaurus novus anecdotorum</u> III, 1717, col. 1390. The new church was begun by Abbot Odolric in the time of King Henri III (1030-1060), and near enough completion to transfer the relics of St Faith into it before Odolric´s death in 1065. In 1040-1052 indulgences were accorded by bishops of the surrounding dioceses to those contributing to the works and illumination of the church. After 1058, and perhaps c.1080-1090, were written Books III and IV of <u>Liber Miraculorum sancte Fidis</u>, ed. A. Bouillet, 1898. In Book IV the monk Sallust is reminded by the need to repair parts of arcades and vaults that a miracle had taken place when capitals and bases were needed for the construction, long ago, but still within his lifetime. In 1099 a series of privileges was obtained from Urban II: there is no mention of building works. Bégon III (1087-1107, but deposed during 1095-1097) built the cloister. Boniface (1107-1119) made a reliquary of leather and enamel discs for the relics of St Faith. Extensive restorations took place in the mid-19th century. The 11th and 12th century enamels and metalwork preserved in the Treasury show close links with Spain (M.M. Gauthier, <u>Rouergue roman</u> and in many later writings).

163. The extensive restorations initiated by Prosper Mérimée, carried out from 1837 to 1879, were strictly controlled, and the different types of design appear to have been respected: M. Aubert, <u>op.cit</u>., p. 12. J.-Cl. Fau (personal communication) would use the criterion of diversity to confirm authenticity: Mérimée "supervised the restoration work very closely" and is never suspected of an excessive use of misplaced imagination like Abadie, or even Viollet-le-Duc.

164. G. Gaillard, in <u>Rouergue roman</u>,p. 41.

165. J.-Cl. Fau: <u>Les Chapiteaux de Conques</u>, 1956; "L´apparition de la figure humaine dans la sculpture du Rouergue et du Haut-Quercy au XIe siècle" <u>Actes XXVIIe Congrès des soc.sav.Montauban</u>, 1972; "Un décor original: l´entrelacs épanoui en palmette sur les chapiteaux romans de l´ancienne Septimanie..", <u>CSMC</u> 9, 1978.

166. E. Erlande-Brandeburg, <u>AduM</u> 1972, reviewing J. Bousquet, <u>La sculpture à Conques</u>..(see following note) considers the first decade of the 12th century "too early and not necessary for any of the sculpture at Conques". He quotes M.M. Deyres, "La construction de l´abbatiale Sainte-Foy de Conques", <u>BM</u> 1965, who says the capitals of the east end and transept are not in their original positions.

167. J. Bousquet, <u>La sculpture à Conques aux XIe-XIIe siècles, Essai de chronologie comparée</u>, Lille 1973; <u>id</u>., "La sculpture de Conques dans ses rapports avec l´art méridional", <u>CSMC</u> 1971.

168. Z. Swieckowsky, <u>La Sculpture romane de l´Auvergne</u>, Paris 1978; introduction by L. Grodecki: on p. 10 he supports Swieckowsky´s "new thesis", and also the anteriority of the choir and nave capitals of Mozac "c.1095" over the rest of the Auvergne. This theory is strongly opposed by Erlande-Brandeburg in a review of an earlier work by Swieckowsky, <u>Sculpture romane d´Auvergne</u>, Clermont-Ferrand 1973, in <u>BM</u> 1976, pp 156-7. An influence on Auvergne sculpture from Conques and from Arles, coming up the Rhône, was proposed much earlier by L. Bréhier, "Les origines de la sculpture romane en Auvergne...", Rev.Mabillon 1923.

169. Pierre d´Andouque, often styled Pierre or Pedro "de Roda" (more recently and properly interpreted as "de Rodez"), Bishop of Pamplona 1082-1114. His favour and appointment followed the disgrace of García, brother of King Sancho Ramirez and Bishop of Jaca. Peter had been educated at Conques and Saint-Pons-de-Thomières and his devotion to Conques was shared by the Aragonese court, where he stood in high regard. He was not only active in the kingdom of Aragon, but of sufficient distinction to be chosen to dedicate the altar of St Faith at Santiago in 1105 and the altar of St Gabriel at Cluny in 1100. He was frequently in Toulouse. J. Saroïhandy ("La légende de Roncevaux", Mél. Menendez Pidál 1928, pp 259-284) suggested that he invented and promoted the legend of Roland at Roncevaux to encourage pilgrims to use that route to Compostela and bring revenue to Conques, to which foundation a church, mill and hospital with its oven, all at Roncevaux, had been presented by Count Sancho of Erro (G. Desjardins, Cartulaire..Conques, p. 347). Other possessions in Navarre acquired by Peter for Conques included Caparroso, Murillo and Garituain. Peter was present in 1091 at the foundation of San Pedro de Castellar, built as a threat to Zaragoza, at the siege of Huesca in 1094 and at its occupation in 1096. The kings of Aragon favoured combining a military and religious foundation on the model of the Islamic ribat, as at Loarre and Montearagon; Peter filled well the rôle of warrior priest. In 1101 at the fall of Barbastro the largest mosque, after the one destined to become the cathedral, was given by King Pedro I to Conques, and the whole kingdom put under the protection of St Faith. A monk Pons from Conques

was appointed first bishop of Barbastro after this reconquest in 1101.

170. I am indebted to Christopher Bailey for his observations on the transept doors, which I have been able to confirm. The masonry of the jambs of the north door is mixed red sandstone and yellow limestone to the level of the capitals which are sandstone. Above, the masonry is yellow but the hood moulding which continues the red billet imposts is red. The outer bases are limestone. On the south door the masonry is sandstone to one course below the capitals. The inner columns are sandstone. The footings to the inner columns are red, the jambs are yellow a third from the ground, then red until two courses below the lintel when they are yellow again. There ae some red sandstone voussoirs in the inner archivolt. Both north and south the nave wall blocks off part of the arch and cornice, on the south a witness hole has been made to free the end corbel.

171. Quarried two leagues away at Nauviale, and limestone from Lunel, a league further distant, which was used when the quarry at Nauviale was exhausted (Rouergue roman, p. 41). Sandstone has continued to be used extensively in the region from mediaeval to modern times, and the change cannot be explained by it being impossible to find. As Gaillard comments, there is no indication of a break in the work between the two materials.

172. The ox-head corbel is similar to one at Anzy-le-Duc. At Varen (Haut-Languedoc roman, figs 128-131; J.-Cl. Fau, Les chapiteaux de Varen 1972, figs 6 and 115) it is associated with pine cones and spits beaded and chip-carved interlaced palmettes. A cornice fragment at Saint-Sernin in the north nave tribune (T. Lyman, AB 1967, fig. 2Q) contains one bucranium corbel with the horns rising to the top of the first roll and interrupting it. At Loarre the corbels set over the doorway are the same. An almost contemporary Islamic corbel is illustrated by Creswell (MAE pl.66.6): on the Bab al-Futuh in Cairo, dated 1087 (480H) the second corbel from the right over the arcades figures an ox head with a leaf scroll hanging from it. (See n. 78).

173. The square-topped wings are probably an influence from carvings at Montecassino (Henry and Zarnecki, "Romanesque arches.." p. 5). It is perhaps this association with Italy that explains why the majority of figure corbels are not roll corbels, since the roll corbel never found favour in Italy. There are square-topped wings in Moissac cloister, and Moissac has no corbels, but the angels of the apse reliefs at Toulouse have square-topped wings, and the roll corbel there is dominant. On the Conques tympanum the tops of the angels´ wings are a rounded point. Spanish wings are all round-topped.

174. GG 1938, pls LXV,21; LXXVII,8; LXXXVI, top right.

175. J.-Cl. Fau, "Le bassin roman de serpentine du cloître de Conques", Actes du Congrès d´études de Rodez 1975, pp. 319 ff. The imps belong with the masked figures on capital 17 of Moissac cloister, the frieze at Le Puy, and pilaster capitals and tympanum at Saint-Martin d´Ainay in Lyon. This affiliation traces the route postulated by Bréhier of influence from Conques up the Rhône.

176. M.-M. Gauthier, Rouergue roman, pp 111,119, 143-145. The pervasive influence of Muslim metalwork and textile designs on the Conques atelier is referred to frequently in her authoritative writings on enamels, eg. Emaux du Moyen Age, Fribourg 1972; "Les décors vermiculés..", CCM 1958, pp 349-369.

177. Rouergue roman, pl. 59. Imitation Kufic is of course common on later enamel work.

178. J.-Cl. Fau, "Un décor original.." CSMC 1978, p. 133. Fau invokes· the iconostasis of St Luke in Phokis with interlace capitals and facetted colonnettes. St Luke also has strong Islamic associations (Grabar, CRAcIBL 1971, art. cit.).

179. Rouergue roman, p.38. (Aimoin, "Historia translationis sancti Vincentii" Acta Sanctorum ordinis sancti Benedicti, Saeculum IV, pas I, 1977.

180. In the Chartres manuscript of Book III of the Miracula (see n.162) p. 242: "a Sarracenis capto, quem cum sociis suis sancta Fides liberavit" is the story of Arnaldus: he came from Cardona, and went trading to Balaguer while waiting for the weather to improve, joining up with other merchants. The party was captured by pagans after having transacted its business, and duly released by St Faith. Cf. J. Duplessy, "La circulation des monnaies arabes en Europe occidentale.." Rev. numismatique 1956, pp. 119-120, "the great period of Muslim gold began in the 11th century and goes on to the mid-13th, and this gold is Spanish and African in origin". The great transhumances recorded by Leroy-Ladurie for the late 13th century in Montaillou, 1982, from France deep into Spain, were based on centuries of smaller scale movement during which also "..les idées, les hommes, les troupeaux, la monnaie y circulent.." (p. 28); there was no segregation by religion (eg. pp 156-158, 450).

181. Defourneaux, p. 130, n.3.

182. Devic and Vaissète, Hist. du Languedoc XLV, p. 466. L. and J. Hill, Raymond IV de St Gilles, Toulouse 1959, p. 16 accept this fact (without comment, though no Spanish historian mentions it) and deduce that the succession to Toulouse had aleady been decided by William to be due to Raymond´s house, since William had no male heirs. Philippa later disputed this.

183. The Cartulary (n. 170) shows donations flowing in from an ever wider area. Restricted to the immediate vicinity in the 9th and 10th centuries, in the 11th they come from the north of Auvergne, Agde, Carcassonne, Narbonne, Nîmes, Avignon, Orange, Tulle, Périgueux, Roussillon, Toulouse and its environs, Vivarais, Limousin, Albigeois, Uzès, Comminges, Gévaudun, Brie, Agen, Bordelais, Bazadais, Dax, Auch. Priories were founded in Normandy, Burgundy, Champagne, Brie, Alsace, London, Italy, Spain and Liège (Rouergue roman, p. 68). Concerning Liège, connexions with the south are already shown in the Death Roll of Guifred of Cerdagne, which assembled 50 signatures in 1050 from ecclesiastical establishments in the Liégeois (J. Stiennon, "Histoire et archéologie:.." CSMC 1971, p. 68). The collection of indulgences conceded by neighbouring bishops for the construction of the abbey of Sainte-Foy was signed by Géraud of Rodez, Etienne of Le Puy, Guillaume of Albi, Géraud of Périgueux, Adalbert of Viviers.

184. Durliat has referred, in this connexion, to the importance of gold from Spain in several articles. In Histoire du Roussillon 1962 he quotes G. Duby on the continuity of a trade route from the Rhône into Andalusia through Roussillon and the Languedoc. Northward a passage by Conques and Clermont would be as practical as up the Rhône, for travel by boat upstream was not feasible.

185. For examples: Saint-Benoît: the Ulysses theme, sirens, centaurs.
        Le Puy: angel heads: fragments from the cloister in Le Puy museum. The Monopoli doorway suggests the common inspiration was in Italy.
        Le Monastier: mermaids.
        Loarre: angel impost, downturned leaf.
        Moissac: angel impost; the scroll of the south doorway capitals at Conques anticipates the linked scroll capitals in Moissac cloister, returning to Conques cloister as the headless bird scroll (fig.135); the cat-headed imp of the Conques basin belongs with the masked figures on capital 17 impost in Moissac cloister, also the cloister frieze at Le Puy, and pilaster capitals and tympanum figures at Saint-Martin d´Ainay in Lyon, (CA 1935, p. 108 and pl. opp. p. 110).
        Poitiers: cornice slabs.

186. P. Monjoin, "L´oeuvre toulousaine de Viollet-le-Duc", Mons hist..France, NS XI, 1-2, 1965; and under the same title, Mem.soc.arch. Midi..France 1957; T.W. Lyman, "Saint-Sernin de Toulouse: `Que faire du XIXe siècle´", BM 139/2, 1981; id., "The sculptural Programme of the Porte des Comtes Master at Saint-Sernin in Toulouse", JWCI 1971.

187. R. Rey, "Pierres romanes toulousaines.....d´une collection parisienne", Bull.soc.arch. Midi..France, NS IV, 1940, pp 10ff. (Collection of M. Brime de Laroussilhe).

188. Lyman, JWCI 1971, p. 24, says the corbels over the
Porte des Comtes may be a 19th century rearrangement, but
the repertoire of heads is the same along the entire length
of the apsidal cornices: "two human and two animal types: a
beardless youthful, a bearded aged man, goats, bears".

189. T. W. Lyman, "Notes on the Porte Miègeville Capitals
and the Construction of Saint-Sernin in Toulouse", AB March
1967, fig. 20.

190. Artistic styles reflect the position of Gascony
between France and Spain at a time when all the routes
across France converged on the western passages over the
Pyrenees, and contacts with Spain were growing in
intensity. The transient influences are usually well-
defined, since there was no previous local building
tradition. The region south of the Garonne valley had
remained outside the Carolingian empire and untouched by
the Carolingian cultural renaissance. Church administration
appears to have collapsed: Cabanot notes that virtually
every document of the 9th and 10th centuries mentioning
monasteries is a fake. The fact that the episcopal lists
are blank until the end of the 10th century appears to
represent a real hiatus. At the end of the 10th century
there is at last mention of a "bishop of the Gascons": a
member of the ducal family and responsible for five
dioceses (Les débuts de la sculpture romane.. Paris 1987,
pp. 22-28).

Menendez Pidal (Esp.Cid, p. 106) quotes evidence that
Count Sancho-William followed the court of Sancho the Great
of Navarre (1000-1035); after this the main pressure came
from Aquitaine.

By the mid-1060s Gascony was annexed by the counts of
Poitiers into the Duchy of Aquitaine. The Chronicle of
Saint-Maixent describes how Gui-Geoffroi went in 1044 to
subdue the county, and succeeded armis et industria.
Archibald, abbot of Saint-Martial in Limoges, was appointed
archbishop of Bordeaux shortly afterwards. When Bernard
Tumapaler claimed and fought for the succession to the
county he was finally paid 15,000 solidi for potestatem
totius Gasconie by Gui-Geoffroi; thus both civil and
ecclesiastical power was assured. By the time the latter,
now Duke William VIII of Aquitaine, led his army to the
siege of Barbastro in 1063 he was the acknowledged ruler of
the province (J. Martindale, op.cit.)

Cluny also at this time was "developing her monastic
empire by the absorption of religious houses". A number had
been founded during the 11th century by local nobles:
Saint-Sever by the Duke in 993; Saint-Jean-Baptiste by
Raymond of Saint-Mont in the first decade of the 11th
century; Nogaro by Austinde, bishop of Auch. From Moissac
Cluny expanded to Layrac, Moirax, Mezin, Auch, Saint-Mont:
"all stages on the routes followed by the black monks from
Moissac to Spain...not to mention the intermediary stops

244

provided by smaller houses, such as the dependencies of Saint-Orens of Auch: Saint-Michel de Montaut-les-Créneaux, Saint-Martin in Touget, Saint-Mamet in Peyrusse-Grande, Saint-Luper in Eauze, Saint-Orens in Lavedan" (Durliat, <u>CA</u> 1970, p. 12). Gregory of Montaner, of the house of Bigorre, was a monk at Cluny before being appointed abbot (1028-1072) of Saint-Sever by Duke Sancho-William. His links with Spain are evident in the illuminations to the copy of the "Beatus" manuscript which he had made at Saint-Sever (BN lat. 8878). There is also, naturally, an influence from northern Aquitaine and the court of Poitou after 1052: Dubourg-Noves (<u>Guyenne romane</u>) notes elements from Anjou at Sérignac and from Angoulême on certain Gascon façades.

191. This is also noticeable at Lescure on the doorway corbels (<u>fig</u>.273), and the animals resemble those of Saint-Sever.

192. Bordeaux will have been another. Very little Romanesque sculpture survives. A few capitals are illustrated in <u>Guyenne romane</u>; the "second phase" is contemporary with Saint-Sever and La Sauve corbels, to judge from the scrolls.

193. J. Cabanot: <u>CA</u> 1970; <u>Gascogne romane</u>; a series of articles on the capitals of Saint-Sever, <u>Bull.Soc Borda</u>, 1963, 1966-1969; most recently <u>Les débuts..</u> 1987 brings all this together with full bibliography. The abbey was founded in 993, flourished under the rule of the Cluniac Gregory of Montaner. A building was begun after a fire in the early 1061s and had progressed far enough for Gregory to consecrate the high altar before his death. This church is thought by Cabanot to have been superceded by an unrecorded new building of the late 11th century. Cabanot shows that the north apses and transept were decorated before the south. The series of capitals begins with a local sculptor´s large smooth acanthus, then in the south chapels comes a workshop "with connexions in the Agenais and Bordelais" to be followed there by "a group trained by the master of the Porte des Comtes at Saint-Sernin in Toulouse, but also influenced by Bernard Gilduin". Durliat gives more emphasis to elements from Santiago ("The Pilgrimage Roads Revisited? <u>BM</u> 1971, p. 113).

194. J. Gardelles, <u>Sculpture médiévale de Bordeaux et du Bordelais</u>, Bordeaux 1976, Section II, from which <u>fig</u>. 219 is copied.

195. Their delicacy recalls ivory carving, eg. the border of the 8-lobed medallions on the casket <u>EK Elf</u>, no 31; <u>JBCC</u> pl 16, but drilled in the case of the ivory.

196. <u>Gascogne romane</u>, pp. 20-22.

197. It is logical that the roofing of the earlier chapels should be completed while work was already in progress for the next parts.

198. op.cit., p. 116. Garcia Romo, AE 1954, argues for a strong Cordoban influence.

199. G. Marçais "Sur un lion de marbre trouvé à la Qal´a des Beni Hammad", Rev. africaine, 1939. Marçais quotes this in AMO p. 117, and mentions more lions.

200. Nogaro, Gascogne romane, fig. 95. Sévignac, ibid., p. 303; Tasque, ibid., fig. 111; there is a beading left as the last vestige of rolls.

201. P. Dubourg-Noves, "Moirax", CA 1969; bibliography, p. 295.

202. Abadie did his worst on the exterior of Saint-Caprais.
.

203. Guyenne romane, fig. 100 (Saint Vivien); Angoûmois roman, fig. 51 (Plassac); Saintonge romane, figs 60, 67 (Fenioux, Corme Royale). The decoration and styles of decorated soffits and metopes needs more study for clarification. Neither the early example of Saint-Hilaire in Poitiers nor that of Conques provoked immediate imitators. In Poitiers at Saint-Hilaire after the tower cornice the corbel tables have single animal reliefs. Only later, in the 12th century does Notre-Dame-la-Grande (Poitou roman, figs 16-18) adopt the luxuriant plant scrolls found also in the 12th century in Saintonge and Angoûmois (Angoûmois roman, fig. 51, Plassac). In the Rhône valley a cornice on corbels on the west tower of Saint-Pierre in Vienne has square flowers and scrolls like the cornice fragments of Le Puy. The soffit fragment with a scroll from Ile Barbe (BM 1936, p. 302) is another example of a tradition of decorated corbel lobes in the Rhône valley.

204. Dubourg-Noves, Guyenne romane, p. 26 dates this upper part of the apse not earlier than the mid-12th century, but perforated metopes otherwise belong to cl100 (pp.253-4), and there seems no reason to make an exception here.

205. ibid., figs 107-115. The connexion with Limousin manuscripts is clear. There are very similar "Arabs" holding columns in the Second Bible of Saint-Martial (Limousin roman, "Manuscrits", pl. 3, BN lat.8, VolI, fol. 4v).

206. Limousin roman, Beaulieu, fig. 5; Chambon, fig 15; Solignac, fig. 33; Saint-Léonard, fig. 1. Saint-Léonard is said by Jackson, Romanesque Architecture, CUP 1920, p. 132, to have roll corbels.

CHAPTER VI

THE CONTRIBUTION OF ANDALUSIA TO ROMANESQUE DESIGN

The foregoing investigation of Andalusian influence in Romanesque has centred on three features: Kufic or mock-Kufic lettering, lobed arches and roll corbels. In each case their assimilation has proved to imply a wider context in which they are incidental:

1. In chapter III the flat two-plane technique of carving in which all the examples of <u>Kufic lettering</u> were executed was found to be characteristic of a distinct craft tradition that was valid for centuries in an area including both Iberia and France. The technique was applied to diverse materials and objects or building parts both religious and secular, and it is everywhere associated with a distinct body of decorative conventions among which Kufic motifs had a place. In Andalusia its practitioners worked in marble, plaster, wood and stone. It is nowhere more in evidence than in the workshops concerned with roof and ceiling work, and hence with the corbel system discussed in Chapter V. Kufic and corbels are not now found together on any building in France. Nevertheless it is workshops with this same decorative tradition and the same links with Andalusia that must be responsible for bringing both features to France.

2. The <u>lobed arch</u> (Chapter IV) entered France primarily as part of far-reaching innovations in the decorative, structural and symbolic function of doorways, and therefore as part of a system of façade design. The earliest example of this new function and setting for a doorway is the Puerta San Esteban, the west entrance to the late 8th century part of the Great Mosque of Cordoba, the Mezquita, on which all subsequent doorways in Andalusia were modelled. Romanesque façades too bear witness to the influence of Andalusian doorway design upon them.

3. The <u>roll corbel</u>, a form invented for the first Great Mosque of Cordoba in the late 8th century, became subsequently a component of a method of roofing which originated in Andalusia and is unknown in France before the Romanesque: that of carrying overhanging eaves on wide horizontal slabs or panels supported on corbels. Furthermore the earliest roll corbels at Vendôme, Poitiers, Tournus and Conques are all associated with decoration in the flat two-plane technique of carving always associated with "Kufic" inscriptions.

Thus the unmistakably Islamic decorative feature, be it Kufic, or the lobing of an arch or corbel, far from being an extraneous ornament culled from chance encounters with a foreign culture, is rather the detail that reveals the Andalusian links or roots of a craft or building

practice that has become essential, and in the absence of
the detail would appear to be "purely" Romanesque.

FEATURES AND MOTIFS

Appendix I lists a selection of architectural features
and decorative motifs that are common to Andalusia and
Romanesque France. Many more could be added. Not a few of
the motifs belong to a traditional repertoire shared with
East Mediterranean or earlier western decorative arts, so
that a derivation for the French example independent of
Andalusia is possible in some, perhaps even in many cases;
this the proponents of the view that French Romanesque
styles are untainted by Islamic influence are ever ready to
point out. Nonetheless the presence of all these motifs in
Andalusian decoration is particularly relevant to
Romanesque architectural decoration, for in Andalusia they
were executed by sculptors, and for the decoration of
buildings, considerably earlier than elsewhere in Western
Europe. Their presence demands acceptance of Andalusia as
an integral part of the whole development of architectural
decoration in the West. The meticulous copy of a Kufic
inscription, evidently from a piece of metalwork, in the
notebook of Adhémar of Chabannes(4) is clear evidence that
motifs could be shared and notions of design disseminated
across the political and religious frontiers. Patently
Islamic elements were evidently studied and current at
Limoges in the mid-11th century; their acceptance is born
out by the frequency of allusions to Kufic in the
decoration of Limousin enamels for several centuries to
come. The elements adopted into architecture however
require further the existence of workshops which had
experience of Andalusian practices and decorative motifs
such that the frontiers had little relevance to their
activities.

The references throughout the previous chapters to the
list of Appendix I represent for most items only a fraction
of possible examples; even so the persistence and diffusion
of the examples of decoration quoted should be enough to
demonstrate that the potential Andalusian contribution was
not limited to exotics in the repertoire, but included
motifs from Andalusia, both dynamic and static, that
appealed widely to Romanesque designers. We can take
treatments of foliage as an example of such dynamic motifs,
and rosettes for the static.

Foliage Motifs

The fluency of Andalusian plant pattern played a large
part in liberating Carolingian interlace from its rigidity:
the essential process is enacted dramatically in the
decoration of the capitals of San Pere de Roda (figs 83-89,
151), in an environment dominated by the flat two-plane
technique; later in the 11th century running scrolls on the
capitals of Conques, Saint-Sernin in Toulouse and Moissac

248

cloister show them heirs on the one hand to the interlace of plait capitals, descendants of a long local tradition, on the other to the Andalusian treatment of the circular leaf scroll D5 (AHIII figs 270c, 273b-d)(figs 92, 105)(1). Such an ancestry is confirmed by the illuminated manuscripts of the region, which depict foliage that has close analogies in Andalusia(2); they have long been understood as imitations of the local sculpture(3).

Rosettes

The rosette, closed and static, is a counterweight to the sinuous moving plant arabesque. It made a dramatic début in Islamic art on the 7th century façade at Mschatta (5), where its vast scale makes it dominate the façade, and it remained popular throughout the Christian and Islamic Near East for some two more centuries. After this it tended there to be overtaken by rectilinear medallion forms, whereas in western Islam it retained supremacy over geometric interlace medallions well into the 12th century. A leading model was that sanctified in the domes of the Mezquita (fig 11) and doubtless modestly emulated in the now vanished pierced domes of countless bath houses in every city of the peninsula (LTB 1957 pp 617-618). It is echoed in miniature in soffits at Madinat az-Zahra´ and Segovia (figs 20, 46) and between roll corbels on the eaves of Auvergnat churches (figs 222, 284). Poitiers (figs 237-239), Lyon and Conques (figs 278-279) adopted floriated cornices like Madinat az-Zahra´ (fig.20), with less static scrolls in the soffits; at Saint-Sernin in Toulouse the more sober ancestral Roman model holds sway, nonetheless it is associated with roll corbels and the eaves system of Andalusian inspiration. Enriched cornices came into fashion once more in later façade decoration in western France, following the example of the Abbaye-aux-Dames in Saintes, Angoulême cathedral or Notre-Dame-la-Grande in Poitiers, with many versions of the rosette among more organic forms.

More flamboyant versions of the rosette, without any connotation of classical soffits and metopes, found favour in other regions. In the Rhône valley they are framed in arches, exactly as in Andalusia (AHIII fig.242); in Burgundian Romanesque they are used in numerous contexts continuously from an early date (6); in Normandy they are applied to capitals, as at Jumièges (7).

Another characteristic Andalusian application in addition to dome and soffit decoration is as a spandrel motif; it is interpreted on al-Hakam II´s mihrab as a great palm flower on a stem, at Zaragoza as a vertical inset coupolette or bacino. It is usurped by figures at Cluny III (8): this modification was already effected on the Platerías doorway at Santiago and the Porte-des-Comtes in Toulouse. It may be surmised too that the constant practice of placing a small rosette boss in the spandrels of arches over figures, as at Santiago, Toulouse or Moissac, is not only the skeuomorph of a jeweller's nails but at the same time an observance of the Andalusian spandrel convention. Rosettes continued to play a striking rôle on doorways even after they were abandoned at Cluny III, for example in Burgundy (fig.153), or in Quercy on the large-scale rosette lintels of Moissac and Thézels. These have a parallel if not a precursor in the doorway of Saint-Jean-le-Vieux at Perpignan (fig.150), now, reconstituted from fragments, in the Palais des Rois de Majorque Museum. It had large rosettes carved at either end of its horizontal members (9). Another use of the motif is exemplified at Jaca, where the chrism of the west door tympanum is studded with smaller rosettes (Aragon roman fig.36).

DOORWAY DESIGN AND LOBED ARCHES

The West Door of Cluny III

Quite apart from its rosettes the Perpignan doorway fragments can indicate the direction from which came some features of the Cluny III façade (the complete doorway might have furnished more). The principle of using the entrance to a religious building in a declamatory manner to proclaim distinguishing features of the inner sanctuary was first expressed in western architecture in the design of the Puerta San Esteban. It was already being adopted into Christian architecture in the early 11th century: the lintels of Saint-Genis-des-Fontaines (inscribed 1020) and Saint-André-de-Sorède (Roussillon roman, figs 19-23) and the Perpignan fragments of disputed date, all reproduce an altar or altar furniture. At Perpignan the torus surrounds even have the guilloche moulding of the altar tables of Gerona, Rodez and Toulouse; in its turn this moulding recalls the border of the Carolingian Narbonne ivory Crucifixion panel (10).

At Cluny III the declamatory principle is extended from the doorway to embrace a whole façade. The doorway is conceived on a monumental scale to reproduce an apse interior with its arcading and wall paintings (11). One of the archivolts on the Cluny door has lobes containing figures, adopting a device seen on the altar-like doorway at Perpignan and on the Roda doorstep (figs 150,151): that of containing carvings within lobes; the convergence with Andalusian lobes is unlikely to be fortuitous, for the designers of the Cluny doorway returned to Andalusia for yet more elements of their great façade. The Puerta San Esteban had established the model: projecting massif, recessed opening, lintel below the diameter line of the arch, alfiz, arched recesses on either side of the massif with windows above.

Other Romanesque Doorways

The Andalusian element at Cluny is further confirmed by the recognizable Andalusian inspiration apparent in many church doorway designs that imitate Cluny in widely varying ways. Treatment of the alfiz is a telling example; the motif has many interpretations (figs 3, 307). Paray-le-Monial and Salles-en-Beaujolais may stress its remote origin in Roman architecture (figs 311,312) but at Loupiac, Château-Larcher, Corme-Ecluse (figs 313, 317, 315) or Rioux (Saintonge romane fig. 182) the Andalusian connexion is undisguised. On more modest façades only a projecting massif and a corbelled weather roof or cornice may be retained, yet often buttresses provide vertical sides to emphasize the line of a rectangular frame (figs 318- 20). Innumerable façades in Poitou, the Angoûmois, Saintonge and Bordelais: Angoulême cathedral or Notre-Dame-la-Grande in Poitiers for example, start out from the basic Cordoban composition of Cluny III: they multiply the cornices and arcades horizontally, sometimes vertically as well, showing as much indifference to the ordering of the building within, its arcades, aisles, tribunes or openings as is notoriously manifest in the Mezquita: there one may enter through an ostentatious doorway only to be confronted by a column almost blocking the way. This type of western French façade coincides with the proliferation in this region of the distinct type of sculpture that started about the third decade of the 12th century (12), exemplified by the capitals of the crossing in Saint-Eutrope in Saintes which show their own selection of Andalusian themes and are noticeably Andalusian in character (Saintonge romane, figs 12-14).

At Corme-Ecluse the alfiz can be read as including the arcading in its frame; at Rioux and Riqueuil, Esnandes or Genouillé (op.cit. figs 199, 206), and in the Berry also (Lurçis-Lévis, fig.314), twin or superposed columns are further Andalusian details; at Saint-Hilaire in Melle (fig.324) the inner archivolt is carved with leaves in relief that recall the lobes of Cluny's triforium. These may be a response to the same current of influence from Cluny that affected Montbron with its series of lobed archivolts (fig.160).

Church doorways depicted in the Bayeux Tapestry make no claim to monumentality (fig.124), but at Jumièges we see the new ideas beginning to take effect in Normandy: the twin columns F6 at the entrance are a sober expression of the solemnity of the entrance. The two transept doors at Conques (?before 1070)(figs 125,132) and the west door at Iguácel (?1072)(Aragon roman, figs 51,53) already display the basic Romanesque composition. Their immediate model is lost. The compositions of the Porte des Comtes at Toulouse (Haut-Languedoc roman, fig.16) and the south door at Marcilhac (fig 6) are experimental attempts to increase the monumental aspect of a doorway, evolved before Cluny III established the dominant model. This we see fully developed at Saint-Sernin in the Porte Miègeville (op.cit. fig.36). The earlier Porte des Comtes has figures in the spandrels (F19) with relief inscriptions (F2) and a roll corbel table above, but it gives no insistent evocation of Andalusian design; the weather roof on corbels and the roll form of the latter may have come at second hand from Conques. At Marcilhac the reliefs of figures are arranged in steps, and remind us of the stepped niches of the San Esteban door; the sun and moon symbols flanking the small Christ figure under an arcade at the top correspond to spandrel bosses (13). The composition is more closely related to spandrels with figures in North Spain than to any French design. The relief inscriptions on the arcades however connect both Toulouse and Marcilhac with Andalusia; they bear out once again the contention that Andalusian methods and motifs were pervasive in many guises in Romanesque craft and design (14).

The doorway of Saint-Michel-d´Aiguilhe in Le Puy (fig.175) is unique. The trilobe, saw-tooth motif, arcading and polychromy can all be referred to Andalusia but they were all well established in Romanesque decoration by the time the chapel was built. Reference to the alfiz is not stressed unequivocally and the design is unlike any in Andalusian architecture; yet there is no doubt that the composition alludes forcefully to Cordoban doorways: it uses what by the later 12th century were purely local elements to produce the most exotic composition in Romanesque decoration.

The Lobed Arch

Apart from this late tour-de-force at Le Puy the modest trilobes of the Velay have only a faint connexion with Andalusia. As originally designed the arcading at Le Monastier along the nave walls (fig.177) would certainly have struck a more emphatic note than the usual small trilobes of the area, but not sufficient to suggest the Velay as the pioneer in establishing the motif in France (15).

Cluny III is more likely to have been one of the prime movers in the dissemination of the lobed arch in France, and this supposition is warranted by historical events. Long before the start of Cluny III Andalusian methods and motifs were reaching France, and were doubtless current at Cluny, it might be through the wood and marble workshops of the east Pyrenean region, or from Montecassino, or direct from Andalusia. But lobed arches were not among them. It is legitimate to see their adoption for the new abbey church around 1088 as indicating a new phase in artistic relations with Andalusia. The appropriate moment would be the occupation of Toledo in 1085 by Alfonso VI, with the lobed arches marking a celebration of that victory, since it brought such enormous benefits in wealth and influence to Cluny. Materially the Muslim gold lavished on Cluny by Alfonso allowed the new building to proceed apace (16); administratively Cluny gained control of the metropolitan see of Toledo through Bernard of Sédirac, at the expense of

the independence of the large Mozarab community in the
city, confirming Cluny´s already forceful authority in the
ecclesiastical and political affairs of North Spain.

With Bernard from the Agenais supreme in Toledo, it is
not surprising to find Toledan elements introduced at
Moissac also, and the agency of Moissac may be postulated
for disseminating more structural and monumental
interpretations of the lobed arch than are now found at
Cluny: those of the "Cahors" group with voussoirs carved to
create an imaginatively shaped intrados, and jambs, with
mouldings that emulate the plasterwork of Andalusian
palaces, shaped into lobes (remarkably similar to the
exterior of the 9th century dome of the Great Mosque of
Sousse in North Africa). At Santiago the same mouldings are
worked on the lobed consoles and the lintels of the
Platerías doorway, and a further link between Santiago and
the "Cahors" group of lobed arches is suggested by the
practice of separately jointing the trilobed and polylobed
arch soffits, at Santiago, a practice seen to greatest
perfection at Cahors.

ROLL CORBELS AND GENERAL PROBLEMS OF DISTRIBUTION

One of the main problems outstanding in connexion with
all the varied Andalusian features found in Romanesque
decoration is that of correlating the patterns of
distribution throughout France. No overriding logic has so
far emerged; however, the appearance of stone roll corbels
at Vendôme, Poitiers, Tournus, Jumièges and Conques before
or very soon after the middle of the 11th century justify
the belief that other Andalusian features or motifs must
have been current in France during the earlier 11th
century.

Two Early Types of Roll Corbel

Even the presence of the roll corbel does not indicate
a single simple current of influence. From the start in
France two distinct styles can be observed, and their
connexions are intricate. One is represented at
Jumièges(fig.225): the corbels are shaped with heavy plain
fillets and the cornice they support is plain. Also at
Jumièges are some capitals of a type associated with the
Narbonne marble atelier, descending from Roda, with
interlace and palmettes (17), as well as other types,
including a "Toledan" (see n. 7). The same type of corbel
and of capital is characteristic of the north transept door
at Conques, of about the same period, while Tournus has the
corbels with a plain cornice, and there are analogous
capitals there as well.

The second style of roll corbel is that of the cornice
and corbels on the tower of Saint-Hilaire in Poitiers (figs
237-239). The single known "Cordoban type" corbel at
Vendôme can be classed with them. The corbels are varied

and carved with delicacy - sculptor´s as opposed to mason´s work. The decoration of the soffit slabs is similar to that of the south door at Conques, which also has corbels of this type. Similarities between carving at Saint-Hilaire and at San Miguel de Fluviá were noted in Chapter V. The capitals on the south door at Conques invite comparisons with examples in north-west Spain, at Frómista and Nogal for instance, where Fluviá evidently also had artistic relations. Their scroll work is of the type which was later much in evidence in Moissac cloister and associated with the Toledan-style Kufic inscription on capital 50 (18). The corbels of the south transept door at Conques (less Cordoban than the non-figural corbels at Poitiers and less ambitious than the figured) have horizontal curl stems as at Poitiers, and their design is again delicate rather than robust. The type has developed far from its precursors at Madinat az-Zahra´, and nothing survives that fills the gap in the development. No French corbel has any close affinity with Andalusian wood corbels, and there are no stone corbels from 11th century Andalusia.

AGENTS OF TRANSMISSION

Our comparison of details of the Velay doors with the Fez panel, and even more tellingly with Andalusian wooden corbels and ceiling members, has established that the decoration of the doors shares its techniques and many characteristic motifs with Andalusian woodwork. The doors and the Andalusian examples are all patently products of a single craft tradition. The constant association of this kind of decoration with ceilings in Andalusia gives strong reason for attributing the introduction into France of the Andalusian system of corbel tables to craftsmen like the makers of the Velay doors, who were evidently acquainted with Andalusian techniques and decoration. Although they are unlike Andalusian wood corbels, the early stone corbels in France are associated with cornices and capitals which are decorated with Andalusian-like motifs, some in the flat wood technique. A trace of the Andalusian wood tradition remains too in the down-turned leaf motif (D16) of numerous Romanesque capitals. A stage of direct transfer of this motif from corbel to capital is met in stone before the end of the 10th century, at Ripoll; it is found later at Santiago, Conques and Moissac, with the culmination of its development in France in the grandiose sweeping flourish of movement of the foliage on capitals at Charlieu, Vézelay or Saulieu (19). These however are products of specialized capital sculptors. The corbel table had come to France when workshops undertook more widely varied tasks (20).

The spread of the lobed arch has a quite different history. Whether traced from Cluny (group I) or Santiago (group 2) it was a phenomenon that took place mostly after 1100, primarily in areas left relatively untouched by the roll corbel: in the Rhône valley, Burgundy, Velay, at Moissac, Cahors and in the Limousin. Toulouse and Conques,

which have roll corbels, did not adopt it, and lobed arches
are far from standard in the Auvergne which has the
greatest concentration of roll corbels in France (21). It
was in Gothic decoration that the potentialities of lobing
the arch were most fully exploited.

In the Romanesque context the original decision to
decorate an arch with lobing is to be interpreted as a
deliberate choice made in the light of serious symbolic
associations, at the highest intellectual ecclesiastical
level. Canon tables and other illustrious manuscript
renderings, altars, literary references to arches, and to
doorways too, will all have contributed to the suitability
of lobing, but only in Andalusia was it part of building
practice. The choice was made at centres of authority like
Cluny and Santiago (22); a rôle is proposed here for
Moissac also, as Cluny´s greatest scion on the road to
Spain, where the models were to be seen.

The roll corbel on the other hand came as part of a
technical system which happened to bring with it its
established decorative traditions; the choice or rejection
of the precise details of its form is unlikely to have been
a matter of high policy and probably rested with the master
builder rather than the patron, or even the artisans on the
work site. Wooden roll corbels are likely to have been
introduced into France early in the 11th century.

These elements are but two of the many diverse
dimensions in which Romanesque France can be seen to have
drawn on the earlier cultural achievement of Andalusia
(23). A large measure of mobility is implied, of craftsmen
and of practices as much as of the secular and
ecclesiastical patrons whose activities and opportunities
for acquaintance with Andalusian culture are alone
recorded. The variety, in both scale and type, of features,
motifs and concepts current in Andalusia and adopted into
Romanesque, from the symbolism of a great façade to the
shape and growth pattern of a single leaf, is matched by a
similar variety in the patterns of distribution and mutual
association in which each is found. The conclusion must be
that Andalusian elements are among the integral components
of Romanesque architectural decoration.

CHAPTER VI. NOTES

1. Saint-Benoît, as so often, is involved in the
development. The mandorla of St Martin on the tower-porch
capital fig.57 is covered with the scroll in flat two-
plane relief. There are early versions also at Nogál and
Frómista.

2. Quercy roman, fig. 63: New Testament, B.N.lat. 254,
fol. 10, from the Agen-Moissac region.

3. _Quercy roman_, p. 140: "the drawing and the illumination here are copying sculpture". In this case it may be ivory sculpture, but Porcher´s argument is that painting and stone sculpture were moving in close concert; in J. Porcher, _Byzance et la France médiévale_, Paris 1958, the same scholar lays stress on the influence of Andalusia, as well as of Italy.

4. UL Leyden, Voss 8o 15. See Chapter III, n.1.

5. Creswell, _EMA I_; E. Kühnel, _Islamic Art and Architecture_, London 1966, pls 6 and 7. The popularity of the motif in early Islamic art infected Byzantium also.

6. The use of rosettes on a capital at Payerne in conjunction with the "fir tree" motif reflects their importance at Cluny and in Burgundy: G. Zarnecki, "La sculpture à Payerne", _Studies...1979_, VIII, pl. 8 and 11; p. 161: Payerne as a reflection of the stage reached at Cluny before the Third Church. Both motifs can be added to the Spanish connexions of early Cluny referred to throughout this article. J. Evans, _Cluniac Art_ gives a number of examples of Burgundian rosettes among the illustrations.

7. Capital with flower cross and birds in circular leaf scroll, in the technique of D9: G. Zarnecki, "1066.." _Studies..._, I, pl. VIIa; compare with Toledo: _AHIII_ figs 271c, 272 a-c, 273 c-d.

8. K.J. Conant, _Cluny...1968_, figs 180, 184.

9. M. Durliat, "Une porte romane de Perpignan", _Mél. Crozet_ I, 1966; id., _La sculpture romane en Roussillon_ III, 1950, pp. 40-42; _op.cit._ IV, 1954, pp. 93-94; P. Ponsich, "Saint-Jean-le-Vieux de Perpignan", _Etudes Roussillonnaises_ 1953, pp. 129-131; id., _CA_ 112, 1954, pp. 114-115 and bibliography p. 118. The Thézels lintel: D. Fossard, "Sur la postérité des sarcophages d´Aquitaine" _BSNAF_ 1962, pp. 134-136, with a bibliography of discussion on the dating. Durliat in 1966 revokes his previous support for the generally accepted early dating of the Perpignan door and proposes the reform of Saint-Jean-le-Vieux as a collegiate church in 1102 as the date for the door fragments; this is because of the classical genius on the side of the lintel, holding a shell mandorla for the Lamb, which Durliat sees as part of the classical revival represented by the work of Gilduinus at Toulouse, but "more backward looking". P. Ponsich, "Les plus anciennes sculptures médiévales du Roussillon (Ve-XIe siècles)", _CSMC_ 11, 1980 gives closely argued stylistic and historical reasons for retaining the 1025 dedication of the church as the date of the doorway.

10. Goldschmidt I (1914), no 31; P. Lasko, Ars Sacra, p. 271; J. Hubert et al., Carolingian Art, fig. 209. Compare the outer border with the Louvre casket, JBCC, pls 14-17.

11. K.J. Conant, "The Theophany in the History of Church Portal Design", Gesta 1976, p. 127 ff. In "The Third Abbey Church at Cluny", Essays ..A. Kingsley Porter I, Conant refers to the considerable use of red and blue background and of gold on the doorway. This is like the sculpture in al-Hakam II´s mosque. The origin of the mediaeval doorway has a growing bibliography, but the Puerta San Esteban is rarely mentioned: R. Hamann Maclean, "Les origines des portails et façades sculptés gothiques", CCM 1969, pp. 157-175; Y. Christe, Les grands portails romans, Geneva 1969 (examines the apse/tympanum connexion); P. Héliot "Observations sur les façades décorées d´arcades aveugles dans les églises romanes", Bull.Soc.Ant.de l´Ouest 4, 1958, p. 367-458 cites Meymac and Le Monastier as two of the earliest examples of using the entrance itself as an element of decoration; M. Durliat, "L´apparition du grand portail roman historié dans le Midi de la France", CSMC 8, 1977, pp. 7-14; U. Monneret de Villard, "Per la Storia del Portale Romanico", Essays..A. Kingsley Porter I, refers to the influence of the mihrab on doorway design, but is mainly concerned with oriental examples; T.W. Lyman, "L´intégration du portail dans la façade méridionale", CSMC 8, 1977, gives further bibliography.

12. Caliphal ivories are often cited as the models for the sculpture; this is valid for the figures (cf. the hair of the figures on capitals at Saint-Eutrope in Saintes (Saintonge romane, fig. 15) and the necks of lions, (fig. 14), but the foliage is equally close to caliphal architectural carving, and the treatment of columns, outlined extrados, and motifs like the Head in a V (D17) noticed by Henry and Zarnecki, ("Arches decorated..." in GZ Studies..VI, fig. 6), triangular drilling (Saintonge romane, fig. 141), floriated cornices (ibid., fig. 117), naturalistic leaf scroll (D9), show familiarity with Andalusian architectural decoration, and already in the crypt of Saint-Eutrope (consecrated 1096) the capitals have such motifs as down-turned leaf, crossed stems and rows of rosettes (ibid., figs 1-10). There is certainly also an admixture of the elements present in Limousin manuscripts (these not necessarily remote from Andalusian connexions) and also in such work as the ivory cross of Fernando and Sancha of León (fig.111). A strong case for the link with caliphal ivories can be made for such foliage carving as that in the porch at Moissac, at Collonges and Cahors (fig.301).

13. The stepped composition is explained by M. Vidal, Quercy roman, as an archaicizing re-use of earlier sculpture. Other Romanesque doorways affect the same composition however; there is even a hint of it in the Moissac tympanum; the stepped pattern is emphasized further

257

on the tympanum of Cahors, and at Saint Ours in Loches (figs 326,327). The latter doorway has radiating voussoirs (F14) as well; separate vertical figures reminiscent of the Platerías doorway at Santiago are combined with fillets.

14. Another illustration of this is the sporadic occurrence of twin columns which Lyman associates with the "sacred portal" ("The function of an ancient architectural ornament and its survival in Mediaeval Spain and France", Actas...Granada 1978), referring to their non-structural use at the threshold of Germigny ("related to Spanish architecture"); Grodecki ("Les chapiteaux de Bernay", BM 1950) thinks with Conant of the blind arcading with twin columns in the apse of Cluny II; at San Millan de Suso twin columns certainly allude to the mihrab of the Mezquita. At Jumièges and at Conques they coincide with alternating supports (F7) and roll corbels (F1); at Toulouse and Solignac with roll corbels, at Solignac also with lobed arch decoration (F22); at both these and at Conques with superposed ·columns (F9). Tabulation of the motifs coinciding with one such feature might produce telling patterns.

15. To depose Le Puy from its pre-eminent pioneering status for the lobed arch is not to dismiss the cathedral as devoid of inmportance as a monument where Andalusian features are found. The wooden doors make its other features specially relevant. The early capitals belong among the group with Catalan connexions; there are twin columns in the east end (F6) and polychrome masonry and voussoirs (F14) in the 11th century parts. Le Puy´s relations with Italy and Sicily brought it into close touch with the Rhône valley, and fragments in the museum show that it also had relations with Conques and Moissac.

16. Defourneaux, p. 21.

17. E. Vergnolle, "Chronologie et méthode d´analyse: doctrines sur les débuts de la sculpture romane en France", CSMC 9, 1978, fig. 5. Some progress is being made in clarifying the development and distribution of "plait" capitals, especially in the south (J.Bousquet, Les chapiteaux de Conques,1973; J.-Cl. Fau, "un décor original.." CSMC 9, 1978, with bibliography). The Jumièges example can be compared with the illustrations to the article by Fau: the pendant pine of his fig. 2 (Roda) recurs between crossed stems (D1,2) at Autun (Grivot and Zarnecki, Gislebertus.., capital 60; fig. B8), at Moûtier-Saint-Jean with downturned leaf volutes (ibid, fig B7).

18. Some of the alabaster capitals from the Galiana palace in Toledo (AHIII , fig. 270a, and especially 270d) have an incipient horizontal leaf motif which may have some part in the evolution of the Berry cylindrical version (Berry roman figs 56. 93; found earlier in Gascony: Gascogne romane, fig.32 (Saint-Sever). A capital from Saint-Nazaire (Aude),

(Fau, op.cit.1978, fig. 3) is a perfect intermediary between the "Berry" motif and the caliphal inturned hollow leaf (D4), as found on the console of the caliphal capital of the Salon Rico, AHIII , fig. 110 and on the console of the capital from Segovia LTB 1957 fig. 480, which is reproduced exactly on the hollowed corners at Saint-Nazaire. Another version is on the volutes of a capital from the Aljafería, AHIII, fig.279c.

19. J. Evans, Art in Mediaeval France, 1948, pl. 29b.

20. Cahn (Doors, p.148) speculates on the makers of the Velay doors as follows: "If Theophilus is to be believed, the arts of joinery and wood carving had not yet emerged at the beginning of the twelfth century into a distinct professional calling. The artisan envisioned by this writer, though primarily a goldsmith, was at the same time a practitioner of woodwork, able to assemble doors, various types of furniture as well as the case for an organ, casting for these and other purposes his own nails"...."there were men of Theophilus´s broad capacities within the circle of the cathedral builders...In Le Puy itself, the association of carpentry with building remained in force to the end of the Middle Ages.." and again "The illustration of the carpenters´characteristic activities furnished by the texts ranges from shipbuilding to the construction of timber frames and roofs of houses." I propose the inclusion among these craftsmen of decorators and roof builders whose techniques stemmed from acquaintance with Andalusian practices, acquired within some kind of international freemasonry, similar to the age-long "freemasonry" implied by the lives of the shepherds of Montaillou (E. Le Roy Ladurie, Montaillou, village occitan de 1294 à 1324, Paris 1982).

21. If Santiago was a determinant influence for the lobed arches of the Velay the roll corbel might be expected there too; but no corbel tables of any kind found favour in the Velay. There must have been other models for lobed arches, now vanished, available in the reconquered cities. The examples in the Rhône valley will have played a mediating part in some cases.

22. At Santiago it is not the doorways but windows that receive the lobing. Lyman op.cit. 1978 stresses the symbolism of windows as purveying (divine) light, and their placing high on façades, which would accord with the lobes on the axial chapel window and on the transept gables. The doorway at Moissac represents further evolution towards the animation of the entrance sought in Gothic architecture. The original design has been transformed, but continuity from the Puerta San Esteban is unbroken.

23. There is a parallel to be drawn with the topic of Andalusian elements in troubadour poetry, which cannot be embarked on here.

APPENDIX I

A NUMBERED LIST OF SOME ANDALUSIAN FEATURES AND MOTIFS
SHARED WITH ROMANESQUE
(Only a few examples of each feature or motif are cited)

FEATURES 1-11, various

F1. Roll corbel. See Chapter V.
F2. Inscriptions in flat two-plane relief. See Chapter
        III; figs 5-7.
F3. Thick acanthus leaf tip on capitals. Mezquita,
        Mozarabic, Zaragoza; Santiago, Moissac; figs 4,
        40, 105.
F4. Stud medallions in relief figs 11, 162. Mezquita,
        Asturian, Mozarab (AHIII fig. 441); Les Aix
        d'Angillon.
F5.   Upwards concentration of decoration. Mezquita,
        Zaragoza; Moissac, Le Puy; figs 18, 114, 195. (cf.
        T.W. Lyman, CSMC 1977: high arcades and high windows
        as the point of departure for façade design in
        Carolingian and early southern French Romanesque; the
        high parts as "lieux privilégiés" before doorways were
        given any dominant rôle).
F6. Paired or twinned columns. Mezquita (fig. 4); Germigny
        des Près; Arlanza, Jaca, Jumièges, early Le Puy
        cathedral, Conques, Nant, Saint-Pierre-de Rhèdes
        fig.16, Larrede (specially frequent in High Aragon and
        Rouergue), Aunay, Melle. Lyman (Granada, XXIII
        Congr.Hist.Art vol. 3) refers to the "sacred portal"
        with a threshold flanked by pairs of columns.
F7. Alternating supports. Green and red columns, with
        Corinthian and composite capitals, in the Mezquita;
        Saint-Nazaire in Carcassonne, Jaca, Ripoll, Bozouls,
        Carennac; the following have roll corbels, F1, as
        well: Jumièges, Saint-Hilaire in Poitiers, N.-D. du
        Port in Clermont, Issoire, Orcival, Saint-Saturnin (E.
        Lambert, "L'Ancienne église du Prieuré de Lay-Saint-
        Christophe et l'alternance des supports dans les
        églises de plan basilical", BM 1942).
F8. Slender columns and colonnettes. Mezquita, Malaga
        (AHIII fig.303); Silos reliquary, Arca Santa, Moissac
        doorway. figs 299, 81, 18.
F9. Superposed columns. Al-Hakam II's extension; Roda
        interior arcades, Cluny III nave, exterior of chevet
        at Toulouse and Conques, fig. 12.
F10. Window or niche on colonnettes. Mezquita domes,
        flanking al-Hakam II's doorways; Iguácel; Le
        Monastier, Saint-Pierre Toirac (fig. 15) with early
        trilobes as at Santiago.
F11. Twin window or niche with central colonnette (ajimez).
        Torre San Juan (late 9th-early 10th century), Mezquita
        doorways; Muzols (fig. 14), Champagne (fig. 171),
        Saint-Antonin (fig. 49).

FEATURES 12-22, arches

F12. Alfiz: rectangular frame surrounding arch. Andalusian from Puerta San Esteban onwards. Often interpreted in Romanesque doorway design with column buttresses and a weather roof or cornice above: Peujard, Loupiac, Le Puch, figs 307, 313, 319. Cluny III and certain Burgundian churches adopted it more explicitly. Some inspiration is suggested from early Asturian openings in rectangular recesses, particularly for versions on the churches of High Aragon (Crozet, CCM 1969, pp 287-289), but the Andalusian development also plays a part.

F13. Alternating voussoirs, Figs 2, 3, 18, 175, 176: contrasts of colour, plane, and of decorated with plain surfaces. Used throughout Andalusian architecture. THe most insistent Romanesque example is at Montivilliers fig. 329; the parallel with Andalusia was first noticed by Zarnecki, ("1066 and Architectural Sculpture", PBA 1966 [pls XIIIa and b]). The caption to pl.XIIIb should read mid-Xth century). The detail of the carved voussoirs resembles Italian interpretations of this Andalusian method of decorating arches. Le Puy, Vézelay.

F14. Outlining and separation of voussoirs. This is more usual in France than F13. At Saint-Aubin in Angers, fig. 330, each voussoir is carved, but separated by an outline. Adopted early at Saintes, and frequent in Saintonge. Combined with the stepped arch, F18, at Saint-Ours, Loches, fig. 327.

F15. Emphasis on extrados by outline, moulding, decoration etc. This is constant in Andalusia; on lobes of arches in France it indicates a new awareness of Andalusian examples, not present in the first examples of lobed arches in Romanesque. Figs 210; 202.

F16. One aspect of F5: raised centre to the extrados. Characteristic of 10th century Andalusian arches, less frequent in 11th as the pointed form gains in popularity. Infrequent in Romanesque, but clear at Vigeois and Meymac. Heavy tympana on lintels, as at Moissac or Collonges achieve something the same effect. Figs 142, 188.

F17. Arcading over entrance, or other main arch. Standard in Andalusian doorway design and frequent in Romanesque. Cluny, Corme-Ecluse, figs 310, 315.

F18. Stepped profile to arch. Puerta San Esteban niches; Marcilhac, Loches, composition of some historiated tympana (Cahors); figs 326, 327.

F19. Motif in spandrel. One of the earliest examples is the bosses in the Puerta San Esteban niches, mihrabs; Cluny, Saint-Sernin in Toulouse, San Isidro in León, Château-Larcher fig. 317.

F20. Intersecting arches. Mezquita, Toledo, Zaragoza; mainly Norman, some in Saintonge.

F21. Lobed arch: see Chapter IV. Mezquita; Santiago, Cluny, Le Puy, Cahors.

F22. Rectangular section ribs in domes. Perhaps contribute to similarly ribbed vaults also. Mezquita, Cristo de la Luz in Toledo; direct copies at Hôpital-Saint-Blaise and Oloron Sainte-Marie; simpler at Loches, Moissac, Jaca, Aubiac etc. <u>figs</u> 11,14-17.

DECORATIVE MOTIFS

D1. <u>Crossed stem scroll</u>.

Mezquita, Madinat az-Zahra´, Zaragoza; Ripoll, Roda, earliest imposts and capitals at Santiago with linked half-palmettes, Saint-Sever, La Sauve, Conques, Bordeaux on the earliest capitals at Saint-Seurin, with Dl6.

a. Mezquita mihrab capitals

b. Madinat az-Zahra´ West Palace. c. Puerta San Esteban

d. Salon Rico, Madinat az-Zahra´

e. Cluny transept capital

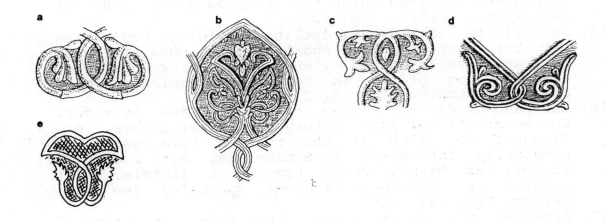

D2. <u>Pine cone</u>.   Derived from classical vine scroll, branching from stems or framed in a heart-shaped double stem. Mezquita dome arcades; Roda, Conques.

a, b. Mezquita dome arcades

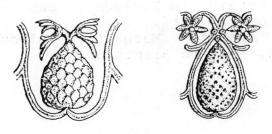

262

D3. <u>Miniature florets in relief</u>, with four or more petals. Flat, as nail heads or in rings. Mezquita: a band under the shell dome of the mihrab (<u>fig</u>.5), Madinat az-Zahra´ as a border for interlocking stars, for metope and soffit panels, as filling for scrolls or volutes, Aljafería as border of plaster ceiling panels, Fez door. On all surviving 11th century Andalusian wooden corbels; Velay doors, Toulouse, with D11 on impost in ambulatory of Saint-Sernin.

D4. <u>Incurled hollow leaf</u>, single or double. Throughout maqsura carving in Mezquita, characteristic of Cordoban ivory carving. The illustration here is composite, to suggest how the Andalusian motif is ancestral to the "Berry" horizontal leaf cylinder (<u>Berry roman</u>, figs 56, 93 and <u>Saintonge romane</u> fig. 32). Also on Hildesheim doors (H. Swarzenski, <u>Monuments</u>, pl. 107), on a capital at Saint-Nazaire (<u>CSMC</u> 1978, fig.3 after p.140), capital at Jumièges as the half-palmette into which the interlace opens <u>op.cit</u>, fig.5 after p. 162, Matha-Marestay doorway (<u>Saintonge romane</u>, fig.100), Moissac, Collonges (<u>figs</u> 301).

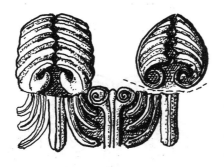

D5. Circular half-palmette scroll, a version of the
universal running half-palmette scroll D7. Three or more
folioles. The leaf is flat, unlike D4. The foliole end, as
in b., or stem running beyond the framing circle is adopted
at Nogál, Moissac and Conques (figs 43, 105, 92). A version
at Saint-Benoît in the tower porch (CSMC 1978, fig. 15
after p. 162).

a. Cordoba, filling a capital volute

b. Toledo. In larger compositions foreshadowing arabesque

c. Tudela, roll corbel end, showing Andalusian tendency to
enclose a double motif, approaching Dl4,b.

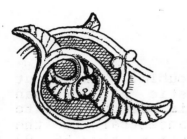  

D6. Split palmettes: two half-palmettes back to back.
Mezquita, Madinat az-Zahra´, Tudela, Segovia, Fez panel
(fig.44); Mozarab (Art Mozarabe, fig. 30); Velay doors,
Angoûmois and Saintonge (Saintonge romane fig. 129). The
Santiago, or Gascon tendril scroll, not always entwined,
arises from it.

a, b. Madinat az-Zahra´

c. Aunay, crossing capital

D7. <u>Meander or wave stem sprouting half-palmette</u>. Throughout Andalusian decoration, single and double with every elaboration. Not much in Mozarab but occurs in early Romanesque. An alabaster capital from the palace of Toledo (<u>AHIII</u> fig.270c), about contemporary with the Toledo well-head <u>fig</u>.71, shows a model for the "Moissac" scroll of cloister capital 50, though not encircled.

a. Mezquita, Puerta de la Chocolata

b. Mezquita, ceiling

c. Madinat az-Zahra´ voussoir

a

b

c

D8. <u>Asymmetrical plant scrolls</u> approximating to Kufic lettering. Mezquita, Madinat az-Zahra´; implication of Kufic strong oon early altar tables: Quarante, Gerona, Rodez, Sorède, and Roda imposts.

a. Mezquita voussoir

b. Madinat az-Zahra´ voussoir

a

b

D9. <u>"Naturalistic" free flowing stem</u> with curling indented leaves. Mezquita mihrab surround. Frequent in Poitou, Angoûmois, Saintonge: La Couronne, cornice <u>fig</u>.39.

D10. <u>Flower or trefoil cross</u>. Mezquita, often as relief medallion F4, Madinat az-Zahra´, sometimes refined there to units of split palmettes radiating from a central floret, Tudela; Le Puy cornice, <u>fig</u>.90, Lavoûte-Chilhac door.

a. Mezquita mihrab panel

b,c. Madinat az-Zahra´

D11. <u>"Heart and Dart" scroll</u>. The palmette in a heart offers an ambiguity of open and closed form that was readily exploited. Throughout an decoration. Fez panel and Malaga wood battens show transition to lam-aliph. Imposts at Roda, <u>figs</u> 83-89, Santiago and Toulouse. Cf. <u>Débuts</u>, pp 20-21 on the break-up of acanthus leaf into "fleuron in an inverted heart, separated by a lance" and then to a fleuron under an arcade. <u>AHIII</u> fig.110 shows the process well under way at Madinat az-Zahra´. Carolingian MS border, <u>Corvey</u> pl.160.

a. Mezquita, mihrab panels

b. Saint-Sernin, Toulouse, ambulatory impost

c. Fez mimbar panel

D12. <u>Border motifs</u>. As is to be expected, many simple traditional border motifs are common to Andalusia and Romanesque: cording, hatching, reel and dart, billet, plain fillet, ovulo, alternating trefoil, interlace of two or more strands. On the faces of corbel fillets are grooving, chequers, lattice, palmette-in-heart, and notably a straight stem with branching curls, transposed from metalwork like the filigree decoration on Asturian crosses (<u>AHII</u> figs 418-420). This is the "fir-tree" motif a. which on capitals at Payerne probably reflects its presence on now destroyed capitals at Cluny II (Zarnecki, <u>Studies</u>, VIII, capitals nos 6,7,I,VII). On a capital at Valdedios, late 9th century, at Dijon early 10th. In mid-11th century on a corbel at Poitiers (no 9, <u>fig</u>.237) and on capitals at Consac (<u>Saintonge romane</u>, figs 50-58), later in Burgundy (Anzy-le-Duc, <u>CSMC</u>1978, fig.13 after p.162) and Vézelay. Saw-tooth: over upper arcading in Mezquita, Mozarabic MSS; Saint-Michel d´Aiguilhe door, in mosaic on Le Puy façade. On Andalusian capitals acanthus stems are interlaced and sometimes twisted into spirals (<u>LTB 1957</u> figs 475,487,499,503), and there are the same spiral stems on Mozarabic capitals and on capitals at Saint-Benoît (<u>fig</u>.91) and Roda. These were cited by Garcia-Romo to trace a "Mozarab" influence on early capitals in the Loire region.

a. Mezquita, fillet of corbel in`Abd ar-Rahman´s patio

b. saw tooth

c. Madinat az-Zahra´, pilaster base.

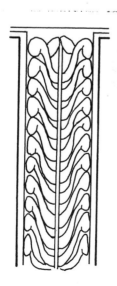

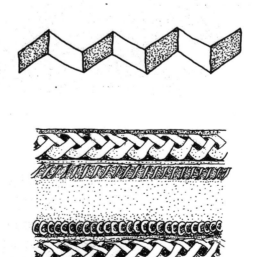

D13. <u>Geometric medallions</u>. They echo patterns of the
Mezquita dome ribs. Mezquita in maqsura, on panels
from palaces of Toledo and Zaragoza; in Cordoba often
with central rosette, a form found again on late
Romanesque soffits at Lérida. Some of the Aljafería
panels combine them with inscriptions. Only secondary
to plant motifs until Almohad and later; Moirax,
Marignac, Lescure metopes, doorway of St Genès in
Châtaumeillant (<u>Berry roman</u>, figs 61,62).

D14. <u>S-divided circle or circular stem scroll</u>. Islamic
artists had a preference for containing a double motif
within the stem circle, two leaves or fruit and
leaves. Qairawan, Madinat az-Zahra´, Seville basin,
Aljafería panel (<u>AHIII</u>, figs 209,249,291,316), Tudela
corbels (here illustrated), Fez panel. The mosaic
floor (<u>CSMC</u> 1972, fig.7 after p. 130) and cloister
capital no 72 at Moissac.

D15. Rosette. Mezquita dome, Aljafería mihrab spandrels, Madinat az-Zahra´ and Segovia soffits (figs 20,46), Pamplona casket medallions; Auvergne and Toulouse soffits, Rhône valley and Burgundy: all sizes and uses, Perpignan door, Moissac lintel. Rose windows: Balaguer (fig. 47); bacini (figs 48,49); linked, on Poitiers and Conques cornices (figs 131-2, 237-9, 278-9), Nogál and Moissac imposts (figs 120, 22).

a,b. Mezquita domes

c. Tudela cornice.

D16. Down-turned leaf. Mezquita, mihrab panel consoles, Aljafería dome supports, many Andalusian wooden corbels. Romanesque capitals: Ripoll, Moissac cloister, Saintes crypt, Conques, many others (figs 21,22,24,26).

a. Mezquita mihrab panel

b. Aljafería dome supports

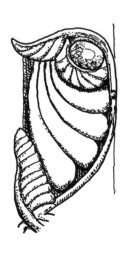

D17. Animate motifs.   Secular subjects which were at times given symbolic meaning. Most themes are taken from portable objects and textiles, but the lion is different. Lyman (T.W. Lyman, "The Sculptural Programme of the Porte des Comtes Master at Saint-Sernin in Toulouse", JWCI 1971) notes there is no major architectural application of the recumbant lion motif in France before the late 11th century. Lions support the columns of a prince's throne at Sedrata (AMO, p.117, and several others). In Cordoba the lion mask spitting foliage on a capital volute (AHIII, fig.245) connects two themes not always combined in Romanesque: i. the usually jawless mask spitting foliage (or sometimes jewels, ribbons, columns etc), as on the façade of Notre-Dame-la-Grande in Poitiers, and ii. the ambiguous lion or human face with a line across the brow implying a cap with ears. Carolingian and later manuscripts have many examples of the (originally classical) lion mask associated with foliage, birds' wings etc (Chapter II, n. 103); the Cordoban volute and a knocker (AHIII, fig.395), bronze mortar (ibid., fig. 394) together with many references to lion images in literature, need to be included in the documentation. The mosaic floor at Die has the Four Rivers issuing from such masks (X. Barral i Altet, "Les débuts de la mosaïque de pavement romane dans le Sud de la France et en Catalogne", CSMC 1972, (with full references to publications of mosaics) fig. 9 after p. 130. This is another craft which shares technical and decorative traditions with Andalusia, as Barral observes). Mosaic motifs include an elephant with howda, animal combats and at Lascar a peg-legged Moor with oliphant. Animate motifs have been numbered as follows:

a. birds, confronted, addorsed, crossed, in profile.
b. small bird frieze (AHIII, fig. 245).
c. fish.
d. Spread eagle.
e. animal attack.
f. lion mask i. spitting foliage; ii. face in eared cap.
g. superposed animals.
h. lions or other felines, pacing, confronted, addorsed, crossed.
i. Gazelles; othr horned or antlered quadrupeds.
j. animal head in V frame, or alone.
k. snake.
l. harpy.
m. griffon.
n. peacock.
o. elephant.
p. beard-pullers.
q. tilting knights.
r. atlas figure.
s. wrestlers.
t. confronted dancers.
u. animal dompter, lion vanquisher, "Gilgamesh".
v. falconer.

APPENDIX II

"CAHORS TYPE" LOBED ARCHES

a.   <u>Intrados with Volute, Split or Elaborated Points.</u>
All these doors have outer archivolts with Limousin moulding.

Limousin

<u>Allassac</u>.   Door, 5 lobes, separately voussoired. Limestone points. Spring from up-curled point.

<u>Bénévent l´Abbaye</u>. Door, 11 lobes, separately voussoired. Split points. <u>fig</u>. 190.

<u>Chamberet</u>.   Door, 3 and two half-lobes, separately voussoired.

<u>Collonges</u>.   Door, two trilobes, separately voussoired. Triple points. Spring from upper volute, <u>fig</u>. 142.

<u>Condat</u>. Door, 5 lobes separately voussoired. Top lobe larger.

<u>Ladignac</u>.   Arcade of five trilobes round apse. Similar to Le Dorat tower.

<u>Lagraulière</u>.   Oculus.

<u>La Souterraine</u>.   Door, 9 lobes, split points, voussoirs radial, <u>fig</u>. 169.

<u>Le Dorat</u>.   Arcade of trilobes round tower.

<u>Les Rosiers d´Egleton</u>.   Blind arch on apse exterior, 7 lobes, separately voussoired, <u>fig</u>. 189.

<u>Meymac</u>. Door, 5 lobes, separately voussoired. Spring from point, <u>fig</u>. 141.

<u>Palisse</u>. Door, 5 lobes, limestone. Spring from up-curled point, <u>fig</u>. 143.

<u>Saint-Bonnet-près-Bort</u>. Door, 5 lobes. Spring from up-curled point.

<u>Saint-Robert</u>. Oculus

<u>Saint-Symphorien</u>.   Door, 4 and 2 half-lobes. Motifs on points. Radial voussoirs.

<u>Saint-Yrieix</u>. Arcading on columns round tower, trilobes separately voussoired. Spring from up-curled point, <u>fig</u>. 203.

<u>Tulle</u>.   Door, 7 lobes, top lobe narrow. Spring from up-curled point. Radial voussoirs, <u>fig</u>. 144.

<u>Vigeois</u>. Door, 5 lobes separately voussoired. Motifs on points. Horseshoe archivolt. Outer archivolts progressively more pointed, <u>fig</u>. 188.

Quercy
Lot, Tarn et Garonne

<u>Cahors</u>.   Door, 3 lobes, separately voussoired, <u>figs</u> 185-187

<u>Moissac</u>. Door, two trilobes, separately voussoired, <u>fig</u>. 191.

<u>Saint-Antonin</u>. Window, twin trilobes, separately voussoired, <u>fig</u>. 49.

Dordogne and the West
Charente, Charente Maritime, Gironde

Aubeterre.   Door, 6 lobes with triple points, radial.
Bassac. Door, 7 lobes, triple points, radial.
Blanzac. Door, 7 lobes, volute points like Palisse, fig.
        205.
Châtres. Door, 7 lobes, triple points, damaged. Spring was
        originally from upper volute. fig. 198.
Chalais. Door, 7 lobes.
Echebrune.   Window, 4 lobes.
Les Eyzies de Tayac.   Door, 5 and 2 half-lobes; convex
        principal points.
Montbron. Door, 6 lobes, fig. 160.
Montmoreau.   Door, 6 lobes, spring from up-curled point,
        fig. 196.
Neuillac. Door, 6 lobes, convex points, fig. 199.
Petit-Palais. Door, 5 lobes; two 5-lobe arcades; a niche
        with two trilobed archivolts; arcade with three 5-
        lobed archivolts over a window. The two flanking
        arcades beside the door are horseshoe-shaped, fig.
        197.
Puisseguin.   Door, 5 lobes, triple points.
Rioux.   Apse windows, double row of multiple lobes,
        triple points.
Vandré. Arcade beside door, multiple lobes, triple
        points, fig. 168.
Villemartin.   Door, 7 lobes, spring from up-curled points
        (Ill. BM 1974).

        b. Archivolts With Lobed Limousin Moulding.
                see Map II

Blanzac. Interior apse windows; fig. 205
Celles-sur-Belle.   Door, five-lobed archivolts, the inner
        four with moulding. By widening the radius of the
        central lobe progressively towards the exterior, the
        outer archivolt is more pointed than the introados,
        which is little raised above the semi-circle.
Déols.   Door, recessed, framed by enriched hood
        moulding and two courses of slabs laid longitudinally
        and shaped to the curve. [?]8 lobes, the two lowest
        wider than the rest, perhaps two restored as one.
        Distinct horseshoe archivolt. Lintel and nambs look
        new, and probably the original profile had jambs level
        with the widest part of the arch; fig. 195.
La Souterraine.   Door. Three orders of Limousin
        moulding, lobed, frame the lobed intrados already
        contained in an unlobed Limousin moulding archivolt on
        capitals and slender columns; these three outer orders
        are lobed to the ground. There is disturbance right
        across at the impost level, where perhaps small
        capitals have been removed. A double hood moulding
        over the whole, ending on corbels at the impost line,
        detracts from the effect of the pointed arch in the

composition: the archivolts are progressively rounder towards the exterior. THe two inner lobed archivolts have an outer line of unlobed Limousin moulding. With the double hood there are fifteen different planes; the voussoiring is consistent throughout; _fig_. 169.

Le Dorat. Door. Four archivolts of lobed Limousin moulding frame a plain double entrance. The moulding turns to the vertical, like the columns of the Moissac and Souillac trumeaux, to meet simple capitals over slender nook shafts of the same diameter as the moulding. A hood moulding like that of La Souterraine surrounds the arch. (_Limousin roman_ fig. 3, p. 215.).

Saint-Bonnet-de-Cray. Window. An outer archivolt with 9 lobes.

Thouars. Door. Three 7-lobed archivolts over a plain two-centre intrados, similar to the two arches of Le Dorat. The lobes are uneven; the central lobe, already narrower than he rest at Le Dorat, is here taller and narrower still. A hood moulding with plant carving introduces a Poitevin element; _fig_. 170.

Tulle. Door. The innermost of five two-centred archivolts of Limousin moulding has 7 lobes; _fig_. 144.

Vigeois. Door. One archivolt of 5 lobes follows the lobed intrados from the same centre above the impost. There is an unlobed archivolt outside it, two-centred on the bottom points of the intrados. A hood moulding turns horizontal to run to the wall return. The whole doorway is recessed into the wall; _fig_. 188.

Saint-Pierre-Toirac. Interior blind arcades, trilobes with torus moulding on the extrados; _fig_. 15.

Beaulieu, _Moissac_ and _Souillac_ have lobed torus moulding down the trumeau to the ground. _Brive_ also had it.

Moissac and _La Souterraine_ have torus (Limousin) moulding down the jambs to the ground.

APPENDIX III

DOCUMENTED DATES FOR EARLY ROMANESQUE SPANISH BUILDINGS
(see WMW for references)

1056   Sa Maria la Reál de Najera, endowed by Garcia, King of Navarre, 1052, consecrated by the Archbishop of Narbonne. Destroyed. (Fita, "Santa Maria la Real de Nájera" BRAH xxvi (1895) pp 157-171).

1063   San Salvador de Nogal de las Huertas: inscriptions at doorway and inside: "Elvira Sansez fecit", and "...era millesima centessima prima.." (WMW pp 213-214).

1066   San Martin de Frómista, mentioned in the will of Mayor, mother of King Fernando of León, "...in hoc monasterio sancti Martini quem..edificare cepi in Fromesta". The will is dated 1066.

1067   Consecration of cathedral of Roda de Isabena (First Romanesque style). Completion of San Millan de Yuso. Destroyed.

1069   Consecration of cathedral of Astorga. Destroyed.

1072   Na Sa de Iguácel: inscription on west front.

1073   Dedication of cathedral of León to San Pelayo by Bishop Pelayo, who restored the church "in quo oratorio altare cum sua abside erexi a fundamentis", built baptistry, refectory, cloister, houses for the canons, bought books, had made a silver cross, procured vestments and ornaments and summoned Alfonso VI, his sisters Urraca and Elvira and all the bishops of the province for the ceremony (ES XXXVI, pp lvii-lxiii; XXXV, pp 110-116). Destroyed.

1074   San Salvador de Ona (Chronicon de Cardena I). Destroyed.

1075   Alfonso VI gave his palace in Burgos for the new cathedral, finished before 1096 when he refers to it as finished. (ES XXVI, pp 197, 458-463). Destroyed.

1076   San Pelayo de Perazancas. Inscription in north wall of nave: "Pelagio Abas fecit in era MCXIIII". First Romanesque corbel table but engaged columns not pilaster strips between the arched tables, and sawtooth and billet moulding above.

1080   San Pedro de Arlanza begun. Inscription in wall of south apse: "..era MCXVIII".

1082   San Pedro de Siresa given the title of Capilla Reál by Sancho Ramirez.

1086   San Caprasio de Santa Cruz de la Serós given to San Juan de la Pena.

1087   San Miguel de Neila. Inscription in south wall.."Abbas Nunnuest..fecit". A small church, "built of well-cut stone and completely Romanesque in style".

1088   Montearagon; the castle finished in 1088 and the canons moved from Loarre in 1089. Destroyed.

1093   San Salvador de Sepúlveda. Inscription in the apse foundation. Town repopulated by the fuero of 1076.

1094   San Juan de la Pena. Consecrated by the Archbishop of Bordeaux and the bishops of Jaca and Maguelonne.

1095   Sa Maria, Loarre. Mortuary inscription in the door jamb. Documents signed from the castle in 1082.

          Sa Maria la Antigua, Valladolid, consecrated by Bernard, Archbishop of Toledo and the bishops of Palencia, León, Burgos, Astorga, Oviedo and Lugo.

1098   Consecration of San Salvador de Leire

1099   Consecration of Sa Maria, Alquezar, a royal chapel within the castle. Destroyed.

          San Benito, Sahagún consecrated. Destroyed.

1100   San Esteban de Corullón completed. Inscription in north wall of tower.

          San Frutos, consecrated by Bernard Archbishop of Toledo: inscription at foot of a buttress of the south wall.

In the last years of the 11th century: Santa Cruz de la Serós; .San Miguel and El Rivero in San Esteban de Gormaz; the tower adjoining the Camera Santa in Oviedo; Sant Andrés (destroyed), Santo Tome, San Cebrian, San Claudio de Olivares, Santiago el Viejo, Sa Maria la Nueva, all in Zamora. Sant Andrés begun in 1093, the rest about contemporary.

APPENDIX IV

A CHRONOLOGICAL LIST OF MILITARY ENCOUNTERS IN SPAIN WITH PARTICIPANTS FROM FRANCE
(compiled from M-P Cid and Defourneaux)

1064   Occupation of Barbastro for one year. Thibaut de Semur, Hugues de Châlons, Guillaume VIII, Robert Crespin, Guillaume de Montreuil.

1073   An expedition from Champagne led by Ebles de Roucy (son-in-law of Robert Guiscard and brother-in-law of Sancho Ramirez (king of Aragon 1063-1094). He is recommended by Pope Gregory VII to hold lands in Spain under the Papacy (Defourneaux p. 138 n.4). He "raised a mighty army" (RHGF XII, 140) but it never arrived in Spain.

1076 and 1080.   Expeditions of Burgundians under Duke High (RHGF XIII, p. 1). Two campaigns that yielded booty and captives, not otherwise recorded.

1080   An expedition of Aquitanians under Duke William VIII arrived at the frontier of ARagon "et gloriosus rex Sancius fecit illum reverti in patria sua" (A. Duran Gudiol, Iglesia p. 116, with references).

1086   The troops of Alfonso VI and some Aragonese set off to meet the Almoravid army newly landed; with them were "Christiani a partibus Alpes, multique Francorum" (Chon. Lusitano, ES XIV, 1786, p. 418).

1087   Alfonso VI, after the defeat of Sagrajas, threatens to let Muslim armies into France if no help is sent. A great army assembled under Duke Eudes of Burgundy (RHGF XII, p. 2), joined by Aquitanians under Hugh of Lusignan (Chr. St. Maixentm qu. RMP p. 340, "many knights from Normandy, Limousin and Poitou"). Normans under Guillaume le Charpentier (P. Boissonnade, "Les premières croisades d´Espagne", Bull. Hisp. 1934, pp 33-34). Boissonnade and E. Petit, ("Les croisades bourguignonnes contre les Sarrasins d´Espagne", Rev.Hist. XXX, 1886) add Provençals and Languedocians under Raymond de Saint-Gilles. There is no document to prove it (Hill 1959), but J.H. and L.L. Hill are "inclined to approve it" even though in April Raymond was already probably in Le Puy with Bishop Adhémar, witnessing a gift by the latter of the church of Usson to the abbey of La Chaise-Dieu (p. 17). The Almoravids had already crossed back to Africa and Alfonso invited the French contingents to return home. They secured some reward by pillaged and joined Sancho Ramirez who was besieging Tudela, but without success. They then broke up with dissensions. The three Burgundian lords went to León to visit their relative, Queen Constance.

1094   Raymond of Burgundy defeated at Lisbon by Almoravids.

1096   Battle of Alcoraz, outside Huesca. Gascons under the exiled Fortuna fought for Pedro I of Aragon. This was the turning point in the fall of Huesca, defended by al-Mostain of Zaragoza with help from Castile. As well as the (french) bishop of Pamplona, the bishops of Bordeaux, Oloron and Lascar were present at the siege, and consecrated the Mosque. The chapel royal was given to Frotaire, abbot of Saint-Pons-de-Thomières.

1100-1101   Fall of Barbastro. The largest mosque was given to Sainte-Foy de Conques to found a monastery, the church of Sainte-Eulalie and lands given to Saint-Gilles-de-Provence. How the Mozarabs reacted to these gifts is not recorded. Pons, from Thomières, was appointed bishop, and was followed at his death in 1104 by Raymond, previously prior of Saint-Sernin in Toulouse (ES XLVI, pp 48 ff).

1106   Fall of Ejea to Alfonso I of Aragon, with Gascons under Centulle de Bigorre, the viscount of Lavardan and Gaston d´Aspe. Gifts to La Sauve Majeure (Defourneaux p. 154 n.).

1108   Battle of Uclès: death of Alfonso VI´s heir, defeat of Alfonso by Almoravids. These, now in Zaragoza, threaten Barcelona. (The Chronicle of Saint-Pierre-le-Vif reports an appeal to Louis VI the Fat, not recorded elsewhere, and considered dubious (Defourneaux, p. 152n.). Muslims retreat after marauding.

1109   Henry of Burgundy, now "of Portugal", recruits French support for his own ambitions, but Burgundians are less in evidence in León from now on.

1110   Henry of Châlons is reported present at the victory at Valtierra near Tudela, wher al-Mostain of Zaragoza is killed.

1110-1115[?]   Expeditions of Pisans to the Balearics, joined by Ramon Berenguer of Barcelona, supported by his clients from Languedoc and Provence (he had just married Douce of Provence), including Guillaume of Montpelier, Aimery of Narbonne, Raymond des Baux, the towns of Arles, Nîmes and Béziers (Defourneaux p. 155). They fail to rout Muslim pirates, but return with "glory and booty".

1117   Siege of Zaragoza by Alfonso I of Aragon. The city now the stronghold of the Almoravid Holy War. Normans present under Rotrou du Perche include Robert Burdet (later "Prince of Tarragona") and many Gascons; Gaston of Béarn and Rotrou are well rewarded in the city at its fall. This was followed by the fall of Tarrazona, Borja, Magallon, Catalayúd. Rotrou possibly at the taking of Tudela soon after (Defourneaux p. 158 quotes Lacarra, P.de V.XXII). William of Aquitaine arrives with Talleyrand of Périgord, Raymond of Turenne, Geoffroy of Rochefort and more Gascons.

1124   Defeat of Almoravids at Cutanda.
1131   Alfonso I besieges Bayonne with the Gascons.
1134   Defeat of Alfonso I at Fraga: death of Centulle de Béarn, Aimery de Narbonne, Augier de Miramont and Bertrand de Laon "...et fortes multi auxiliares

Franciae et multi alienigenae" (Chron. of Alfonso VII, ES XXI, 339). Bishop of Lescar taken prisoner. Robert Burdet from Normandy also present.

1135   Alfonso VII of León/Castile, son of Raymond of Burgundy and Uracca, daughter of Alfonso VI, crowned emperor.

For some decades French military intervention ceases.

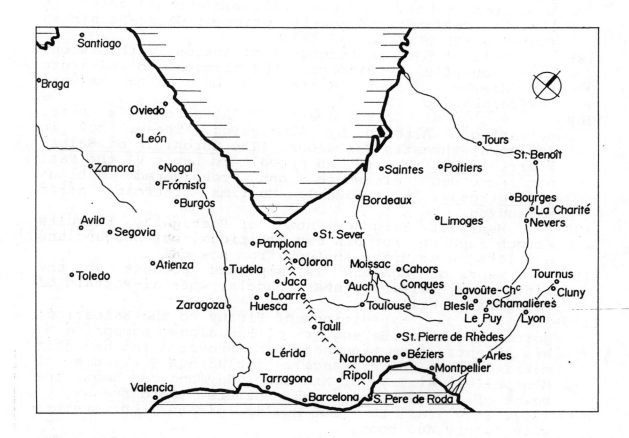

BIBLIOGRAPHY

The principal abreviations used in text and footnotes are the following:

Periodicals

AARP   Art & Archaeology Research Papers, London.
AB   Art Bulletin of America
AduM   Annales du Midi
AE   Arte Español
AEA   Archivo Español de Arte
AEAA   Archivo Español de Arte y Arqueologia
al-And   al-Andalus
An Est Med Anuario de Estudios Medievales, Barcelona
Anth An   Anthologico Anua, Rome

BM   Bulletin Monumental
BRAH   Boletín de la Reál Academia de la Historia
BSNAF   Bulletin de la Société Nationale des
            Antiquaires de France
BSAOuest   Bulletin de la Société des Antiquaires de
            l´Ouest
Bull Arch.   Bulletin Archéologique
Bull. hisp.   Bulletin hispanique

CA   Congrès Archéologiques (Soc.Fr.Arch)
CCM   Cahiers de Civilisation Médiévale
Cah Arch   Cahiers Archéologiques
CRAcIBL   Comptes-rendus de l´Académie des
            Inscriptions et Belles-Lettres
CSMC   Cahiers de Saint-Michel de Cuxa

EEMCAragon   Estudios de la Edad Media de la Corona
            de Aragon, Zaragoza
EHR   Economic History Review
ES or EX   España Sagrada: Teatro Geografico-historico de la
            Iglesia de España, 52 vols, Madrid, 1747-1879
GBA   Gazette des Beaux Arts
GX   Gallia Christiana

Inf Hist Art   Informations d´Histoire de l´Art
JBAA   Journal of the British Archaeolgical
            Association
JWCI   Journal of the Warburg and Courtauld
            Institutes

MF, MM   Madrider Forschungen, Madrider Mitteilungen,
            Deutsches Archäologisches Institut, Madrid,
            published in Berlin
MGH   Monumenta Germaniae Historica
Mons Hist   Les Monuments historiques de la France

Pat lat   Patrologia Latina
PBA   Proceedings of the British Academy
PdeV   Principe de Viana, Pamplona

Rev. hist.   Revue historique
RHGF   Recueil des Historiens des Gaules et de la France

B.N.   Bibliothèque Nationale, Paris
MAN   Museo Arqueológico Nacional
Volumes of the Zodiaque series La Nuit des Temps published
      at La Pierre-qui-Vire (Yonne) are referred to by
      title only:
Angoûmois roman: C. Daras, 1961
Aragon roman: A. Canello Lopez, A. San Vicente, 1971
Berry roman: J. Favière, 1970
Bourgogne romane: R. Oursel, 1979
Castille romane: L.M. Lojendio, A. Rodriguez, I,II, 1966.
Catalogne romane: A. Junyent, I, 1968; II, 1970
Forez-Velay roman: O. Beigbeder, 1962
Gascogne romane: J. Cabanot, 1978
Guyenne romane: P. Dubourg-Noves, 1969
Languedoc roman: R. de Saint-Jean, 1975
Haut-Languedoc roman: M. Durliat, 1978
Limousin roman: J. Maury, M.-M. Gauthier, J. Porcher, 1940
Navarre romane: L.M. Lojendio, 1967
Normandie romane: II, L. Musset, 1974
Poitou roman: R. Crozet, Y. Labande-Maillefert, 1962
Pyrénées romanes: M. Durliat, V. Allègre. 1969
Quercy roman: M. Vidal, 1969
Rouergue roman: G. Gaillard, M.-M. Gauthier, L. Balsan,
            1963
Roussillon roman: M. Durliat, 1964
Saintonge romane: F. Eygun, J. Dupont, 1970
Val de Loire roman: A. Surchamp et al., 1965
L´Art Mozarabe: J. Fontaine, 1977

Other works

AH   Ars Hispaniae, Historia Universal de Arte
      Hispanico, Madrid:
    II. B. Taracena, Arte Romano. P.B. Huguet, Arte
    Paleocristiano. H. Schlunk, Arte Visigodo, 1947
    III. M. Gomez Moreno, El Arte Arabe Español hasta los
    Almohades. Arte Mozarabe. 1951
    IV. L. Torrés Balbas, Arte Almohade, Arte Nazarí,
    Arte Mudéjar, 1949
    V. J. Gudiol Ricart, J.A. Gaya Nuño, Arquitectura y
    Escultura Romanicas, 1948
    VI. J. Gudiol Ricart, W.W.S. Cook, Pintura e
    Imaginería Romanicas, 1950
AMO   G. Marçais, L´Architecture musulmane
      d´Occident, Paris 1954
ARE   M. Gomez-Moreno, Arte Romanico Español,
      Esquema de un Libro, Madrid 1 934

Cahn,Doors   W. Cahn, The Romanesque Wooden Doors of
      Auvergne, New York 1974
Camps, Modulo   E. Camps Cazorla, Modulo, Proporciones y
      Composición en la Arquitectura Califal Cordobesa,
      Madrid 1953

Conant, Cluny   K.J. Conant, <u>Cluny, les églises et les</u>
    <u>maisons du chef d´ordre</u>, Mâcon 1968
Corvey   B. Korzus, <u>Kunst und Kultur im Weserraum</u>
    <u>800-1600</u>, Exhibition at Corvey, Munster 1966
CRA   K.J. Conant, <u>Carolingian and Romanesque</u>
    <u>Architecture</u>, Harmondsworth 1966
Crozet, ARB; ARP; ARS: <u>Art roman en Berry</u>, Paris 1932;
    <u>Art roman en Poitou</u>, Paris 1948; <u>Art roman en</u>
    <u>Saintonge</u>, Paris 1971
Débuts   see GG 1938
Defourneaux   M. Defourneaux, <u>Les français en Espagne aux</u>
    <u>XIe et XIIe siècles</u>, Paris 1949
Demus   O. Demus, <u>Romanesque Mural Painting</u>, London
    1970
Duran Gudiol, Iglesia   A. Duran Gudiol, "La Iglesia de
    Aragon durante los reinados de Sancho Ramirez y
    Pedro I (1062? - 1104")́, <u>Anthologia Anua</u> 9, 1961.
Doors   see Cahn
EK Elf   E. Kühnel, <u>Die Islamische Elfenbein-</u>
    <u>skulpturen VIII - XIII Jahrhundert</u>, Berlin 1971
ELP   E. Lévi-Provençal, <u>Histoire d´Espagne</u>
    <u>musulmane</u>, I, II, Paris 1950; III, Paris 1967
ELPInscr   id., <u>Inscriptions arabes d´Espagne</u>, Leyden
    1931
EMA   K.A.C. Creswell, <u>Early Muslim Architecture</u>, I
    parts 1 and 2, 2nd ed., Oxford 1969; II, Oxford 1940
EMA short   id., <u>A Short Account of Early Muslim</u>
    <u>Architecture</u>, Harmondsworth 1958
EV 1972   E. Vergnolle, "Les chapiteaux de La
    Berthenoux et le chantier de Saint-Benoît-sur-Loire
    au XIe siècle", <u>GBA</u> 1972
EV Saint-Benoît   id., <u>Saint-Benoît-sur-Loire et la</u>
    <u>sculpture au XIe siècle</u>, Paris 1985
Ewert, Cordoba, Malaga, etc. C. Ewert, <u>Spanisch-islamische</u>
    <u>Systeme sich kreuzender Bögen</u>
            I. <u>Die senkrechten ebenen Systeme sich</u>
    <u>kreuzender Bögen als Stutzkonstruktionen der vier</u>
    <u>Rippenkuppeln in der ehemaligen Hauptmoschee von</u>
    <u>Cordoba</u>, MF2, Berlin 1968
            II. <u>Die Arkaturen eines offenen Pavillons</u>
    <u>auf der Alcazaba von Malaga</u>, MM7, Berlin 1966
            III. <u>Die Aljafería in Zaragoza</u>, MF12, Berlin
Ewert, Bal.   id., <u>Islamische Funde in Balaguer und</u>
    <u>die Aljafería in Zaragoza</u>, MF7, Berlin 1971
Fikry, Le Puy   A. Fikry, <u>L´Art roman du Puy et les</u>
    <u>influences islamiques</u>, Paris 1934
GG 1938, or Débuts   G. Gaillard, <u>Les débuts de la</u>
    <u>sculpture romane espagnole</u>, Leon-Jaca-Compostelle,
    Paris 1938
GG Premiers Essais   id., <u>Premiers essais de sculpture</u>
    <u>en Catalogne aux Xe et XIe siècles</u>. Paris 1938
GG Etudes   id., <u>Etudes d´art roman</u>, Paris 1972
Goldschmidt   A. Goldschmidt, <u>Die Elfenbeinskulpturen in</u>
    <u>der Zeit der karolingischen...Kaiser</u>, VIII-XI
    <u>Jahrhundert</u>, I and II, 1914, 1918

Granada   Actas del XXIII Congreso Internacional de
          Historia de Arte 1973, Granada 1976

GZ Payerne   G. Zarnecki, "La Sculpture à Payerne",
          L´Abbatiale de Payerne, Lausanne 1966 .Repr.in

GZ Studies   id., Studies in Romanesque Sculpture, London
          1979

GZ 1066   id., "1066 and Architectural Sculpture", PBA
          1966. Repr. in GZ Studies

Hernandez 1930   F. Hernandez, "Un aspecto de la
          influencia del arte califal en Cataluña (Basas y
          capiteles del siglo XI)" AEAyA XVI/4, 1930

Hill 1959   L. and J. Hill, Raymond IV de Saint-Gilles,
          Comte de Toulouse, Toulouse 1959

Ig.Moz.   M. Gomez-Moreno, Iglesias Mozarabes, Madrid
          1919

JBCC   J. Beckwith, Caskets from Cordoba, London
          1960

LTB 1935   L. Torrés-Balbas ("TB"), "Restos de una
          techumbre de carpintería musulmana en la iglesia de
          San Millán de Segovia", al-Andalus III, 1935

LTB 1936   id., "Los Modillones de Lobulos" I, II,
          AEAA, Jan.-April, May-August 1936

LTB 1957   id., Arte Hispanomusulmàn hasta la Caïda del
          Califato de Córdoba in Historia de España ed. R.
          Menendez Pidal, Vol. V, Madrid 1957

MAE   K.A.C. Creswell, The Muslim Architecture of
          Egypt, Oxford 1952

Maldonado Memoria   B. Pavón Maldonado, Memoria de las
          excavaciones en la Mezquita Mayor de Madinat al-
          Zahra´, Madrid 1966

Maldonado Toledo   id., Arte Toledano Islámico y Mudéjar,
          Madrid 1973

Mâle Art et Artistes   E. Mâle, Art et artistes du moyen
          âge, 3rd ed., Paris 1968

Mél.Marçais   Mélanges d´histoire et d´archéologie de
          l´Occident musulman...Georges Marçais, Algiers 1957

M-P Cid   R. Menendez Pidal, La España del Cid, 7th
          ed., Madrid 1969

Mesplé 1961   Toulouse, Musée des Augustins, Les
          Sculptures Romanes, Paris 1961

Palol & Hirmer   P. de Palol and M. Hirmer, Early
          Mediaeval Art in Spain, London 1967

Tudela   B. Pavon Maldonado, Tudela, Ciudad Medieval, Arte
          Islamico y Mudéjar, Madrid 1978

WMW 11th C.   W.M. Whitehill, Spanish Romanesque
          Architecture of the Eleventh Century, Oxford 1941.